FOOT REGIMENTS OF THE BRITISH ARMY

A History of the 109 Infantry of the Line Regiments 1633–1899

J. A. Miles was born in London in 1938. He spent his National Service in the Royal Military Police before qualifying as a structural engineer when he worked on the civil construction of three nuclear power stations. Miles then moved to the Channel Tunnel where he built a factory on the Isle of Grain for the manufacture of concrete tunnel linings, before moving to Denmark. He retired in 1989.

Throughout his life, Miles read many histories of battles, and wondered who the 42nd Foot, the 19th Foot, etc. were. In 1972, he decided to investigate their origins and actions – hence this book, mainly through information from regimental secretaries and museum curators, who were most helpful.

J. A. Miles

FOOT REGIMENTS OF THE BRITISH ARMY

A History of the 109 Infantry of the Line Regiments 1633–1899

Olympia Publishers
London

www.olympiapublishers.com
OLYMPIA PAPERBACK EDITION

Copyright © J. A. Miles 2015

The right of J. A. Miles to be identified as author of
this work has been asserted in accordance with sections 77 and 78 of the
Copyright, Designs and Patents Act 1988.

All Rights Reserved

No reproduction, copy or transmission of this publication
may be made without written permission.
No paragraph of this publication may be reproduced,
copied or transmitted save with the written permission of the publisher,
or in accordance with the provisions
of the Copyright Act 1956 (as amended).

Every effort has been made to trace copyright holders and to obtain their permission for the use of copyright material. The publisher apologises for any errors or omissions and would be grateful if notified of any corrections that should be incorporated in future reprints or editions of this book.

Any person who commits any unauthorised act in relation to
this publication may be liable to criminal
prosecution and civil claims for damage.

A CIP catalogue record for this title is
available from the British Library.

ISBN: 978-1-84897-345-9

(Olympia Publishers is part of Ashwell Publishing Ltd)

Published in 2015

Olympia Publishers
60 Cannon Street
London
EC4N 6NP

Printed in Great Britain

To the ex-military personnel mainly from the Regimental Museums, who since 1972 have furnished me with details of areas where their regiments and others have taken part. Without their assistance this history would not have been possible.

CONTENTS

PREFACE   15

INTRODUCTION   17

THE ORDER OF PRECEDENCE AND NUMERICAL DESIGNATION
OF REGIMENTS OF INFANTRY OF THE LINE   23

COLOURS AND BATTLE HONOURS   29

LATE 17TH CENTURY RECRUITMENT, FOOD, WIVES,
DISCHARGE   35

CHAPTER 1   41
   1633 TO 1660
   CHARLES I
   ENGLISH CIVIL WAR
   COMMONWEALTH

CHAPTER II   45
   1660 TO 1685
   CHARLES II
   RESTORATION

CHAPTER III 50
    1685–1688
    JAMES II
    RELIGIOUS CONFLICT
    SEDGEMOOR

CHAPTER IV 59
    1688
    WILLIAM III
    INVASION

CHAPTER V 64
    1688–1691
    SCOTLAND

CHAPTER VI 69
    1689–1691
    IRELAND

CHAPTER VII 74
    1689–1702
    WILLIAM III AND MARY II

CHAPTER VIII 84
    1702–1714
    QUEEN ANNE
    WAR OF THE SPANISH SUCCESSION

CHAPTER IX   108
1714–1719
GEORGE I
1st JACOBITE REBELLION

CHAPTER X   122
1702–1744
WEST INDIES

CHAPTER XI   128
1715 – Until
IRELAND – 1742, MINORCA – 1748 and GIBRALTAR – 1727.

CHAPTER XII   134
1739–1745
GEORGE II
EUROPE – WAR OF THE AUSTRIAN SUCCESSION

CHAPTER XIII   144
1745–1746
GEORGE II
THE SECOND JACOBITE REBELLION

CHAPTER XIV   161
SEVEN YEARS WAR 1756–1763
GEORGE II
NORTH AMERICA

CHAPTER XV   **194**
    SEVEN YEARS WAR 1756–1763
    GEORGE III
    WEST INDIES 1759–1762

CHAPTER XVI   **201**
    SEVEN YEARS WAR 1756–1763
    GEORGE III
    INDIA

CHAPTER XVII   **210**
    SEVEN YEARS WAR 1756–1763
    GEORGE II
    MINDEN

CHAPER XVIII   **215**
    SEVEN YEARS WAR 1756–1763
    GEORGE III
    BELLE ILE AND WILHELMSTAHL

CHAPTER XIX   **220**
    CANADA 1763–1767
    GEORGE III

CHAPTER XX   **223**
    AMERICAN WAR OF INDEPENDENCE 1775–1783
    GEORGE III

CHAPTER XXI 246
    AMERICAN WAR OF INDEPENDENCE 1775–1783
    GEORGE III

CHAPTER XXII 254
    FRENCH REVOLUTIONARY WAR 1793–1801
    GEORGE III
    MARTINIQUE – ST LUCIA – EUROPE – EGYPT

CHAPTER XXIII 269
    NAPOLEONIC WAR 1809–1810
    GEORGE III
    WEST INDIES – MARTINIQUE, GUADELOUPE

CHAPTER XXIV 272
    PENINSULAR WAR 1808–1814
    GEORGE III
    THE SPANISH PENINSULA AND PYRENEES

CHAPTER XXV 305
    THE HUNDRED DAYS – WATERLOO 1815
    GEORGE III

CHAPTER XXVI 312
    EMPIRE EXPANSION

CHAPTER XXVII 322
    NEW ZEALAND 1846–1866
    QUEEN VICTORIA

CHAPTER XXVIII 325
    INDIA 1843–1853
    QUEEN VICTORIA

CHAPTER XXIX 331
    CRIMEA 1854–1856
    QUEEN VICTORIA

CHAPTER XXX 336
    INDIAN MUTINY 1857–1859
    QUEEN VICTORIA

CHAPTER XXXI 344
    ZULU WAR 1879
    QUEEN VICTORIA

CHAPTER XXXII 355
    1881–1899
    QUEEN VICTORIA

EPILOGUE 366

ACKNOWLEDGEMENTS 373

PREFACE

This is the history of the British Army, the infantry. Apart from a few minor references, it does not cover the foot guards or cavalry regiments; neither does it refer to the happenings after 1899.

Where possible, contemporary titles have been used. Throughout, regiments have been referred to by their name at raising, followed by their regimental number prior to the reforms in 1881, and their title immediately after, e.g. 1685 Colonel John Granville's Regiment of Foot (10th Foot, the Lincolnshire Regiment). However, instead of using colonels' names prior to 1754, for clarity the title of 2nd Foot etc. has been used.

J. A. Miles

INTRODUCTION

The story of the modern Army started in 1633 when Sir John Hepburn raised what was later to become the 1st Regiment of Foot, the Royal Scots. Any attempt by regiments to claim earlier origins cannot really be justified and so the year 1633 is the first reference used.

The growth of the Army commenced firstly during the English Civil War, which gave the basis of regimental ties and a certain conformity of uniform, although for a long time the Army remained poorly paid and badly equipped. By 1694, many regiments had been formed such that it was considered necessary to clarify the rules relating to the Order of Precedence of these regiments of foot. This was drawn up in Flanders by a Board of General Officers, numbers were to be given to English regiments to commence from the time when they were placed on the English establishment. Likewise Scots and Irish regiments were so numbered, but as the Act of Union with Scotland did not take place until 1707, some non-English regiments carried lower regimental numbers than they would have wished – for instance, the Royal Scots Fusiliers were the 4th Infantry Regiment to be raised, but as they did not march into England in support of King James II until 1688, they ranked twenty-first in seniority of the Line. A few years later the Army just withstood a call by Parliament to be disbanded, but with the turn of the century and a new war breaking out with France, regiments recruited and new ones were formed.

In 1715 the numbers that had earlier been given to the regiments of foot were confirmed by Royal Warrant. However these were not used as a regimental title because until 1754 regiments were still known by the name of their colonels.

With the failure of the Jacobite Rising in 1746 and the subsequent events in Scotland following Culloden, the British Army rallied to the British flag, maintaining this allegiance unaltered for nearly 200 years; then only to be affected in 1922 when the Irish regiments from the south of the border were disbanded.

To assist recruiting during the American War of Independence a successful scheme was used in England. Lord lieutenants of counties and various noblemen raised local men to fight in volunteer corps named after their county. This not only assisted recruiting but gave the soldier a tie with home. Therefore in 1782 all colonels were required to choose their area or county for recruitment. This was followed by a Royal Warrant dated 31st August 1782 giving the chosen county titles to all regiments except those with special designations: the King's Own or the Queen's. The use of the regiment number was to continue to be used in the title of the regiment.

The Army organisation continued in much the same manner until 1881, when under the joint control of Mr Edward Cardwell the Secretary of State for War and Garnet Wolseley, his chief military advisor, the Territorial System was inaugurated. On 11th April by General Order No. 41 dated 1st May, the reorganisation of the regiments of foot was given in that all regiments of the Line should drop their regimental numbers and adopt Territorial titles.

With General Order No. 69 issued at the end of June, an appendix was published giving the composition and titles of Territorial regiments. Regiments which had only one battalion were linked together in pairs under one Territorial designation, each of four battalions for Great Britain and five for Ireland, the 1st and 2nd battalions of each being Line and the remaining two or three being Militia.

As the first 25 regiments of the Line already had two battalions it was not necessary to link them with other Regiments.

Excluding the two world wars when many regiments were enlarged, amalgamated or reshuffled, only to be disbanded when peace returned, the military organisation remained as set out in 1881, until during the middle of the twentieth century nearly all foot regiments came under the axe; some in the space of ten years amalgamated twice. It was possible for a new regiment to be formed from three or four original Line regiments until by 1975 the organisation contained only 30 regiments formed into five divisions. Some of these new regiments were formed from nine or ten of the original 109 regiments of foot. Later amalgamations have lowered this even more, hence this history ceases just before the war in South Africa at the beginning of the twentieth century.

What then, made the British Army the great force that we now believe it to be? What made the British square so invincible? The British volley so devastating? How was it that men were prepared to die to save their regimental colours? How did the regiments establish their fine traditions? Why were they given the nicknames that they so proudly bore? Why did men enlist into this volunteer Army knowing that socially they were outcasts, that they would probably be sent to some of the most unhealthy places on Earth, there to die from one of the local diseases or a native lance, club or rifle ball from a European rival in a war of which most of the population of the island had never heard? Or if there were no wars and Parliament so decreed the regiments be disbanded, men were discharged to roam the streets of England without pension or privilege, for the civilian at home did not care about the outcome or even the men who fought in some fancy foreign war. The men that is, and not the officer class who purchased their commissions and in many cases were totally unfit to lead – and to lead what? Wellington, during the Peninsular War referred to his men as 'the scum of the earth' and so they probably were.

To find the answers to these questions we must travel back, past the Second World War which set the seal on the Empire, back past the Great War which set the seal on feudal England, back to the seventeenth century and the mercenary troops who fought for King and Country, although both King and Country may have changed depending on whose purse was the heaviest. As the needs of Empire grew, so there became a need for an Army of regular troops.

Where were the men to fill the ranks of the newly formed or established regiments? They were here, here in the streets of our towns and cities, here in our villages, here in the highlands of Scotland and the valleys of Wales, and here in the ever open recruiting ground of Ireland, where many fine regiments were raised and many fine Irishmen were signed on for the English establishment – for this was the British Army.

The recruiting sergeants did a good job, for the people at home cared little about their Army and indeed why should they? Life was hard and they had their own problems. In any case the soldiers seen in garrison towns were probably better clothed and better fed than the general public. The Factories Act of 1833 brought in a shorter working day in that it forbade employment of children under nine years of age and enforced a nine-hour day for the under thirteen-year-olds, for prior to this children often started work at the age of five or six and worked in the mill or mine from six o'clock in the morning until seven o'clock in the evening. Was it then not obvious that many found their way into the Army, the only home they would ever know?

Regimental ties were strong because the regiment was their family. If they did desert, where could they run? They had no civilian clothes and in most cases the enemy or local population would have killed them or returned them for a bounty to the regiment where the penalty was harsh and in some cases final.

Discipline was maintained with the lash. Even this, however, was to become a source of boast. The Northamptonshire Regiment earned the nickname of 'the Steelbacks' from the amount of punishment taken. During the late 18th and early 19th century sentences of 1000 strokes of the lash were not uncommon. In January 1807 by Royal Order of His Majesty George III a private in the 54th Foot (West Norfolk Regiment) awaiting 1500 lashes for mutinous conduct heard that His Majesty had been graciously pleased that no sentence for corporal punishment should exceed 1000 lashes. This did not extend to India where one private in Bengal received 1500 lashes within three months of this Royal Proclamation. Successive governments courted the youth of the country, the fine deeds were later commemorated on Regimental Colours, and to fill the ever open jaws of ranks depleted by death the recruiting parties sang in praise of the regiments.

Newspaper reporters did not travel with the regiments to record the actions or non-actions of the day and so blunders, mismanagement of troops, troop movements and battle reverses were not penned until years afterwards.

In fact, the Battle of Corunna in 1809 was covered by a lawyer who worked for *The Times* newspaper and later claimed to be the first official war correspondent. His reports however were gathered from local writers and therefore resulted in poor and inaccurate details. Even this coverage was short-lived, as the Duke of Wellington did not allow further reports during the Peninsular War.

By the middle of the 19th century, newspapers sent representatives to report on the deeds of the armed forces, and so the public, with growing awareness of the often senseless waste of life, were once again duped by a master stroke of Victorian propaganda – the Victoria Cross. This was and still is a medal to be awarded to all ranks of the Army, Navy and lately the Royal Air Force, for exceptional bravery and extreme devotion to duty in the presence of the enemy. It was established in 1856 by Queen Victoria, and made the ideal weapon with which to counter the ever-growing doubtful public regarding the activities of the Army in the Crimea. Most regiments present has someone of whom they could boast a deed of valour, and indeed since in those days when the award could not be given posthumously, most regiments soon had a live recipient.

This practice was to hold the Army in good stead, for if it needed to advertise an obscure minor action it awarded a Victoria Cross, if it required to turn an act of massacre into an act of glory, it awarded a Victoria Cross – the actions at Isandhlwana and Rorke's Drift are excellent examples, a large defeat at the former, overshadowed by many Victoria Crosses awarded for the latter. Glory for the living indeed!

With the passing of the red jacket at the turn of the century, so came the passing of the small wars, world wars were to become the highlights of the twentieth century – these however have not been covered, suffice to say that valour, death, cowardice and life sprang from them.

Did they herald the end of the British Army, or the beginning of another chapter in its long history?

THE ORDER OF PRECEDENCE AND NUMERICAL DESIGNATION OF REGIMENTS OF INFANTRY OF THE LINE*

It is vital that the precedence of regiments is explained, as confusion often follows when accounts of events are read where regiments are referred to by number, prior to 1754. The reason for this is that the numerical designation was not necessarily the Order of Precedence of regiments.

In marked contrast to battle honours, which have never really added to the status of regiments until many years after the action for which they were awarded, are the Order of Precedence of regiments of infantry of the Line where colonels of Line regiments have, since the Civil War, taken an extremely active role to ensure that the seniority of their regiment was the highest they could possibly attain.

The first Order of Precedence is that laid down in the Warrant of King Charles II, dated 12th September 1666:

'For the preventing of all Questions and Disputes that might arise for or concerning the Ranks of the several Regiments, Troops and Companies which are now or at any Time hereafter shall be employed in our Service··· We have thought good to issue out these following Rules and Directions.

'First, as to the Foot, that the Regiment. Of Guards (i.e. Grenadier Guards) take place of all other Regiments···the General's Regiment (i.e. Coldstream Guards) to take Place next the Admiral's (the Admiral's Regiment i.e. the Duke of York's as Lord High Admiral of

---

* Precedence of Regiments Part II from the *Army Quarterly* vol. 23, dated 1931, and The Order of Precedence of Regiments from *Journal of the Society for Army Historical Research*, vol. V, dated 1925.

England) immediately after and all other regiments and Colonels to take place according to the date of their commissions···'

The next Order of Precedence is given in the Warrant of King Charles II dated 6th February 1684, '··· After which Our Scotch Regiment and Tangier Regiment, Our Brother James Duke of York's Regiment are to have Precedency as they are here ranked.'

The regiments referred to here are those that were finally numbered 1st Foot, 2nd Foot and the Prince George of Denmark's Regiment which, following the 1688 English Revolution, was disbanded in 1689 because it was considered that it was too favourable to the ousted King James II.

This Order of Precedence is followed by a general ruling: 'That all other Regiments of Foot take place according to their respective Seniorities from the time they were raised, so as that no regiment is to lose it Precedency by the Death of their Colonelle.'

The next warrant was dated 3rd August 1685 and was probably rushed through following the raising of regiments for the Monmouth Rebellion for it generally repeated the 1684 ruling and fixed the following Order of Precedence:

Regiment	Later
The Royal Regiment of Foot	1st Foot
The Queen Dowager's Regiment	2nd Foot
Prince George of Denmark's Regiment	(Disbanded 1689)
The Holland Regiment	3rd Foot
The Queen's Regiment	4th Foot
Royal Regiment of Fusiliers	7th Foot
Princess Ann of Denmark's Regiment	8th Foot
Henry Cornwall's Regiment	9th Foot
Earl of Bath's Regiment	10th Foot
Duke of Beaufort's Regiment	11th Foot
Duke of Norfolk's Regiment	12th Foot
Earl of Huntingdon's Regiment	13th Foot
Sir Edward Hale's Regiment	14th Foot
Sir Wm. Clifton's Regiment	15th Foot

A note appended to this Warrant reads: 'This Order was cancelled and the matter of it contained in the Declaration,' (1694 Warrant).

On 10th June 1694 the following Warrant was issued by William III after being drawn up at Roosbeck Camp.

'Order for Settling the Rank of the Foot. William R.

'A Report having been made unto Us by a Councill of Warr of the Generall Officers of Our Army touching the Rank of Several regiments of Foot now in the Low Country's and for the setling for the future the Precedency of such Regiment's as may hereafter be raised or taken into Our Service, Wee have thought fit hereby to Declare our Royall Will and Pleasure.

1s. That an English Regiment shall take place of all other Regiments, being otherwise in the same circumstances.'

(On 19th June 1708 the Board of General Officers amplified this Rule by the addition of the following:
> 'That no regiment raised in England is to be deemed
> an English regiment unless placed, at the same time
> of raising, on the Establishment of England.)

2ly. That an Irish Regiment shall have Rank from the Day it comes upon the English Establishment, and not lose it afterwards by their return to Ireland, or being putt upon the Establishment of that Kingdom.

3ly. That a Scots Regiment coming upon the English Establishment shall take Rank with other regiments from that time.

4ly. That any regiment of what Nation soever being raised in England, shall have Rank from the time of its raising.

5ly. That the Three English regiments that have lately Served in Holland (i.e. 5th, 6th, and Cutt's Foot, disbanded in 1699) take their Rank immediately after the Queen's Regiment of Foot (i.e. 4th Foot), in respect of the Capitulation that was made for them by the Earl of Ossory in the year 1668, with the allowance and Direction of Our Dearrest Unkle King Charles the Second, which is likewise to have effect as to the Rank, with the Scots regiments (i.e. of the Scots Brigade in Holland) among themselves: Upon which considerations Wee Do hereby Declare, Our Will and Pleasure is, that the Rank and Precedency of the Several Regiments Serving Us in the Low Countries be as follows, vizt.'

Here follows a list of regiments as the 1685 list with the following additions):

Regiment	Later
Colonel J. Stanley's Regiment	16th Foot
Colonel F. Collingwood's Regiment	Disbanded
Sir G. St George's Regiment	17th Foot
Colonel F. Hamilton's Regiment	18th Foot
Brigadier Erle's Regiment	19th Foot
Colonel Lander's Regiment	Disbanded
Colonel Mackay's Regiment	Disbanded
Colonel Graham's Regiment	Disbanded
Colonel F. F. O' Farrell's Regiment	21st Foot
Colonel Ingoldsby's Regiment	23rd Foot
Maj-Gen. de la Meloniere's Regiment	Disbanded
Comte Marton's Regiment	Disbanded
Colonel Belcastel's Regiment	Disbanded
Colonel Maitland's Regiment	25th Foot
Colonel Ferguson's Regiment	26th Foot
Colonel Tiffin's Regiment	27th Foot
Earl of Argyle's Regiment	Disbanded
Colonel Buchan's Regiment	Disbanded
Earl of Strathnaver's Regiment	Disbanded
Colonel G. Hamilton's Regiment	Disbanded

'Which Rules and Rank of the Severall Regiment's above-mentioned Wee Do hereby Direct to be hereafter observed and all persons whom it may concern are to govern themselves accordingly.

'Given at our Camp at Roosbeck this 10 day of June 1694. In the Sixth Year of our Reign.

By His Majestys Command. W.B'

In 1712 much correspondence flowed as Queen Anne caused a major upset by the issue of a new rule:

<u>Whitehall</u>

<u>28 July 1712</u>

'Her Majesty having been moved upon the Affair relating to the Ranks of Sevl. Regimts. Now Settling by the Board of General Officers, I am to signify to you Her Pleasures That Regard is to be had to the Dates of Raising the said Regimts. and not to the time of Their coming upon the English Establishment. Which You are Desired to Communicate to the Board.'

Basically this meant that Scots and Irish regiments should take rank from raising, not as William III's ruling from the date of joining the English Establishment. The effect of this was that regiments were placed (using later numerical designations) 1st to 4th, 7th to 18th, 21st, 25th, 20th, 19th, 22nd, 23rd, 24th, 27th, 26th, 35th, 36th, 28th, 39th, 29th, 30th, 31st, 32nd, 37th, 33rd, 34th, 38th, note that Colonel Harrison's Regiment (6th Foot, the Royal Warwickshire Fusiliers) and the Major-General Pearce's Regiment (5th Foot, the Northumberland Fusiliers) 'had no post, but as Dutch Regiments' and they were placed junior to all other regiments.

Although 22 colonels petitioned the Board on 13th November 1712 complaining that their regiments had lost precedence owing to the new rule, the petitioners on this occasion were unsuccessful and had to wait until 11th January 1715 when they were invited to acquaint the Board of General Officers at their next meeting.

'...that They may Govern Themselves accordingly, And also that they would hear and give their Opinions upon such Petitions as shall be referred to Presented to Them on this subject, and when They have settled the Rank and Seniority of the sevl. Regimts. as They will stand by this Rule, you do Transmit to my Office a List thereof for my laying the same before His Majty.

                              (sd). WILLIAM PULTENEY'

This appears to have been carried out, for on 19th February 1715 a list was submitted to King George by the Board. It contained the Order of Precedence of the 1st to 39th Foot Regiments. No subsequent alterations in relative rank taking place, it was on this Order of Precedence that the numerical designations of regiments were finally fixed.

It should be accepted that so far reference has only been made to the Order of Precedence of regiments of infantry of the Line. Following the re-instatement of the King William III rules in 1715, the Order of Precedence was not subjected to major revisions and that the Order of Precedence of regiments then, was to become the numerical designation of those same regiments later, probably as late as 1742 for when renumbering of certain regiments took place just after this date, it was almost certainly the numerical designation which was adjusted. However, regiments continued to be referred to by the name of their colonels until 1754.

COLOURS AND BATTLE HONOURS

A battle honour is not merely a record of battle in which a regiment has taken part. It is only awarded if the regiment had distinguished itself in battle and if the headquarters of the regiment was present.

Although there are many types of battle honours, they generally fall into two categories. The first category is the distinction in the form of a badge.

The first infantry regiment to receive such an award was Colonel Hamilton's Regiment of Foot (the 18th Foot). William III granted this regiment the honour of bearing his arms – the lion of Nassau. This took the form of the golden lion on a blue field surrounded by golden billets and the motto VIRTUTIS NAMURCENSIS PRAEMIUM for service at the Siege of Namur in 1695. The remaining ten infantry of the Line regiments and three foot guards regiments active in Flanders at that time and especially at the siege and capture of Manur, had to wait until 1910 when, along with the Royal Irish Regiment (18th Foot), they were granted the battle honour NAMUR 1695.

Colonel Edward Lloyd's Regiment of Foot (5th Foot) were not so lucky, for they failed to receive the award in 1910 and again in 1934 when, following an invitation by the War Office to colonels of regiments to 'review their honorary distinctions and to submit applications for further distinctions where they would appear justified', their colonel submitted that, although he conceded that the Fifth had only acted as a covering force, they had in fact contributed greatly towards William III's successful campaign in Flanders. For this he requested a general honour of FLANDERS 1694-1697 be granted. 1934 could not have been a year advantageous for the release of further honours, for the request was not granted.

Personal colours have been in existence ever since men decided to band together to fight. Certainly by the time of the English Civil War, miscellaneous banners had been totally superseded by the flag, which mounted on a staff was for the Line infantry to be referred to as colours.

Until 1707 an infantry regiment had many colours. Regiments were at this time raised and maintained by noblemen who took command as colonel and, apart from furnishing the regiment with his names, virtually controlled its every action and was responsible for its uniform and equipment. To both of these were affixed family crests and various heraldic devices associated with the Colonel. This practice ceased with the issue of the 1747 Clothing Regulations in which colonels were forbidden to fix personal motifs to uniforms or equipment.

1707 was also the year of political union between England and Scotland. To demonstrate this unity the red cross of Saint George and the white saltire of Saint Andrew on a blue field combined to form the Union Flag. The white field from the English flag was maintained as a strip to surround the red cross thereby effecting the striking contrast of red, white and blue. The regimental system was also reorganised with the many standards being reduced to just three for each regiment.

The 1747 Clothing Regulations which were confirmed by Royal Warrant in 1751, required that the number of colours for each battalion be reduced to two and the makeup of colours was given in the following detailed manner:

'The First or King's Colour to be The Great Union and the Second or regimental Colour to be the colour of the facing of the regiment (i.e. the colour of the lapels, collar, cuffs and trimmings of the uniform coat) with the Union in the upper canton.' The Rank (precedence) of the regiment was painted or embroidered in gold Roman characters within a wreath of roses and thistles on the same stalk.

The Regulations also carried a list indicating special badges awarded to 1st, 2nd, 3rd, 4th, 5th, 6th, 7th, 8th, 18th, 21st, 23rd and 27th Regiments of Foot which they would be allowed to fix to their colours.

Six Marine regiments, 44th to 49th of the Line were to have on both colours, a ship with sails furled and the rank of the regiment underneath. This number was again in Roman characters and was to be the Order of Precedence number, not the unofficial 1st Marines to 10th Marines titles. The first six Marine regiments were raised in 1739 with a further four raised in 1740 (50th to 53rd Foot), they were all disbanded in 1748. Their second colour was again the colour of their facings, in the case of the 44th, 46th, 48th, 51st and 53rd Regiments of Foot this was yellow.

The next Royal Warrant to affect colours was in 1768. The size of Colours was fixed at six feet six inches horizontal by six feet vertical and the staff at nine feet ten inches including spear and ferrule. Regiments with black facings also had black colours. There were only four regiments in 1768 with black facings and the Warrant stated that their second colour should be Saint George's Cross throughout; union in the upper canton with the other three black.

In 1801 the red saltire of Saint Patrick was added to the Union flag of England and Scotland with the result that the new Union flag then was as we know it today. Colours were therefore changed to include the new Union flag and the Union wreath, where the shamrock had joined the roses and thistles.

The most common badge on Regimental Colours was awarded on the 6th July 1802, following the successful campaign against the French the previous year, and was the sphinx mounted on a plinth and superscribed EGYPT.

The second category and by far the most common, was the award of a single name, which is sometimes followed by the date of the action. Both are normally inscribed singly or together in a scroll and arranged on the Royal Colour in decorative formation on the cross of Saint George, usually symmetrically placed on the Union wreath where this occurs on the Regimental Colour.

The first infantry of the Line battle honour GIBRALTAR was awarded to the 12th, 39th, 56th and 58th Regiments of Foot on the 14th April 1784, for the defence of Gibraltar between 1779 and 1783. It is usual that these dates follow the distinction although they were only added in 1909.

MINDEN follows next. Fought on the 1st August 1759, it was awarded to the six Minden Regiments – the 12th, 20th, 23rd, 25th, 37th, and 51st Regiments on Foot – on the 1st January 1801 in remembrance of the battle in which the regiments honourably distinguished themselves. Awards to other infantry regiments engaged in the Seven Years War were not granted until much later. The most extreme case was BELLE ISLE (7th June 1761) which was awarded to the regiments concerned in 1951.

The granting of MINDEN in 1801, 42 years after the battle, appears to have set the fashion, for during the nineteenth century awards followed closely after the event. This is especially so for the Napoleonic Wars, the Peninsular War, Waterloo, the Crimea and the host of African, Egyptian and Far Eastern campaigns.

Probably to keep up public interest in the affairs of Empire, and the prospective recruit's eyes from the boredom he may encounter if he joined a regiment engaged in India, Indian awards were promptly given for any action after 1810, although the award to Indian foot regiments were not always simultaneous with that of their British counterparts.

The Victorians certainly knew the value of battle honours, for battles and campaigns prior to 1801 provided them with propaganda to heighten any flagging spirits amongst the populace.

Queen Victoria's reign soon heralded changes, for in 1844 regulations were issued which formalised colours. The First Colour became the Royal Colour and the second became the Regimental Colour. Colours generally became more uniform and laid out in regular pattern. The size of Colours was changed several times during the reign of Victoria, until in 1881 by the time of the Cardwell reforms they were three feet nine inches by three feet.

As if to herald the introduction in 1881 of all regiments formed into 1st and 2nd Battalions, Queen's Regulations of 1873 ordered that the inscription II BATT be placed below the Union wreath for second battalions.

The Cardwell reforms obviously necessitated changes in colours. Where two regiments were joined to form a common regiment their battle honours were shared and facings had to be rationalised. This was done on a national basis. Blue was still to be the colour for Royal regiments whilst English and Welsh took white, Scottish yellow and Irish regiments green. The Territorial designation with the Royal or other title was incorporated with the Imperial Crown on both colours and the number of the battalion was placed in the upper canton (slightly modified later from the upper canton to inside the crimson circle bearing the regimental title).

1882 saw 51 awards to infantry regiments for services at:

BLENHEIM 1704, RAMILLIES 1706, OUDENARDE 1708 and MALPLAQUET 1709 under John Churchill, Duke of Marlborough during the War of the Spanish Succession and a further twelve awards, again in 1882, for regiments which took part in the Battle of Dettingen in 1743, in which King George II became the last British monarch to actively lead his army in battle. George awarded the White Horse of Hanover to be affixed to the Colours of some regiments for their part in the battle.

FONTENOY 1745 was never awarded as an honour, for the British under William Augustus, Duke of Cumberland were defeated. The Duke, who was the second son of George II, had served under his father at Dettingen and had been appointed Captain General of the British Army in Europe in 1745.

Defeats were not honoured but certain defensive actions could be termed honourable and instances exist where honours have been awarded for abortive but gallant defences. On the other hand successful battles and campaigns have not always been recognised. If it was not in the interest of political unity to grant an honour, it was discreetly forgotten. Instances of this are Sedgemoor and Culloden. Neither were battle honours presented for the American War of Independence; regiments having lost a colony could hardly hope for awards! Except that some honours were awarded in 1908 and 1909 for 'fringe' actions at Gibraltar and in the West Indies, presumably by 1908 and 1909 it was considered that sufficient time had elapsed for these awards to be honourably presented.

Honours for the French Revolutionary Wars between 1793 and 1802 do not appear to have been awarded to any pattern and were filtered to regiments periodically from 1802 until 1909.

The earliest battle honour to be found on any infantry Colour is TANGIER 1662-1680 but this was only awarded to the Queen's Royal Surrey Regiment (2nd Foot) in 1909.

Battle honours were further exploited during the two world wars when so many were earned and given that it was impossible to affix them all, hence only a selection were chosen to be carried on the colours.

Colours remain much the same today, although with the many amalgamations, they are in some cases solid with battle honour scrolls from the many constituent regiments and the twentieth century wars.

It was at Laing's Nek in South Africa on 28th January 1881 that the 2nd Battalion of the Northamptonshire Regiment became the last regiment to carry their Colours in action. Colours then became solely ceremonial.

LATE 17th CENTURY RECRUITMENT, FOOD, WIVES, DISCHARGE

Billet – *An order requiring a householder to board and/or lodge soldiers upon his premises.*

Life at the end of the seventeenth century was vastly different from that experienced today; therefore, it may be very difficult for people who have accepted as commonplace the luxuries of the late twentieth century to understand how relatively primitive life must have been three hundred years earlier. One only has to look at life in Britain immediately after the Second World War, most working-class families had no bathroom and for many a bath tub was filled by kettles and saucepans from the stove. An outside toilet, in some cases shared by several families was not uncommon, whilst central heating was almost unknown. Only one room would be heated by a coal fire, barricaded from the rest of the house by curtains and draught mats against the door.

Imagine then, life 250 years before, a life at the lower end of society for one must be directed at the type of person to which the recruiting sergeants cast their attentions. This was a time when life, certainly by modern standards, seemed cheap, where for crimes against the State men were hanged, drawn and quartered, public executions were entertainment and for those lucky enough to escape the death penalty for trivial offences, there was the experience of prison where conditions were appalling.

Barracks did not exist and when a regiment was raised or moved into an area, an order was issued requisitioning accommodation for the soldiers. They were therefore billeted upon a population which resented their presence; this usually resulted in the men in the service of the Crown being lodged in ale-houses or the unoccupied parts of a house, such as the attic or outbuildings which would generally be cold and damp. However, these may have been an improvement in living conditions, which the men may have experienced in their own homes, prior to enlistment.

The basic military diet consisted of ground peas or beans mixed with a roughly ground grain, this would have been eaten with a coarse bread or biscuit sometimes accompanied with cheese. Neither the soldier nor the civilian from the same class background ate green vegetables. However on active service or during the occupation of areas recognised as being hostile to the regiment, extra rations were often obtained by the poaching of fish or the killing of chickens, rabbits, pigeons and other game. Root crops were another victim of the soldiers' thefts and although the plundering of civilians by soldiers carried the death penalty, it was known that, although men from the regiments were often responsible, so too were members of the civilian population. Therefore, unless caught red-handed, the culprit remained unpunished.

Campaigning was generally carried out during the summer months. Therefore, during the inactive winter period, recruiting parties returned to England, Scotland, Ireland and Wales. It was important that enough men were lured into service thereby keeping the regiments up to strength. Two main differences existed depending on where the regiment was stationed, firstly for those in England, where the recruitment of men could be carried out all the year round and secondly for those in Flanders, where the winter months only were used. The recruiting party, normally led by a sergeant, would take lodgings in an inn or tavern when the hunt for men would begin. It could not have been easy to persuade suitable men in towns or villages that life in a regiment serving overseas, would be preferable to that which they currently experienced. Or would it?

Some young men would be carried away with thoughts of grandeur probably brought on by too much ale, but this method of recruitment did not raise sufficient men and schemes both in England and Scotland were introduced whereby men who were debtors or those convicted of petty crimes were encouraged to join the colours as an alternative to prison. The Scots were slightly different as they would generally be recruited into the Clan regiment. Sometimes recruiting parties used tactics similar to the naval press gang but this was not condoned by the authorities, so much so that in 1693 every recruit had to be taken before a Justice of the Peace to ensure that coercion had not been used.

Having enlisted, the recruits would be escorted to regimental headquarters or, if the regiment was overseas, taken on board ship, the precaution of the escort was necessary to stop the more unscrupulous slipping away with the bounty they had received for enlisting. The bounty had been introduced as a further enticement in an effort to gather suitable young men. The scheme was administered by the Treasury from whom each company commander, usually a captain, claimed the bounty money for the number of recruits raised. This was unfortunately open to abuse as the recruit, probably unused to dealing in sums of money as large as that being offered, would accept figures well below the official rate of one pound.

Recruiting parties were forbidden to take married men into service mainly because there were no provisions for wives. Serving soldiers were likewise strongly advised not to marry. However towards the end of the seventeenth century, two or three wives were taken on to company strength and permitted to travel with their husband's regiment. Their position ceased if their husband was killed or died. Most would try to marry another soldier from the regiment, preferably a corporal or even better, a sergeant. However, some wives with children returned to the parish they had left, in the hope that the authorities would look after them.

Men who left the Army after their period of service only received fourteen days' pay as well as a small bounty, and those who could no longer serve the regiment through illness, or had become maimed through action, and may have even spent time in one of the so-called hospitals where treatment was basic, in conditions where low hygiene and inadequate sanitation prevailed, could only look to a life as a general labourer, as most would not have learnt an earlier trade, or to the mercy of the Justice of the Peace for any hand-out to keep them from starving.

In 1681 King Charles had recognised the need to look after men who had been discharged, especially those with more than twenty years' service when he established the Royal Hospital in Chelsea which was capable of taking nearly 500 men, however in less than ten years it was full. It had been a start, but for many, many years the professional soldier had little prospect for a happy future when discharged.

FOOT REGIMENTS OF THE BRITISH ARMY

'Infantry: The least spectacular arm of the Army. Yet without them, you cannot win a battle, without them you can do nothing at all. Nothing.'

Field Marshal Viscount Montgomery.

CHAPTER 1

1633 to 1660
CHARLES I
ENGLISH CIVIL WAR
COMMONWEALTH

Musket – *A heavy, large carbine shoulder firearm with smooth bore. From mousquet, Middle French (1301–1600)*

There are no infantry of the Line regiments which survived the Civil War of 1642 and the Commonwealth which followed. The only regiment which precedes this time is the 1st Regiment of Foot, the Royal Scots, raised under warrant from the Privy Council of Scotland at Edinburgh on 24th April 1633, receiving royal sanction from King Charles I at Whitehall on 28th March 1633, being 1200 men for use in France by Louis XIII. It was not until the restoration in 1660 that Charles II asked Louis XIV to restore the regiment to this country. The Civil War therefore does not enter into the history of the infantry of the Line except that it produced certain events worthy of note.

Prior to the Civil War there was no standing Army, only a feudal militia, which raised from each county its quota of men who mustered once a month during the summer. This muster was a poorly organised affair; the men often arrived late from distant areas and therefore had little time for drill and the county even less money with which to buy powder for musket practice.

Due to the island remoteness of England her frontiers were the sea, duly guarded by the Navy. Any Army which was raised under the command of the King – in this case Charles I – had to be carried out by Parliament who themselves could not assemble the Army unless requested by the King, each in turn held control over the other.

When Charles's reign began, he inherited a war with Spain. His first act was to call Parliament to supply funds to continue, but the new Parliament did not support the war of his predecessor and refused him the money. Charles, relying on the advice of George Villiers, Duke of Buckingham, not only continued the war but also unwittingly involved the French. Buckingham, a poor manager, plunged the King into further debt with ill-conceived expeditions against Spain. Parliament attacked both the King and Buckingham whom they also tried to impeach, Buckingham was murdered (a separate incident) following which the King successfully sued for peace. A well-balanced time followed where Parliament, although still smouldering, remained quietly observant, whilst the King ran the economy. The effect of this was to leave the country without an army.

During this time Charles attempted to reform the Scottish Kirk which he believed to be his right as King. The Scots would have none of this and in 1638 drew up the 'National Covenant' against which the Kirk would oppose interference by the King. The Scottish General Assembly took an extremely hard line when it rejected all of Charles's appointments and indeed some made during the reign of James I. This was followed by a Scottish invasion of England by veterans from the Continental wars. Charles unsuccessfully attempted to arrest the advance by calling upon his militia but then took the only course open to him and, at Berwick in the mid-summer of 1639, he signed a treaty of pacification with the Scots.

This brought Charles time; firstly to ask Parliament for money and secondly to arrange for an army from Ireland under Thomas Wentworth, Earl of Strafford to assist in his struggle against the Scots. Parliament refused to finance the raising of any army, believing it would strengthen their hand against the King. The second string in his bow failed as miserably as his efforts to raise money, when Wentworth was taken ill and therefore unable to bring his army to the King's aid. The Scots now advanced 100 miles further south and reached the River Tees. Charles, unable to stand against this second Scottish advance, again consented to pacification but this time the cost was higher, and Charles agreed to pay nearly £6,000 every week to the Scots.

Parliament had now achieved its aim and the Parliamentary areas of the country, which included London, stood against their King. In January 1642 a much discredited monarch left London. Another Parliamentary town was Hull whose gates were closed to Charles and, despite demands for admittance by the King, remained so. By this act on St George's Day, 23rd April 1642 the Civil War regrettably commenced.

From both parties the call for militia went out to a country ill-prepared for war. The King's forces were better led and morale was higher, especially in the cavalry. It was probably for this reason that Parliament developed what was the first attempt by the British at uniformed regimentation and so, during January 1645 the New Model Army was born. Its infantry consisted of twelve regiments each with 1200 men, a total infantry strength of nearly 15,000. This scheme was so successful that within four years all Parliamentary militia were re-formed and all Parliamentary forces thereafter belonged to the New Model.

Prior to the forming of the New Model Army, uniforms were not supplied and troops used various motifs to distinguish themselves from the enemy and identify them to their own side.

Mercenaries from the Continent fought on both sides, and it was teachings from these seasoned troops which led to the successful development of Parliamentary forces. Weapons of course have generally dictated battle formations and tactics. The New Model was no exception, thus the infantry was formed from pikemen and musketeers whose role was dependent upon each other, although there were many times more musketeers than pikemen. The combination of pikemen/musketeer formed an ideal defensive/attacking formation, the sixteen-foot long pikes presented a very formidable barrier against advancing troops whilst the musket was effective up to almost a quarter of a mile, although it should be added that it was not accurate at most of that distance. It was also extremely heavy, required a prop to hold it in the aim position and took an age to load. During this time the musketeer was shielded by pikemen or by other musketeers who were generally formed six ranks deep.

The Civil War continued at disjointed intervals for regrouping, chase and politics until, in January 1649 the King's trial and execution left England at peace, whilst Oliver Cromwell in the same year turned his attention to Ireland, then in 1650 to Scotland, following the proclamation by Charles II as King of Scotland. Charles had travelled south but was beaten at Worcester in 1651 and as a fugitive left England six weeks later.

Cromwell assumed ever more regal titles until his death in 1657 by which time he was King in all but name. During the latter part of his rule in 1655 he took the Island of Jamaica. Also, in the same year he commenced a war against Spain where in 1658 in the Spanish Netherlands the New Model carried the day with a pike charge during the Battle of the Dunes. This was to prove its last action, for the Restoration of the monarchy followed in 1660 and shortly afterwards the New Model Army was disbanded.

CHAPTER II

1660 to 1685
CHARLES II
RESTORATION

Fusilier *– The title given in the late seventeenth century to those regiments armed with the 'fusil', a light flintlock musket. In battle such regiments were originally charged with the protection of the artillery, which in those days fired from the infantry Line, however being very cumbersome was a favourite target for enemy cavalry.*

All Fusilier regiments wore the badge of the grenade in flames representing the ignited spherical artillery shell or grenade.

The Restoration and the subsequent rule of Charles II until his death on 6th February 1685 did in itself little or nothing at all for the establishment of a standing army and it was not until his brother James succeeded him that we see the need for a standing army based in England.

It is true to say that the 2nd, 3rd, 4th, 5th, 6th and 21st Regiments of Foot were all raised during the time of Charles II, but with the 1st Foot returning to France, the 2nd Foot raised for the defence of Tangier, the 3rd, 4th, 5th and 6th Foot raised for Dutch service and the 21st Foot kept in Scotland, there had been a finer array of English Line regiments with the New Model. It would however be unfair to take the prestige of early raising away from any of these regiments. One must now look into the course of events which led to their raising and also the religious background that was for a long time to dominate the life of this Country.

Charles II returned to England when he landed at the port of Dover on 25th May 1660. The mood of the people following his return was one of disillusionment at Puritanism and fear that Parliament would usurp power again. Yet equally fearful were the landed classes, regardless of which side they had chosen in the earlier troubles for they were nearly all impoverished and they certainly did not intend to allow the King to reverse the power taken from the monarchy and lodged with the people.

As Charles did not require a standing army, Parliament were content that any militia required to defend the country could be raised and controlled by the county lord lieutenants. Charles therefore did not bother the 'Long Parliament' for money for an army but his extravagant ways meant that he was continually short of money. The situation was saved when the hand of Catherine of Braganza was offered to Charles by the Portuguese. She brought a dowry of over £300,000 also the naval bases of Tangier, which turned the eyes of the Government to Mediterranean trade, and Bombay, with similar opportunities for Oriental trade.

In 1661 the Earl of Peterborough raised the Tangier Regiment of Foot, (2nd Foot, The Queen's [Royal West Surrey] Regiment). The purpose of its raising was to defend Tangier from the Moors from whom it has been taken by the Portuguese. The marriage of Charles and Princess Catherine took place in 1662. The Tangier Regiment of Foot then garrisoned Tangier. For eighteen years they remained in the North African outpost, holding the area against pirates and Moors. During those eighteen years the regiment was to have five different colonels and fully deserved its first battle honour – TANGIER 1662-1680 which can have been of no satisfaction to the men at the time as it was not granted until 1909.

Lord George Douglas's Regiment (1st Foot, the Royal Scots) returned to England for a short time in 1662 at the request of Charles, before returning to Louis XIV in France where they remained until 1676.

In 1664 English soldiers in the pay of the Dutch were disbanded and made their way to England where they arrived in 1665. The reason for their disbandment was that the British Government was short of money, the defence of Tangier was expensive, the Governor of Bombay was rather slow to assist in the establishment of the dowry base in India. The dowry itself remained unpaid, in fact eighteen years passed before full payment was made. Cromwell's foreign policy of European greatness which maintained the port of Dunkirk for £400,000 which although at the time drawing ridicule, proved a sound move.

During the early years of Charles's reign Holland grew strong from her overseas trade, together with the Dutch East India Company with fleets of Dutch ships transferring wealth from the East Indies via the Cape, from the West Indies and from the North Sea fishing grounds.

As the English forgot their Civil War, Charles cast his eyes upon the trade of the Continent and under pressure from the Duke of York, Parliament voted over two million pounds to boost England's naval strength by over 100 ships, until in 1664 war at sea broke out with Holland off the African coast, spreading in 1665 to the Channel where, in June off Lowestoft 25,000 men manning 150 ships met the Dutch fleet in a fierce battle. It was the outbreak of this war which led to the English troops in the service of Holland to return to England in the spring of 1665. It is claimed that the forerunners of these troops were 300 volunteers who 90 years earlier had been raised by London guilds and subsequently transferred to and for the Netherlands in their religious conflict with Spain. Upon their return they were reformed, named the Holland Regiment and, because England was engaged at sea, came under the naval authorities for the next two years, together with the Lord High Admiral's regiment formed a few months earlier and which, had it not been disbanded in 1689 would have taken precedence as the 3rd Regiment of Foot[†], instead to the Holland Regiment went this title, therefore in 1665 the 3rd Foot of the East Kent Regiment of Foot was born.

[†] *During the war of Austrian succession in 1745 two regiments had colonels with the same surname, one General the Honourable Sir Charles Howard and the other Lieutenant General Thomas Howard. To avoid confusion in the issue of orders, because regiments were at that time known by the name of their colonel, the regiments were known by the colour of the facings on their uniforms. General the Honourable Sir Charles Howard – The Green Howards (19th Foot)*

    Lieutenant General Thomas Howard – the Buff Howards (3rd Foot) later 'The Buffs'.

The honour of the 4th Foot went to a regiment raised by the Earl of Plymouth from men of the Royal English Regiment on 13th July 1680 although at the time of its raising it was called the Second Tangier Regiment. It had been raised to augment the garrison at Tangier where it remained for four years. This regiment was later to be called the King's Own (Royal Lancashire) Regiment of Foot.

Europe was changing, France with four times the population of England and ably led by Louis XIV was taking over as the premier power; Spain and Austria were on the decline. It was in this climate that France, who had agreed to assist Holland if she was attacked, declared war on England. Thus, although Charles claimed that this Dutch war was due to Dutch aggression, England found herself alone with an expensive war on her hands. The only saving was that both sides found the war crippling and therefore following a drawn-out indecisive conflict, peace was gained in 1667. The squabbles and intrigue continued whilst crisis followed crisis and France secretly negotiated with England against the Dutch and three years later war again broke out, but this time it was between England and France against Holland alone and lasted until early 1674, when England and Holland patched up their differences and the States General again requested permission to raise men from England and Scotland for service against France. England although not really wishing to become entangled in another land war, granted permission for the formation of a land force and appointed Sir Walter Vane to command. Vane, who had earlier fought for the States General, had returned in 1665 to England where three years later he was to become colonel of the Holland regiment. But it was as a major general in the Dutch service that in April 1674 he returned to Holland where his force was formed into four regiments – two English, one Irish and one Scottish.

One of the English regiments stationed at Bar-le-Duc in the Netherlands following the end of the Third Dutch War, became the 5th Regiment of Foot (Northumberland Fusiliers). The second English regiment at the same time became the 6th Regiment of Foot (the Royal Warwickshire Regiment), at that time carrying the title of Lillington's Regiment after its first colonel.

In 1676 Colonel Douglas was to return to England from France with his regiment (1st Foot) a stay which lasted for four years until it was embarked along with two Guards regiments for Tangier where it won its first battle honour TANGIER 1680. This was only granted to the regiment in 1909. Probably of greater significance to the regiment was the granting of the title in 1684 of the Royal Regiment of Foot, an honour still carried by the regiment today.

Charles Erskine, Fifth Earl of Mar, received a commission to raise a regiment of foot to re-establish law and order in Scotland. On 23rd September 1678 the 21st Foot (Royal Scots Fusiliers) was raised, although at that time in line with other regiments it took the name of its colonel, and was therefore known as the Earl of Mar's Regiment. During its ten-year stay in Scotland it became known as Mar's Grey Breeks because of its coarse woven cloth trews.

This is where one must bear in mind that precedence was fixed from the date that regiments were first placed on the English establishment. Thus the Earl of Mar's Regiment which did not cross the border until it marched south to support its Stuart king against William of Orange in 1688, became the 21st Foot not the 4th Foot which, had they been an English regiment, would have been their title.

Another regiment affected by this ruling was Granard's Regiment (18th Foot, the Royal Irish Regiment), which first saw service for the Commonwealth during the time of Cromwell. At the time of the Restoration when the New Model was disbanded in England, the Irish Foot Regiment was formed into one eighty-company regiment called the Royal Regiment of Ireland. Early in 1684 it was decided to form ten regiments from the original one regiment and on 1st April 1684 the newly created Earl of Granard was commissioned to become the colonel of one of these. This regiment did not cross the sea to England until the Monmouth rebellion and even then immediately returned to Ireland without moving further than Chester, so it came under the 1694 ruling – 'that an Irish Regiment shall have rank from the day it comes upon the English Establishment'. Thus Granard's Regiment would become the 18th Foot.

CHAPTER III

1685-1688
JAMES II
RELIGIOUS CONFLICT
SEDGEMOOR

Protestant – *A Christian who denies the universal authority of the Pope and affirms the principles of the Reformation.*

Following the strict rule of puritan England, the return of the monarchy enabled a certain liberal attitude to spread across the country. This was encouraged by Charles II who although a sympathiser with Catholicism showed compete disregard for matters of the spirit and indifference as to whether people belonged to either church. For more than ten years the people of England had not been persecuted for their faith and in 1672 Charles, taking advantage of the fact that monarchy had never lost its power of proclamation, issued a Declaration of Indulgence which tolerated Catholics and dissenters and gave freedom of private worship to its people. Later this had to be withdrawn but the seed of Charles's liberalism was sown. The Roman Catholic Church on the other hand required a more formal setting, France was Catholic and Catholics were present in many high positions, Charles's Queen, Catherine, was Catholic, his brother James and his wife were Catholics, some of his councillors were Catholic, Catholicism was practised by many of Charles's nobles.

Charles's marriage to Catherine proved barren, although this cannot be said of his many affairs, one of whom with his Welsh mistress Lucy Waters produced an illegitimate son James, Duke of Monmouth. In the absence of an heir the line of succession passed to Charles's brother James, Duke of York, a Roman Catholic. The majority feared the return to the stricter Catholic way of life and then in 1678 at first rumour and then panic as an alleged plot was uncovered – the Popish plot, testified to by Titus Oates. The plot was to apparently murder the liberal Charles and suppress Protestantism. Charles was wary of the evidence but many Catholics were brought to trial and executed as a wave of anti-Catholicism swept the country. One of the results of the plot was to attempt to exclude James from the succession. Charles although believing very strongly in hereditary succession, apparently went to extreme lengths to be seen to appease the country and its fear of a Popish king, these were however mostly show.

The Protestants proposed several schemes, all designed to ensure that if the Crown passed to James, the administration would remain Protestant. Lord Shaftesbury demanded that the Protestant Duke of Monmouth should succeed. Charles would not agree and refused to name his illegitimate son as heir. By 1680 the Popish Plot had been exposed and with it the loss of the anti-Catholic cause. In the same year Charles sent James to Scotland as Governor, a position which, being intelligent and shrewd, he ably filled. James returned to England and from 1683 took a leading part in the administration of the realm, until on 6th February 1685, his brother died after receiving his last rites of the Roman Church.

It was now the turn of the Protestant population to fear the succession of James, especially one, namely Titus Oates who was brought to trial and severely punished for the plot largely fabricated by himself. James II now pursued the establishment of the Roman Catholic Church, but he decided not to rush matters. A gradual takeover would produce better results and so a tolerant James held out his hand to the Protestants.

At this time James, Duke of Monmouth was enjoying court life in Holland, when Lord Shaftesbury together with nobles from the 1681 purge at present in exile, urged Monmouth not to wait for the country to call him, but to take what was after all rightly his. Were not the people of England waiting to flock to his side and the Protestant cause? Also with the assistance of the Scottish people who were waiting to join Archibald Campbell, ninth Earl of Argyll, who had departed for Scotland in early May and already landed in the Western Highlands.

Monmouth sailed for England to land unopposed at the small harbour at Lyme Regis on 11th June 1685. It was with a hastily gathered, ill-armed band of followers (it would be incorrect to describe the rebels as an army), that Monmouth entered Taunton on 19th June to be proclaimed King. It appears likely that this was not entirely to Monmouth's liking, as he would probably have wished for more support from the nobility before any such proclamation was made. He must have felt that his cause was lost as he led the rebels cautiously around the West Country avoiding clashes and major towns. Support from London and other areas of power had not been forthcoming and Argyll had been captured in Scotland.

It took two days for the news of the landing to reach James II, who by this time was firmly established in Whitehall. James looked for support from the militia but he knew that it was regular troops that would be needed to repel his nephew.

Two foot regiments, the Queen Dowager's Regiment under a Colonel Kirke (2nd Foot) and the Trelawney's Regiment, to become a Royal regiment later in the year referred to as the Queen's Regiment (4th Foot), were available having returned from Tangier when the base was given up. The Royal Regiment of Foot (1st Foot) has also had companies in Tangier in 1683 but now the whole regiment was in the south of England. These three regiments, together with three foot guard regiments, were the only ones to take part in the Battle of Sedgemoor. The Earl of Granard's Regiment (18th Foot) was called from Ireland but was not sent against Monmouth. The 5th and 6th Regiments of Foot landed in England from the Dutch service, too late however to assist in the suppression of the rebellion.

Whilst Monmouth continued his advance in the West County, King James decided to raise more regular troops and towards this end commissioned nine gentlemen to raise regiments for the Crown. A Royal Warrant dated 11th June 1685 (the day of Monmouth's landing) commissioned Lord Dartmouth to raise a regiment. Companies were established by 27th June 1685 but the regiment, destined to become the 7th Foot (the Royal Fusiliers), did not leave London until 1688. On 20th June 1685 Lord Ferrars raised a regiment in Derbyshire which was given the title of The Princess Anne of Denmark's Regiment of Foot (8th Foot), (the King's Liverpool Regiment) as a compliment to the future Queen. The 19th June 1685 was the date of the officers' commissions in Colonel Henry Cornwall's Regiment of Foot (9th Foot), (the Norfolk Regiment).

The unique feature of John Granville, Earl of Bath's Regiment of Foot (10th Foot), (the Lincolnshire Regiment) was that it was clothed in blue and for some years after its formation on 20th June 1685 it was the only regiment to be so clad. Red was the chosen colour probably because red dyed cloth was the cheapest material available. The recruiting ground was Derbyshire and Nottinghamshire, but these recruits were soon to join the Plymouth garrison with troops under the command of the Governor of Plymouth Fort where they remained for just over four years. It was also on 20th June 1685 that the 1st Duke of Beaufort, currently in charge of the Gloucestershire militia, received orders to raise a regiment, the 11th Foot (the Devonshire Regiment) from men from the counties of Devon, Somerset and Dorset with the depot at Bristol.

Following an order dated 23rd June 1685, Henry Howard, 7th Duke of Norfolk, raised a regiment, the 12th Foot (the Suffolk Regiment) which was recruited from Norwich in the form of only one company of foot, although 20th June is now accepted as the official date of raising. Another Regiment raised on 20th June 1685 and commanded by Theophilus, 7th Earl of Huntingdon was to become the 13th Foot, (Somerset Light Infantry).

Sir Edward Hale's Regiment, the 14th Foot (the Prince of Wales's Own [West Yorkshire] Regiment) was raised at Canterbury on 22nd June 1685 with companies formed from several towns in Kent. The last of the nine regiments came from Nottingham and adjoining counties and was raised by Sir William Clifton whose commission as colonel of the regiment which was to become the 15th Foot (East Yorkshire Regiment) was dated 22nd June 1685. As the nine regiments each consisting of ten or eleven companies of foot and each containing one hundred 'private men' of pikemen and musketeers were still being formed when Sedgemoor was fought, none actually took part in the fighting although the 13th Foot was employed in guarding prisoners taken after the battle.

Monmouth had a force of between 7,000 and 8,000 men, consisting of hastily recruited poorly armed militia. It must be stated that the militia raised by James differed little with ancient pikes, scythes and general paraphernalia that one associates with the peasant stock of the day. Monmouth had had a few early local successes but the regular army of James forced a retreat on Bridgewater. Lord Feversham was now in command of the Royalist forces and set up camp on Sunday 5th July at the small village of Westonzoyland, four miles from Bridgewater.

Monmouth's plan, born of desperation, knowing that in a set-piece battle his army could not hope to match the regular troops of the King and also the belief that Feversham would be caught totally unprepared, was to attack the Royalist troops during the night. Shortly before midnight, Monmouth's leading infantry at the head of 3,000 foot and 800 horse left Bridgewater. Three hours later they had travelled the six miles through extremely difficult country in what must rate as one of the most formidable marches ever undertaken. For his army to pass Royalist outposts undetected was a feat worthy of praise in its own right. Then events began to go sadly wrong for Monmouth as the Royalist troops became aware of his presence and with the early dawn the Royal forces began riding down the rebels, in the general melee a broken Monmouth fled the field. The Royal troops were in no mood for compromise and when the King's troopers scoured the area, Monmouth was captured and escorted to James. After a very undignified interview, Monmouth was taken to Tower Hill where on 25th July 1685 he was executed.

After the suppression of the rebellion, King James reviewed his troops at Hounslow Heath and thanked both officers and men for their readiness to support his Crown during the recent troubles.

The corps so soon to become either disbanded or at best reduced to ten companies each of approximately fifty private men must have looked a colourful sight at the review with at least twelve different flags being carried by each regiment. These flags belonged to colonels, majors and captains of the companies forming the regiment; this of course was before the innovation of the King's or regimental colours.

The abortive attempt by the Protestant faction to gain power and the apparent prevention of yet another civil war, strengthened the hand of James who took advantage of the popularity which followed and the upsurge of support for the Crown, to suppress the Protestant religion and subvert the constitution of the Kingdom.

As Judge Jeffreys (the hanging judge) was busy dealing with the West Country supporters of the Duke of Monmouth, King James II was considering his first essential, namely, that Parliament should not be allowed to interfere with his ambition. He set into operation his plans for the replacement of Protestants by Catholics in the key appointments, but firstly in early November 1685 he laid his plans before Parliament for a strengthened and regular standing army and as his example he cited his own militia which had shown badly when opposed by Monmouth and also Monmouth's own rebels who at Sedgemoor had not stood against James's regular regiments. He also made it clear that Catholic officers, who had recently been commissioned by him to assist him in his latest struggle, would not lose their commissions.

Parliament, wishing not to have their consternation interpreted as disloyalty granted an additional £700,000 to boost the fleet and strengthen the standing Army, whilst respectfully expressing the wish and hope that James should not attempt to suppress the Protestant religion. The actions so far demonstrated by the King prompted the House of Lords to invite the judges to act regarding the route upon which James appeared to be travelling. James could not call upon the judges to support his actions and he certainly could not count on either theirs or the House of Lords supporting his hoped for domination by the Roman Catholic religion, therefore within two weeks James had entered the House of Lords and prorogued Parliament. It was never again called during his reign.

James was now free to concentrate on the replacement of the Protestants; his easiest path was Ireland and the Irish regiments which already carried many Catholics. The Army was to be remodelled and the instrument chosen by James was another Papist, a Colonel Richard Talbot, who displayed a burning desire to see Roman Catholicism control the standing army. In the summer of 1687 Colonel Talbot, newly created as the Earl of Tyrconnel took office as Lord Lieutenant and inspected regiments in the Irish Corps on the Curragh of Kildare, dismissing Protestant officers and men and replacing them with men of Roman Catholic persuasion. One of the regiments so affected was Lord Forbes' Regiment, the 18th Foot, (Royal Irish Regiment). Colonel Lord Forbes was allowed to retain more Protestants than any regiment in other Irish Corps, probably to avoid undue conflict with this popular young noblemen.

James continued with the rebuilding of his army in England. He also used his dispensing power to frequently prorogue Parliament, thus ensuring that the Bench was sympathetic towards his cause. The Privy Council was also encouraged to admit Catholics. The effect of James's narrow-minded, unforgiving and unconstitutional methods upon those who had remained loyal to him during the Monmouth troubles, was the loss of many of his former supporters including Parliament which James now realised, had to be constantly prorogued to avoid conflict.

It was into this climate that a further two regiments came into being, for on the 27th September 1688 a commission was given to Colonel Solomon Richards to form a regiment of foot comprising of thirteen companies each of the sixty men was to become the 17th Regiment of Foot (the Leicestershire Regiment). This was followed when a special commission dated 9th October 1688 was raised on Archibald Douglas to bring a cadre of officers, NCOs and men from the Royal Regiment of Foot (1st Foot) to form a Regiment of Pikemen and Musketeers at Reading. It became the 16th Foot (the Bedfordshire Regiment).

The position in the country was worsening and was certainly not improved when the lieutenant-colonel and five captains of Princess Anne of Denmark's Regiment (8th Foot) were tried by courts martial for refusing to allow Roman Catholics into their companies.

The Protestant people of England had hoped that the Catholic line would die with the King and they were prepared to wait until his natural death (he was 55 years old in 1688). However on 10th June 1688 a male heir was born. The circumstances surrounding the birth were sufficient to allow certain doubts about the parents of the child, but without any firm evidence to the contrary it had to be accepted that a Catholic heir now existed.

The scene was now set for civil war. On the one side the King with a standing army of fifteen Line regiments and foot guards totalling twenty thousand men at a cost of over half a million pounds a year.

On the other side were a growing band of influential Whigs and Tories who were uniting to oppose the King. The leaders of a group which called itself 'The Party of Action' met on 30th June at the house of Charles Talbot, Earl of Shrewsbury and there together with six other people, Talbot signed and sent a letter inviting the Protestant William of Orange to come to England, pledging support if he should do so. Individual pledges were also given secretly, the most notable was from John Churchill, later to become the First Duke of Marlborough, who wrote to William in August renewing an earlier pledge but safeguarding his position by remaining with James until after William's November landings.

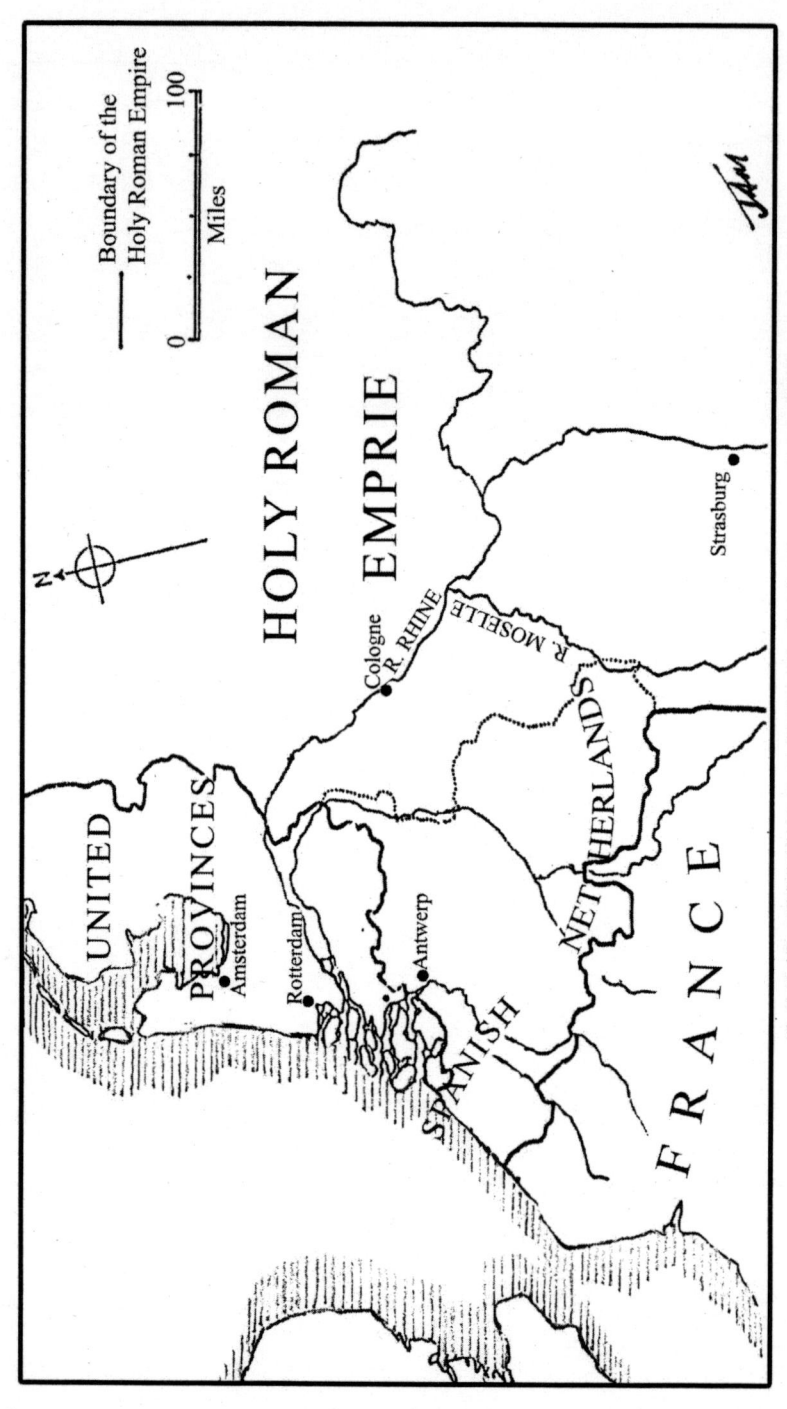

NORTHERN EUROPE - 1688

CHAPTER IV

1688
WILLIAM III
INVASION

Jacobite – *Supporter of James II of England after his enforced abdication.*

In order to be able to understand why William, Prince of Orange, should be interested in England, it is necessary to look at the history of Europe and how those events influenced the succession to the throne of England.

For several centuries the House of Hapsburg, which was led by a confederation of German princes who had the right to elect the Emperor, ruled the Holy Roman Empire. It had control over Spain and her overseas possessions including part of America, the Netherlands and part of Italy. The Hapsburgs had divided during the middle of the sixteenth century. One part of the family had then taken control of Spain, leaving the other branch the remainder. In 1648 the United Provinces of the Netherlands gained independence from Spain. The ten Southern Provinces remained under Spanish rule as the Spanish Netherlands.

Since 1672, William had been Captain General of the United Provinces. He was the nephew of James II, his mother Mary was the sister of both Charles II and James II, she had died in 1660 and William had been brought up under the guidance of his uncle, Charles II. To confuse matters William married Mary, the daughter of James II. Unlike James, Mary was a Protestant.

By the end of the seventeenth century, each of the European neighbours were casting greedy eyes across their borders, yet each was fearful that the other would move against them. The French under Louis XIV were looking eastwards to increase their dominion whilst hoping that the divisions remained in the Holy Roman Empire, now lesser than its former glory, who in turn feared French aggression, whilst Louis being a Catholic, had more than an interest in keeping England, Scotland and Ireland Catholic. The English, who under James had strong Catholic ties, wished to draw strength from the Catholicism of France, whilst the United Provinces eyed possible movement from the Holy Roman Empire and a more realistic fear of invasion from the French, who since 1672 had rebuffed their attempts to agree a peace treaty. It was into this background that the succession to the English throne was linked to the power struggle in Europe and the religious conflict in both Europe and England.

James had pressed for Catholic domination, increasing daily his suppression of the Protestant cause, until William was invited to redress the situation. William was also seen by some of the English as the man to stop any invasion of England by the French. Before he could be sure of success, William had to solve another problem, that of winning over the merchants of Holland who believed that French trade was preferable to an alliance with England. He also had to convince the people of England that their European partner should be the Protestant Dutch and not the Catholic French.

In 1688 several events took place of major importance to the English succession. In June, the Catholic heir to James was born. Also in June, the invitation to invade England was received by William, who in response commenced preparations for an invasion whilst quietly worried lest Louis should attack the Netherlands. Louis, on the other hand, believed that should William invade England, he would be engaged in battle with James who might possibly defeat him. Whatever the outcome William would be out of the way, leaving Louis to march his troops into the Rhineland without Dutch interference, which is what he did in September.

Thomas Osbourne, Earl of Danby, was one of the signatories of the invitation to William and he believed that the route to a successful landing was to invade through the north. However, a Protestant wind had driven the transports of William not north but on a westerly course, whilst more importantly it held the fleet of

James in Essex. William was to land in Devon and even as the English fleet sailed against him, the storm intervened again and drove the ships of James back into the shelter of Portsmouth. It was on 5th November 1688 that William landed at Brixham, Torbay, with what was undoubtedly the largest disciplined military force ever to land on English soil; 24,000 men drawn from mixed British and European soldier classes.

Two regiments (5th and 6th Foot) who had returned to Holland after the 1685 Monmouth rebellion, returned with William. However, the unique distinction of wearing the Lion of England as its cap badge went to the 4th Foot, the King's own [Royal Lancashire] Regiment) as the first Royal Regiment to change allegiance from James to William on his arrival in England. The regiment (4th Foot) had become a Royal Regiment in 1685, referred to as the Queen's Regiment. Later, in the reign of Queen Anne it was to be called the Queen's Own.

Less than 30 miles from Brixham, James had regiments stationed in Plymouth under the command of the Earl of Bath and any fear that William may have harboured, that regiments loyal to James would oppose his landing were dispelled when news reached him that Bath had paraded his garrison and almost without demur they declared for the Prince of Orange, thus the 10th Foot (the Lincolnshire Regiment) and the 13th Foot (Somerset Light Infantry – Prince Albert) were two of the first regiments to desert their Catholic King.

Had James not pursued his anti-Protestant policy with such vigour and had he not carried this policy into his army and had he not shown such weak resolution in resisting the invasion, James may well have held his crown. The 21st Foot (Royal Scots Fusiliers) were ordered to march south to join James. Lord Forbes Regiment, 18th Foot, (the Royal Irish Regiment) were also one of the regiments ordered by James to proceed to Salisbury from London where it had been quartered since the summer of 1688. Lord Forbes completed the march to join the army of James and swell its numbers to nearly 30,000 trained full-time troops. This should have been sufficient to enable James to resist the invasion but he was deserted by some of his regiments of horse. Word also reached him that the revolt had succeeded in several counties and when he heard that the Navy in Portsmouth had deserted him, James realised that with Protestant support within his army, he could not oppose William, especially as many men had actually refused to fight in the cause of Papacy and had joined William.

While James was forced to withdraw to London with what was left of his army the 7th Foot (the Royal Fusiliers – City of London Regiment) who were encamped at Hounslow Heath did not return with him to London but, almost to a man, joined the cause of the Prince of Orange, who had on 19th November 1688 commissioned Francis Lutterell of Dunster Castle in the county of Somerset to raise a regiment, the 19th Foot, (the Green Howards) and the very next day Colonel Sir Robert Peyton raised his regiment, the 20th Foot, (the Lancashire Fusiliers).

His decision to retreat encouraged many powerful figures to sign an association for a free Parliament and join William as he made for London. Prince George of Denmark carried his regiment over to William and even John Churchill finally decided that the time had arrived to openly declare for William when he left the camp of James at Salisbury.

James returned to London and received details of the steady advance of William. His attempt to negotiate from such a weak position decided James that his wife and son should leave the country. Two days later on 11th December 1688 James left Whitehall to flee abroad but, having boarded his ship at Sheerness, he missed the tide and was subsequently forced by local people and Faversham fisherman to return to London. James was not to be denied: he escaped, possibly due to William's desire that bloodshed on English soil should be avoided, and finally sailed from Rochester on 23rd December, arriving in France two days later. Upon the flight of James, the recently appointed Colonel of the 16th Foot (the Bedfordshire Regiment), a sympathiser of the King, resigned and was replaced by Colonel Hodges at the direction of the Prince of Orange.

Lord Forbes (18th Foot) also under the direction of William disbanded 500 Catholic officers and men leaving fewer than 200 Protestants with the colours. The strength of the regiment was soon recovered by a draft of Protestant officers from Hamilton's Irish Regiment and immediate recruitment of Protestant rank and file.

Panic spread throughout the South of England when rumour falsely suggested that recently discharged Roman Catholic Irish troops were responsible for looting, murder and arson. For their own safety these troops were rounded up and sent as prisoners to the Isle of Wight before being transferred to the service of the Catholic Emperor of Germany.

CHAPTER V

1688–1691
SCOTLAND

Covenanters – *Those who belonged to a religious sect of strict Puritans, who had been outlawed and persecuted during the reigns of Charles II and that of his brother James.*

The Declaration of Rights, which had been drawn to prevent a monarch from maintaining a standing army in peacetime, was accepted by William and Mary on 13th February 1689. This agreement led in April 1689 to their coronation as King and Queen of an England with a population of five million. James (albeit absent) was still King of Scotland.

In March 1689, David Leslie, 3rd Earl of Leven who had travelled to England with William, was then authorised to raise a regiment (25th Foot, King's Own Scottish Borderers) in Edinburgh to guard the city. In two hours, by beat of drum, 800 men were enlisted and paraded near St Giles.

Colonel George Viscount Castleton's* Regiment (30th Foot, 1st Battalion East Lancashire Regiment) was issued with beating orders on 16th March 1689 following a commission dated 8th March to raise a regiment that was to consist of twelve battalion companies each of 69 privates, three sergeants, two corporals and one drummer with one company of grenadiers. A few days after the issue of orders, passes were granted for Lord Castleton to proceed to York where at

---

* Sir George Saunderson, Baronet of Saxby, Lincolnshire and Fifth Viscount Castleton in the Kingdom of Ireland.

the beginning of June the regiment was clothed, armed and all companies united.

In Scotland, John Graham of Claverhouse 'Bonnie Dundee' had served James well and in recognition of that service, in 1686 he had been made a Major General and Provost of Dundee.

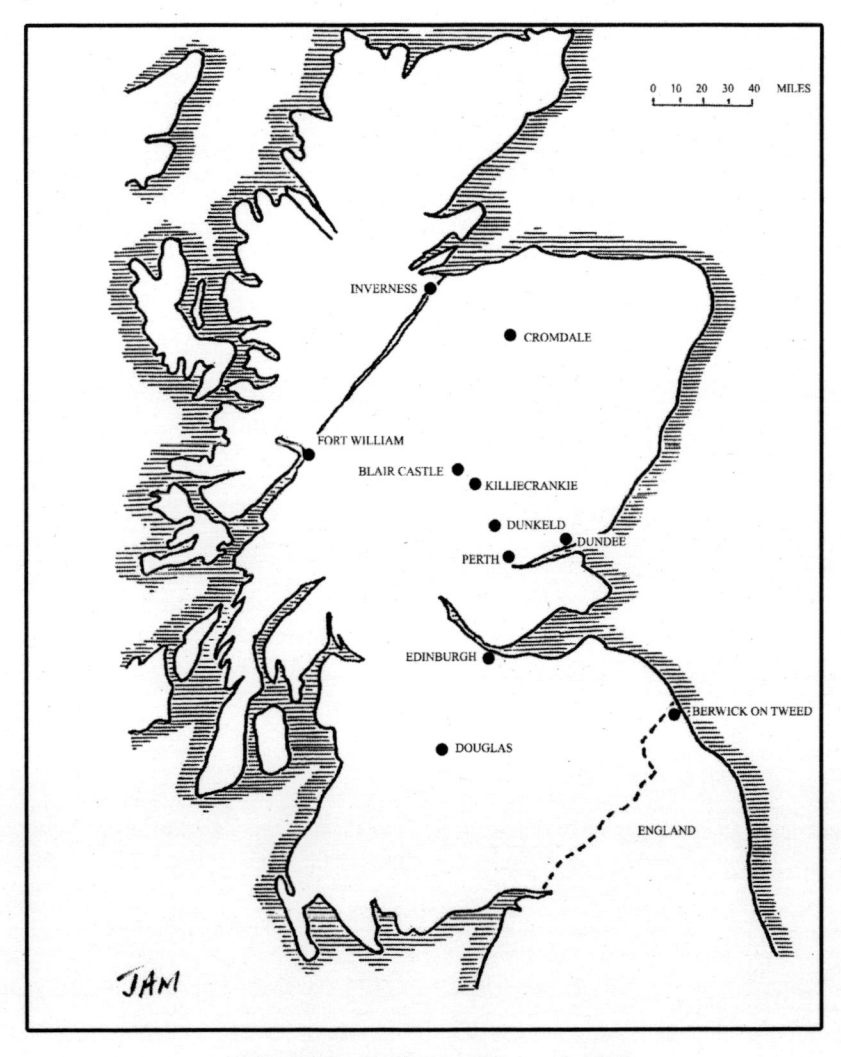

SCOTLAND 1688 - 1690

In November 1688 he was created Viscount Dundee. As William's successes swept through England, Dundee urged James to stand against him. James refused the advice and this enabled the Convention of Estates in Scotland, which had been summoned in Edinburgh in April 1689, to declare that James had forfeited his throne and a majority showed for William and Mary, who were proclaimed King and Queen of Scotland. Dundee, who had attended the Convention, rode north from Edinburgh to raise clans loyal to the man they considered their legitimate monarch. His intention was to set up a rival Convention in Stirling, resulting in the Government in Edinburgh offering a reward of £20,000 for his capture dead or alive. Dundee, who believed that reinforcements would arrive from Ireland, moved further into the Highlands with his ever-increasing Stuart army.

At Douglas in Lanarkshire on 14th May 1689 the Earl of Angus Regiment (26th Foot, 1st Battalion, the Cameronians) was raised in one day without beat of drum, nor expense of levy money. The only regiment of the British Army born of religion 'for service of the King's Majesty in the defence of the nation' was raised from the ranks of the Covenanters by the Earl of Angus and later called the Cameronians after Richard Cameron, one of the most notable leaders of the Covenanters.

William sent lowland Scot Major General Hugh Mackay, veteran of the Dutch Wars to watch Dundee's movements and put down the Highland Jacobites. The 13th Foot (Somerset Light Infantry) having joined Mackay and Leslie's regiment (15th Foot, East Yorkshire Regiment) also marched from London in June 1689 to Berwick-upon-Tweed. Mackay pursued Dundee to Inverness only to find that he had doubled south intending to loot Perth and, in June, mustered the clans in Lochaber. Although he had difficulty keeping them together, he was able to create a Jacobite army despite the indiscipline of the untrained collection of clansmen who only responded to their clan chiefs. Those who supported Dundee were those who feared and therefore hated the Campbells – Cameron of Locheil, the MacDonalds, Stewart of Appin and Macleans of the Isles.

Warned of the approach of William's Government forces under Major General Mackay, Dundee trapped them just north of the dark, narrow ravine of Killiecrankie near Pitlochry in Perthshire. Mackay, who outnumbered Dundee by nearly two to one was in command of a force of 4,000 men of which 3,000 were foot, the remainder cavalry and dragoons.

At sunset on 27th July 1689, within half an hour, Mackay's troops had broken under the fierce charge of the rebel Highlanders. Lord Leven's regiment (25th Foot, King's Own Scottish Borderers) claims to have held its ground until ordered to withdraw, an action which afterwards caused the Lord Provost and magistrates of Edinburgh to confer the right to recruit forever in Edinburgh without asking leave and to march through the city with bayonets fixed and colours flying. Hasting's regiment (13th Foot, Somerset Light Infantry) also claim to have stood fast amid the general rout.

It is doubtful if either side could claim a victory. There is no doubt that Mackay's force retreated. However, about 600 Highlanders were killed, and more important was the death of Dundee who had been hit by a Government bullet in the first charge. He was carried into Blair Castle where he died later that evening. As the Government troops retreated, the Highlanders were intent on plunder and made no effort to pursue Mackay's broken forces. Instead, leaderless, they moved southwards to the cathedral town of Dunkeld.

About this time, the Government's intention had been to use Castleton's regiment (30th Foot) in Ireland, but following Mackay's setback at Killiecrankie the regiment was ordered to march to Berwick-upon-Tweed.

On 21st August 1689 in the churchyard of Dunkeld, 1200 officers and men of Angus's regiment (26th Foot) under the command of Lieutenant Colonel William Cleland, faced a Jacobite force of 5000 Highlanders. Cleland's regiment distinguished itself by the doggedness of its defence, during which Cleland was killed. The Highland army fired Dunkeld as it was driven from the town.

Leslie's regiment (15th Foot) followed the retreating Highlanders to the wilds of Lochaber, afterwards proceeding to Inverness. During this uncertain period the officers were ordered to wear their swords at all meals, a tradition carried on (even after the amalgamation in 1958) by the orderly officer wearing his sword before dinner in the mess.

To control the Highlands, the Government forces under the command of Sir Thomas Livingstone had a firm control of Inverness. Major General Mackay constructed a fortress at Inverlochy, to be given the name of Fort William after the new King. This was garrisoned under the command of Colonel Hill.

On 1st May 1690, Livingstone with Leslie's regiment (15th Foot) surprised and routed Buchan at Cromdale on Speyside. Angus' regiment (26th Foot) was on its way to reinforce Livingstone when it heard news of the victory. The Jacobite cause in the Highlands was checked for the time being, as James fled to France. Beveridge's regiment, the 14th Foot, the Prince of Wales's Own (West Yorkshire) Regiment stayed in the south of Scotland until 1692 when it sailed from Leith for Flanders. Leslie's regiment was in Scotland until the end of 1693.

CHAPTER VI

1689–1691
IRELAND

Huguenot – *A 16th Century French Protestant.*

King James sailed from France, and on 12th March 1689 arrived at Kinsale in the south of Ireland with French diplomats and military advisors, some French troops and the promise of more. He certainly had no desire to be King of Ireland, but saw a defeat there for William as a route for his return to England because he believed that Louis XIV would strike into the Low Countries, thereby drawing the Dutchman back to his homeland.

On 24th March, James entered Dublin and called for an Irish Parliament. His Lord Lieutenant, Tyreconnel raised an army of 50,000 poorly armed and undisciplined men who held all of Ireland except where members of the Protestant faith had rallied behind the walls of Londonderry and Enniskillen.

On 3rd April, to support the people of Londonderry, the 17th Foot (Leicestershire Regiment) and the 9th Foot (Norfolk Regiment) were directed to Ireland under the command of Colonel Cunningham. Unknown to Cunningham, the Governor of Londonderry had secretly planned to give up the town to King James and had given false statements to the Council regarding provisions available to the troops. Believing this, Cunningham returned in April to England with both regiments only to find that William had deprived him of his commission for desertion of the garrison. On 1st May, William Stewart took over command of the 9th Foot and, unlike the 17th Foot, returned with his regiment to Ireland where it took part in the relief of Londonderry. Another regiment to lose its colonel was the 18th

Foot (Royal Irish Regiment) when Colonel Sir John Edgeworth was found guilty of irregularly procuring clothing by purchasing the old uniforms of disbanded Roman Catholic soldiers to supply recruits instead of providing them with new. Edgeworth was replaced by Edward, Earl of Meeth on 1st May 1689.

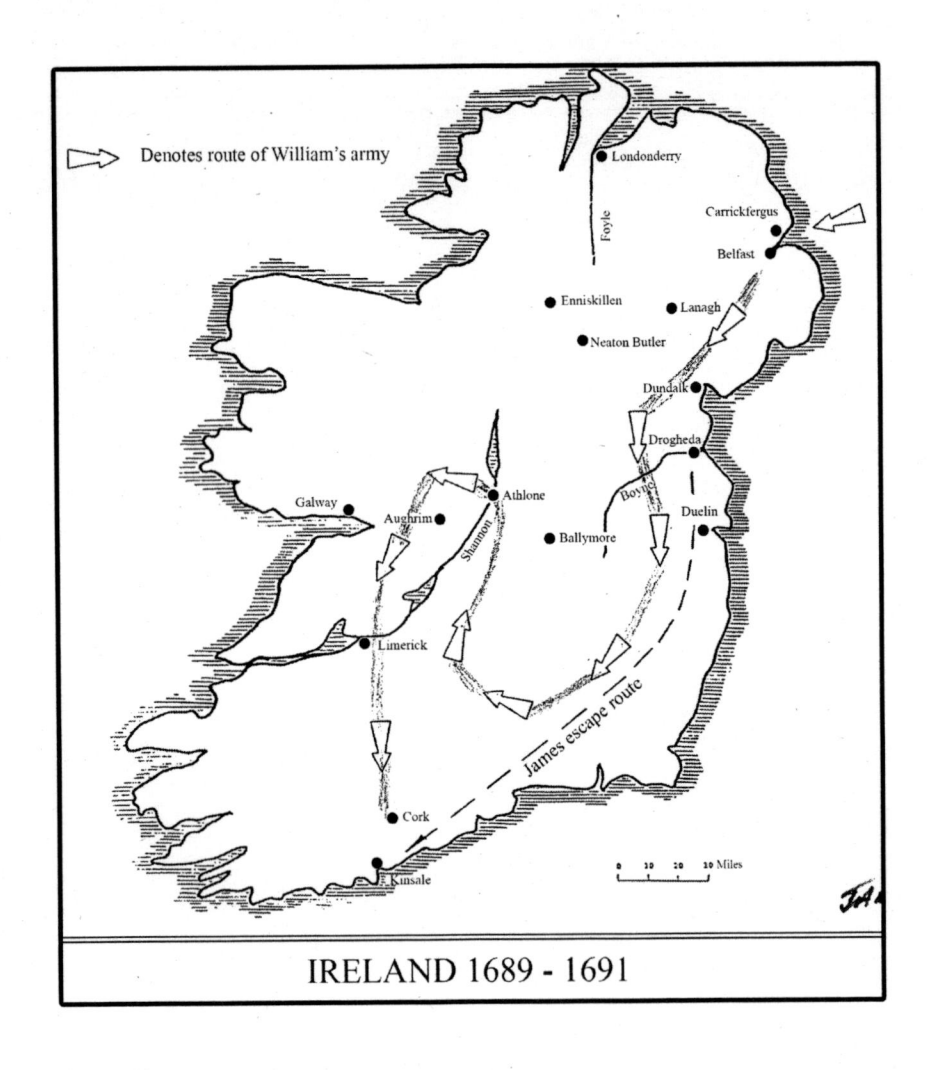

IRELAND 1689 - 1691

The strength of William's new army was further increased when on the 8th March 1689, Sir Edward Dering, Baronet of Surrenden in Kent, was issued with a commission requiring him to raise a regiment of foot. This was achieved and the first muster took place on 28th March with Dering as the colonel. The establishment was fixed at three sergeants, three corporals, two drummers and 60 private soldiers, in all 884 NCOs and men. The regiment was to become the 24th Foot (South Wales Borderers). Another regiment was formed by Henry Howard, 7th Duke of Norfolk. This regiment was raised on the Wirrel Peninsular and became the 22nd Foot (Cheshire Regiment). Lord Herbert of Chirbury also received a Warrant on 16th March to raise volunteers for a regiment. It became the 23rd Foot (Royal Welch Fusiliers), the oldest infantry regiment in Wales.

In April, James had invested Londonderry, a siege which was to last 105 days. The Protestant defence was inspired by George Walker, an elderly Anglican priest. Food supplies were nearly exhausted, only horseflesh and meal remained when, in July, William's ships broke the boom over the River Foyle.

James had also invested Enniskillen (Inniskilling) and the town was to become the birthplace of another regiment, from the original band of irregular levies who, whenever the opportunity was presented, probed the surrounding Catholic forces. From foot soldiers led by Colonel Tiffin was born Tiffin's Inniskillings, later to become the 27th Regiment (1st Battalion Royal Inniskilling Fusiliers). In July 1689 the men of Enniskillen routed the Catholic supporters at the battle of Newton Butler.

To challenge James, King William chose the men who had led his troops at Torbay nine months earlier. In August 1689 an army was assembled at Chester under the command of the old Huguenot, Marshall Frederick Duke Schomberg. Sailing to Ireland with his army, which included the 22nd and 24th Foot, Schomberg landed at Bangor in Antrim on the south side of Belfast Lough. He laid siege to the fortress of Carrickfergus which surrendered shortly after.

The army then advanced to Dundalk to make camp on low wet ground. The winter quarters for the inexperienced recruits were spent in great hardship. The rains were continuous and sickness was rife, the men were badly fed and clothed and many died. It may have been a different story had the regiments been composed of veterans of the Dutch wars more able to cope with the bad weather. However, to fill the depleted ranks, Schomberg called for replacements and also for regiments who had gained experience from the Scottish campaign.

In the early summer of 1690, Marshall Schomberg established a bridgehead in eastern Ulster for King William who landed on the 14th June with a powerful army of 36,000 men, made up from English, Dutch and Danish regiments. William also had experienced Dutch generals and several Hugeunot battalions. Although his army was formidable he had risked much in his passage to Ireland, for the French fleet controlled the Channel and had the chance been presented they would have crushed him at sea.

Within a fortnight William reached the Boyne. James with 7,000 French troops supporting his Irish army faced him. James's centre of Irish troops broke under the advance of William's right flank. The Battle was fought on 11th July and was a mixed success for William, as Schomberg was killed, but at the head of his regiments William pressed for victory, driving into the left-flank regiments of James's army.

Had battle honours been awarded for the Boyne the 4th, 6th, 8th, 9th, 11th, 12th, 14th, 18th, 20th, 22nd, 23rd and 27th would carry the name.

For most of the regiments it was their first action. This was certainly the case of Tiffin's Inniskillings who at the Boyne fought as a regular regiment in the original colour of their uniform. Thus, under their new name of 'Grey Inniskillings' they were blooded in action. It was undoubtedly the actions of theses soldiers, which led to the badge of the 27th Foot being composed of the Castle of Inniskilling flying the flag of St George.

The 7th Foot arrived in Cork in September 1690 and the 25th Foot from Scotland in the spring of 1691.

From the Boyne, William's army moved towards a Dublin held by James's troops without the ex-King who had not tarried but, arriving before his demoralised army, fled to Kinsale, thence on to France, a defeated King who was never to return to England. Within days Dublin had fallen and, without James, one would have expected a collapse of the Catholic cause. However, stands were made at Athlone,

Aughrim, Ballymore, Galway and Limerick, the latter was defended by Patrick Sarsfield who rallied the Catholic supporters. In August 1691, following a short siege, Sarsfield was forced to surrender Limerick. He and 10,000 crushed Irish troops sailed for the Continent.

Some British regiments left Ireland almost immediately, whilst others stayed for varying periods over the next few years.

CHAPTER VII

1689–1702
WILLIAM III and MARY II

Bayonet – *A blade attached to the muzzle of a firearm. French – baionnette. From Bayonne, city in France.*

Whilst William was suppressing the Catholic cause in Scotland and Ireland, events in Europe were dominated by the French, where King Louis XIV had become a problem to the rest of Europe. So much so, that what was known as the Grand Alliance was formed against him. England, Spain, the Netherlands and Germany made up the coalition which spent the summer of 1689 on the defensive against the French, who were determined upon seizing the Spanish possessions in the Netherlands. However, the English Parliament, anxious not to spend unnecessary funds on a large standing army at a time when peace through stalemate seemed just around the corner and believing that it was not a time for the raising of further regiments, agreed to increase its army by only 8,000 men. Therefore, between June 1689 and 1694, no new regiments were formed.

King William's progress in Scotland had been relatively swift and even though the deposed James had arrived in Ireland having left France in March 1689, it was believed that William had the strength with which to overcome any Catholic threat from the former King or his French supporters.

Although Louis XIV had an efficient army which far exceeded the size of the Grand Alliance, he was nevertheless committed on several fronts to such an extent that the people of England began to feel that he would not be able to carry out an invasion, especially as they believed that the English Navy controlled the seas around Britain.

In 1689 two battalions of the 1st Regiment of Foot (the Royal Scots) went to the Netherlands, where they were to remain for six years. The same year saw the arrival in the Low Countries of the 16th Regiment of Foot (the Bedfordshire Regiment) and the 21st Regiment of Foot (Royal Scots Fusiliers) who both saw their first action against the French at the Battle of Walcourt on 25th August, where the 16th Foot under Colonel Hodges bore the brunt of the battle, and held the French Army at bay for three hours. Their reward was an even longer stay than the 1st Foot, as they remained in the Low Countries until 1697.

On 30th June 1690, just off Beachy Head in the English Channel, a naval battle took place where the English were soundly beaten by the French but Louis was unable to press his advantage and invade England, due to the over-commitment of his land forces in Europe, and the lost cause in Ireland, from where, at the end of 1690 a defeated James returned to France urging him to invade England.

Campaigning on land was generally carried out in the late spring and during the summer. The Admiralty also believed it unwise to unnecessarily keep its ships at sea after the middle of September until at least the middle of March. It was, therefore, able to refurbish and refit the fleet during the winter months.

Towards the end of 1690 the course of events enabled King William to leave command in Ireland to Baron Ginkell. The defeat of James did not however bring wars to an end, because for William, since his possessions in the Netherlands were threatened by the French, further action had to be taken.

The threat from the French enabled William to persuade Parliament to raise their sights regarding the strength of an army to defend Britain. They agreed that 70,000 men were needed to curb any designs that Louis may have against their country, although the merchants, whose ships were increasingly harassed by the French, would have to finance the new King's expedition. Parliament would have preferred that William brought all regiments back from the Netherlands to defend England. Instead William returned to the Low Countries at the head of some 23,000 British troops. In January 1691, the 7th Fuzileers (the Royal Fusiliers) were ordered to Flanders, embarking on the 11th January.

The 10th Regiment of Foot (the Lincolnshire Regiment) had remained in the Channel Islands until 1691 when they moved to Ostend, where they joined with the 16th Foot and Fitzpatrick's Fuzileers, a brigade under General Churchill, afterwards the Duke of Marlborough. In command of the 10th Foot was the Earl of Bath's nephew, Lieutenant-Colonel Sir Beville Granville. Although not actively engaged in the opening months of the campaign, it formed part of a reserve corps, composed of twelve squadrons of cavalry and six battalions of infantry – two British and four foreign.

The 30th Regiment of Foot (1st Battalion, the East Lancashire Regiment) was assembled at Hull to march south and join the expeditionary force having been almost completely re-armed in March 1691. All musketeers receiving the firelock which was certainly a great improvement on the old matchlock, but shared with it one great defect in that the ramrod or 'scowrer' was made of wood, supplied at seven shillings a hundred, and it was certain that sooner or later these would break. It is possible that their new bayonets were of the socket and ring pattern, which enabled the soldier to fire with the bayonet fixed. This was an enormous improvement on the earlier plug bayonet which was pushed into the muzzle, preventing the weapon being used as a firearm.

In April 1691, Louis moved his army eastwards and overran the fortress of Mons, signalling that the main focus for his land conflict had moved to the Low Countries. Later in 1691, the 25th Regiment of Foot (the King's Own Borderers) left Ireland and, for the first time since their raising, went to the Continent of Europe in support of William against the French.

Early in 1692 events took another twist because, whilst Louis was continuing his land war, he was also in his final preparations to invade England, which he believed to be badly short of troops. Therefore, a large French fleet including transports and store-ships was being assembled in northern French ports. At this time, too, ex-King James with his exiled Jacobite Court boasted the support of 10,000 Irish and 10,000 French troops all ready to restore a Catholic to the throne.

To combat these threats, King William was ordering English and Scottish regiments to sail for Flanders:

The 3rd Regiment of Foot (the Buffs or East Kent Regiment)

The 4th Regiment of Foot (the King's Own or Royal Lancashire Regiment)

The 14th Regiment of Foot (the Prince of Wales' Own Yorkshire Regiment)

The 19th Regiment of Foot (Alexandra, Princess of Wales' Own Yorkshire Regiment)

The Green Howards and the 26th Regiment of Foot, 1st Battalion the Cameronians (Scottish Rifles) were to join regiments already in the Low Countries preparing to meet the French advance. This was the year when most regiments would first see real action and be blooded in the art of European warfare.

It was not until the middle of April 1692 that the English Government realised the French intention, and made preparations to defend by land and sea. The Earl of Meath's 18th Regiment of Foot (Royal Irish) and several other regiments embarked at Waterford in Ireland, for England.

On 19th–20th May, the English and Dutch fleets destroyed fifteen French ships of the line off Cape La Hogue, thereby depriving Louis of his invasion plans.

The land war began with the French laying siege to the great fortress at Namur which was taken by them in June. William attempted to recapture the fortress, but bad planning, ill prepared troops and bad weather were responsible for his army being bogged down in flooded countryside. The attempt was aborted.

Abandoning the relief of Namur, William moved towards Brussels, where in late July after marching throughout the night, he attacked the French who were relaxed after occupying a strong position near the village of Steenkerke, believing that the country was too enclosed to permit any advance in the close formation adopted by the regiments of those days. In the early morning William surprised the French. In their confusion he initially overwhelmed their advanced regiments, inflicting heavy casualties. The French commander, Marshal Luxembourg, rallied his troops and ordered a stand against the advancing British, who were held. The eight British regiments commanded by General Mackay, being in the forefront of the action, took the brunt of Luxembourg's Household troops who launched a spirited counter-attack against them, changing what should have been a decisive victory for William into a defeat. French reinforcements drove from all sides and two British generals were killed as the regiments sustained heavy casualties.

The 10th Foot and 3rd Foot were called upon to redress the balance. The 10th advanced under their colonel who had given orders that not a shot should be fired 'until they were muzzle to muzzle with the Frenchmen'. They went forward and after beating off several attacks by the French battalions, finally drove the French in the front line back to their camp. Elsewhere, the fight had gone ill for the Allies. Colonel Hodges of the 16th Foot was killed at the head of his Regiment, as was Sir Robert Douglas, who, with one battalion of the 1st Foot, drove back four French battalions, unfortunately losing one of his Colours. It was in retrieving the Colour that he was killed. The 26th Foot also lost the young Earl of Angus. The British foot regiments had been left unsupported by the Dutchman Count Solms, to suffer the French onslaught unaided. By noon the battle was lost and the army, watched by William, was in full retreat. Some semblance of order was maintained by the Dutch General Overkirk who was later to play a prominent part in Marlborough's campaigns. Although casualties on both sides were similar, the day belonged to the French.

On 22nd August, the 2nd Regiment of Foot (the Queen's [Royal West Surrey] Regiment) landed at Ostend. They were followed in September when the 8th Regiment of Foot (the King's [Liverpool] Regiment) also joined those already in Flanders, who had spent the weeks after their first European action, marching and counter-marching before being ordered into winter quarters to regroup and fill their depleted ranks with recruits.

The inaction of Count Solms was debated in the English Parliament where the fact that he appeared to care little for the non-Dutch regiments, prompted a call in the House of Lords that no English general should be subordinated to a Dutchman, whatever his rank. It was however strongly argued that no English officer had the experience with which to conduct a European campaign. Marlborough, whose time was yet to come, had been sidelined.

With the defeat of the French naval force at Cape La Hogue, British merchants felt confident that their ships could trade unmolested and, in order to save them more money, called for a reduction in the strength of the army. This was narrowly defeated in Parliament, who voted to carry the war into next year.

In 1693 the French onslaught continued with the fall of the fortress at Huy on the River Meuse, and also at a former village called Charleroi located near the River Sambre, which had been turned into a fortress in 1666 by the Government of the Spanish Low Countries.

In early July, the 10th Foot and other regiments were detached from King William's main army. This unfortunate reduction in strength resulted in his being outnumbered by the French in unfavourable countryside. The 10th had joined a force commanded by the Duke of Wurtemberg, which was to attack the French between the Rivers Scheldt and Lys. However, incessant rain meant that the men marched through mud up to their knees. The lines to be attacked were near the town of Doignies, and consisted of a long earthen rampart with an outer ditch. The nearby stream of Espierette, greatly swollen, formed a second ditch. On the 8th July, the 10th Foot led the left column, and although the water of the Espierette was up to their necks, some of the French lines were captured.

In the meantime William, realising that the French were in greatly superior numbers, constructed a system of strong entrenchments and palisades along the Landen stream. The claim of the 16th Foot is that the King spent that July night in their lines. The ensuing battle, referred to as LANDEN in which King William III led his army in person was probably the bloodiest that century. The King's army initially resisted the might of the French but was eventually driven from its positions. William lost nearly 20,000 men. The 3rd Foot lost its three colours when two of its ensigns were killed and a third was taken prisoner. The 2nd Foot and the 26th Foot were both engaged in furious fighting as William rallied the remainder of his army to stem the French advance.

Marshall Luxembourg, with losses less than half that of the Alliance, believed that William's army was a broken force and therefore failed to press his victory. This allowed William to retire to winter quarters, mostly in and around Bruges. The French were content to know that they now held an impregnable position in the area.

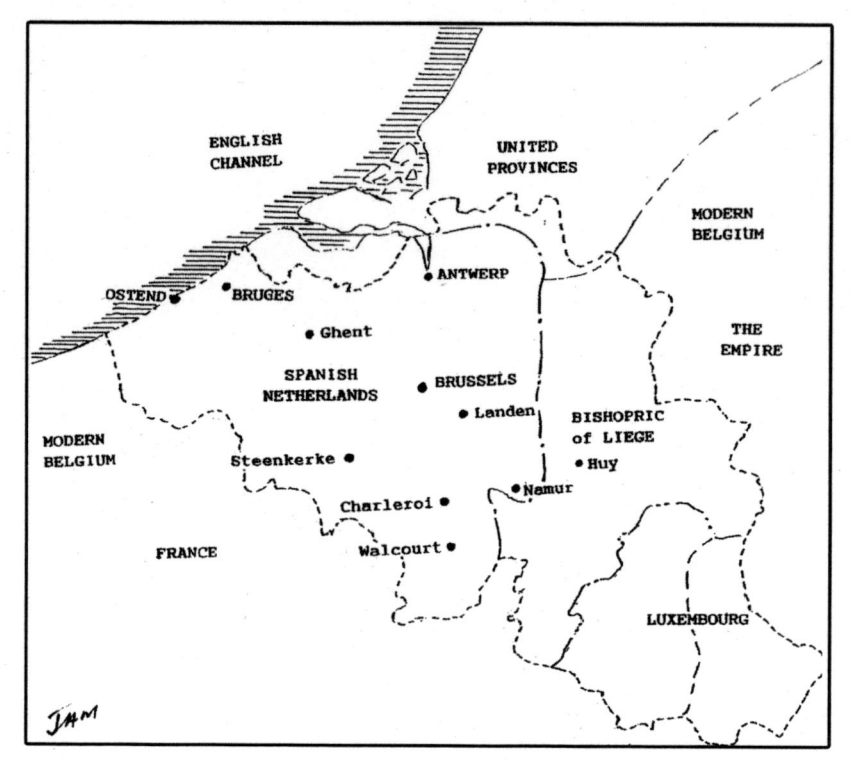

THE LOW COUNTRIES 1690

As if to remind the French that their overseas Empire was also vulnerable, the 5th Regiment of Foot (the Northumberland Fusiliers) carried out a commando-style raid on the French held island of Martinique, whilst the 24th Regiment of Foot (the South Wales Borderers) was employed chiefly at sea and in attacks on points of the French coast.

Leaving his army in winter quarters, William returned to England where early in 1964 he reviewed regiments in Hyde Park prior to some embarking for Flanders. In the spring, the 15th Regiment of Foot (the East Yorkshire Regiment) embarked in Scotland, bound for Ostend. The 17th Regiment of Foot (the Leicestershire Regiment) and the 23rd Regiment of Foot (the Royal Welsh Fusiliers) also arrived in Europe to support the army of William.

Two regiments were raised in 1694. The 28th Regiment of Foot (1st Battalion the Gloucestershire Regiment), was raised by Colonel John Gibson, Lieutenant-Governor of Portsmouth, and the 29th Regiment of Foot (1st Battalion the Worcestershire Regiment) raised in London on 1st June by Colonel Thomas Farrington, an officer of the Coldstream Guards. Neither regiment was sent to Europe.

The campaign of 1694 did not open until May. The army failed to bring the French to action and no conflict of any importance was fought. William turned west towards the Channel ports. To block this advance, the French moved their army from one end of the front to the other. Both sides were on the defensive. The troops however, suffered many privations from the dearth of supplies. The major event of 1694 was the death through smallpox of Queen Mary. King William would carry on alone.

The main object at the start of campaigning in 1695 was to recapture the city and fortress at Namur, which had been taken by the French in June 1692. As the siege of Namur began, William's main army was supported by covering forces. The 10th Foot formed part of one force, who as the French advanced against them in far superior numbers, retreated to Ghent under their leader, the Prince de Vaudemont. During this retreat, Liuetenant-Colonel Godolphin commanding the 10th Foot, together with some of his men, was captured. The 15th Foot was in another covering force engaged at the siege of Huy. They returned to garrison Dixmunde, thereby missing action at Namur.

The siege and recapture of Namur against a stubborn, strong French presence, who'd had three years to consolidate their position was bound to be a bloody affair, and so it was. Colonel John Courthope, two officers and 101 rank and file of the 17th Foot were killed, as were twenty officers and five hundred men of the 25th Foot, who were killed by the explosion of one of the enemy mines. Despite heavy losses, the Grenadier Company of the 18th Foot distinguished itself during the final assault on the fortress, while the honour of taking the main gates was assigned to the 23rd Foot. The fortress surrendered on 22nd August.

For their direct action at the siege and capture, the 1st, 2nd, 4th, 6th, 7th, 14th, 16th, 17th, 18th, 23rd and 25th Regiments were awarded the Battle Honour NAMUR. (In 1910). The 26th having been reinforced from Scotland, the 5th, 19th, and a detachment of the 27th saw engagements to varying extent in the campaign. When the Battle Honour was awarded, it was considered that although they played a major part as a covering force, their involvement was not direct enough to receive the award. In 1934, the 5th appealed against the decision following an invitation by the War Office to review their honourary distinctions, but were again rejected. During 1695, the 22nd Regiment of Foot (The Cheshire Regiment) arrived in the Netherlands for a short period.

By 1696, the war was drawing to an inconclusive end. Both sides were running into financial difficulties and it therefore appeared prudent to gently sabre-rattle whilst evading any direct actions. Although the 8th Foot, who had returned to England in 1693, went back to the Netherlands to garrison Dendermonde, several regiments, including the 10th Foot returned to England. Stalemate was the word, as both sides were weary of the struggle. Against William's wish, the Grand Alliance began to fall to pieces. The 17th Foot and the 22nd Foot returned to Ireland.

The Peace of Ryswick was signed on 10th September 1697. By the terms of the Treaty, Louis XIV was to give up all of the conquests made during the preceding nineteen years and acknowledge William as King of England. William's troops had gained experience of war, which was to be of the greatest value to them in the struggle with the French in a few years' time.

Thoughts of peace were also endorsed by Parliament. Ten regiments were disbanded, including the recently formed 29th Foot, who were reduced to cadre status, with officers on half pay.

Not all regiments were disbanded or reduced. Colonel Gibson's 28th Foot, which had only been raised in 1694, was in 1697 sent to Newfoundland, where it found that the French had left the colony in ruins. Colonel Gibson left 300 men to rebuild the outpost when he returned to England. Unfortunately, of the men he left, 214 died of sickness and exposure due to the appalling winter conditions.

To understand the rundown of the army, it is necessary to look at the differing attitudes of the Whigs and Tories in the Parliament of the day. The Tories, mostly landowners, had financed the war through existing land taxes and were therefore against a continuation of

Continental involvement, requiring instead, economy and disarmament. The Whigs, conscious of French aggression in Europe, were quite prepared to form a War Government. These ideals led to their administration being driven out in 1697.

William unsuccessfully urged a Parliamentary coalition to save the 87,000 regular British soldiers under arms following Ryswick, believing that he still needed 30,000 men plus a considerable number of officers to sustain a viable army. Despite his arguments, Parliament voted for only 7,000, forcing William to send away his Dutch Guards.

Should William die, Anne, the second daughter of King James II was certain to succeed. She was a Tory and also dedicated to the High Church. Married to George of Denmark, they had seventeen children, although none survived to adulthood. In 1698, Anne's surviving son, the Duke of Gloucester, was nine years old. William invited the man that he had neglected during the recent crisis, and now supported him in his desire to resist the reduction of the army, by restoring Marlborough to his previous army rank and to be governor to the boy Prince. Unfortunately, this was short lived as the young Duke of Gloucester died of smallpox, aged eleven in 1700.

The future descent of the Crown was regulated to ensure a Protestant succession. Under the Act of Settlement of 1701, the following were amongst those proclaimed:

The House of Hanover, who descended from Elizabeth, the daughter of James I, was declared next in succession after Anne.

Every future Sovereign be a member of the Church of England.

No foreign-born monarch should wage Continental war, nor go abroad, without the approval of Parliament.

CHAPTER VIII

1702–1714
QUEEN ANNE
WAR OF THE SPANISH SUCCESSION

Marlborough – Born John Churchill in 1650, his father Sir Winston, had suffered for his support of the Royalists in the Civil War. Upon restoration, John at the age of seventeen obtained a commission in the 1st Foot Guards, subsequently transferring for his first overseas action in Tangier. Returning in 1672 he went with the Duke of Monmouth to support the French against the Dutch. His positive actions encouraged Louis XIV to promote him Colonel of an English Regiment in his service, where Marlborough spent the next two years acquiring great knowledge of French tactics and of the French language. Until he joined King William in 1688, Marlborough very carefully played the political situation.

In 1689, William rewarded him with the Earldom of Marlborough. After France declared war on the Dutch, William sent ten battalions under the command of Marlborough who actually transformed dispirited British Regiments into a strong force. His fortunes under William were up and down until Anne became Queen when, within two weeks, Marlborough was appointed Captain-General of all her forces.

Following his successes during the War of the Spanish Succession, he fell out of favour and stayed on the Continent, returning on the death of Anne in 1714.

He died in 1722, probably our greatest general.

When King Charles II of Spain died on 1st November 1700, the whole of his dominion in Spain, the Netherlands and the Americas were accepted by King Louis XIV for his grandson Philip V of Anjou.

One of Louis' first actions was to move large forces into the Spanish Netherlands. Fortresses which had formed the main barrier against a French invasion surrendered without a shot being fired. This was because, although they were garrisoned by the Dutch under the rights of the Treaty, they were commanded by supporters of Louis and therefore strongly agreed with the accession of Philip, hence their loyalty to the invasion force.

King William III recognised this act by Louis as a direct threat to the security of Britain. However, he could not at first induce Parliament to take any action. Eventually England took up the cause of Charles, Emperor of Austria who was the rival claimant to the Spanish throne and they therefore formed an alliance with the Austrians, Dutch and Germans.

Early in 1701 two regiments of foot were raised in Ireland. Major General Arthur Chichester, 3rd Earl of Donegall, raised a regiment at his own expense in return for which William, as a special mark of his favour, gave permission for the officers and soldiers of the regiment to wear orange facings. It was first known as 'The Belfast Regiment' later the 35th Regiment of Foot (1st Battalion Royal Sussex Regiment), and the 36th Regiment of Foot (2nd Battalion the Worcestershire Regiment) who were raised by Lord Charlemont in Ulster.

On 31st May 1701, William proclaimed John Churchill, Duke of Marlborough, as the Commander in Chief of the British forces being assembled in the Netherlands. Amongst them were the 8th, 15th, 17th and 24th Regiments of Foot. However, once in the Netherlands the Allied and also the French armies manoeuvred and counter-manoeuvred in an effort to place each other at a disadvantage and no active operations were really undertaken. Later, regiments were reviewed at Breda Heath by King William.

It was not until ex-King James II died on 16th September 1701 that, contrary to the Treaty of Ryswick, Louis announced to the exiled Court that he recognized James's son as King James III of England and would support his rights. This led to indignation in England.

Preparations were at once made to raise a large army to fight France. 48,000 men would be needed in anticipation of the declaration of war.

Regiments which had not recently been reduced to cadre status were reinstated and new regiments were formed. On 12th February 1702, the 34th Foot were raised as Lord Lucas's Regiment of Foot (1st Battalion, the Border Regiment).

With the prospect of another war against France, it was the intention of King William to take command of his troops. However on 20th February whilst riding in the park outside Hampton Court his horse stumbled, William was thrown to the ground breaking his collarbone. Complications set in and sixteen days later on 16th March, William died at the age of 52.

Anne was born on the 6th February 1664 and was therefore 38 years old when she succeeded William. It was generally accepted that she was slow and obstinate, nevertheless she was proclaimed Queen.

The Duke of Marlborough became overall Commander of the British Army and, on 4th May 1702, war was declared.

In 1702 six regiments were placed on the establishment of the Navy for sea service. They were not just to serve on board as marines, but as land forces to make landings as required. Following its disbandment in 1698, the 30th Foot was reformed as a Marine regiment, followed by the raising of the 31st Foot, Colonel George Villiers' Regiment of Marines (1st Battalion, the East Surrey Regiment), the 32nd Foot, Colonel Edward Fox's Regiment of Marines (1st Battalion the Duke of Cornwall's Light Infantry), the 33rd Foot, The Earl of Huntingdon's Regiment of Marines (1st Battalion The Duke of Wellington's [West Riding] Regiment). The 35th Foot was included as a regiment placed on the establishment of the Navy, whilst the 6th Foot was also allocated for sea service.

Three regiments were selected to become 'Fusilier' regiments. One English (7th), one Scots (21st) and one Welsh (23rd), they were to be used to protect the artillery. Their officers no longer carried pikes, but were armed with a light fusil. All companies wore mitre-shaped caps and were armed with flintlock fusils, swords and bayonets.

In 1702 a British fleet sailed for Spain in what was a badly managed and unsuccessful expedition. Landing near Cadiz the ill-conceived operation failed. Regiments boarded the ships which had brought them and hurriedly sailed away from southern Spain.

The 3rd Foot, which had taken part in the expedition, was in the fleet returning home when it shared in the capture of some Spanish treasure ships at Vigo Bay. The gold and silver bullion taken from the Spanish was minted into coin with the word VIGO placed below the bust of Queen Anne, with most of the coins dated 1703.

The 35th Foot was another regiment that had the misfortune to have been on the expedition. They left Spain and with a smaller force, sailed for the West Indies in order to attack French and Spanish settlements. Again, this was not a happy experience, as by the Autumn of 1703, the expedition had suffered so many casualties from yellow fever that it was forced home to recruit.

The 22nd Foot had a better experience in the Caribbean. They had been in the Netherlands until 1702 when they went to Jamaica, where they spent twelve years not only on land against the French and their supporters but also at sea manning HM ships.

Two other regiments were formed in 1702. Colonel Richard Coote's Regiment of Foot (39th Foot – 1st Battalion, the Dorsetshire Regiment) who did not see action with Marlborough, and Colonel Meredyth's Regiment of Foot (37th Foot – 1st Battalion, the Hampshire Regiment). Colonel Meredyth was to become a Brigadier-General in 1704 following which the regiment saw action in all of Marlborough's major battles.

In the autumn of 1703, Portugal joined the Grand Alliance against France mainly through the Methuen Treaties, which were named after the Allied envoy who that year conducted the negotiations. These affected both trade and policy, in that Portuguese wine shipped to Britain would carry less duty than French wine. In return, Portugal would import its cloth requirements from Britain. Politically, the Duke of Savoy joined the Alliance, whilst Portugal, fearing French designs, not only asked for money and troops but also that Archduke Charles of Austria should be placed on the throne of Spain. Towards this end in February 1704 Admiral Sir George Rooke commanding a large fleet accompanied the Archduke from England bound for Lisbon, together with several regiments whose transfer had been agreed with Marlborough.

In May, the force under Rooke consisting of 30 English and nineteen Dutch ships together with 2,400 troops under the supreme command of Prince George of Heese-Darmstadt, an experienced soldier, sailed with Rooke into the Mediterranean. However, the French fleet was off Toulon, necessitating a withdrawal back to Portugal. Sir Cloudsley Shovell, who commanded a further 23 ships joined Rooke, but although their eyes were set on another attack on Cadiz, memories of the earlier encounter forced a rethink. It was therefore to the easier target of the poorly garrisoned, rundown fortress of Gibraltar that they turned their attention. A force of about 2,000 English and Dutch Marines stormed the garrison and in one day, the 4th August 1704, took possession in the name of Charles of Spain.

The French resolved to recover Gibraltar and therefore during the winter of 1704/5 the garrison under Prince George of Hesse-Darmstadt withstood siege conditions and frequent attacks by French troops.

For the capture and defence of Gibraltar, the following regiments were awarded the battle honour GIBRALTAR 1704-1705. This award was, however, only made 200 years later in 1909!

The Queen's Own Regiment of Marines (4th Foot – The King's Own [Royal Lancaster] Regiment) under their Colonel, Lieutenant-General William Seymour who had been appointed in 1703 to command the new brigade.

The Earl of Barrymore's Regiment of Foot (13th Foot, the Somerset Light Infantry).

Colonel Thomas Sanderson's Regiment of Marines (30th Foot – 1st Battalion the East Lancashire Regiment).

Colonel George Villier's Regiment of Marines (31st Foot – 1st Battalion the East Surrey Regiment).

Colonel Edward Fox's Regiment of Marines (32nd Foot – 1st Battalion the Duke of Cornwall's Light Infantry).

The Earl of Donegall's Regiment of Foot (35th Foot – 1st Battalion the Royal Sussex Regiment).

Events in Europe were rapidly coming to a head when in 1704 having abandoned the Emperor, the Elector of Bavaria joined the French, who seizing the opportunity sent a large army under Marshal Marsin to assist the Elector and thereby press for the capture of Vienna. Discovering this, the Duke of Marlborough obtained the approval of the Dutch States-General who hitherto had been unwilling to consent to any offensive action. They agreed that a Dutch force should be left to guard the Netherlands whilst Marlborough, hoping to defeat the French plan, embarked on a march of just over 250 miles, probably one of the greatest marches ever undertaken by the British Army. Leaving an area east of Maastricht on 19th May, he marched 40,000 men along the Rhine south east into the heart of Germany.

The aim of the French Marshal Villeroi had been to intercept Marlborough and force combat north of the Moselle. However when, ten days later, Marlborough reached Coblenz, instead of turning west along that river as was expected by all, he crossed the Rhine on a bridge of boats before heading south on to the River Main at Frankfurt, then crossing the River Neckar on 3rd June. All the time moving steadily through splendid countryside, his Redcoat regiments, adequately supplied with food and equipment were travelling at the relaxed pace of approximately ten miles each day. Once across the Neckar, Marlborough moved further south until, north of Ulm, he was joined by Prince Eugene, the Austrian Commander and Prince Louis of Baden, Commander of the Imperial Army of the Rhine. As Marlborough neared the Danube, Marshal Tallard with his command was moving through the Black Forest to support the Elector of Bavaria and Marsin's French force.

Map of Spain

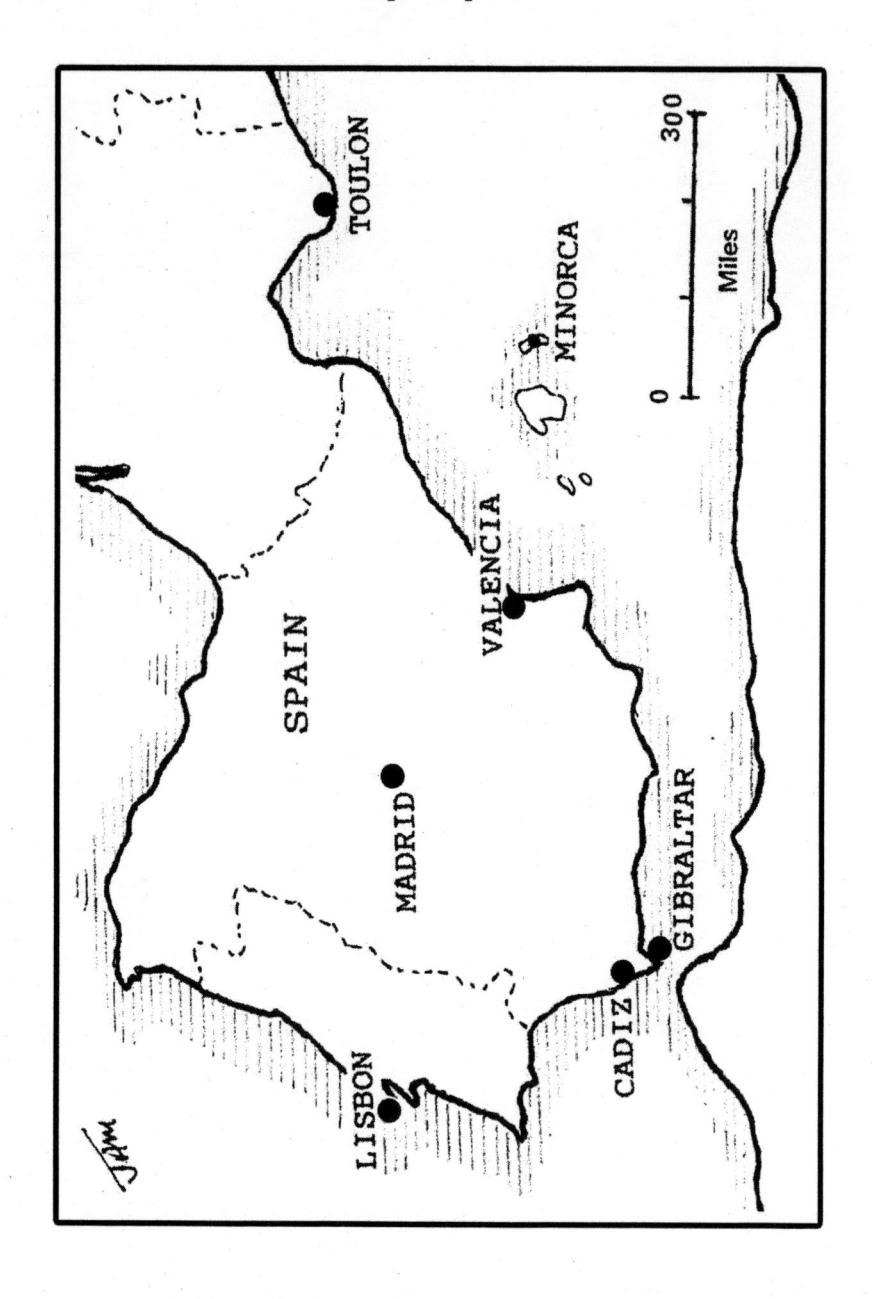

Planning their action, the Allies agreed that Eugene would hold the Rhine while Prince Louis and Marlborough turned towards Donauworth where early in July they came across a force of French and Bavarians in an entrenched camp on the Heights of Schellenberg. The Allies agreed that an immediate assault should be made on the strongly held position and so an attack took place with an Army that included:

The Royal Regiment of Foot (1st Foot).
Churchill's Regiment of Foot under Colonel Charles Churchill (3rd)
Brigadier-General Webb's Regiment of Foot (8th Foot) although in 1702 it was titled the Queen's Regiment of Foot.
Lord North and Grey's Regiment of Foot (10th Foot)
Brigadier-General Howe's Regiment of Foot (15th Foot)
The Earl of Derby's Regiment of Foot (16th Foot)
Lieutenant-General Ingoldsby's Regiment of Fusiliers (23rd)

In the evening, a determined Allied attack overcame the resistance of the enemy and drove them into the Danube, capturing many guns and colours and much of the Bavarian baggage. Although this was the first major victory for Marlborough, it was not without a price. Lieutenant-General Ingoldsby's Fusiliers lost sixteen of its officers and all regiments lost many rank and file.

Following his victory at Schellenberg, Marlborough had hoped that the Elector would cede but this did not happen. Neither could he be brought to conflict knowing that Marshal Tallard was moving through the Black Forest to support him and as Marlborough did not have heavy cannon, the British would be unable to force entry into Bavarian strongholds. During this time the frustrated Allied troops caused much consternation to the opposition and its supporters, but it was not until six weeks later that on the early morning of the 13th August the forces faced each other.

The French had moved into position on the 12th, having the Danube, some mills and the village of BLENHEIM on their right. On the left, about two miles away, was the village of Lutzingen. Protecting their entire front were the swampy banks of the Nebel, a tributary of the Danube. Early the following morning Marlborough deployed his army.

The strength of the combined French and Bavarians under Marshal Marsin, the Elector and Marshal Tallard was just under 60,000 men, comprising sixteen battalions of foot, four regiments of dragoons with a reserve under Marshal de Clerambault of eleven battalions; at the same time some 10,000 men drawn up following the recognised order of battle of the day with foot in its centre and the cavalry on its wings. In this instance both Marsin's and Tallard's armies were drawn up separately over a three-mile front. The effect of this was to leave the villages of Oberglau and Blenheim defended only by foot whilst the centre, Marsin's right and Tallard's left, consisted of cavalry.

Tallard was ready, and the early morning mist was clearing as he looked across the Nebel. On Marlborough's right, Eugene was not in position, having been delayed due to moving his force through difficult country. Therefore Marlborough held his position until Eugene had joined his right flank. His plan, based on the weak disposition of the French, was to take advantage of the wide space between Oberglau and Blenheim, too wide for effective French crossfire from either village, thus enabling an attack on the French centre drawing Tallard's cavalry from the Nebel. This would allow the Allies to re-form after crossing on the bridges that Marlborough's pioneers were constructing over the stream.

Allied troops endured heavy cannon fire until Eugene was finally in position. Lieutenant-General Lord Cutts was entrusted with the assault on the enemy's right. Lord North and Grey's (10th), the Duke of Marlborough's (Late) Regiment (24th) under its Colonel William Tatton, Howe's (15th) and his own Regiment of Fusiliers (21st) were amongst the regiments in Brigadier-General Row's brigade who cleared the defenders from the mills. Seeing the British infantry moving across the Nebel, de Clerambault moved his entire French reserve to reinforce the defenders of Blenheim leaving Tallard weak in foot troops.

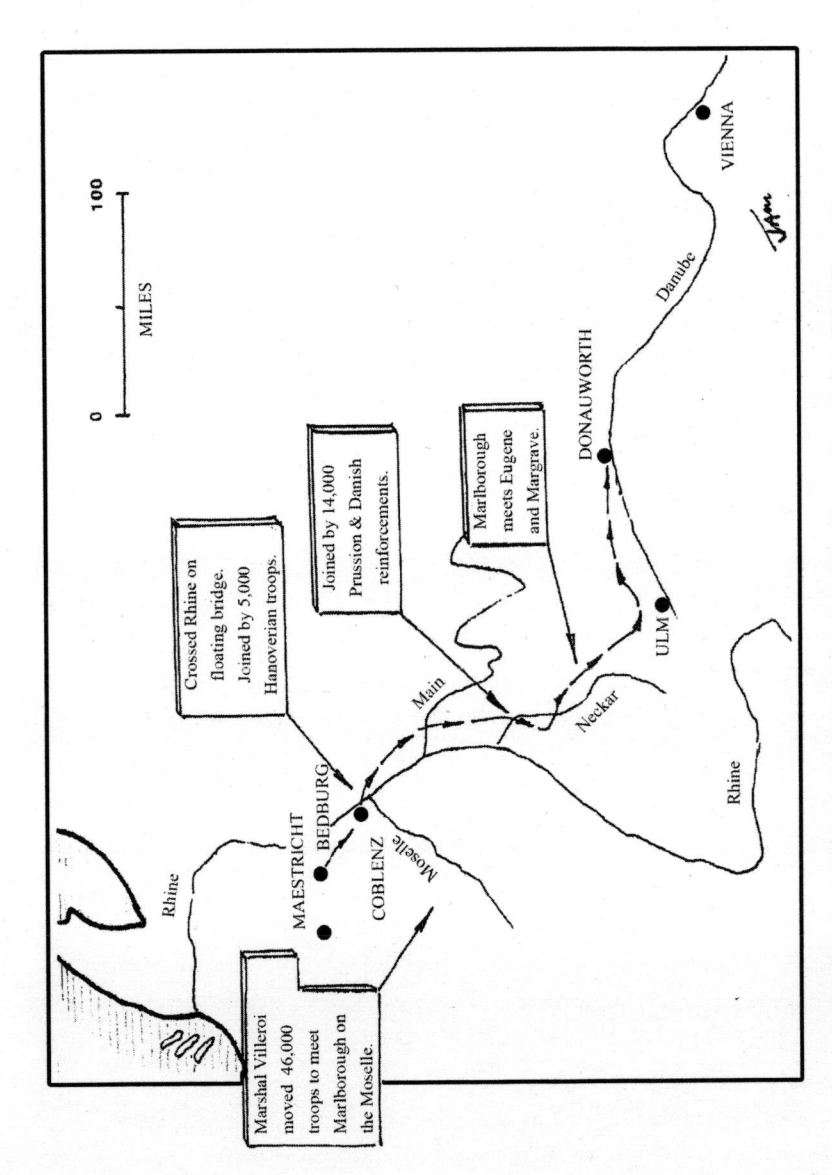

MARLBOROUGH'S MARCH TO SAVE VIENNA

Meanwhile, Marsin was having difficulty holding the Allied attack on Oberglau, whilst on the French right Row's brigade was advancing against Blenheim, the five battalions under orders to reserve their fire crossed the meadow separating them from the French palisade. As the brigade moved to within 30 paces, the French poured heavy fire into the leading file where one in three fell, the line continued forward until Row, who was Colonel of the 21st, plunged his sword into the palisade giving the signal to fire. A volley crashed out from the British regiments and men tore at the planks using their swords, when another French volley ripped into them causing heavy casualties. Row was mortally wounded, Lieutenant-Colonel Dalzell aided by Major Campbell, both of Row's regiment, tried to carry him to safety but both were struck and killed by accurate French firepower.

Brigadier-General Ferguson (26th Foot) moved his brigade forward whilst Row's brigade regrouped and charged again and again until Marlborough ordered them back saying that they had 'done enough for valour'. Heavy fighting was taking place in other parts of the line with varying success. Eugene prepared to attack Oberglau with ten battalions as the Elector moved against him.

Marlborough ordered his men to prevent the defenders from coming out of Blenheim and also to defend the crossing points of the Nebel for the cavalry to pass, thereby enabling the Allies to pierce the enemy centre at the junction of Tallard's and Marsin's wings. French Guards tried to break through the position held by Webb's (10th Foot) but they failed and the regiment took over 1,000 prisoners.. The final act was brought about as Allied cavalry charges and infantry aggression caused 30 Squadrons of French cavalry to panic. They were driven into the Danube where many perished. Thousands who were not killed by the muskets of the British infantry of cavalry swords were taken prisoner.

The French troops in Blenheim attempted to escape but found their retreat was cut off. Twenty-seven French battalions surrendered en-bloc at about 9.00 p.m. including two generals, 18,000 men, many guns and over one hundred stands of colours together with vast quantities of tents, transport and baggage.

The losses to the Franco-Bavarians were 38,000 men. Those suffered by Marlborough and Eugene being about 12,500. Howe's

Regiment (15th) lost eighteen officers killed or badly wounded. Ingoldsby's Fusiliers (23rd) having previously lost sixteen officers at Schellenberg had now lost a further nine officers, whilst Lord North and Grey lost a hand leading his regiment.

One of the indications of the severity of losses was reflected by Colonel Tatton's Regiment (24th) where 85 officers and men were killed and an equal number wounded which was a total of nearly one third of the strength of the regiment.

French prisoners were so numerous that five British battalions were employed to take them to the Hague. With his victory at Blenheim, Marlborough had removed the immediate threat to Vienna.

*

In 1704, the Allies tried unsuccessfully to break out of Portugal into Castile with a total force of over 20,000 foot and 700 horse, but their efforts were thwarted by French troops commanded by Marshal de Tesse assisting the Spanish.

Early in 1705, following secret talks with certain Catalan leaders, in an invasion fleet commanded by Sir Cloudesley Shovell accompanied by a military force under the Earl of Peterborough took on board the Archduke Charles who was the Allied candidate for the Spanish throne.

In early August the whole force had entered the Mediterranean. By mid August, the Allies launched an attack by land and sea on the Levant coast; forces were put ashore at Altea 60 miles south of Valencia, whilst the fleet anchored off Barcelona and laid siege to the city. Moving north, the Allies attacked the citadel of Montjuich where, after a long siege, Barcelona capitulated. It was here that although the 35th Foot was not present, it lost its first colonel, the Earl of Donegall.

Other Spanish fortresses which were captured following sieges were Valencia and, further west, Alburquerque and Badajoz where Major-General Holcroft Blood's Regiment (17th Foot) took part; they also gained distinction at the siege of the fortified town of Alcantara in 1706. It should be remembered that although the campaign appeared successful, the provinces were inadequately garrisoned and poorly defended.

During the early part of 1706, Marshal de Tesse marched towards Barcelona where, having been joined by Philip V, they laid siege to the city, only to withdraw in May when Allied relief arrived by sea. This withdrawal by the Franco-Spanish troops allowed the Allies to rapidly move across the Peninsula. Saragossa was taken in June, followed by Madrid where the Archduke was proclaimed Charles III. The stay was short lived, as pursued by the Duke of Berwick (an Englishmen closely related to the deceased James II), the Allies hastily returned to the area of the Levant coast of Spain.

In the spring of 1705 some regiments were reviewed in the Netherlands by the Duke of Marlborough. Most regiments saw some skirmishing but generally the year was spent attempting to fill their ranks with drafts of recruits from Britain.

During the early part of May 1706, information reached Marlborough in Maestricht that Marshal Villeroi who had been sheltering behind the River Dyle had crossed the river and was moving eastwards with a French force.

Marlborough moved his army until at dawn on the 23rd May, his leading troops came upon the French near the village of RAMILLIES about twelve miles North of Namur. On discovering the approach of the Allies, Villeroi took a defensive position on high ground, stretching from the village of Autreglise in the north to Taviers four miles distance in the south with the villages of Offus and Ramillies equally spaced between. His force of 60,000 men slightly outnumbering that of the Allies.

Marlborough's troops were deployed just before noon; his first push came with a feint to the north. The effect of this was for Villeroi to move his reserves from the centre to cover the attack. Having used similar tactics at Blenheim this was exactly what Marlborough had anticipated, which displayed his generalship and set him apart from his contemporaries. He was to exploit the good undulating cavalry terrain in the south between Ramillies and Taviers, as he hurled the whole of his Dutch, Danish and British cavalry, 25,000 men, at the French cavalry who were located between the villages. At one stage Marlborough personally joined the cavalry attack to urge the Allies to greater efforts. 40,000 horsemen from both sides battled for ground, until the French line south of Ramillies was broken.

Marlborough ordered the advance of his whole force. His main infantry attack under the Brigade of the Earl of Orkney charged the area near Ramillies sweeping everything before them, whilst the cavalry, forming at right angles, swept along the rear of the French line. The French force was destroyed and fled the field in chaos.

Allied losses were less than 5,000 men. Nightfall shielded the remains of the French army as fewer than 15,000 retreated to Ghent in disorder, a distance of 60 miles closely pursued by Marlborough's cavalry supported by his infantry.

French casualties during the battle and retreat were more than 15,000. The victors collected 80 standards or colours and over 50 cannon.

Within two weeks the effect of this victory and the Allied advance was the fall of Flanders with the French falling back to their own frontier.

In 1707 Charles Churchill, the brother of the Duke of Marlborough was appointed colonel of the Coldstream Regiment of Foot Guards. Major-General the Duke of Argyll succeeded him as colonel of Prince George of Denmark's Regiment (3rd Foot) and as Prince George was the Consort of Queen Anne, the Regiment acquired the Royal Dragon badge.

Following much debate and assurances, leading Scotsmen finally approved the Articles of Union between their country and England. These were presented to Queen Anne who together with Scottish representatives accepted the merging of the two Parliaments. It should be remembered that these representatives were generally lowland Scots. In the north, Jacobite feeling was very strong, such that in the spring of 1708 some regiments were recalled to England to defend against the fear of a suspected invasion by Louis XIV in support of the Pretender. However this came to nothing. Regiments including Lord North and Grey's (10th Foot) and Howe's (15th Foot) were sent back to the Continent, arriving in April.

The merger of 1707 necessitated a change in the design of Colours of all regiments. The red St George Cross which covered the entire flag was joined by the white saltire and blue field of St Andrew.

The campaign in Spain was resumed in the spring of 1707, when Mordaunt's Regiment (28th Foot) landed at Alicante as part of the force including Dutch, German, Portuguese and British troops under the command of the Earl of Galway, who was French.

On 25th April, Galway's men attacked the Duke of Berwick's Franco-Spanish Force at Almanza which lay about 43 miles inland. The battle began with the Allied force including Colonel Thomas Pearce's Regiment (5th Foot) assaulting the enemy with vigour using deadly fire and bayonet. Berwick saw that the Allied right had fled early in the battle, which left them badly outflanked; he therefore committed his reserves with great success.

In this battle several Allied regiments were almost wiped out or capitulated. Blood's Regiment (17th Foot) fought until hardly a man was left standing, Colonel Blood was badly wounded and died a few months later. It was said that Marlborough in a despatch, refers to him as being 'much lamented for his bravery and experience'. The 35th Foot were almost wiped out and lost their colours. These were recovered from a church in Madrid about three years later.

In 1707 Queen Anne awarded the badge of the figure of Britannia to Colonel William Stewart's Regiment (9th Foot) for their outstanding gallantry at Almanza. The defeat was a disaster and some indication of the casualties which were inflicted on regiments; show that Mordaunt's Regiment (28th) lost 300 officers and men out of a total strength of 532.

As a result of the rout the Archduke was driven back, as slowly during the rest of 1707 and in 1708, Philip recovered Valencia.

1708 was a depressing year for the Allies, where the only success was in September when a fleet under Sir John Leake took Minorca.

In the early summer of 1708, Marshal Vendome and the Duke of Burgundy with a French army of about 80,000 men were moving to reinforce troops who were besieging the fortress of OUDENARDE. Oudenarde lay on the River Scheldt which flowed through the fortress in a northerly direction past the village of Gavre about six miles away. Two miles to the west roughly parallel to the river, and for the entire distance from Oudenarde to Gavre, was high ground.

Intent on preventing the French from achieving their object, Marlborough who was 50 miles away moved his men in the direction of Oudenarde. The march took just under three days. Meanwhile the French, not suspecting that conflict was imminent, were crossing the river at Gavre at an unhurried pace with the Duke of Burgundy taking a route along the high ground, whilst Marshal Vendome the lower ground nearer the river.

On the 11th July 1708, Marlborough's advance guard under General Gadogan was moving across pontoon bridges over the river to place itself between the French and Oudenarde. He was followed by 80,000 men under Marlborough and Eugene.

Vendome, who was not on good terms with Burgundy, could not believe that the Allies were close at hand and advancing towards him. Confusion spread throughout the French as Burgundy moved his troops down from the heights to face the Allies, whereupon fierce fighting followed. An attack by Marlborough which penetrated the French flank, carried on until it divided the French army in two. At least half of the French were surrounded by the Allies. The remainder were never brought into action but remained on the heights.

The route that Vendome had taken earlier in the day to attack Oudenarde, was the route taken when darkness allowed him to escape, thereby saving his army from complete destruction. The French suffered about 8,000 men killed with a further 7,000 taken prisoner, against only 3,000 Allied casualties.

The victory at Oudenarde led Marlborough to believe that it was the time to advance into France. After all, as well as his seasoned troops he had a force of over 7,000 men waiting with transports in England. Eugene did not agree but believed that the important fortress of Lille should be captured before enlarging the operation into France. Thus followed the siege of Lille. Marshal Boufflers with a force of 15,000 men defended the city.

The siege was conducted by Eugene, with Marlborough concentrating on his major role of supplying the besieging forces with all the requirements that were needed to take the city and citadel whilst keeping the largely superior French relieving force at bay. The French did manage to cut the original supply line, although Marlborough's organizational ability had created an alternative route from Ostend.

Vendome moved his army to the south of Lille where he joined Berwick. Marlborough kept between them and the city where he linked with Eugene who in a strong position, held the French at bay as they again tried to cut the Allied communications with a frontal attack in the woods near the chateau of Wynendael. This was rebuffed by heavy fire from regiments under Lieutenant-General Webb (Colonel of the 8th Foot).

The city of Lille capitulated in October 1708 after Sergeant Littler of Colonel Godfrey's Regiment (16th Foot) swam across the Scheldt in the face of heavy fire to cut the ropes which held the drawbridge thus enabling the Allied troops to gain access to the city. Littler was subsequently awarded a commission with the 1st Regiment of Foot Guards (Grenadier).

After a gallant defence, on 9th December 1708 Marshal Bofflers was obliged to surrender the citadel.

The fall of Lille was a blow to the French, and it was not the last, as Marlborough, having dragged his cannon the great distance, recaptured Bruges at the end of December. In early January, Ghent too fell once more to the Allies.

During the early summer months of 1709, the Allied army under Marlborough and Eugene was at its greatest strength and though the weather was poor with overcast conditions and heavy rain, it did not prevent their intention to capture what was probably one of the strongest fortresses on the French frontier, the town and citadel of Tournai had been fortified by the engineer Vauban and was located 36 miles from Ghent.

The British regiments were all at first with the covering army, but when the town surrendered, Lord North and Grey's Regiment (10th), Howe's Regiment (15th) under Lieutenant-Colonel Andrew Armstrong and Godfrey's Regiment (16th) became part of the force laying siege to the citadel, a difficult task due to its underground defences.

With trench warfare raging above, mining and counter-mining in the tunnels below ground led to hand-to-hand fighting together with loss of life through explosions, smoke, collapsed passages and drowning from water which poured in from the flooded tunnels above. The siege carried on until the garrison surrendered on 3rd September.

After the surrender at Tournai, several regiments joined Marlborough and Eugene, who having invested Mons, were moving to the south when they encountered the French under Marshals

Villars and Boufflers with about 95,000 men and 80 guns, in a strongly fortified position in the gap between the forest of Sars and the wood of Laignieres near the village of MALPLAQUET which lay about nine miles southwest of Mons. The Allies were slightly stronger with something over 100,000 troops, however the formidable nature of the French entrenchments and the physical features of the countryside made an outflanking move impossible.

At about 7 a.m. on the 11th of September 1709 the battle which proved to be the most costly of the Duke's victories began. The tactics which Marlborough had used at Blenheim were generally repeated as both French wings were attacked. On Marlborough's left, his Dutch troops took terrible slaughter as the French in the wood of Laignieres held firm, whilst on the right Eugene was more successful. After many hours of fighting, much of it hand-to-hand, he broke through the defences in the forest of Sars reaching open terrain beyond. The French moved men from the centre to cover, thus giving Marlborough his chance. Regiments under Lieutenant-General, the Earl of Orkney moved against the depleted French who still remained at the redoubts, where the position was forced, enabling Marlborough to move his 30,000 cavalry against them. Although the French defended with great courage they were driven from the field.

Fifty French standards and colours were taken by the Allies who, with this victory, counted the cost at over 20,000 killed or wounded. French losses were slightly fewer and such was the carnage that only about 500 prisoners were taken.

The Prince George of Denmark's Regiment under Lieutenant-General the Duke of Argyll (3rd Foot), Lieutenant-General Webb's Regiment of Foot (8th) and Major-General Lord North and Grey's Regiment of Foot (10th) who all formed a spearhead, suffered heavily. Lieutenant-General Howe's Regiment of Foot (15th) were spared, as they arrived just as the battle was beginning and were placed in reserve and thereby only received a few casualties. Her Majesty's Royal Regiment of Foot of Ireland (18th) had met and defeated their fellow countrymen who were serving as the French Royal Regiment of Ireland.

This victory prevented any further attempts on the part of the French to interfere with the Allies besieging Mons, which fell on 23rd October.

In 1712 as a reward for its disciplined gallantry in these great battles, the Royal Regiment of Welch Fusiliers (23rd) was so named. In view of its association with the Prince of Wales it was granted the right to wear on their colours the Red Dragon, the Rising Sun and Prince of Wales's Feathers which were the three badges of His Royal Highness.

Several British regiments remained on the Continent until 1714 taking part in minor operations at Douai, Aire, Bethune and Bouchain.

In 1710 the Allies had virtually left the Peninsula to the Spanish whose troops failed to emulate the discipline and fire-power of the British, when at the Battle of Almenera in July and Saragossa on 20th August, the Allied army of Philip V was defeated as the Archduke retook the capital.

At Saragossa the 6th Foot had been in the forefront of the charge which broke the enemies' ranks and although they captured 22 heavy guns and more than 30 standards and colours, this sole act did not save Philip. It is said that in recognition of the bravery displayed by the regiment, Queen Anne was pleased to bestow on them the antelope badge which had been the royal badge of one of the Moorish regiments.

During December, the last significant battle of the Peninsular War was fought, as on 8th December, English troops under General Stanhope were caught by the Duke of Vendome at Brihuega where after a brief encounter, having lost 300 dead and another 300 wounded the English surrendered. 2,000 men including General Stanhope were taken prisoner.

By 1710, Europe had been at war for a decade, England and France were weary. Therefore both sides decided on secret talks designed to end hostilities. This change of heart was largely because in England the Whigs had lost control to the Tories who wished to follow a policy of peace, a course of action supported by Queen Anne. In the pursuit of negotiation, Marlborough was sidelined on false charges of financial irregularities.

Talks continued, Nova Scotia and Newfoundland would be ceded to the British. Gibraltar and Port Mahon were to be naval bases, together with several trading deals mostly favourable to Britain. This did mean that her Allies during the recent campaigns were deserted in the interest of peace.

It is wrong to think that there were only one or even two treaties, those of Utrecht in 1713 and Rastadt in 1714. There were in fact a series of agreements with France and Spain which ran parallel during the entire negotiating period.

On Sunday 1st August 1714, the last Stuart sovereign, Queen Anne died at Kensington. She had achieved the Union and because of Marlborough's victories, the power of France to dominate Europe had been checked.

Under the 1701 Act of Settlement, succession was no longer in dispute, the Crown would pass through to the Protestant niece of King Charles I, the Electress Sophia of Hanover, however she had died two months before Anne. Consequently it passed to her eldest son George Louis, Elector of Hanover, passing over many Catholics and problems with Jacobite supporters.

In 1882 a committee was appointed under Major General Archibald Alison to review the claims of regiments who had been involved in the campaigns of the Duke of Marlborough, On 13th March the awards of BLENHEIM, RAMILLIES, OUDENARDE and MALPLAQUET were made. These were to be borne on the Colours of the following regiments:

EUROPE 1702 - 1704

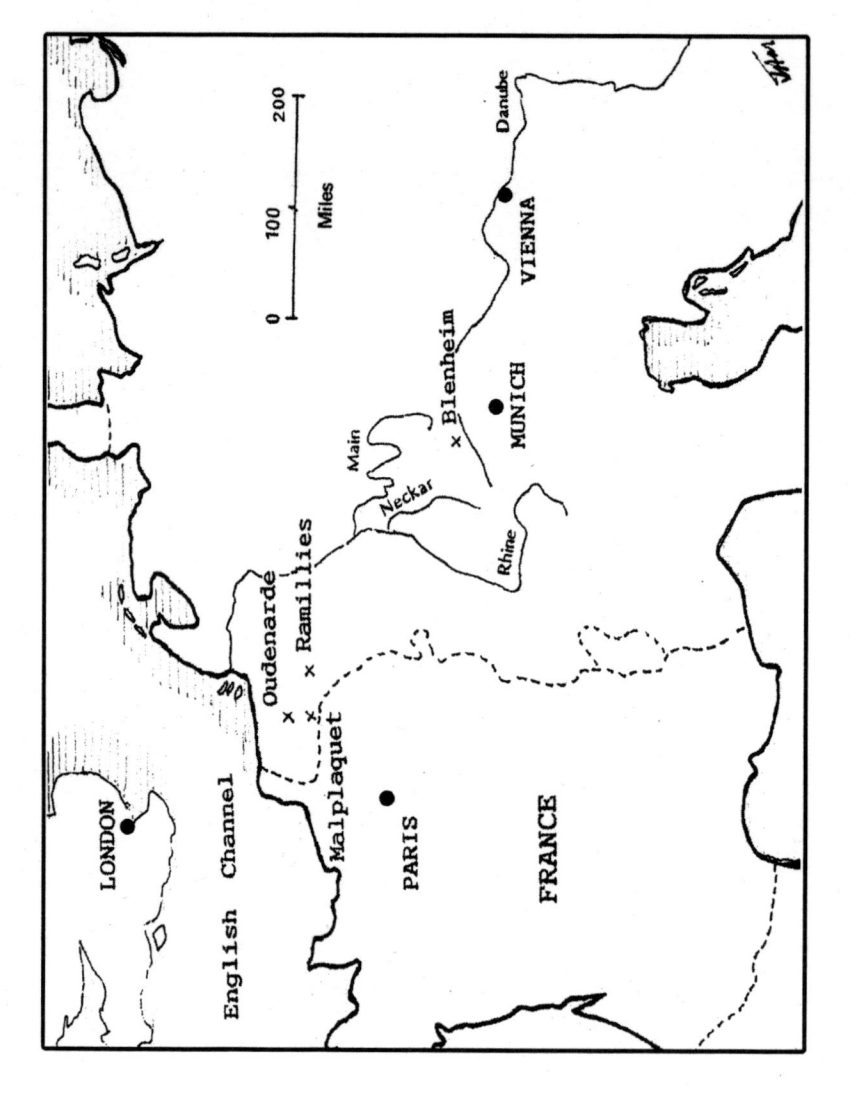

BLENHEIM

The Royal Regiment of Foot (1st), Colonel: The Earl of Orkney.
General Churchill's Regt of Foot (3rd),   Col. Charles Churchill.
Brig-Gen Webb's Regt of Foot (8th) Col.   John Richmond Webb.
Lord North & Grey's Regt of Foot (10th)   Lord North and Grey.
Brig-Gen Howe's Regt of Foot (15th) Col.   Emmanuel Howe.
Earl of Derby's Regt of Foot (16th) Col.   Maj-Gen Earl of Derby.
Royal Regiment of Ireland (18th)   Brig-Gen Frederick Hamilton

Brig-Gen Row's Regt of Fusiliers (21st)   Archibald Row.
Lt-Gen Ingoldsby's Regt of Fusiliers (23rd)   Richard Ingoldsby.
Duke of Marlborough's (late) Regt (24th)   William Tatton.
Brig-Gen Ferguson's Regt of Foot (26th)   James Ferguson.
Brig-Gen Meredyth's Regt of Foot (37th)   Thomas Meredyth.

RAMILLIES

The Royal Regiment of Foot (1st) Colonel.   The Earl of Orkney.
Gen Churchill's Regt of Foot (3rd) Col.   Charles Churchill.
Brig-Gen Webb's Regt of Foot (8th) Col.   John Richmond Webb.
Lord North and Grey's Regt of Foot (10th)   Maj-Gen Ld North & G.
Brig-Gen Howe's Regt of Foot (15th) Col.   Emmanuel Howe.
Col Godfrey's Regt of Foot (16th)   Colonel Francis Godfrey.
Royal Regiment of Ireland (18th) Col.   Lt-Gen Richard Ingoldsby.
Royal Regt of Scots Fusiliers (21st) Col.   Lord Mordaunt.
Her Majesty's Regt of Welch Fus. (23rd)   Brig-G Joeseph Sabine.
Col Tatton's Regt of Foot (24th) Colonel   William Tatton.
Brig-Gen Lord Dalrymple's Regt of Foot (26th)   Lord Dalrymple.
Col de Lalo's Regt of Foot (28th) Colonel   Sampson de Lalo.
Brig-Gen Farrington's Regt of Foot (29th)   Thomas Farrington.
Brig-Gen Meredyth's Regt of Foot (37th)   Thomas Meredyth

OUDENARDE

The Royal Regiment of Foot (1st)	Col. Lt-Gen Earl of Orkney.
HRH Prince George of Denmark's R of F (3rd)	Lt-G Duke of Argyll.
Lt-Gen Webb's Regt of Foot (8th) Colonel	John Richmond Webb
Lord North and Grey's Regt of Foot (10th)	Maj-Gen Ld North and G.
Maj-Gen Howe's Regt of Foot (15th) Col.	Emmanuel Howe.
Col Godfrey's Regt of Foot (16th) Colonel	Francis Godfrey.
HM Royal Rgt of Foot of Ireland (18th)	Lt-Gen Rich. Ingoldsby.
HM Regt of Royal (North) British Fus. (21st)	Sampson de Lalo.
HM Regt of (Royal) Welch Fusiliers (23rd)	Brig-Gen Joseph Sabine.
Brig-Gen Primrose's Regt of Foot (24th)	Gilbert Primrose.
Col. Preston's Regiment of Foot (26th)	Col. George Preston.
Lt-Gen Meredyth's Regt of Foot (37th)	Col. Thomas Meredyth.

MALPLAQUET

The Royal Regiment of Foot (1st)	Col. Lt-Gen Earl of Orkney.
HRH Prince George of Denmark's R of F (3rd)	Lt-G Duke of Argyll.
Lt-Gen Webb's Regt of Foot (8th) Colonel:	John Richmond Webb.
Lord North & Grey's Regt of Foot (10th)	Maj-Gen Ld North & G.
Lt-Gen Howe's Regt of Foot (15th)	Colonel Emmanuel Howe.
Col. Godfrey's Regt of Foot (16th)	Colonel Francis Godfrey.
HM Royal Regt of Foot of Ireland (18th)	Lt-G Rich. Ingoldsby.
Lt-Gen Erie's Regt of Foot (19th)	Colonel Thomas Erie.
HM Regt of Royal (North) British Fus. (21st)	Brig-G Sampson de Lalo.
HM Regt of (Royal) Welch Fusiliers (23rd)	Brig-Gen Joseph Sabine.
Brig-Gen Primrose's Regt of Foot (24th)	Gilbert Primrose
Col. Preston's Regiment of Foot (26th)	Col. George Preston.
Lt-Gen Meredyth's Regt of Foot (37th)	Col. Thomas Meredyth

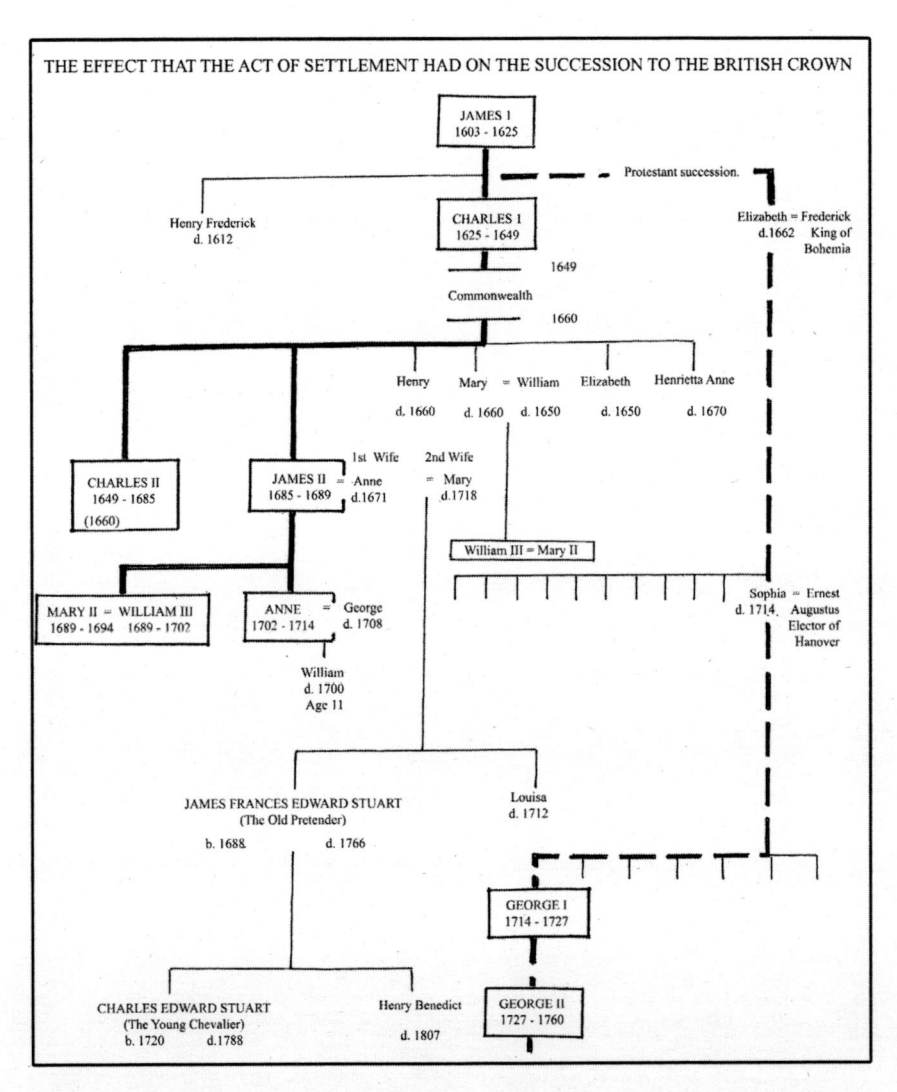

THE EFFECT THAT THE ACT OF SETTLEMENT HAD ON THE SUCCESSION TO THE BRITISH CROWN

```
                              JAMES I
                             1603 - 1625
                                                    Protestant succession.
   Henry Frederick            CHARLES I                         Elizabeth = Frederick
      d. 1612                 1625 - 1649                        d.1662    King of
                                                                           Bohemia
                                    1649
                              Commonwealth
                                    1660

              Henry    Mary = William   Elizabeth   Henrietta Anne
             d. 1660  d. 1660 d. 1650   d. 1650      d. 1670

                             1st Wife   2nd Wife
   CHARLES II      JAMES II  = Anne    = Mary
   1649 - 1685     1685 - 1689  d.1671   d.1718
     (1660)
                                 William III = Mary II

   MARY II = WILLIAM III   ANNE    = George              Sophia = Ernest
   1689-1694  1689-1702  1702-1714   d. 1708             d. 1714  Augustus
                                                                  Elector of
                                    William                       Hanover
                                    d. 1700
                                    Age 11

         JAMES FRANCES EDWARD STUART       Louisa
              (The Old Pretender)          d. 1712
           b. 1688.       d. 1766

                                           GEORGE I
                                           1714 - 1727

   CHARLES EDWARD STUART    Henry Benedict  GEORGE II
    (The Young Chevalier)                  1727 - 1760
    b. 1720    d.1788         d. 1807
```

Under the Act of Settlement of 1701, the future descent of the Crown was regulated to ensure Protestant seccession. After Anne, the heiress presumptive was the Electress Sophia of hanover and her protestant descendants. As she predeceased Anne by two months the Crown passed to her eldest son, George Louis Elector of Hanover, passing over the Catholic Stuart line.

CHAPTER IX

1714–1719
GEORGE I
1st JACOBITE REBELLION

George I – *A great grandson of King James I, George Ludwig (George Louis), Elector of Hanover, since 1698 was 54 years old when he succeeded Anne in 1714. He was small shy and retiring, could speak no English and believed that British power and position would serve to aid his domain in Hanover and his pretensions regarding Europe. He died of a stroke in 1727.*

In the summer of 1715 the Catholic son of King James II, James Francis Edward Stuart who, with his second wife Mary, had been sidelined by the 1701 Act of Settlement, wrote from France to John Erskine, Sixth* Earl of Mar, Secretary for Scotland calling on Mar to raise the clans in support of him without further delay.

Mar had earlier declared himself for George, but was disappointed with the cool response contrary to that which he had expected. On receiving the letter from James, he disguised himself as a workman and at London docks boarded a collier for Scotland where at Castletown in Braemar on 6th September 1715 he proclaimed the Pretender James as King James VIII of Scotland and III of England.

Following the Proclamation, on the 8th September the Jacobites raided Edinburgh. The raid failed, but without difficulty a week later Colonel John Hay captured Perth with a Jacobite army largely

---

* In Colonel John Davis's – *History of the 2nd (The Queen's Royal) Regiment of Foot* written in 1895, he states that it was William Erskine, Eleventh Earl of Mar. This would appear to be incorrect.

composed of Highland clansmen. General Gordon of Auchitoul had gone into the Western Highlands to bring in the clans from those parts. The whole country north of the Tay was soon in the hands of the rebels as armed Jacobite clansmen rallied under their chiefs in support of James. Had Mar been a more determined commander, he would have acted swiftly to overwhelm his numerically inferior opponent by driving him back over the Tweed, but he waited on events in England as he expected news that the Northumberland Jacobites and Scots supporters from the Western Borders would signal their support by joining the cause. Instead, every day's delay added to the strength of the King's position.

George I at once sent the Duke of Argyll to North Britain to take control of operations. He arrived at Edinburgh on the night of the 14th September. Four days later at Stirling, he reviewed his small force of about 1,000 infantry and 500 horse, consisting of two regiments of dragoons with Colonel Forfar's (3rd Foot – Royal East Kent Regiment) who had been called from Ireland. Colonel Montague's (11th Foot, the Devonshire Regiment) who had arrived in London from Flanders in August 1714 and were ordered to Scotland where, at Stirling in October 1714, they had paraded for the Coronation of King George I. Colonel Richard Boyle Viscount Shannon had taken over as colonel from William Breton on 27th January 1715 therefore as Shannon's (25th Foot – King's Own Scottish Borderers) and Orrey's (21st Foot, the Royal Scots Fusiliers) they were the only regiments present at Stirling.

Due to this shortage of regular British regiments, Argyll asked Lord Townshend for more troops. He waited impatiently for reinforcements, firstly from Ireland in the shape of two regiments of dragoons and four of foot and secondly from Holland where, because of the situation in Scotland, George I reluctantly asked the States General for Dutch troops. His request was later answered when they authorised the dispatch of 6,000 men.

1st JACOBITE REBELLION
1715 -- 1716

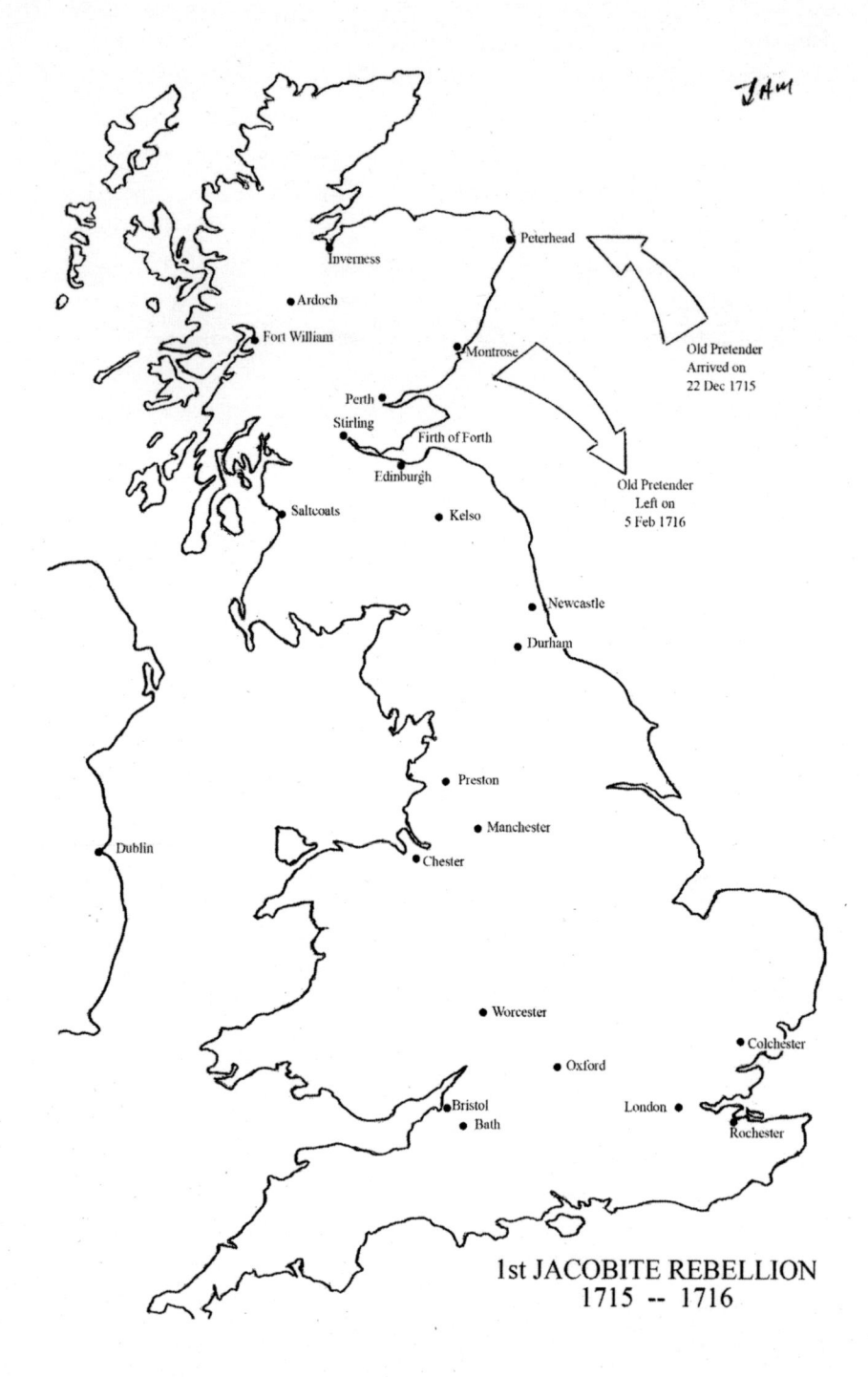

The camp at Stirling was commanded by Major-General Joseph Wightman, whose regiment (17th Foot, Leicestershire) had arrived in Ireland on 24th April 1714. Less than a year later, on 23rd March 1715 they were ordered to Dublin, where together with Morrison's Regiment (8th Foot, King's Liverpool) and Clayton's Regiment (14th Foot, West Yorkshire) they now awaited a fair wind to take them to Scotland, They landed at Saltcoats, Ayrshire in the early summer, arriving at Stirling on the 29th September where they joined the troops already there. To further boost the support at Stirling, Egerton's Regiment (36th Foot, Herefordshire) had sailed from Ireland on 23rd October, Richard Viscount Irwin's Regiment (16th Foot, Bedfordshire) was in Stirling early in October but moved to the protection of Fort William, the key to the Western Highlands.

Before 1715, Borr's (32nd Foot, 1st Battalion the Duke of Cornwall's Light Infantry) had nearly been disbanded, but was revamped on the Irish establishment. Sankey's Regiment (39th Foot, 1st Battalion Dorsetshire) was one which had its soldiers and resources divided between policing duties in Ireland and acting as marines on board HM ships in the Mediterranean.

In order to sweep the supporters of James to power across the whole of Britain, it was planned by the Jacobites that the uprising from the Highlands would support a simultaneous main thrust which would come from the southwest of England. It was here in early October that James would land, followed by a successful march by the Jacobite army to capture London. This was not to be, because the Whig Government stamped out rebel supporters in the West Country. Place after place which showed in favour of the insurrection was crushed with its leaders arrested as Lord Berkeley, Lord Lieutenant of Gloucestershire secured Bristol with three regiments of foot and a detachment of horse, while Major-General Wade took Bath. Oxford, which showed sympathy for the cause, was taken by General Pepper.

Grove's Regiment (10th Foot, the Lincolnshire) who had been serving in Flanders, returned to England and when the rebellion broke out were at Colchester where they were instructed to act as bodyguard for the Royal Family and spent time in this capacity at Hammersmith, Kensington and Chelsea.

Despite the reputation which Mar had earned as a good organiser, there is a dearth of evidence about any detailed schemes for the rising and the lack of co-ordination which his prolonged time in Perth reveals, epitomises the rebellion as a whole. A month after he raised the standard at Braemar, Mar was still in Perth, although he did take some action for on the 9th of October 1715: he sent Brigadier McIntosh of Borlum with a Highland force of about 2,000 men to cross the Forth by boat. This method of transport was necessitated because Argyll's troops held the only bridge crossing, at Stirling.

Borlum crossed between 12th and 14th of October with minimal interference from Government troops. However, instead of Mar instructing him to gather in the sympathisers in revolt on the Borders and attack Argyll from the rear, he left it to Borlum to decide what he should do once he was across the Forth. On the 19th October Borlum left for the Borders, where on the 20th he met up in Kelso with the Northumberland Jacobites.

The insurgents believed that the Roman Catholic landowners of Lancashire would come out in support, therefore Borlum headed south, reaching Preston on the 9th November. Hearing of this move General Wills, the garrison commander at Chester decided that he must attack 'these Rebels at Preston'. He left orders that Handasyd's (22nd Foot, the Cheshire Regiment) should secure the town of Manchester, known for its sympathy towards the Jacobite cause. This was confirmed when difficulty was encountered finding billets for officers and men of the regiment, until the town constables were informed that the town would be fired if the refusal continued. Needless to say, accommodation was soon found.

General Carpenter had been sent by the Government to Newcastle. Upon learning the intention of the insurgents he hurried south by forced marches and at Durham was joined by a detachment of the royal forces under General Wills. Having received information that Carpenter was advancing from the opposite side of Preston, Wills arrived before the town, determined to immediately attack the rebels. He put his forces in position in front of the Town on Friday 11th November and found to his surprise that the rebels had neglected to secure the bridge over the River Ribble which led to a narrow lane between steep banks. Here in this confined pass a fierce struggle took place, but Wills pressed forward and soon came near to the town where Forster had attempted to erect some form of defence.

The Royal troops here suffered much loss as they were met by a heavy fire from the rebels. Undeterred, they rushed at the barricades, two of which were carried. The struggle went on nearly the whole of the Friday night, but the Highlanders and their supporters fought so well that General Wills at first thought it prudent to withdraw. Despite this the rebels considered their position hopeless, therefore, on the morning of Sunday 13th, following Carpenter's arrival, Forster, without consulting his principal officers, sent Colonel Oxburg to propose terms of capitulation. Wills was not at first disposed to treat, owing to his now superior position, but agreed at last that he would do the best for them if they surrendered.

The Highlanders were at first very indignant and wanted to cut their way through the Royal troops but were persuaded by their chiefs to yield. Lord Derwentwater and McIntosh went over as hostages for the peaceful surrender.

Meanwhile in Scotland, Mar had stayed in Perth since the uprising began, all the time receiving reinforcements, until on the 10th of November he at last moved his army out. His plan was to take Edinburgh before moving south into England. From Perth he would have to cross the Forth. The route taken by Borlum nearly a month earlier was not now possible, so Mar decided that he would cross the river above Stirling.

Intelligence reached Argyll that Mar was moving with intent to take Edinburgh. He would reach Dunblane then send 3,000 clansmen to engage Argyll, keeping him at Stirling. On reaching Auchterarder, Mar reviewed his rebel army before moving south on the 12th of November, Argyll moved north to meet him, choosing as the battle site the rising ground of Sheriffmuir just north of Dunblane.

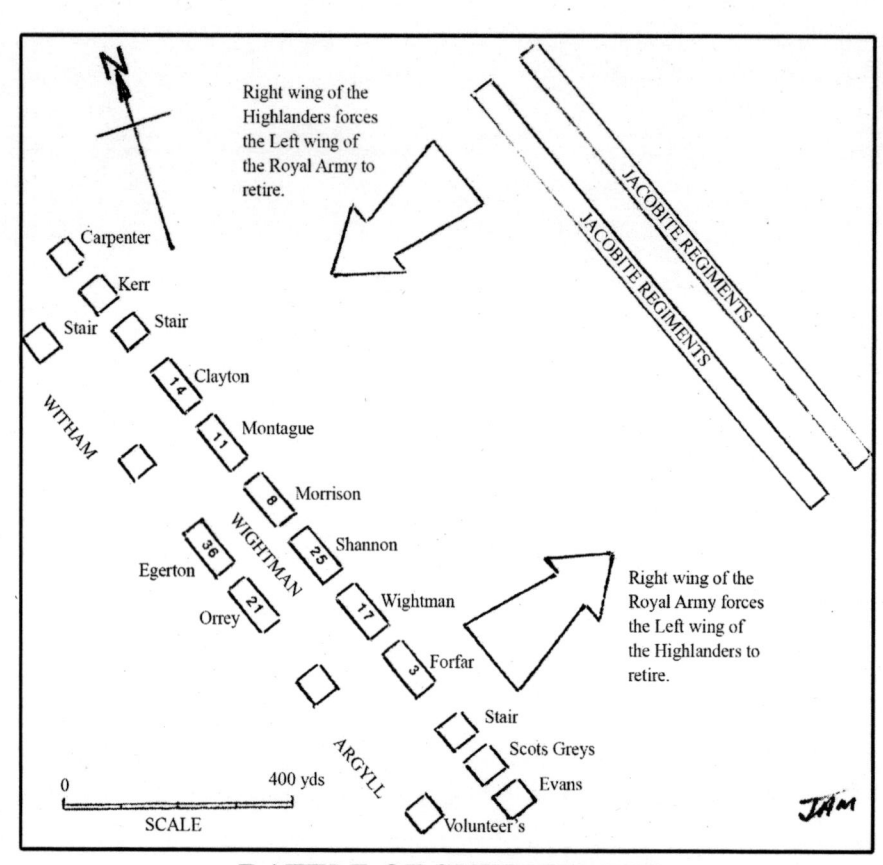

BATTLE OF SHERIFFMUIR
13th November 1715

On the morning of Sunday the 13th of November, the same day that Preston was lost, the rebels, just under 9,000 strong were advancing on high ground in order of battle. Both rebel lines containing ten clan battalions of foot with horse on each flank. The King's troops had three squadrons of dragoons on the flanks of his front line, with six battalions of foot, commanded by Major-General Wightman, who was colonel of the 17th Foot. From the left flank in the front line the infantry were:

Clayton's 14th Foot   (West Yorkshire Regiment).
Montague's 11th Foot   (Devonshire Regiment)
Morrison's 8th Foot   (King's, Liverpool Regiment)
Shannon's 25th Foot   (King's Own Scottish Borderers)
Wightman's 17th Foot   (Leicestershire Regiment)
Forfar's 3rd Foot   (Royal East Kent Regiment, the Buffs)

The second line consisted of two battalions of foot again flanked by horse.

Egerton's 36th Foot   (Worcestershire Regiment)
Orrey's 21st Foot   (Royal Scots Fusiliers)

    Argyll saw Mar's clansmen march from the left, and therefore gave orders to march to the right in order to counter the enemy's move. As a result, just before noon, the two armies set about re-organising themselves. Mar moved his line up the hill in two columns. On the Government side the process of right-forming took longer than it should have done, and while this lengthy operation was taking place, it was attacked by a furious charge from Mar's right wing. The two armies arrived not squarely facing each other but echeloned or offset, so that the right wing of each outflanked the left wing of their opponent.
    This resulted in the right wing of the royal army chasing the left wing of the rebels from the field, whilst the right wing of the rebels forced the left wing of royal army to retire. Each of the leaders was with their own right wing and therefore in that sector fought a

successful engagement, unaware that his other wing was being defeated.

Wightman's regiment reported that the rebels 'received them very briskly' but after some resistance, Argyll charged with his cavalry and pushed them back across the Water of Allen, after which he returned to the field only to find that the colonel of the 3rd Foot, Forfar had been severely wounded (he would later die). The fighting was now virtually over. Each leader, realising his situation, did some manoeuvring in the face of, and close to, the enemy, but as darkness began to fall, both commanders retired, Argyll to Dunblane and Mar to Ardoch. Argyll returned to the field the next day and carried his wounded off to Stirling. Mar returned to Perth from where he wrote to the Pretender explaining his withdrawal whilst still awaiting his arrival.

The battle is often referred to as no side gaining an advantage. This is not really true, for although Mar was not beaten, he was prevented from crossing the River Forth thereby taking Edinburgh. He was also thwarted in his attempt to move south into England. It is difficult to assess exact losses but is generally accepted that the Government army lost 663 killed, wounded or taken prisoner, while the figure for the rebels was only 232.

In the far north, Inverness which had fallen to the rebels in mid-September, changed hands back to the pro-Government Whigs. At about this time, on 29th November, Colonel Harrison's Regiment (15th Foot, the East Yorkshire) was ordered to march to Worcester, they had arrived from Flanders, landing in London then marching to Rochester before their move to the West Country.

At long last, on 22nd December the Pretender arrived at Peterhead, but immediately took to his bed for the next five days. On 2nd January 1716 he set out for Perth where on the 9th of January he made a public entry where, for a while, new life was infused into his supporters.

Reinforcements were still joining the Royal army, except for Sabine's (23rd Foot, the Royal Welch Fusiliers) who were in Ireland in 1715. They were so anxious to take part in the action that they offered to defray the charges of their own transportation to the scene of the fighting. Disappointingly for them, the rebellion was over before they arrived and the cost was probably borne by their Colonel Joseph Sabine, a rich man who had led them at Schellenburg, Blenheim and Ramilies.

The rebellion dragged on without hope of success as more troops joined the royal army at Stirling, where Clayton's, Egerton's, Forfar's and Orrey's were grouped under Brigadier Morrison.

On 29th of January 1716, royal troops now numbering 10,000 men including militia, marched on Perth, although due to heavy snow it was three days before they arrived.

Without any attempt at a fight, the Jacobite army slipped out of Perth, and on 5th February, the clansmen were deserted by the Pretender, who went aboard a small French cutter at Montrose taking Mar with him. The Highlanders dispersed back to their clan areas.

The 1715 rising was over.

Despite his hasty retreat from Montrose in February 1716, the Pretender and his Jacobite supporters still had designs on the throne of Britain. Due to the alliance between France, the Dutch, Germany and England, in line with the Utrecht Treaty, James could no longer look for support from the French. He had, however, managed to interest Sweden in his cause.

Baron Gorty, a minister and adviser to the King of Sweden, believed that an invasion of England would be successful especially as Spain was also enthusiastic about the scheme – which was that there would be an insurrection in England in favour of the Pretender and an invasion of Scotland by James in person. After all, the clansmen were still ready for a fight and even though the recent Act of Parliament by the English forbade the possession of arms, many Highlanders still openly carried muskets, broadswords, pistols and dirks whenever they went to church, to market or to fairs.

In England, Count Gyllenborg and Baron Spaar were the Swedish ministers who were assisting with Gorty's plan. Unfortunately for them, letters were intercepted by the Government who set in motion preparations to counter the danger, with a force being assembled under the command of Lieutenant-General Wills.

Clayton's (14th Foot) was in Fort William, while in October, Kirk's Regiment (2nd Foot, the Queen's Royal West Surrey) went into quarters in Manchester, with 108 men sent north to Lancaster to relieve Brigadier Preston's Regiment (26th Foot, the Cameronians [Scottish Rifles]), who were guarding rebel prisoners from the Earl of Mar's earlier rising.

Early in 1717 Count Gyllenborg was arrested and a search of his house disclosed papers exposing the plot. It therefore followed that at its assembly on 20th February, great indignation was expressed in Parliament regarding the Swedish plot, so much so that some members proposed that war should be declared against Sweden.

Although for the remainder of the year it was considered that an invasion was unlikely, relations with Spain remained strained. Lord Stanhope sent his cousin Colonel Stanhope as ambassador to Spain, and the Prince Regent of France, who still favoured a peace policy sent the Marquis of Nancre. Both men tried extremely hard to prevent war, but Cardinal Alberoni the Prime Minister of Spain, remained stubborn, determined on an attack against Britain. This brought matters to the point where it was deemed necessary that actions should be commenced for a British fleet to be sent to Spain. These preparations reached the ear of Alberoni who ordered the assembly of a strong Spanish naval force of 29 ships of war, with transports for 38,000 soldiers with adequate stores, weapons and ammunition.

From the British side, plans were in hand for the collection of a land force at Portsmouth and a fleet which would be under the command of Admiral Byng, who had received instructions to sail for the Mediterranean with 20 sail of the line. Kirk's (2nd Foot) and Whetham's (27th Foot, Royal Inniskilling Fusiliers) were two of the regiments ordered to Portsmouth.

The Spanish fleet began operations by taking Sicily. This attack had been anticipated and Byng had been instructed to obstruct, if possible. On 11th August 1718 the two fleets were in sight of each other off Cape Passaro, the southern-most point of Sicily. Byng at once sent Captain Walton on to intercept a division of the Spaniards which had gone in towards the coast. Walton was successful and the Spaniards were completely defeated.

War was declared in December 1718. With his sanctuary in France denied, James arrived in Madrid which was the signal for the despatch of the force assembled by the Spanish minister Cardinal Alberoni, consisting of five men of war, 20 transports and 5,000 soldiers on board, mainly Spanish but some Irish. The expedition also carried arms for 30,000 more in anticipation of the Jacobite and Highland clansmen who were due to join them once they landed in Britain.

In England, troops were moved to cover any landings which might have been attempted. On 6th March 1719, five companies of Kirk's (2nd Foot) were ordered to Bristol. Three days earlier Wightman's (17th Foot) was directed to Hull, earlier Clayton's (14th Foot) had left Fort William for Perth, then on to Inverness. Egerton's Regiment (36th Foot) embarked at Cork for Britain in March of that year.

On 1st March, Edmund Fielding was given a commission to raise ten companies from out-pensioners of the Royal Hospital, Chelsea who moved to Portsmouth as garrison troops. They would later become the 41st Foot (the Welsh Regiment).

Once again the latest attempt by James was doomed to failure. Ahead of the main invasion force sailed Earl Marischal with Spanish regular troops. The main fleet encountered fearful storms which raged for nearly two weeks in the Bay of Biscay. Stores, guns, and even horses were cast overboard in an unsuccessful attempt to save the ships. However, one by one they limped into Spanish ports in very poor condition, so much so that the enterprise would have been abandoned had not Marischal sailed in front of the storm. With two ships he reached the Western Highlands with 400 Spaniards and about 100 Scottish and English gentlemen, landing at Kintail on the mainland within Skye, where he encamped opposite the castle of Donan where the hoped-for clans would add support. The support never came as they were only joined by about 1,500 clansmen.

To oppose this force, General Carpenter directed Major-General Wightman from Inverness on 5th June, with three troops of Scots Greys and the regiments of Montague's (11th Foot), Clayton's (14th Foot) and Harrison's (15th Foot). At about 4 p.m. on the 10th June, they arrived at Glenshiel. The Spaniards and Highlanders fell back and took up a position amidst the Pass of the Streichell, where an hour later they were attacked by Wightman's Troops. The insurgents were soon dislodged and driven off with little loss to the Royal army. The Lords Tullibardine, Marischal and Seaforth escaped as did most of the Highland clansmen, but the entire Spanish contingent surrendered as prisoners of war.

On 21st April 1719, Cholmeley's (16th Foot) received orders to march to Newcastle. A month later under directions from the Lords Justices they were sent to Sunderland. During this time, Wightman's (17th Foot) were sent to cover Cholmeley's Regiment in Newcastle and Gateshead. The role of Cholmeley's in Sunderland was to aid the civil magistrates in suppressing any tumults or insurrections. Later they returned to Newcastle, followed by a march to Edinburgh.

The assistance given by the Spanish Court to the Stuart cause so annoyed the British Government that, by way of reprisal, they decided that Spain should be deterred from future similar ideas. To this end an expedition was organised to attack the Spanish coast.

Shannon's (25th Foot) or the Edinburgh Regiment (its title at the time) had only been in Ireland since 1718, but in 1719 was ordered to embark for the Isle of Wight to join the expedition forming there. Due to contrary winds, the transports carrying Shannon's Regiment were driven first into Milford Haven, before limping into Bristol where the regiment landed.

From there the 25th marched overland more than 100 miles to Plymouth where it embarked for the Isle of Wight to meet up with troops being assembled under Richard Temple Viscount Cobham. One of the regiments was Howard's (24th Foot – the South Wales Borderers). Howard had been appointed colonel in 1717 and commanded for 20 years. The regiment was called Howard's Greens due to the colour of its facings (nothing to do with the Green Howards, 19th Foot). Other regiments who joined Lord Cobham's expedition consisted of a brigade of Guards, 4,000 men of the 24th, 25th, 33rd and 34th Regiments of Foot, who embarked on 21st September 1719 and sailed from the Isle of Wight to Spain under convoy of a squadron of ships.

When the fleet reached Corunna it found the place well defended, and therefore coasted along to Vigo where the expedition anchored in Vigo Bay. Cobham landed with the grenadier companies of the 24th Foot on the evening of the 29th September. Next day the rest of the troops were put on shore. Shots were fired from the ships into the city, which submitted without resistance, while the garrison under Don Gonzal de Soto retired to the citadel.

On 5th October, Rondadella was burned and its governor offered to cede. Terms were sent in and guns were landed from the ships at anchor. This covered the honour of the defenders who required that a battery should be erected against them, before they could surrender. The next day de Soto surrendered.

As the weather was poor, the British troops found that their temporary camp was becoming waterlogged due to the heavy rain. The well-being of his men being important to him, Lord Cobham transferred them into the shelter of the city.

Ponte-ve-dra also submitted without a fight to Major-General Wade, supported by 1,000 men who took as trophies: brass ordnance, small arms and military stores. Lord Cobham considered that the expedition had fulfilled its purpose and re-embarked with his troops, returning to Portsmouth.

After this second failed rebellion, the task of the forces in Scotland was to prevent any further rising and they were disposed to guard the building of barracks and to prevent disorder. There were at this time insufficient barracks for the nine British regiments which formed the Scottish command, so a number of them had to be billeted in the larger towns.

Following the death in 1727 of King George I, the Crown passed to his only son also called George, but who, unlike his father was able to speak English. Nevertheless, he was still regarded in Britain as a foreigner. He was to remain on the throne until 1760, a period of 33 years.

CHAPTER X

1702-1744
WEST INDIES

Jamaica – *Discovered by Columbus in 1494 and ruled by Spain until captured by England in 1655.*

What happened to regiments not directly involved in the Jacobite Rebellion or those who were engaged in the defence of Gibraltar or activities in Minorca?

In 1717, Colonel Philips, Governor of the colony of Nova Scotia formed a regiment from several independent companies of foot who were grouped under him. It became the 40th Foot (Prince of Wales's Volunteers, [South Lancashire] Regiment) although in 1782 it was titled the 40th or (2nd Somersetshire) Regiment of Foot.

Another regiment that missed Marlborough's Continental War was the 38th Foot (South Staffordshire) Regiment raised by Colonel Luke Lillingston at the King's Head in Lichfield in 1705. Lillingston took his regiment to Ireland but in 1707 did not accompany it to the West Indies, where in those remote and fever-stricken islands, it spent 57 years based in Antigua, neglected, suffering from tropical diseases and much of its time too fond of drink.

It is difficult to establish the reason for this extremely long stay, except that the establishment required troops to maintain the English presence in the area. Unfortunately the expense of relieving these troops by that of another regiment was high; it was easier to leave the incumbents in their current locations. This period in the life of the 38th is unique in the history of the British Army concerning overseas postings.

Spain had originally held vast possessions on the American continent and throughout the West Indies. These now required large manpower resources which she could not muster, and opportunist European countries including England, fought for possession. Islands and areas of the mainland changed hands, in some cases several times.

During most of its service in the West Indies, the 38th, based on Antigua, was badly neglected. Pay was at best late and in many instances did not arrive at all. Soldiers who left Ireland in 1707 were smartly clad, but after years in these tropical locations, their uniforms were reduced to rags. At one time they had not received replacement clothing for over ten years, and their solution was to improvise by cutting makeshift uniform-type tropical kit from the sacking which was used for packing the locally grown sugar. This practice was later commemorated by the wearing of a brown Holland patch behind the cap badge of their Stafford knot.

During this time their weapons too were not updated. In fact some muskets were over 50 years old, with some firearms damaged to the point where, without adequate repair facilities, it left some of the soldiers unarmed.

As may be expected, under the conditions in which the soldiers lived, hygiene was, certainly by modern standards, non-existent. Food was poor and alcoholic drink, mainly rum but also some local spirits, was too plentiful. For those taken to the so-called hospitals, conditions were even worse, training, cleanliness and a total ignorance to the task in hand, allied to their liking for the same drink as their patients, led to many deaths, most of them from the misunderstood local ailments.

The time spent in the West Indies was not all wasted. Detachments were sent to defend the Leeward Islands which so often found themselves open to assaults from the opponents of England.

The 38th Foot also found that it was ordered to supply the Navy with men to act as marines, so small parties were often embarked on HM ships where there main role was to maintain discipline on board against men who had been enforced for service in the Navy.

When these ships were not fighting the enemy which, most of the time, included the French and Spanish, they were engaged against the privateers and pirates who operated in the area. After all, a British man of war armed and with soldiers on board, was not the sort of prize that pirates were seeking.

During the 57 years that the 38th Foot spent in the West Indies, the officers were replaced many times. Young officers gazetted were the sons of local planters and Government officials. Of the men, because reinforcements from England were often of poor quality, local white men were also recruited. Apart from being in the band, black men were not enlisted.

While the 38th Foot was abroad, hostile feelings were growing in intensity between England and Spain; this was due to the colonial policy of the two countries in the West Indies and South America. As a consequence, in 1739 war broke out. Six hundred men of Blakeney's Regiment (27th Foot, the Royal Inniskilling Fusiliers) set sail and were engaged at Porto Bello on the Isthmus of Darien. Some indication of the severity of conditions is that due to climate, fever and disease only nine men were able to return at the conclusion of this duty.

Guise's (6th Foot – Warwickshire Regiment), who were posted from 1742 to 1744, also suffered terribly from disease.

Sea transport between England and the West Indies could take months. In July 1740, the 15th Foot (East Yorkshire Regiment) and other regiments under the command of General Lord Cathcart embarked for Jamaica. Much delay occurred owing to unfavourable winds and it was not until January 1741 that they arrived.

The Holland patch behind the badge is not the only example of regiments wearing trophies to highlight long periods away from home. The 23rd Foot (Royal Welch Fusiliers) wear five black ribbons on their collar. These are a link to when soldiers wore pigtails, which were powdered and greased, and in order to protect the red tunics, the pigtail was encased in a bag. In 1808 this custom was abolished, the regiment was in Nova Scotia. As communications were slow, the 23rd was the last to wear the bag. When it was finally removed, the five ribbons with which it had been secured were retained.

Admiral Edward Vernon, who had been a Member of Parliament since 1722, told the House in 1740 when England was a war with Spain, that the Spanish Empire in the West Indies was militarily over-extended, so weak in fact he claimed he could take Porto Bello with only six ships. This was required because it was the base of the

Guarda Costas who were raiding British ships in the Caribbean in line with the claim by Spain, that they had 'a right of maritime search' and the subjecting of captured seamen to cruel punishments.

On the strength of this assertion, towards the end of October 1740, Harrison's Regiment (15th Foot, the East Yorkshire), Maj-General Thomas Wentworth's Regiment (24th Foot, the South Wales Borderers) under the command of Lieutenant-Colonel Theophilus Sandford, each raised 1,000 rank and file with part of Chomondeley's (34th Foot, the Border Regiment) together with six new Marine regiments (disbanded in 1748) and a train of artillery all under the command of Lieutenant-General Lord Cathcart embarked and sailed under Admiral Ogle for the West Indies.

Storms in the Bay of Biscay coincided with the death of Lord Cathcart who was succeeded by Major-General Wentworth who was unfortunately not an equal replacement of the same vigour, quality or determination as Cathcart.

The first objective of the expedition was San Juan de Cartagena (now a city in the Republic of Colombia) a place of great importance, because it was the residence of the Spanish Captain-General of the Indies.

The force, aided by American 'Marines' and at least 1,000 slave pioneers, arrived off Carthagena early in March 1741. Bocha China, the name of the harbour, was defended by outlying forts which would require to be silenced before the fleet could enter.

On 25th March, Fort Louis was stormed and the fleet entered the harbour. However, not until April was it decided to attack Fort St Lazar which commanded the town. Preliminary siege-works had been carried out by the white regular troops who were suffering sickness due to the climate. This was necessary as the Negro slave pioneers refused to work whilst under fire.

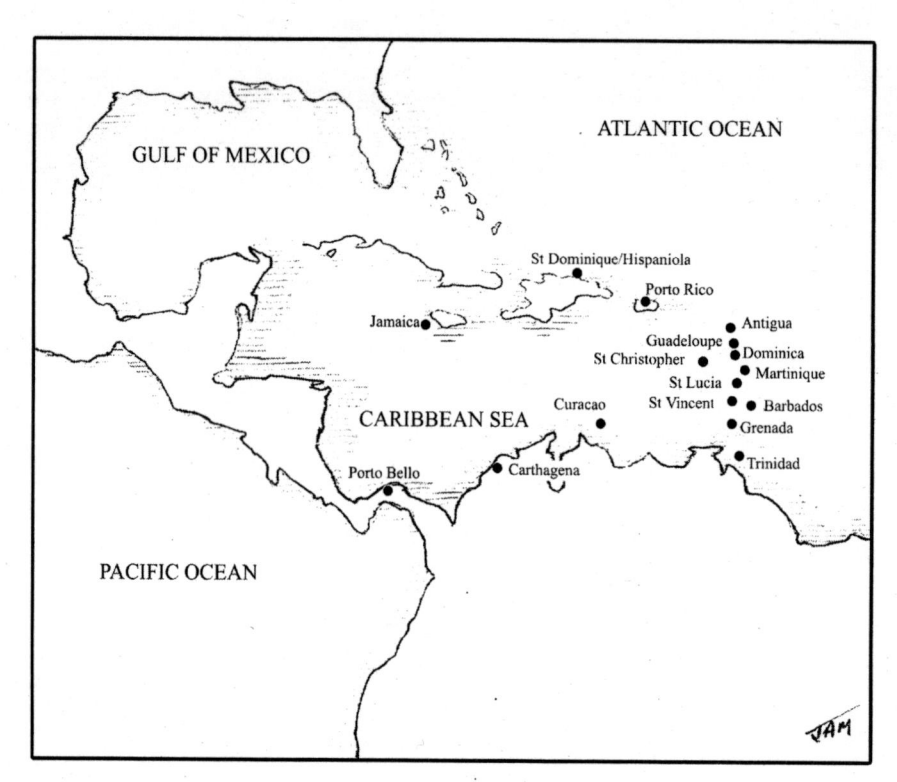

WEST INDIES

To ensure success, General Wentworth pressed for assistance from the fleet but Admiral Vernon declared that the Fort could be stormed without his aid, therefore Wentworth ordered a night attack under the command of Major-General John Guise who led the force of 1,200 men. Due to either poor navigation or incompetence at daybreak the force found themselves attacking the wrong face of the fortress and, although they pressed with great resolve, they were beaten off and forced to retreat leaving a number of officers and 600 men dead or wounded on the field.

As the rainy season had set in, the enterprise was abandoned and on the 16th April 1741 the troops re-embarked. In this short campaign ten officers had been killed and of the original 1,000 NCOs and men only 219 survived. The Commanding Officer of the 24th Foot, Lieutenant-Colonel Theophilus Sandford did not. The toll continued, for many died from local fevers on board the fleet as it made its way to Cuba. The troops were landed on the eastern end of the island where they were employed against the Spaniards at San Jago de Cuba until November 1741, when they returned to Jamaica.

CHAPTER XI

1715 – UNTIL
IRELAND–1742, MINORCA–1748 AND
GIBRÁLTAR – 1727.

Before moving into areas of conflict during this period, it is interesting to note some of the events recorded by the 11th Foot (Devonshire Regiment).

In 1715 at Stirling, several soldiers and drummers deserted but will be pardoned if they return within 21 days.

In 1731 in Edinburgh, Alexander Campbell, an Argyllshire man and sentinel in Captain Petit's Company who was quartered in Leith, was found murdered in the house of James Chrystie of Ireland, who it is believed to be the murderer, having found Campbell in bed with his wife. Also in Edinburgh in 1732, another sentinel John Smith, was shot for deserting, having been twice pardoned by General Wade for the same offence.

In 1738 in Dundee, John Veal a sergeant in the 11th Foot, having apprehended a deserter and within a mile of the town took the fatigued prisoner behind him on horseback. The prisoner drew a knife and stabbed his keeper to the heart, both fell from the horse, while the prisoner remounted, the sergeant with his last breath fired two pistols at him but he rode clean off.

Lt. Colonel D.V. Wakely, 1978

In October 1711 the preliminaries were signed which were to form the basis for the Treaty of Utrecht, enabling the Treaty to be finally settled in the spring of 1713. Included in this were conditions that France should acknowledge the 1701 Act of Settlement, which confirmed Protestant succession for the British Crown. The Treaty also required that the Crowns of France and Spain should never be united. Other clauses secured enormous gains for Britain – Gibraltar and Minorca come under their control, together with St Kitts, Acadia and Hudson's Bay, Newfoundland.

IRELAND

Regardless of the outcome in the mainland of the Jacobite Rebellion, Ireland still presented problems such that many regiments were required to be stationed there. In March 1715, St Clair's Regiment (1st Foot, the Royal Scots) left England for Ireland, arriving on the 26th April 1715 and remaining there for 26 years until relieved in 1741.

Colonel Whetham's (27th Foot, the Royal Inniskilling Fusiliers) who had spent time with Admiral Byng's Fleet, disembarked at Kinsale in August 1720. However on the 22nd March 1725 Richard, Viscount Molesworth became colonel. It was as Molesworth's Regiment they served in many areas of Ireland until 1733.

Colonel the Honourable James O'Hara was created Lord Kilmaine in 1721. Hence as Kilmaine's (7th Foot, the Royal Fusiliers) he moved with his regiment from Cork to Dublin, Due to the troubled state of the country, in September 1723 all officers of the regiment were appointed Justices of the Peace. This was repeated in Galway in 1724 where they were again appointed to oversee justice under both military and civil law. It was in December of that year that Lord Kilmaine succeeded his father; therefore the regiment again changed its name to Tyrawley's Foot and remained on the Irish establishment until 1726. This was also the year that Colonel Middleton's Regiment (25th Foot, the King's Own Borderers) left Ireland having been there since 1721.

Colonel Robert Hayes' Regiment (34th Foot, the Border Regiment) returned to England from Europe only to be sent to Ireland where it remained until the beginning of 1727 when it was embarked for Gibraltar. Even in 1730, regiments were still being sent to Ireland.

Dalzell's Regiment (33rd Foot, the Duke of Wellington's [West Riding] Regiment) arrived in Ireland on 9th July 1730 and under their new colonel returned to England as Johnson's Regiment in 1742.

MINORCA

What of events in the Mediterranean?

One item of importance during the recent war was the capture in September 1708 of the Island of Minorca by Sir John Leake commanding an English fleet. This enabled the establishment of the naval base at Port Mahon.

What has been termed the Treaty of Utrecht took nearly two years to put into place and consisted a series of separate agreements between the individual Allied states on one side and France and Spain on the other.

The terms with Spain especially entitled Britain to hold Minorca and Gibraltar. As a major sea power, Britain now held the entry and control of the Mediterranean at two locations. The fleet could patrol from Port Mahon which was at the eastern end of the thirty-mile-long island. The port was defended by Fort St Philip which was located on the southern side of the entrance to the haven.

In January 1713, Lord Tyrawley resigned as colonel in favour of his son The Honourable James O'Hara. It was as O'Hara's Regiment (7th Foot, the Royal Fusiliers) it was ordered to Minorca in February, where it was to form the garrison with Sankey's Regiment (39th Foot, the Dorsetshire Regiment), Whetham's Regiment (27th Foot, the Inniskillings) and Phillip's Regiment (40th Foot, the Prince of Wales's Volunteers [South Lancashire] Regiment). During its stay, the Fusiliers were quartered at St Philip's Castle, where in July 1718 they witnessed the arrival of Admiral Sir George Byng with his fleet, with relief for the garrison who were to replace both O'Hara's and Sankey's. These regiments having left Minorca, were due for service in Sicily.

Colonel Richard Philipp's Regiment (12th Foot, the Suffolk Regiment) were ordered to Minorca in 1715, ten years later they were joined by Colonel Whightman's Regiment (17th Foot, the Leicestershire Regiment) who were to stay on the island for 25 years.

In 1726 Colonel Roger Handasyd's Regiment (22nd Foot, the Cheshire Regiment) were ordered to Minorca where they were to be stationed alongside (Maj-Gen) Thomas Whetham's Regiment (12th Foot) until they were relieved 22 years later.

All regiments remained in Minorca in a sort of uneasy peace, mainly neglected by the local population until 1756 when 15,000 Frenchmen disembarked at the western end of the island. Being in inferior numbers the British troops were withdrawn to the fortress at Port Mahon, where it was expected that Admiral Byng would relieve the garrison.

Byng, who had an ill-equipped fleet withdrew after an inconclusive action and returned to Gibraltar. This led to the loss of the island and the court martial of Byng and his execution by firing squad for cowardice.

GIBRALTAR

The Spanish were resentful over the loss of Gibraltar to Britain following the terms of Utrecht. Although not at war, Spain set in place preparations with the intention of regaining the fortress. A secret treaty was agreed between the Emperor of Germany and the King of Spain, whereby the Pretender would be placed on the throne of Britain and the fortress of Gibraltar would be returned to Spain.

Several regiments already formed the garrison at Gibraltar, the Earl of Barrymore's Regiment (13th Foot, the Somerset Light Infantry) had been there since 1711, although Stanhope Cotton had taken over as Colonel on the 8th July 1715 only to be succeeded on Christmas Day 1725 by Lord Mark Kerr. Middleton's Regiment (25th Foot, the King's Own Scottish Borderers) who sailed for and landed there in 1726. Thomas Pearce's Regiment (5th Foot, the Northumberland Fusiliers) were also present during the coming siege.

Early in January 1727, the Spaniards under the Conde de la Torres moved against Gibraltar. Their army numbering about 20,000 men camped at San Roque within five miles of the fortress.

Robert Hayes's Regiment (34th Foot, the Border Regiment) left Plymouth at the beginning of 1727, but a severe storm badly damaged their transports such that only six companies managed to return to Plymouth, the remainder of the regiment was lost. The six companies were regrouped and sailed again, arriving there on the 26th March. However, while the regiments were being transported to augment the garrison, on 11th February the Spanish Army had opened an attack from three trenches against the fortress.

The Earl of Portmore, Governor of Gibraltar, his Lieutenant-Governor and several senior officers were all on leave in England and had not realised the significance of the silent withdrawal of the Spanish Ambassador from the Court of St John. However, learning of the investment of their fortress, several regiments were alerted and moves were set up to strengthen the garrison at Gibraltar.

The Lieutenant-Governor was the first to return, bringing with him 500 men from Handasyd's Regiment (22nd Foot, the Cheshire Regiment) who had been ordered to leave Minorca. They arrived on 10th April. The Governor returned on the 26th bringing with him a regiment of foot and a regiment of Guards with a fleet commanded by Sir Charles Wager. These reinforcements raised the strength of the garrison to 6,000 men.

The siege continued for four months, fighting that lasted through the month of May and into June. The Spaniards suffered very badly through sickness owing to their barren location, while the British were well provided by sea due to the considerable strength of the British fleet under Admiral Hobson. Although taking no part in action during the conflict, its very presence kept lines with England open and also kept the garrison supplied with fresh provisions from the coast of Africa. The defending troops, who had heard of the plight of the Spaniards compared to their own situation, looked with contempt upon the besiegers, whom they knew to be suffering.

On 10th June 'a parley was beat' by the Spaniards. The siege was raised thirteen days later following a tremendous cannonade from the besiegers. Losses were high on the Spanish side, possibly as many as 3,000 were killed or wounded, apart from those who perished from sickness.

The British losses were only about 300, due mainly to damage caused by themselves using useless pieces of guns and mortars which had been standing in the Rock galleries since 1704. Many pieces blew up when the British gunners tried to put them into action. Thus the abortive attempt to take the fortress from the British cost many more injuries to the Spanish.

In 1739 Colonel Joseph Sabine (23rd Foot, the Royal Welch Fusiliers) who was a very rich man, died as Governor of Gibraltar.

CHAPTER XII

1739–1745
GEORGE II
EUROPE – WAR OF THE AUSTRIAN SUCCESSION

On the 17th April 1713 the Pragmatic Sanction was published by the Austrian Emperor Charles the Sixth, whereby in the case of his having no male issue, his daughters were to succeed to his hereditary dominions, in preference to the sons of his late brother, Joseph the First.

In 1739 following the requirements of General Wade, a number of independent Highland companies recruited from the young gentlemen of Whig and Jacobite clans, took service in 'Am Freiceadon Dubh' and were formed into a regular regiment, as The Earl of Crawford's Regiment of Foot (the Highland Regiment) or 43rd Foot, later designated the 42nd Foot, the Black Watch, in effect a police unit for the Highlands and so-called due to its dark Government tartan.

Two major events occurred in 1740. In October the Hapsburg Emperor of Austria, Charles VI died leaving his domains to his daughter Maria Theresa. In the same year the Kingdom of Prussia acquired a new ruler in Frederick II, later called The Great, who ascended to the throne of his father. He inherited a formidable army which he was anxious to use to expand his territories. Ignoring the 'Pragmatic Sanction', Frederick attacked and seized the Austrian province of Silesia. France, anxious to challenge the Hapsburgs, encouraged and supported him.

In January 1741, ten Marine regiments were raised by Britain and took rank in the Army, as such they were numbered 44th to 53rd.

Seven additional regiments of infantry were also raised, these were numbered 54th to 60th.

In 1748 when peace seemed secure, the ten Marine regiments were disbanded (certain modern day parallels!!). To fulfil the numbering classification the foot regiments who had earlier been numbered 54th to 60th were re-numbered as follows:

43rd Foot. Originally raised in Winchester in 1741 as Colonel Fowke's 54th Regiment, who were stationed in Minorca from 1742 to 1747. In 1748 they became the 43rd Foot and in 1881, the Oxfordshire Light Infantry.

44th Foot. Raised by Colonel James Long of the 1st (Grenadier) Guards as the 55th Regiment, it became the 44th Foot 1st Marines in 1748 and the Essex Regiment in 1881. Lieutenant-Colonel John Lee from the 4th Foot succeeded Long in 1743.

45th Foot. In 1741, Colonel Houghton raised and commanded the 56th Regiment, serving in Gibraltar from 17th June 1742 with the re-numbering they became the 45th Foot 2nd Marines, and The Sherwood Foresters – Derbyshire Regiment in 1881.

46th Foot. King George conferred the command of the 57th Foot, on Colonel John Price from the 1st Foot Guards. The commission was dated 13th January 1741. The 57th was subsequently numbered the 46th Foot, 3rd Marines in 1751. They became Duke of Cornwall's Light Infantry in 1881.

47th Foot. On the 3rd January 1741, Colonel John Mordaunt was authorised to raise a regiment of foot 'by beat of drum or otherwise' this was achieved by 15th January and titled the 58th Foot. Colonel Mordaunt was then succeeded by General P. Lascelles from March 1743. In 1748 it became the 47th Foot, 4th Marines and in 1881, The Loyal North Lancashire Regiment.

48th Foot. Colonel James Cholmondeley's Regiment was raised in Norwich on 17th January 1741, and took precedence as the 59th of the Line. In 1742 Lieutenant-Colonel Thomas Hopson marched to London, where King George reviewed the regiment before moving to Salisbury where it was to remain until 1744. In 1748 the regimental number was changed to 48th Foot, 5th Marines. In 1881 it became The Northamptonshire Regiment.

49th Foot. Raised in the West Indies by the Governor of Jamaica Edward Trelawney in June 1744. It was designated as Trelawney's Regt. (the Jamaica Volunteers) 63rd Foot. In 1748 it became the 49th Foot, 6th Marines. In 1881, it was titled the Princess Charlotte of Wales (Berkshire) Regiment.

In April 1742, the Spanish fleet joined with the French Squadron at Toulon. Major General Hargrave who was then Lieutenant-Governor of Gibraltar received orders that in the event that Admiral Matthews required troops for service on board his ships, he should be furnished with 500 men from Fowke's Regiment (2nd Foot, the Queen's Royal West Surrey Regiment), Hargrave's Regiment (7th Foot, the Royal Fusiliers), Lieutenant-General Colombine's Regiment (10th Foot, the Lincolnshire), Fuller's (29th Foot, the Worcestershire Regiment) and Houghtori's (45th Foot, the Sherwood Foresters – Derbyshire Regt). Records of the Gibraltar Garrison dated 9th May 1742 indicate that 313 men from the above regiments were serving as marines on board HM *Royal Oak*. During 1743 the fleet continued in Hyeres Bay blockading the French and Spanish fleets in Toulon harbour.

On 29th November 1743 the troops were transferred to another ship HM *Rupert* and took part in the action of the 11th February 1744.

In May 1742 several regiments were embarked for Flanders, mainly landing in Bruges where under Field Marshal the Earl of Stair they were to support the Queen of Hungary and Bohemia, Maria Theresa against the French. In April 1743 King George II prorogued Parliament and announced that his army would support the claims of Maria Theresa.

Regiments assembled in the Netherlands joining the Allied army of 37,000 men consisting of Hanoverians, Austrians and British who, early in 1743, commenced the march south, crossing the River Rhine in May. King George, accompanied by his second son William Augustus, Duke of Cumberland, left England to take part in the campaign. He joined Lord Stair on 19th June at Aschaffenburg. By this action he became the last British monarch to personally lead his army into battle.

The Allied army was operating in the valley of the River Main east of Frankfurt. A French army of 60,000 under Marshal Noailles lay in the neighbourhood. His plan was to cut the Allies' supply route from the Netherlands. Towards this end, he completely outmanoeuvred the Earl of Stair and on the 27th June, whilst conducting a withdrawal Stair was ambushed, and his army trapped near the village of Dettingen on the River Main in Bavaria. The French occupied a strong position, so, believing the Allies to be weak, they moved from their strength to attack.

The French cavalry charged the Allied left and centre but the British line held. They counter-attacked the French dragoons who unable to withstand the disciplined line fire, broke and fled. In trying to cross the River Main, many drowned.

The French infantry failed to retrieve the situation and after a few hours fighting, the Allies had won the day thereby driving the French out of Germany. British losses were less than 2,000 while the French lost twice as many. 25th December 1740, John Huske from the Coldstream Guards was promoted as Colonel of the 32nd Foot, the Duke of Cornwall's Light Infantry. He served at Dettingen as Brigadier and was severely wounded. In recognition of his services he was promoted to Major-General and given command of the 23rd Foot, the Royal Regiment of Welch Fusiliers.

In recognition of their action in the battle, the following regiments were awarded the battle honour DETTINGEN. However it was not authorised until 1882!

Colonel Thomas Howard's Regt. 3rd Buffs	Royal East Kent
Colonel Brig-Gen Richard Onslow's Regt.	8th Kings Liverpool
Colonel Robinson Sowie. 11th Foot	Devonshire Regiment
Colonel Scipio Durore, 12th Foot	Suffolk Regiment
Colonel Henry Poulteney. 13th Foot	Somerset Light Infantry
Colonel Thomas Bligh. 20th Foot	Lancashire Regiment.
Colonel Maj-Gen John Campbell. 21st	Royal North British Fusiliers
Colonel Newsham Peers 23rd	Royal Regiment of Welch Fusiliers

Colonel William Handasyd. 31st Foot	East Surrey Regiment.
Colonel John Huske. 32nd Foot	Duke of Cornwall's Light Infantry
Colonel John Johnson. 33rd Foot	Duke of Wellington's Regiment.
Colonel Henry Ponsonby. 37th Foot	Royal Hampshire Regiment.

In addition to the above, to commemorate the battle the 23rd Foot carry the White Horse of Hanover on their Regimental Colour.

At this time recruits were becoming harder to find, therefore General Order dated 29th April 1744 directed that able-bodied and fit men should be received even if they were under five feet five inches tall.

Although for most of 1744, the activities of Louis XV were taken up by his campaign on the Rhine. However in December Marshal Saxe received orders to prepare a plan of operations for the French army in Flanders. His plan was a simple one, to advance to the Austrian Netherlands through a breach opened on the River Scheldt.

Two years after Dettingen the British Army was still actively involved in Europe, such that Barren's (4th Foot), Cholmondley's (34th Foot), Fleming's (36th Foot) and Ligonier's (48th Foot) were ordered to Flanders along with the 19th Foot commanded by Colonel the Honourable Charles Howard. To command these forces King George II made the Duke of Cumberland Captain-General of all forces on the Continent.

In 1745 the village of Tournai was strongly held by the Allies, but by the end of April, Saxe had besieged the village forcing Cumberland to assemble his entire force of British, Dutch and Austrians to march to its relief with some 65,000 men, of which about 25,000 were British.

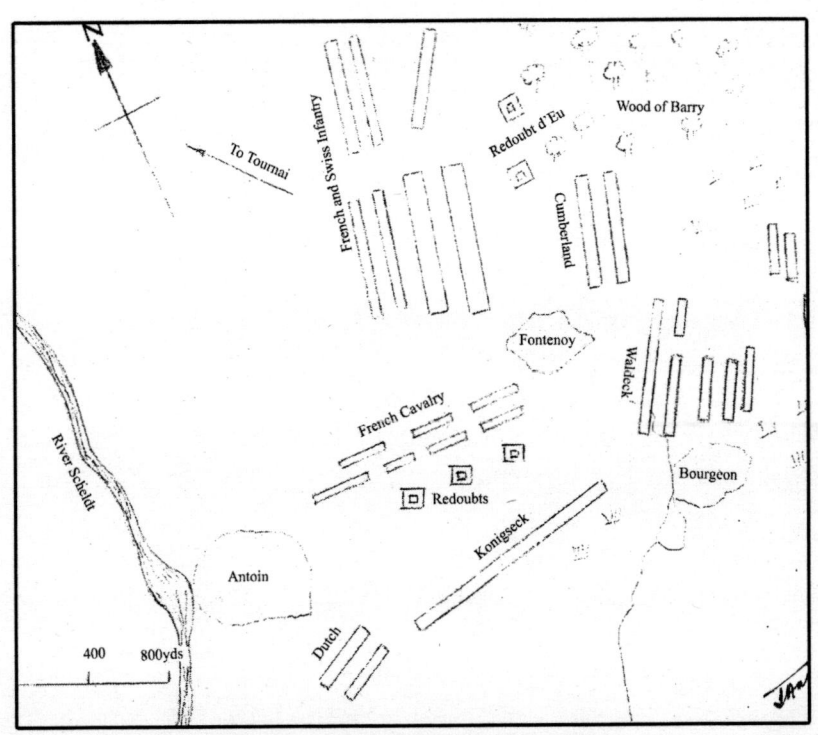

FONTENOY 10th MAY 1745

On 5th May, warned of the Allied movements, Saxe sought a suitable spot to block their advance. He left a besieging force of 20,000 in front of Tournai. About five miles southeast was the River Scheldt, on its right bank lay a broad gently sloping plateau crossed by a ravine. Onto this, Saxe moved 50,000 men to take all of the advantage that the position offered.

To the left of the French lay the village of Antoin overlooking the river. Further to the north lay the Wood of Barry protected by two redoubts. Antoin and Fontenoy were stiff with cannon and many French troops. In addition three redoubts were constructed between the two villages.

Defending this position French Guards were posted in front of the ravine. They were supported by Swiss, Irish and French infantry located behind fortified barriers. 68 squadrons of cavalry were drawn up in two lines parallel to the Scheldt and three regiments of dragoons were in the village of Antoin.

At about 5.30 in the morning the Duke of Cumberland tested the three fortified points. The Dutch moved towards Antoin but were harried by French dragoons and under fire from Antoin, together with cannon from the left bank of the river. The Dutch refused to engage and throughout the day remained where they were, unmoved by events as they evolved.

Saxe had left unfortified a half-mile stretch between the redoubts in the Wood of Barry and the village of Fontenoy. Cumberland, who had drawn his troops in battle order, signalled Ingoldsby's brigade of Highlanders to attack the French near the extreme edge of the wood. Unbeknown to him, the enemy lay in wait concealed under timbers which had been felled by French pioneers. The infantry marched ahead and at fifty paces, the French fired a volley, this did not halt the Allied advance which drove the French from their position. In the centre, Fontenoy was attacked by the English Guards but the artillery and musket fire from the French checked the Allies.

At about 8.30, the main body of 15,000 British and Hanoverian infantry moved through soggy ground and dense undergrowth up sloping ground to cut the French position in two. This move by Cumberland forced the French Guards and Swiss troops who had been surprised by this move to fall back on their two wings while the Allied infantry advanced towards the main French position.

Saxe gave the order for all 68 Squadrons of cavalry to charge the Allies in successive waves but for several hours the Allied infantry held. In fact, after the battle a French officer described their efforts as 'like charging two flaming fortresses rather than two columns of infantry'.

The Allies had not taken Fontenoy and were now exposed, until by the afternoon Saxe believed that the time was ready for a general advance on all fronts. French infantry had by now regrouped and was joined by cavalry from Antoin and Tournai.

The British infantry, now deep inside French lines, outflanked and isolated was forced to retreat leaving large numbers of dead and wounded. Some indication of this was that 20 battalions lost over 4,000 men. Bragg's (28th Foot) lost eleven of its officers and 126 other ranks, Peer's (23rd Foot) lost more – 22 Officers and 301 men, Onslow's (8th Foot) took 137 casualties. The 25th Foot, which until the 25th April was Lord Sempil's Regiment, lost a total of 200 officers and men.

The retreat was accomplished in a fairly orderly fashion aided by aggressive action from the Scots Greys whose assistance was marred by the loss of their colonel who was mortally wounded. The Honourable James Cholmondley's Regiment (34th Foot) also covered the retreat and the other major factor responsible for the successful withdrawal was that the Dutch troops although remaining inactive, held their position, thereby preventing the French from pressing their advantage. As darkness fell, Cumberland was forced to leave the major part of his equipment and abandon the Austrian Netherlands to Louis XV.

The outcome of the battle was indecisive. Overall the Allies lost over 7,000 dead or wounded while the figure for the French and their supporters was probably just over 5,000, of whom 53 were officers killed. Colonel Duroure commanding the 12th Foot died of wounds received at Fontenoy. His place as colonel was taken by Henry Skelton who as well as colonel of the 32nd Foot had also acted as brigadier at both Dettingen and Fotenoy.

One interesting aside is that of a tombstone in a Brighton churchyard, to a soldier who was wounded at Fontenoy whilst with Guise's Regiment (5th Foot); the soldier died in 1821. The main point of interest is that the soldier was a woman, Phoebe Hessel who was 108 years old at her death.

King George II was about to embark for the Continent but when news of Fontenoy reached him, he returned to London dissatisfied with his Dutch ally's lack of effort.

Barren's Regiment (4th Foot) was originally ordered to march to Ghent, however on 17th May 1745 it was redirected to Allmost to join the army the following day, being relieved at Ghent by the remnants of Duroure's Regiment (12th Foot) and Welch Fusiliers (23rd Foot) both of which had suffered heavy casualties at Fontenoy. Many wounded crowded into Ghent, for here and also at Bruges were established two large Allied 'hospitals'.

Despite the retreat after Fontenoy, George II and Parliament still believed in a strong British influence in Europe. Therefore more regiments were to be sent to assist those already there. Price's Regiment (14th Foot) embarked at Tilbury on 15th May 1745, landing in West Flanders before joining the army encamped on the Plain of Lessines towards the end of the month. Other regiments were to be sent to Ostend as this was a vital point of communication for Cumberland's army. Four battalions of infantry were chosen to be sent together with one battalion of foot Guards. In July Campbell's Regiment (21st Foot) received orders for Ostend, so did Harrison's and Handasyd's (15th and 16th Foot) they arrived on the 27th July and the garrison was hastily reinforced. The last of the four to arrive were the Royal Irish Regiment (18th Foot) when on the 9th of August they arrived from Antwerp.

Because the Austrians had allowed Ostend to fall into disrepair it was poorly fortified and to make matters worse for the British, their general who had been appointed to command arrived after the town was invested Therefore de Chancios, who was an Austrian officer of the same rank, assumed command.

By the 15th August the Frenchman Count Lowendahl was responsible for cutting Cumberland's route through Ostend. He erected batteries on the shore to enfilade the harbour and keep British frigates from the port.

Cumberland found that the French were too strong for him to force their lines. Ghent and Ostend were cut off; his only open line was through Brussels and Antwerp.

On the night of the 22nd August the French made a powerful general assault on Ostend such that the commanding officers within the port agreed to capitulate providing that all honours of war were afforded. The garrison would be allowed to evacuate and be escorted to Austrian territory. These terms were accepted and all regiments marched out on the 24th August. In the midst of these rebuffs, news was received that on the 25th July, Charles Edward Stuart had landed in Scotland.

CHAPTER XIII

1745-1746
GEORGE II
THE SECOND JACOBITE REBELLION

The romantic conception of the '45 is misplaced. Charles Edward Louis Philip Cassimir Stuart 'The Young Pretender' generally unaided and unwanted, led a rebellion which subsequently was to lead to the clearances of the Scottish Clan system and way of life in the Highlands.

Charles Stuart made his attempt to seize the throne on behalf of his father, when following his landing from the small French frigate *La Doutelle* on the island of Eriskay in the Outer Hebrides, he was ferried by Antoine Walsh across the Minch to the mainland in July 1745, landing on the shore of Loch nan Moidart.

Jacobite supporters had agreed that if Charles brought ten thousand French troops with him, they would join the rebellion. Instead he landed with only seven companions; consequently the reception that greeted him was not encouraging, Macdonald of Sleat and Macleod for all their professions of loyalty refused to have anything to do with what appeared to be a desperate venture, also the great Whig clans of the north had not, as had been hoped, rushed to his support. Two clan chieftains, Macdonald of Clanranald and young Cameron of Lochiel begged him to abandon the enterprise, however under great pressure they joined the Prince. This meant that their clansmen one thousand strong would come out in force. Therefore, the day after he raised his standard and issued his Proclamation at Glenfinnan, he found himself at the head of 1600 men. The Proclamation, dated from Rome 1734 appointed him Prince Regent.

2nd JACOBITE REBELLION
1745 -- 1746

When Charles landed, both England and Scotland, had been denuded of experienced regular troops for the campaign in Flanders, the only men in the country were two thousand ill-prepared recruits under Lieutenant-General Sir John Cope who at best could be described as an indifferent soldier.

From Glenfinnan, Charles set out for Edinburgh gathering support as he went. The Governor at Fort Augustus, alarmed at reports of the landing and the vulnerability of Fort William sent the Royal Regiment (1st Foot) to reinforce the garrison. When they were within eight miles of their destination they were ambushed. The soldiers under Captain Scott moved to retreat but this was cut off by the Highland rebels. The exhausted troops surrendered, but were subsequently released on parole provided that they did not serve against Charles; a parole which Captain Scott honoured.

General Cope gathered his newly raised regiments, assembling his command at Stirling. From there he marched to Inverness; but by doing so, he had left the south of Scotland unprotected. Charles took advantage and entered Athol, seizing the Castle of Blair before proceeding to Dundee then to Perth, Having captured Perth, the Highlanders marched on Edinburgh.

When Charles landed in Scotland the gravity of the situation appears not to have been fully realised by the Government, but by the end of August orders were sent to the Duke of Cumberland for the immediate despatch of regiments from Flanders. In England the Militia was hastily called out and preparations were made to assemble an army under Marshal Wade at Newcastle-upon-Tyne.

The rebels marched from Perth with 4,000 men and arrived in the vicinity of Edinburgh on the night of the 16th September. At 5 o'clock the following morning the city guard melted away and the city surrendered. The Castle was still held by Royal troops. General Guest who commanded the garrison at the Castle gathered the principal inhabitants into the sanctuary of the fortress. Charles entered the city and celebrated the event with a ball in Holyrood, the palace of his ancestors.

It seems incredible that a disorganised small group of Jacobites has been able to lay siege to the Scottish capital. There were, however, too few rebels to hold the entire country. Their control extended only to the areas actually occupied by the Jacobite array. All through the rebellion, the far north, north-east, south-west and Skye were held for King George II, little support came from anywhere except the Southern Highlands.

General Cope, alarmed at the rebels' progress, marched his regiments to Aberdeen, from there embarked for Dunbar, 27 miles east of Edinburgh which they also reached on the 16th September, too late to save the city.

At Dunbar, Cope reviewed his troops; three of the regiments had only been raised in 1741 and were as yet untried: Colonel John Lee's Regiment, 55th Foot (later 44th), Colonel John Price's Regiment 57th Foot (later 46th) and Colonel Lascelles who became Colonel in 1743 of the 58th Foot (later 47th). The only regiment with any experience was Colonel John Guise's 6th Foot. Cope also met Brigadier-General Fowke who commanded the 13th and 14th regiments of dragoons.

The next day Cope advanced towards Edinburgh to observe the disposition of the rebels, now increased to about 5,000. In the accepted deployment of the day, Cope prepared for battle. On the left was Lee's Regiment, Lee had only succeeded as colonel in 1743. Eight companies of 58th Foot, were joined by two companies in the centre under John Guise (6th Foot), his artillery, poor as it was, on the right of the line. Also on the right were two squadrons of the 13th Dragoons, on the left two squadrons of the 14th Dragoons and in reserve a single squadron from each of the 14th Dragoons and in reserve a single squadron from each of the dragoon regiments.

As Cope realized the size and ferocity of the rebel force against him he knew that his outnumbered, inexperienced troops could not withstand the Highlanders on a location such as Prestonpans* on terrain that suited them. He therefore moved his line to that which he believed would place him in a position to guard Edinburgh, which he did not realise at the time it was in the hands of the rebels.

Preston from Priest's town, the early owners of the land being the monks of Holyrood and Newbattle who erected pans on the seashore to manufacture salt, hence it received the name Prestonpans.

Before Cope could complete his move, the Jacobite left was not exactly opposite his right, therefore the greatly extended rebel line not only gave Cope a mistaken impression of the enemy numbers, but posed a threat to his left flank. He sent his aide-de-camp to fetch two guns from the right of the line, although unfortunately the only gunners he had were one civilian from the Scottish train and three Scottish soldiers from Edinburgh Castle. Their incompetence was shown when they fired their guns once and fled.

Having fired a volley, the Highlanders charged and in their usual fashion they dispensed with their firearms, relying on their broadswords which hit the shaken redcoats who failed to hold their ranks and scattered, thereby avoiding the slashing attack. The cavalry, noting the demise of the foot, fled the field. The skirmish lasted less than half an hour before the army led by Cope had melted away. Royal casualties were about 300 mainly killed in flight, while the rebels lost only about forty. Charles with his victorious clansmen returned to Edinburgh whilst Cope rode to Berwick to raise the alarm that his troops had not halted the rebellion.

With the news of the disaster at Prestonpans, greater urgency was placed on the order for troops to return from Flanders, such that eleven regiments were embarked, and although bad weather delayed their transports, they landed in the southeast mainly in the Thames area. From there Loginier's (59th Foot, later 48th) who had been the first of the newly raised regiments of 1741 to be sent abroad on active service when it embarked for Ostend in June 1744, now found itself back in England where together with Poulteney's Regiment (13th Foot), Price's (14th Foot), Cholmondley's (34th Foot), Fleming's (36th Foot) and Ponsonby's (37th Foot) went north where General Wade, now a Field-Marshal had been sent by King George II. He was at Doncaster before moving to Newcastle-upon-Tyne where infantry regiments assembled with several dragoon regiments, in all about 14,000 men and twenty guns.

Howard's Regiment (19th Foot) and Bligh's (20th Foot) moved to Coventry then Lichfield, whilst Harrison's (15th Foot) stayed in the south along with the Royal Highland Regiment, The Black Watch (43rd Foot, later 42nd) to repel any invasion by the French; also early in November orders were issued for Richbell's Regiment (39th Foot) then being landed at Portsmouth, to move to London finally joining the Royal camp on Finchley Common.

Such was the alarm in England regarding the rebellion, that in October the remaining regiments in Flanders including Sempill's (25th Foot) which had gone into winter quarters the week before, were ordered to embark for Newcastle, the Duke of Cumberland himself hurried home to take command of a force which was to assemble at Lichfield in Staffordshire, an appointment which was to relieve Sir John Ligonier who was the present commander of anti-rebel forces.

After their easy victory at Prestonpans many clansmen returned to their homes with plunder. Charles stayed in Edinburgh for more than a month. By the time the Highlanders returned after their celebrations he had also been joined by many who had hitherto held back from joining the rebellion.

By the end of October the rebels marched south from Edinburgh, Charles had wanted to march on Newcastle to meet Wade before the general could be reinforced by regiments from Flanders. However, he took the advice of Lord George Murray to advance, taking Carlisle, thence into Lancashire where English Jacobites would join the cause, thereby bringing a mighty force against London.

When the Highlanders started their advance southwards, the main body under Charles took the east coast route and advanced as far as Kelso before moving away westwards. On 5th November, Charles, leading the rebels, crossed the border at the River Esk. The next day his advance guard was at the gates of Carlisle where, after a siege of six days, Carlisle surrendered.

The departure from Scotland of Charles Stuart, had allowed his enemies in that country to surface. After all, Edinburgh Castle had never surrendered and was still held by the King's troops. Wade took advantage and despatched two regiments of dragoons and two regiments of foot, Price's 14th and Ligonier's 59th to re-occupy the Scottish capital. This was accomplished without opposition on 14th November. The 59th remained in Edinburgh until the 9th December when they marched to Stirling to assist in holding the line of the Forth.

From Newcastle, Wade was in an excellent position to relieve Carlisle. In so doing he would thwart the Jacobite aim of moving on

London. However information regarding the rebel intention was scarce; he did not know that Carlisle had fallen, he was too slow and when he did move his march began in the midst of a snowstorm, which lay on the high ground nearly three feet thick. When the royal army reached Hexham, news of the surrender was given to Wade who then returned to Newcastle.

By late November the rebels had moved south through Penrith, passed Lancaster, crossed the River Ribble at Preston then on to Wigan. Manchester was quickly occupied where 300 volunteers were formed into a Jacobite regiment, called by Charles, the Manchester Regiment.

As the rebels were moving south through Lancashire, Wade was moving from the northeast with his army via Durham, Darlington, Richmond and Wetherby to cover Yorkshire from the Rebels.

From Lichfield the Duke of Cumberland was unaware of the direction that the Rebels would take, he believed that they would head for Wales, therefore he planned to meet them with an army of 8,000 men at Stone, unfortunately for him this was not their destination.

Early in December, Charles entered Derby with about 4,500 men. He was now only 130 miles from London, When Cumberland heard that the rebels were in Derby he realised that they would reach London before he could. He was not ready to march on Derby; instead he made Northampton his next objective. Sowle's Regiment (11th Foot) and Handasyd's (16th Foot) made for Rugby.

From Derby, Charles wanted to move towards London. However his generals led by Lord George Murray, pointed out that Edinburgh had been retaken and was now in the hands of George II's supporters, also a force of French auxiliaries under Lord John Drummond had landed at Montrose. Cumberland was advancing through the Midlands and Wade was moving south with two armies closing behind him. Murray advised caution and Charles had no alternative but to order a retreat at the end of December. The decision of the rebels came as Cumberland had only reached Coventry, it was there that he heard that they were returning to Scotland.

Leaving Derby the rebels were followed through Lancashire by the Duke as fast as he possibly could, arriving in Lancaster the day after the Jacobites had left.

Wade was at Wakefield when he heard that Charles was retreating northwards. He was not in any position to place his army so that the retreat could be hindered, therefore he hurried north through Yorkshire, retracing his earlier route south, but back through Northallerton, Darlington and Durham rather than across the moors. He arrived in Newcastle on 31st December 1745.

When the royal army under Cumberland arrived at Kendal they learned that the Jacobites had left earlier that day. They therefore continued close upon the rebels who to gain a little time from their pursuers, set Penrith on fire. Instead of immediately following, the army remained in the town to extinguish the flames.

After a few days Cumberland, leading his army, arrived at Carlisle. It was here that Charles had abandoned most of his artillery and reinforced the garrison with 300 men from the newly formed Jacobite Manchester Regiment before continuing his retreat into Scotland.

The royal army invested Carlisle on 21st December, and after a short siege the Jacobite castle garrison agreed on 30th December to capitulate to Brigadier-General Bligh, colonel of the 20th Foot. Immediately after the surrender, Campbell's Regiment (21st Foot) and Sempil's (25th Foot) who had formed the rearguard for the advancing army, received orders to go directly to Newcastle, thence urgently to Scotland to reinforce the army assembling under Lieutenant-General Henry Hawley,

The day after the rebels left Carlisle, they crossed the River Esk into Scotland. They made no attempt to recover Edinburgh but moved towards Glasgow which was reached on 26th December. A week later Charles left Glasgow for Stirling where he was joined by new levies, nearly 800 men mostly Irish troops in the French service. They had landed at Montrose with several heavy guns. The Jacobite strength was now 9,000 as they proceeded to lay siege to Stirling Castle, which was held by General Blakeney, colonel of the 27th Foot.

Having crossed into Scotland, the royal force arrived in Edinburgh in mid-January. Wade and his troops had been there for several days. He was now considered to be old and tired and was relieved by Lieutenant-General Hawley, a strong disciplinarian who with his force left Edinburgh on 13th January for the relief of Stirling.

Following an alarm that the French were about to attempt to invade the South Coast of England, Cumberland headed south. He took with him several regiments leaving Hawley with only three regiments of dragoons and twelve regular infantry regiments to raise the siege of Stirling.

In Edinburgh on 13th January, General Howley sent his second in command Major-General John Huske to march towards Stirling with the vanguard of the royal army. Three days later General Hawley with the remaining battalions of infantry, dragoons and Militia regiments joined the royal camp which was located to the west of Falkirk where they believed the rebels to be seven miles away. In front of the camp was an area of deep, narrow, wet swampy ground and upon its right flank some enclosures and more wet trenches.

On the morning of the 17th January, Charles assumed the offensive. He led his troops in broad daylight to the south of the royal camp concealing his movements by a forced march through by-lanes and over rough fields. Major-General Huske had been watching a small detachment of the enemy when he saw the whole Jacobite force moving towards the high ground of Falkirk Muir, about two miles south-west of the royal troops.

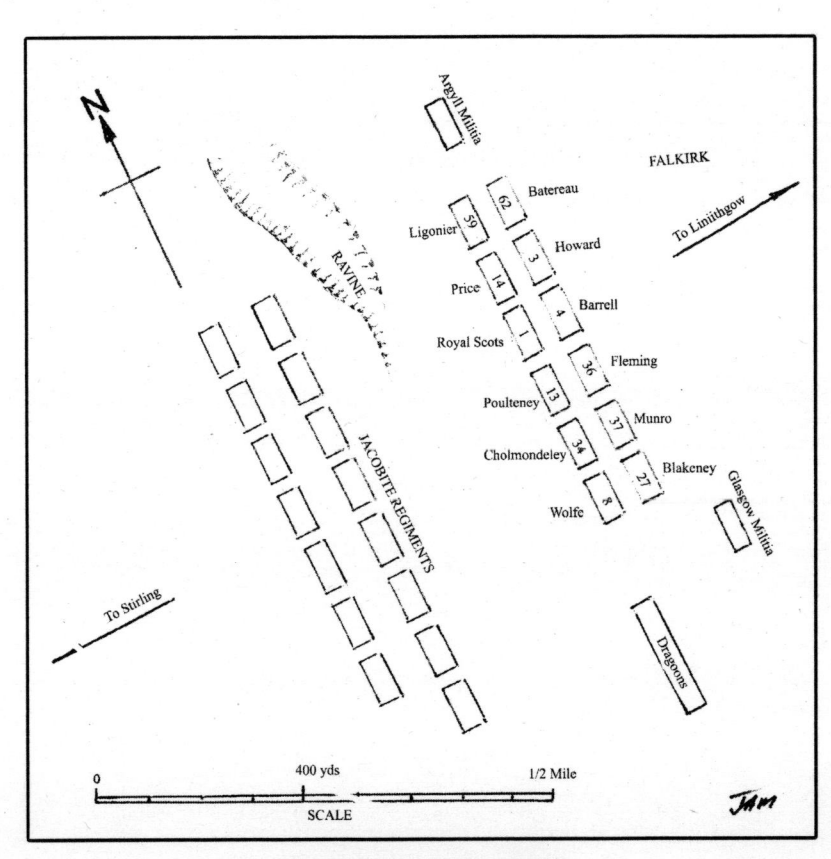

BATTLE of FALKIRK
17th January 1746

Huske alerted the army, drums beat to arms and they hastily proceeded along rugged terrain to the moor where the rebel army with a strength of about 8,000 men appeared in order of battle without interference from Government troops; a further 1,000 men had been left to continue the siege of Stirling.

General Hawley was eating his mid-day meal, but he mounted his horse and galloped towards the scene. Such was the surprise of the Jacobite advance that apparently the General had forgotten his hat. The fact that Charles had reached the high ground forced Hawley, whose troops were of a similar number to that of the Highlanders, to hastily take position, although they were not formed immediately opposite the Jacobite regiments such that the English right considerably overlapped the enemy left.

For some time the armies faced each other, neither being prepared to leave the position. Hawley's front line of infantry was formed by six Regiments of Foot, in the second line were another six Regiments and behind them on the right were the Argyll Militia with the Glasgow Militia to the left, behind the left flank regiments and dragoons.

Hawley, who was himself a cavalryman, held the conviction that the clansmen would not stand against his dragoons, therefore at about four in the afternoon he ordered his three cavalry regiments led by Colonel Francis Ligonier in command of the 13th Dragoons up to the higher ground from where they attacked the Highlanders' right flank, who held their fire until the royal troops were within ten yards. The volley was effective, two of the dragoon regiments fled in disorder, the remaining regiment met the Highlanders, whose tactic was to throw themselves to the ground and use their dirks to thrust into the bellies of the horses, causing the dragoons to wheel about and retire.

The Highlanders then counter-attacked, charging at the infantry as a wild storm broke across the moor. Squalls of sleet and rain drove into the faces of the royal troops. The gloom of the January late afternoon and the darkness of the storm, together with frightened riderless horses were all that the infantry could see before the clansmen were upon them with broadsword and targe.

The royal troops were attacked from the front and flank, their muskets misfiring as the storm grew worse, the troops unable to see, their powder wet, causing the left of the royal lines to turn and flee.

The left flank of the Jacobites was held in check by a ravine in front of, and between them and the English right. The 10th Dragoons appeared to the rear of the Jacobite left and, in the confusion, where their leaders had lost control, many clansmen believed that the battle was lost and were therefore retreating towards Stirling. The retreat was halted as Charles, seeing the dilemma of his troops, ordered up the Irish pickets who steadied the fleeing Highlanders.

The rout of the royal troops was partially saved, at least for a time by Barrell's (4th Foot) and Ligonier's (59th later, 48th) who stood firm, together with Price's (14th Foot) having been formed into one division with the Royal Scots (1st Foot) and Howard's (3rd Foot), prior to covering the retreat before they too retired and fled.

The encounter had lasted less than 30 minutes with the day belonging entirely to the Highlanders, but their check by Hawley's right, the ferocity of the storm, the lateness of the day with gathering gloom, and their lack of discipline deprived Charles of any attempt at pursuit. Instead, the Highlanders passed the night prowling the battlefield trying to collect loot from the bodies of dead royal troops, even stripping them of their clothes.

Jacobite losses amounted to less than fifty, while over 300 royal troops were left dead on the field. Five officers of field rank were killed including the colonel of the 37th Foot, Sir Robert Munro and also the commander of the 34th, Lieutenant-Colonel Powell.

The royalist army abandoned most of its camp equipment as it fled to Linlithgow some eight miles east of Falkirk, which was entered that night by Charles in very high spirits.

The Duke of Cumberland who had returned south after the recapture of Carlisle, left with all haste for Edinburgh when news of the disaster at Falkirk reached London. On reaching the Scottish capital he assumed command of a demoralized army consisting of fourteen regiments of infantry and two regiments of dragoons.

Cumberland spoke to his generals regarding the conduct of the regiments at Falkirk, and heard that Barrells believed that their stand had been due to their holding the Highlanders at bay by, instead of bayoneting the immediate enemy in front, moving against the man on the front right, so as to get under the guard protection of the targe. Cumberland instructed all regiments to follow this procedure. However, had the Highlanders followed the conventional contemporary battle plan where continental armies squared against their enemy, this would appear acceptable. Contrary to this the Highlander's method of attack was speed, ferocity and disorder. This meant that when the clansmen attacked they were not in line, so this method of defence would appear to be suspect. What it did, was to give regiments a feeling that the Highlanders were not invincible and that a method had been devised to beat their undisciplined approach.

From Linligthgow, Cumberland organised an advance west towards Falkirk and Stirling. The rebels were still besieging Stirling Castle, but this they abandoned and crossed the River Forth to fall back towards Inverness. After a day's rest at Stirling, the royal army set out after the Jacobites. The roads were in a poor state and several bridges had been destroyed. Cumberland's wagons and field guns being difficult to move through thick mud enabled the Highlanders to leave Perth on their northward journey a full four days before he arrived there.

The retreat was a fatal blunder for the Highlanders. It meant famine and starvation and above all, the loss of any Lowland support there may have been for Charles and the Jacobite cause. It also gave time for Cumberland to regroup and train his army.

Cumberland halted at Perth for two weeks due to the severity of the weather. He was nevertheless able to obtain supplies by sea and drill his troops. Leaving Perth, as he had Stirling, garrisoned by Hessian infantry under Prince Frederick of Hesse, Cumberland advanced towards Aberdeen which he reached in early March. Finding his progress hampered by heavy rains and snowstorms he decided to spend the rest of the winter there, where the army was drilled and disciplined, for he did not want another Falkirk.

On 8th April he left Aberdeen for Inverness, where he believed that Charles had established his headquarters. The regiments that had fought at Falkirk were now in good shape and had also been joined by Bligh (20th Foot), Campbell (21st Foot) and Sempil (25th Foot).

Charles with his Jacobite supporters was indeed at Inverness and was anxious to prevent the royal army from crossing the deep and rapid River Spey. In this he was unfortunate as they crossed without opposition, reaching Nairn fifteen miles east of Inverness on 14th April.

April 15th was the twenty-fifth birthday of the Duke of Cumberland and here again he showed his generalship as he decided not to give battle that day, resting his men and at his own expense supplying then with bread, cheese and brandy. He had 8,000 infantry and 900 cavalry.

Prince Charles had fewer than 5,000 men, as large numbers of his half-starved Highlanders had dispersed in search of food. Yet he moved his men to Drummossie Moor and, believing that a surprise dawn attack on the royal camp was an excellent opportunity to rout his enemy, formed the clansmen into three columns and marched the twelve miles towards Nairn. Through poor management or incompetence there was no surprise, because they were still two miles away when, at 4 o'clock, they heard reveille sound from the camp. The weary, hungry and dispirited Highlanders retraced their steps to retake their positions on Drummossie Moor.

Following reveille, the royal army tents were struck within the hour and by 11 o'clock in the morning the two armies were in full view of each other, albeit over two miles apart.

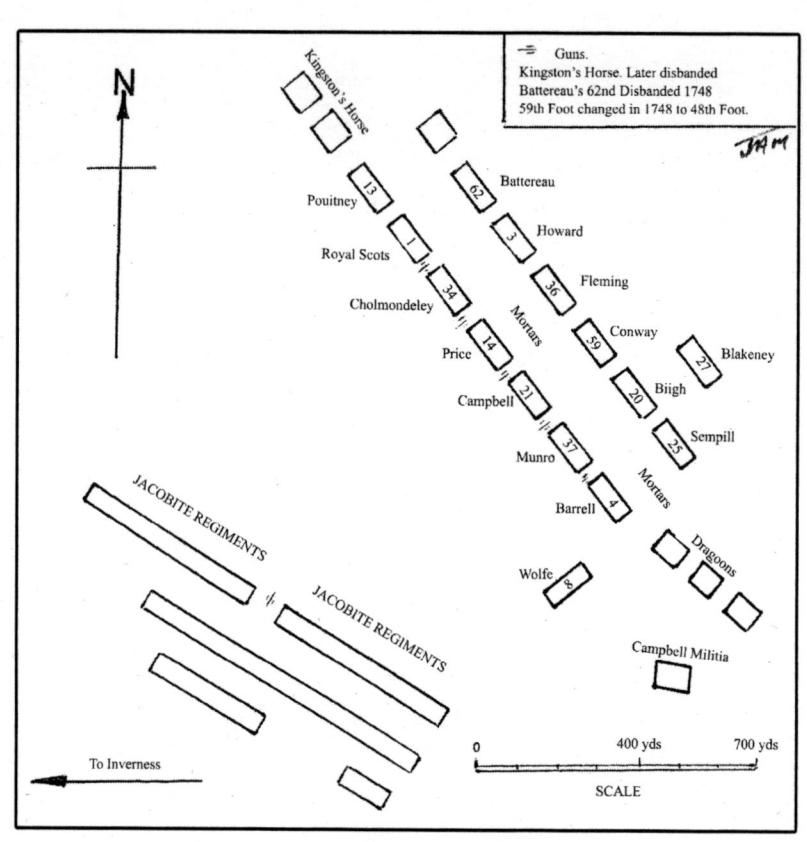

BATTLE of CULLODEN
16th April 1746

The bare, open moorland chosen by the Jacobites offered them little advantage. Charles had hoped that the royal army would be unable to bring up their field guns due to the boggy nature of the ground, but using horses and much manpower, ten guns were brought into play. The Highlanders formed into two irregular lines supported by a few pieces of artillery, while opposite, the royal army formed into an unhurried pace. Cumberland spaced his guns in pairs between his front-line regiments.

The battle started sometime after midday with a fierce cannonade from the royal guns and a lesser response from the Jacobite artillery. Cumberland moved Wolfe (8th Foot) forward on the flank and facing inwards to enfilade any attack on that flank.

The effect on the Highlanders was that the clansmen became impatient as this was not their style of fighting, with their chiefs unable to hold them in disciplined check they attacked the Royal line with the fury and speed which had been so successful at Falkirk. Through the smoke, the whole right and centre of the Jacobite line charged with broadsword and targe. Such was the onslaught, that they broke through Barrell's (4th) and Munro's (37th) in the left flank of the first line, also taking two of the field guns.

Those of the clansmen who had pierced the royal line came across the second line drawn up three deep, front rank kneeling, second rank bending forward and the third standing upright. Holding their fire until the Highlanders were close they fired in a volley. When Cumberland gave the order to advance, the bayonets of the second line drove into the disorientated rebels as they were overpowered and driven from the moor, with dreadful slaughter. The battle had lasted less than an hour.

After the victory, a General Order dated Inverness 6th May 1746 indicated that nineteen regiments were stationed in the Highlands searching for arms and dealing very severely against the clans who had taken part in the rebellion.

Colonel Lee's Regiment (55th Foot, later 44th) were at Edinburgh where they provided the guard when the 14 Jacobite colours taken at Culloden were burnt in June 1746. The standard belonging to Charles was carried by the hangman and burnt first with three flourishes of trumpets amidst loud cheers. Then the rest were carried separately by chimney sweeps from the Castle to the fire at the Cross where heralds proclaimed the names of the traitors.

*

James Francis Edward 'The Old Pretender' died 1st June 1766 aged 78 years leaving two sons. Charles Edward Louis Philip Cassimir 'The Young Pretender' died in Rome 31st January 1788, and Henry Benedict 'The Cardinal York) who in 1746 took holy orders and died in Rome in 1807, were the last male branch of the house of Stuart.

CHAPTER XIV

SEVEN YEARS WAR 1756–1763
GEORGE II
NORTH AMERICA

From 1750, many regiments were raised, allocated numbers and then after a very short time disbanded. Their number was then re-allocated to other newly formed corps. For this reason it is sometimes difficult to follow the history of some regiments numbered 50th Foot and above. Unless disbanded regiments form part of the main story, their passing is not recorded here.

Despite the defeat of the Jacobites at Culloden, and the punitive measures taken by the authorities in Scotland, hostilities against France continued, until war with the French was formally terminated in 1748 by the Peace of Aix-la-Chapelle.

By 1754 the British in North America had established thirteen colonies along the east coast. Such was the pioneering spirit of the colonists and their desire to increase their land holdings, that they were intent on moving both to the north and also westwards.

The land to the north was held by French settlers. Following diplomatic talks in Paris between the two nations, the border between the British and French was unclear. It is not surprising that a solution was not forthcoming, as maps of the region that were used in the discussions were incomplete and inaccurate.

Following what they were sure was their boundary, the French planned to construct forts in the areas of their settlements along the Ohio valley, from the great lakes to the Mississippi. The British colonists were sure that the French were moving into their territory; therefore they hurried to protect what they were sure was their land, especially when they heard that attempts by the French were

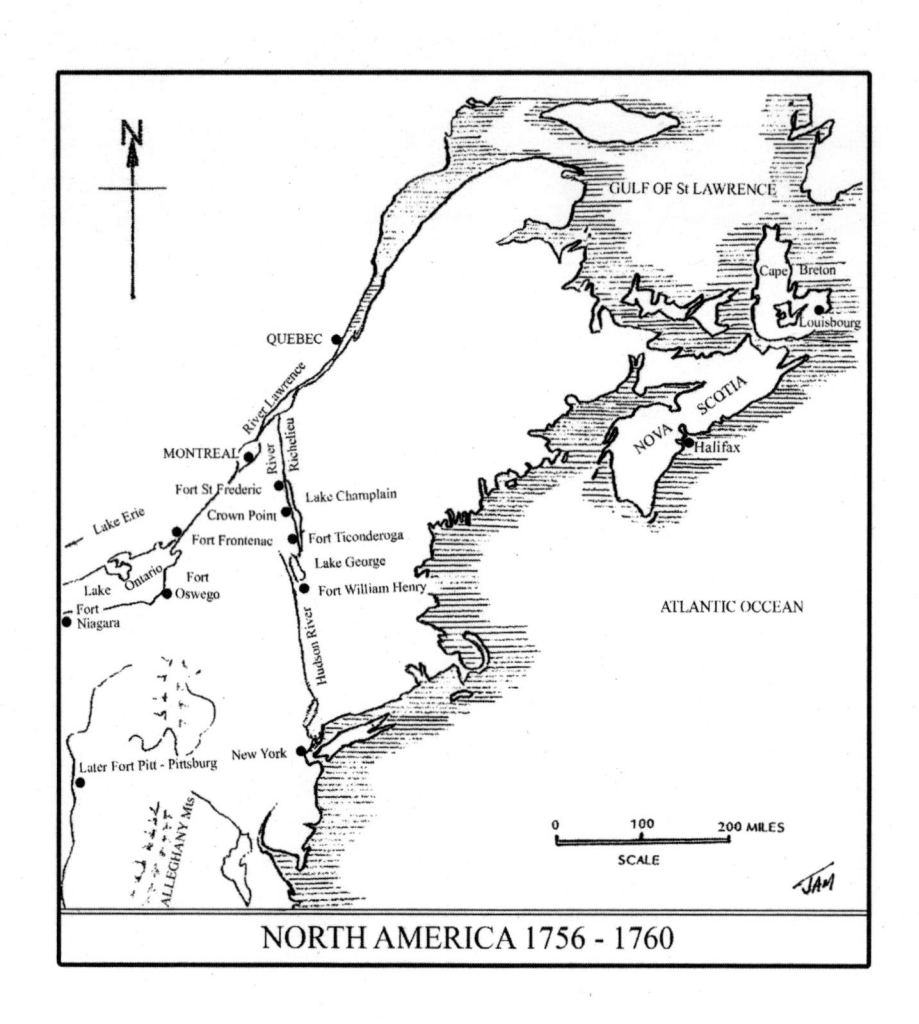

NORTH AMERICA 1756 - 1760

underway to construct Fort DuQuesne, deep in areas which they believed belonged to them.

Two factors would influence and conflict. Firstly, to their advantage, the French held the inland waterways and lakes which formed the main transport routes through the forests and rugged terrain.

Secondly, to their disadvantage, the French had only one outlet to the Atlantic, and that was through the St Lawrence. It was on this route that they relied for their supplies and reinforcements from France.

Both nations were aware of the importance of North America. Although at peace, both were prepared to use force to protect their interests in this faraway land.

France had a population of twenty million from which she had created the greatest military power in Europe. Her strength at sea was well below that of Britain, who with a population of under eight million did not rely on a large standing army, especially during periods of peace. Instead the British had built up a force at sea, which not only commanded the defence of her shores, but also prevented other nations from successful colonial expansion with its associated trade, because their shipping had to run the gauntlet, by avoiding a British fleet.

The situation in North America led the British Parliament to believe that, unless action was taken, the French would command a vast area of this largely unsettled continent. For this reason the Duke of Newcastle, Thomas Pelham Holles, who was the chief British minister, asked the Captain-General of the Army, the Duke of Cumberland, to formulate a plan for the protection of the North American colonies.

Cumberland, who only had experience of the tactics used in European warfare, did not believe that it would be difficult to deal with the French settlers, who after all were only supported by a few savage undisciplined Indians. He recommended that only two regular British regiments, aided by militia from the colonies, would be sufficient to assist the British colonists in their struggle against the French settlers.

Major-General Edward Braddock, a strong disciplinarian, was the choice to lead the operation. He was an officer experienced in the rigid disciplined fire from battalion formations.

In February 1755, Braddock arrived in Virginia. The plan was to capture, in separate independent strikes, the four forts which were under construction by the French. His column consisted of two British regiments of foot, the 44th (Essex) and 48th (Northamptonshire) each about 800 men, together with about 3,200 men from the colonies, mostly with no military experience, especially of the type of tactics proposed by Braddock. Some of the colonists were knowledgeable regarding frontier warfare and amongst these was a 23-year-old officer, George Washington, who had volunteered to join the British general.

The two British regiments were not composed of the finest manpower that the nation could provide. In fact, whilst in England awaiting embarkation, they had largely been made up of rejects from other regiments. A further drawback to the British plan was that, unbeknown to Braddock, as the result of a bribe, the French had obtained a copy of his orders, therefore his intention was known even before he left Virginia.

Following problems with the supply of transport, namely wagons and horses promised from the colonies, Braddock, leading his troops was finally underway on 26th April. His task was to capture Fort DuQuesne which was at the forks of the Ohio river.

It was a poorly planned operation, mainly because Braddock was unaware of the pitfalls that he would encounter on his 300-mile journey. He did not possess a reliable map of the route and therefore was unable to avoid swamps and forested areas, and because there were no roads, a track had to be cleared by pioneers from the colonial troops.

His Indian scouts were generally ineffective, as they didn't really want to get involved either with the British advance or the Indians who supported the French. Braddock's advance was slow, just under twenty miles a day; nevertheless some men from his column became stragglers. These and any others who strayed were ambushed by the Indians loyal to the French.

Word was brought to Braddock by his few loyal Indian scouts, that Fort DuQuesne was defended by only fifty men. Encouraged, he pressed on although it was becoming clear to him that due to the terrain, he would be unable to adopt his tactic of forming square, if and when he was attacked.

By 13th June, forty-eight days into his march, Braddock reached Fort Necessary. Realising that conditions were different from those which he had originally expected, he sought Washington's advice on the best tactic to employ in his push towards his destination. Washington advised him to send a small force forward. Braddock did not really agree, as it was against his military instinct. He did reluctantly accept the advice, and led 1,500 men onto his target. After two or three days he had left his main army over forty miles behind.

Reaching the banks of the River Monongahela on the 9th July, he was now only about eight miles from Fort DuQuesne. Believing that he would be attacked as he crossed the river, he sent a small detachment across expecting an ambush. None came, he therefore cautiously moved the remainder of his troops across. Once they were all on the other side, he moved his men into close formation, as he believed that the terrain here would support this course of action.

The French commander, Captain Jean Dumas, was too experienced to meet Braddock in set formation. Instead he deployed eight hundred of his Indian allies behind rocks and trees. Braddock's highly visible red-coated soldiers were hit by sniper fire from the Indians. The General urged his men to return the fire and act in a disciplined manner, but as they fell, his orders were not heard. His men could not locate the enemy let alone bring concentrated volleys against them. More and more of his men fell as the Indian snipers wrought havoc amongst the troops.

Braddock moved his reserve of eight hundred men forward, but these were met by the retreating front line. Braddock rode forward, again urging his men to form line and face the enemy, but as they saw more and more of their numbers fall from the accurate musketry fire from the invisible enemy, they were in no mood to await death. Seeing the imposing figure of their General hit several times, losing several horses, they too followed the fleeing front line. As Braddock mounted yet another horse, a bullet penetrated his lung. He was carried to the rear where, fatally wounded, he died the next day.

The panic-stricken British troops fled, leaving over 1,000 dead. Any wounded left on the field were soon killed by the advancing Indians.

The Governor of Massachusetts, William Shirley had only reached Albany in central New York, when he heard of the demise of Braddock. The overall command now fell to him although he was no soldier but a lawyer. His role in the operation had been to capture Fort Niagara, located at the junction of the lakes Erie and Ontario. To achieve this he arrived at Fort Oswego, still one hundred and fifty miles from his objective.

The capture of Niagara depended on the success of Braddock. However, his failure released regular French troops against which Shirley's 2,000 raw levies felt that they could not compete so most deserted.

Shirley left seven hundred men from the newly raised 50th and 51st Regiments to repair the defences and hold Oswego. With no Indian scouts and very few experienced troops, he decided to postpone any attack for another year. This decision, although probably correct, cost him the command which was given to Lieutenant-General John Campbell, fourth Earl of Loudon, who arrived too late in the season to save Oswego, which, in 1756 was taken by the French commanded by the Marquis de Montcalm.

The third thrust in the British attack was under the command of Sir William Johnson. His force consisted of Irish troops with 3,000 raw militia. He also had local Indians with the advantage of their knowledge of the region. After a forced march he arrived with his troops at Fort William Henry. Their advance ground to a halt, due to the lack of preparations for the construction of boats or rafts required to take them up the lake.

The French commander, Baron Dieskan, had left a 2,000 militia to meet the British assault on Crown Point. He then sailed with 1,500 regulars landing close to Fort William Henry. There he learned that Johnson had a superior force but he was loath to retreat. He blindly marched into an ambush, losing at least half of his men. Johnson failed to profit from his victory when most of his men deserted.

As winter approached, Johnson was forced to abandon Fort William Henry. He withdrew, leaving only a small garrison, mainly from the 35th Foot (1st Battalion Royal Sussex Regiment) who had sailed to North America the previous year. The garrison was overwhelmed by a superior French force under General Montcalm. It was allowed to march out with honours of war. However, the French were unable to control their Indian allies, who did not understand this code and massacred most of the regiment and their families.

The easiest task fell to Robert Monckton, a British colonel, who was in charge of 2,000 Rangers drawn from several North American colonies. He was to seize Fort Beausejour at the head of the Bay of Fundy. To achieve this he had to transport his rangers by water to the bay and assault the fort which guarded the narrow isthmus joining Nova Scotia to the mainland.

The French garrison surrendered without a blow. It was the first breach in the chain of the 2,000-mile French defence system, which stretched from the Gulf of St Lawrence.

The inconclusive operations of 1755/1756 had failed to resolve the uneasy peace which was to linger for several more years.

The effect of the British defeat and withdrawals on the North American colonists was one of confusion, for they failed to unite in the defence of their own territory.

Back in England, Parliament was worried that events in Europe were requiring much attention, but more importantly, they believed that the French would continue their expansion policy in North America. As a result, in 1755 the raising of eleven new regiments was authorised. These were numbered from 52nd to 62nd.

Colonel James Abercromby formed the 52nd Regiment, although this did not happen until December 1756. Colonel Robert Napier, the 53rd Regiment, whilst the 54th was raised in Coventry by Hedworth Lambton, their first colonel.

William Whitmore of Apley near Bridgenorth, raised the 55th Regiment. The 56th was formed by Lieutenant-Colonel John Campbell. Lord Manners raised the 58th in the same year. The 59th embarked almost immediately for marine service in the Mediterranean. Also in 1755 the 60th Regiment was raised in

Plymouth, while Colonel Sir Charles Montague's Regiment was numbered the 61st.

Of more significance to the conflict in North America was the raising of the 62nd Regiment. The British Government decided that a force should be raised by the colonists in America. Men would be recruited from Massachusetts, New York, Pennsylvania, Maryland and North Carolina, similar to the rangers used by Colonel Monckton. The first commanding officer was a Swiss soldier of fortune, Henri Bouquet, who brought experienced officers and other ranks from Europe.

The only other regiment within this group of numbers was raised in Stirling in 1757, titled the 57th Regiment of Foot.

With the defeat of the army at Oswego, the 50th and 51st Regiments were disbanded and erased from the Army list. Therefore the regiments raised as the 52nd to 62nd were reclassified:

52nd became	50th (1st Bn, the Queen's Own Royal West Kent Regt)
53rd	51st (1st Bn, the King's Own Yorkshire Light Infantry)
54th	52nd (2nd Bn, the Oxfordshire & Buckinghamshire LI)
55th	53rd (1st Bn, the King's Shropshire Light Infantry)
56th	54th (2nd Bn, the Dorset Regiment)
57th	55th (2nd Bn, the Border Regiment)
58th	56th (2nd Bn, the Essex Regiment)
59th	57th (1st Bn, Middlesex Regt, the Duke of Cambridge's Own)
60th	58th (2nd Bn, the Northamptonshire Regiment)
61st	59th (2nd Bn, the East Lancashire Regiment)
62nd	60th (the Royal American Regiment) (The King's Royal Rifle Corps)

*

In Parliament, William Pitt 'the Elder' or the Earl of Chatham as he subsequently became, criticised the conduct of the war, especially the setbacks in North America. Believing that the Duke of Newcastle was weak, albeit an extremely rich man, he refused to serve under him, instead he continued to find fault with Government policy.

On 11th November 1756, Newcastle resigned and the role of First Minister was taken over by the Duke of Devonshire. Pitt joined him to form a rather makeshift Government, which was not to last for many months into 1757.

Pitt told Parliament that he saw the preservation of British influence in North America to be paramount. As such, the colonies should raise a national militia. Britain would raise more regiments, especially from the Highlands of Scotland.

Existing regiments were required to raise second battalions. In 1756 the 3rd, 4th, 8th, 12th, 19th, 24th and 31st Regiments of Foot all complied. Early in 1758, the 20th and 23rd Foot also followed the instruction. Later in 1758, the new second battalions which had been raised in 1756 were numbered in their own right.

The 2nd Battalion of the 3rd Foot became the 61st Foot (2nd Battalion, the Gloucestershire Regiment). The 2nd Battalion, 4th Foot, were re-numbered the 62nd Foot (1st Battalion, the Duke of Edinburgh's [Wiltshire] Regiment). The 2nd Battalion, 8th Foot, were given the title 63rd Foot (1st Battalion, the Manchester Regiment). The 65th Foot (1st Battalion, the York and Lancaster Regiment) had been the 2nd Battalion of the 12th Foot, while the 2nd Battalion, 19th Foot, became the 66th Foot (Princess Charlotte of Wales' [Berkshire] Regiment). The 69th Foot (2nd Battalion, the Welsh Regiment) had been the 2nd Battalion, 24th Foot, and the 70th Foot (2nd Battalion, the East Surrey Regiment) had originally been the 2nd Battalion, 31st Foot.

Of those regiments whose second battalions were raised in 1758, the 2nd Battalion, 20th Foot, became the 67th Foot (2nd Battalion, the Hampshire Regiment), and the 2nd Battalion, 23rd Foot, were re-numbered 68th Foot (1st Battalion, the Durham Light Infantry).

Pitt also stated to the Government, that the removal of the French from North America should be accomplished by a three-pronged attack on the disputed territories. Unfortunately for him, he was taken ill and for some time his proposal had to be put on hold.

In March 1757 Pitt was back at work. He planned that Admiral Holburne would immediately sail from Portsmouth to North America with 5,000 regular troops. Atlantic storms frustrated his plans. Strong westerly winds blew for weeks and it was not until May that his ships passed the Isle of Wight.

Pitt sent orders that the Earl of Loudon should remain in New York until Holburne arrived in Halifax. There the combined force would be seventeen ships of the line and at least 17,000 troops. But by 1st May, Loudon received definite instructions to attack Louisbourg in order to deprive the French of their naval base.

Back in England, Pitt was dismissed, mainly due to his continual conflict with the King. This did not seem to worry the ambitious politician who believed that his popularity made him indispensable.

He waited as Newcastle attempted to form a government, but without Pitt this proved very difficult. Pitt refused to compromise. He demanded to be given complete control as Secretary of State for the current war, both in Europe and North America. On 29th July 1757 the Newcastle/Pitt coalition took office.

Following Pitt's earlier order, as Holburne arrived at Halifax, Loudon sailed from New York intending to attack Louisbourg, For several weeks the area was shrouded in mist, preventing many attempts to establish the strength of the French naval base. Loudon remained frustrated and it was not until 5th August that the mist cleared. Loudon believed that it was now too late in the season, therefore he decided to postpone the attack for another year. When the decision was conveyed to Pitt he was furious at the delay and placed the blame at the overcautious Earl who was recalled to England.

The command fell to Lieutenant-General James Abercromby who had been second-in-command to Loudon. The 52-year-old General was not the choice of Pitt, who believed him to lack the necessary aggression but had to acquiesce to the King, who had insisted on the promotion.

Pitt wrote to each of the American Governors, requesting that 20,000 soldiers be recruited by the colonies. The cost would be borne by Britain. He also wrote that 50,000 men were being raised by the British.

To Abercromby Pitt outlined his plan, also naming the senior officers who would lead. Lord Howe would be the brigadier supporting Abercromby. George Augustus Howe was only 34 years old, but was looked on as a superb officer, who held the support of both the contemporary officers and men.

Pitt's plan for North America was a triple offensive. First Louisbourg, then, when the fortress was secure, through the Gulf of St Lawrence to Quebec. The second was to take Montreal: via the Hudson River, Lakes George and Champlain and the Richelieu river, and the third a flanking movement across Lake Ontario and an assault on Fort DuQuesne.

Abercromby was charged with the conduct of the lakes campaign, especially the crossing of Lake George and the taking of Fort Ticonderoga, which was the most formidable obstacle on the route to Montreal. The fort had to be captured after the river ice on the Hudson had melted, but before the French could rush reinforcements to the area. To achieve this, Abercromby had to sail up Lake George early in May.

Delays occurred as the colonials were late joining the main army. The prime reason was that they were awaiting ships, arms and ammunition which had been promised by Pitt. These did not arrive until the end of June.

The force which had been allocated to Abercromby consisted of the 27th Foot (1st Battalion, Royal Inniskilling Fusiliers), Lord John Murray's Highlanders 42nd Foot (1st Battalion, The Black Watch – [Royal Highlanders]), the 44th Foot (1st Battalion, the Essex Regiment), the 46th Foot (2nd Battalion, the Duke of Cornwall's Light Infantry), the 55th Foot (2nd Battalion, the Border Regiment) and the 1st and 4th Battalions of the Royal American Regiment, 60th Foot, the total amounting to just over 6,300 men. In addition 9,000 men, mainly militia from the American Colonies, also joined the British regulars.

The combined force moved to Fort William Henry, where previous preparations for the gathering of about 1,000 of the long, tapering flat-bottomed boats called bateaux, and nearly 100 whale boats had been made. On the evening of the 4th July, baggage, most of the stores and ammunition were all on board and the whole army embarked in good order on the morning of the fifth.

While the British had been spending much time preparing and despatching their force, the French had executed their plans to strengthen Ticonderoga which hitherto only had a garrison of 1,000 men.

Montcalm with 5,000 fresh regular troops reached the fort at the end of June. He surveyed the terrain and defences and concluded that they had little chance of an effective resistance with the existing arrangement.

He therefore concentrated his forces at the head of Lake George, where it was reported to him that a large fleet of small boats was approaching. His officers estimated that a force of 20,000 men was being carried in the boats.

On 6th July, the British landed on the west bank of the lake. As was the usual European norm, they formed into four columns with the intention of moving to take Ticonderoga from the rear.

Howe led the advance guard into an area occupied by a detachment of French troops, who were sheltering in thick woods. A sharp brief skirmish ensued, the French were scattered and suffered a considerable loss before falling back on the fort's outer perimeter.

Lord Howe at the head of his men was one of the first killed when he was shot through the heart. He was a fine officer who was renowned for the steps he had taken to adapt the infantry to the conditions of the dense woodland which they were encountering in North America. He had cut off their long coat-tails, cut their hair short and made the officers and men wear leggings to protect them from briars, thus adding comfort and speed to their activities. Abercromby, perceiving that the men were fatigued, ordered them to march back to the landing place.

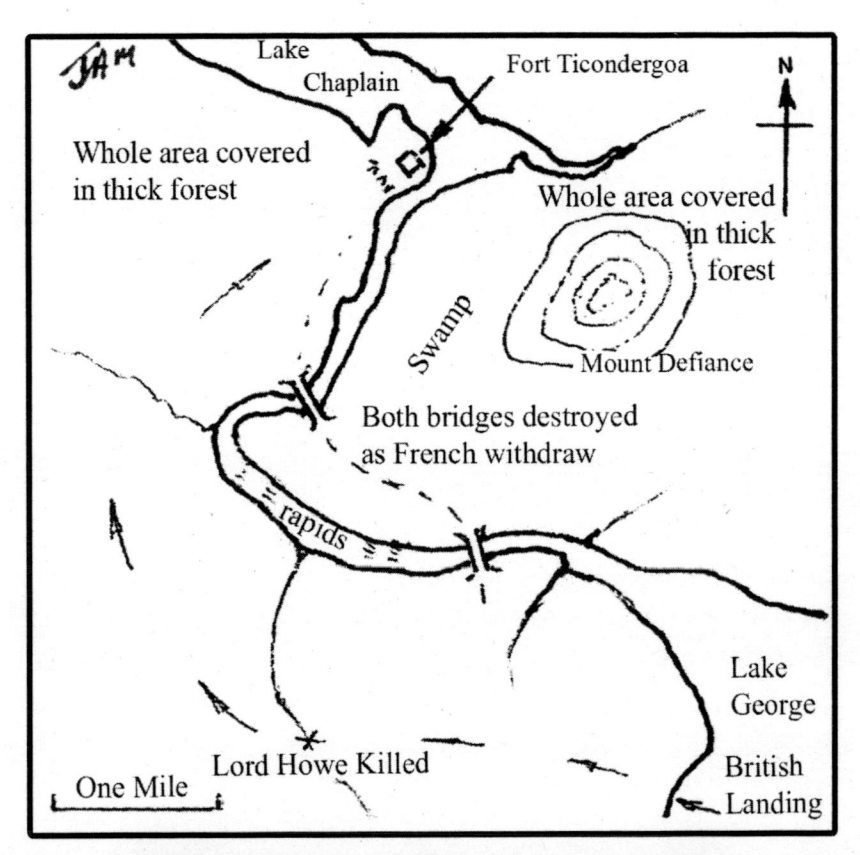

BRITISH ASSAULT ON FORT TICONDEROGA 6TH - 8TH JULY 1758

At dawn on the seventh, while, fortunately for the French, the British General was drawing his troops back, the whole French army fell to their task. Montcalm's pioneers hastily erected a log wall called a abatis, constructed from the intertwined trunks of trees and branches, seven to eight feet high manned by 3,000 regulars. He had received 400 more men led by Brigadier Levis. Even so, the French were outnumbered three to one with provisions for only five days.

The next morning the British advanced again. Following a cursory inspection, an engineering officer reported to Abercromby that the position occupied by the French was weak, the entrenchments were unfinished such that a direct assault would probably lead to success. He was faced with several choices – either to conduct a siege which would entail spending time in bringing up all of his guns, and from the commanding position on the Heights of Rattlesnake Hill, now called Mount Defiance, blast the fort by cannon, or he could engage in a direct frontal attack. Based on the engineer's report and assisted by the rumour that the French were about to be reinforced with 3,000 men, he decided on the latter.

Abercromby drew up his infantry in line of battle. The pickets, made up from light infantry and rangers formed the skirmishing line and would be the first to commence the assault, followed by the Massachusetts Regiment. British regular battalions marched next. Colonial Militia, the 42nd Foot and the regiment which had been Lord Howe's, the 55th Foot, were all held in reserve.

The battle began at 12.30 on the 8th July 1758. The British right, then the centre moved forward in long lines, three deep. As the troops marched up to the entrenchments, they found a strongly fortified breastwork where they were exposed to very destructive fire from the French defenders.

As the leading British ranks became entangled in the abatis, the Highlanders from the 42nd Foot, impatient at being left in the rear, rushed forward attempting to hack their way through the fallen trees with their broadswords. The branches caught fire! This and the height of the obstacles kept the regiment at bay. A few men from the 42nd led by their Commander, Captain John Campbell broke through the breastworks, but were all killed.

At sunset, after four hours General Abercromby gave orders to retreat and withdrew his men back to the landing place for a second time.

French losses were just over 100 killed with over 250 wounded. British losses were high, of the 6,300 regulars engaged nearly 2,000 were casualties. As well as losing their Commander, the 42nd lost 203 men killed and 296 wounded. Lieutenant-Colonel Samuel Beaver of the 46th was also killed as were five officers also from that regiment. The 44th had 205 killed or seriously wounded. The 27th, 55th and both battalions of the 60th all suffered heavy losses.

The British advance on Montreal had been stopped. Abercromby took his army back to the southern end of Lake George.

Montcalm was still worried that the British would mount another attack. After all Abercromby still had more than 13,000 men and might renew the attack with cannon. On the morning of the ninth, volunteers who had gone out to scout the whereabouts of the British, brought back the report that they were in full retreat. It appeared that panic had overtaken the defeated troops. In their haste to leave the area as quickly as possible, they had left behind several hundred barrels of provisions and a large quantity of baggage.

The rashness of Abercromby before and during the assault was matched by his spiritless and cowardly actions after. Such was his terror that, on the evening of his defeat, he sent an order to Colonel Cummings, commanding Fort William Henry, to send all sick and wounded together with all heavy artillery to New York without delay. He followed so closely upon this disgraceful order that Cummings had no time to obey it.

As he withdrew, Abercromby had been asked by Lieutenant-Colonel John Bradstreet to entrust him with 3,600 colonials for an attack on Fort Frontenac. A native of Maine, Bradstreet was in James Wolfe's opinion 'a most remarkable man'.

Bradstreet pushed up the Mohawk river, embarked his men on Lake Ontario and reached Fort Frontenac on the 26th August, a distance of 430 miles. The garrison of just over 100 French regulars was taken by complete surprise and surrendered.

Brigadier John Forbes was already on his way to assault Fort DuQuesne, the same fort which, three years earlier, Major-General

Edward Braddock had failed to capture, and to which operation he had given his life.

Forbes feared that he might fail to reach his main objective before the winter rains put an end to his advance. On the 6th September, still 40 miles from Fort DuQuesne, he sent Major James Grant ahead with 838 picked colonials. They were ambushed and lost about 300 of their number. Ahead, Forbes heard explosions. The French garrison, believing that they could not withstand a full attack, had destroyed and abandoned their fort.

Leaving men to garrison the ruined fort which he had re-named Fort Pitt, later Pittsburg, in honour of William Pitt, Forbes returned to Philadelphia, where he died the following March, a few weeks before the arrival of a letter from Pitt, thanking him for the honour of naming the fort after him.

*

By far the most important operation in the campaign proposed by Pitt, was the assault on the fortress of Louisbourg, the occupation of which would give a free passage through the Gulf of St Lawrence, greatly assisting in the aim of taking Quebec, which Pitt believed would pass total control of Canada to Britain.

To command this phase of the plan, Pitt selected Colonel Jeffrey Amberst of the 15th Regiment of Foot, whom he promoted to Major-General. It was not a popular choice for the King, who believed that an older, more senior officer should be appointed.

Although only 41 years old, Amherst was a very experienced officer having seen action with his regiment during the War of the Austrian Succession, and also with the Duke of Cumberland in Germany.

A large fleet was to be assembled, it would be used to co-operate with the army, and transport the regiments and Marines to Cape Breton Island leading to the capture of Louisbourg. To command this fleet of 35 heavily armed ships of the line, which included fourteen frigates, Pitt chose Vice-Admiral Edward Boscawen.

The strength of the British Army under Major-General Amherst would be over 13,000 regulars, which would be supported by a large artillery train.

The brigadiers to support Amherst were Wolfe, who had earlier been added to the military staff, Whitmore and Lawrence. In 1745, Lawrence had been with the British colonists when they had captured the fortress of Louisbourg from the French. Unfortunately, at the end of hostilities in 1749, the British had exchanged the fortress with the French for Madras in India. Lawrence therefore knew the area well including its weak points. Whether this was of any value is doubtful, for when the French re-occupied the area, they considerably strengthened the defences.

Pitt expected that Louisbourg would be taken by the end of June, when Amherst and Boscawen would sail up the St Lawrence river and take Quebec, where they would meet up with a victorious Abercromby. Towards this end, Boscawen sailed from Plymouth on 23rd February 1758.

On the 9th May, he sailed into Halifax harbour, his voyage had taken nearly three months. There he met eight ships of the line who had wintered there following the campaign of the previous year. It took just over two weeks to water and provision the ships. Boscawen sailed from Halifax to join Sir Charles Hardy who was cruising off Louisbourg.

By 2nd June they had gathered all of their ships and anchored off Gabarus Bay which was about seven miles from Louisbourg, which at the time was stormbound, fog-infested and located above an extremely rocky coastline.

Louisbourg was defended by 6,000 Frenchmen with 240 cannon mounted in batteries. They were also supported by eleven ships of war which were currently in the harbour. Expecting that this latest attack would follow that of 1745 when the New Englanders had come ashore off Garabus Bay, the French had erected fortifications along that area of the beach.

Amherst intended that his three brigades should land along the beach between White Point and Cormorant Cove. He could not land when he wished, because once again the area was shrouded in fog, but more important there was heavy surf and swell along the entire beach.

Due to the conditions, Amherst had to modify his tactics. Instead of sending in the three divisions as planned, with Whitmore on the right, Lawrence in the centre and Wolfe on the left, he concentrated his forces against Cormorant Cove. There Wolfe would lead the attack and the other brigadiers would follow.

At four in the morning on the 8th of June, as it became light, three to four hundred small boats emerged from behind the main British fleet and made for the area of Cormorant Cove, they were covered by the guns of the ships.

The heavy thick smoke from the French gunfire and British guns obscured the vision of the defenders, who were convinced that the invaders had withdrawn. Instead Wolfe was the first to land when he jumped into the sea. Unfortunately driven by the heavy swell, several boats crashed into rocks, overturning and taking with them men from the Grenadier Company of the 15th Foot, together with one of their officers.

Wolfe, whose task was to attack with his division of picked men, thereby covering the landing of the rest of the army, thought that the extreme conditions made it impossible to land more than a few men, so he waved his hat to signal a retreat. This was either ignored or missed, as more men ran onto the beach.

The light infantrymen waded ashore, other boats followed. Men from the 17th Foot came ashore waist deep in the water in the face of heavy French fusillades. Wolfe's men charged ashore with fixed bayonets, then took cover in a small wood where they used their dry powder to reload their muskets.

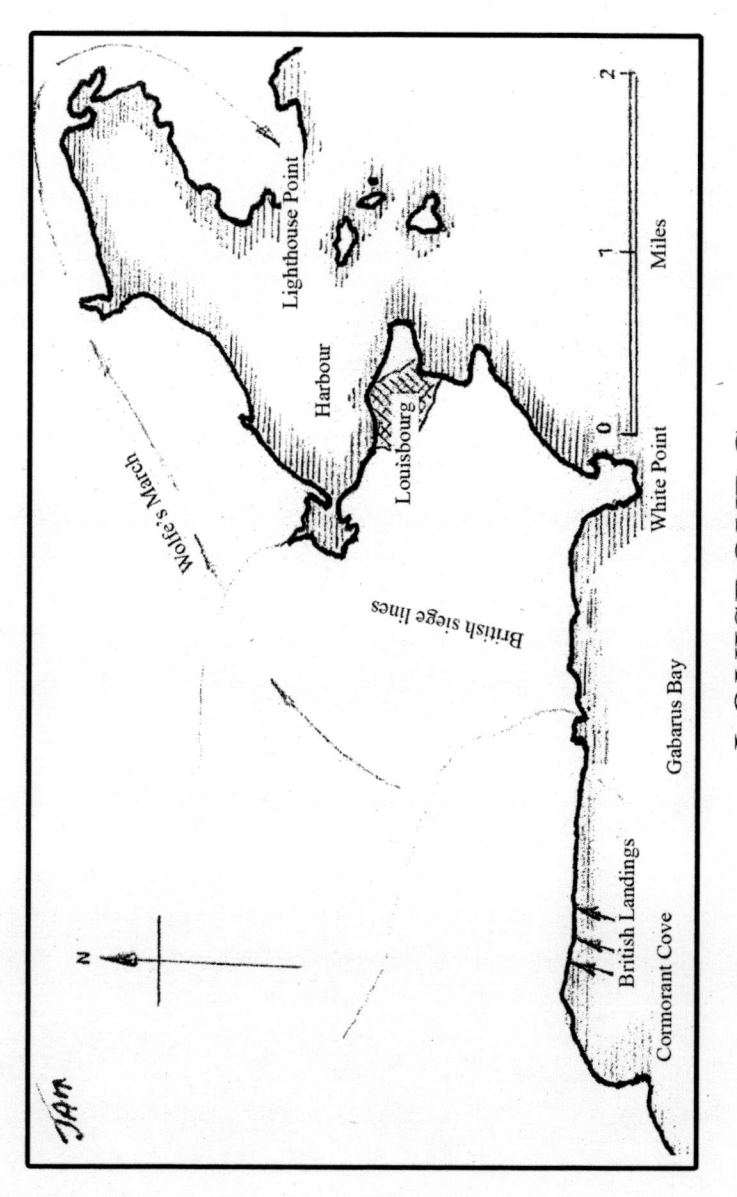

LOUISBOURG
8th June - 27th July 1758

The French advanced against the wood, but were met by British volleys. They broke and 2,000 French soldiers fled the two miles towards the fortifications of Louisbourg.

The landings had only cost the British about 100 men. The other divisions including 400 Marines from the newly formed 62nd Foot landed, but due to the weather, few supplies and no heavy guns could be got ashore.

Amherst had his army on shore by the 12th June but, apart from a few six-pounders which were landed on the 11th, the rest of the artillery remained on the ships.

Having established himself on shore, Amherst sent Wolfe with over 1,000 men to march around the harbour of Louisbourg and secure the area directly north of the town, a journey of over seven miles.

A month was to elapse before Amherst would be able to land all of his heavy guns, meanwhile Wolfe continued with his task, capturing French outposts whilst establishing a road system on his way to Lighthouse Point, where he was able to position a seven-gun battery.

Two islands guarded the entrance to the harbour. From Lighthouse Point, Wolfe was able for two days to fire on the French batteries located on the islands. By the end of this bombardment they were rendered useless.

Amherst requested Boscawen to land a force of marines to relieve Wolfe from Lighthouse Point, such that the Brigadier and his men could join the main attack from south of the town. On 26th June, 260 officers and men landed to relieve Wolfe. This force included the remaining Marines from the 62nd Foot who had not hitherto been landed. The next day, six heavy guns were brought ashore and positioned, before the Marines entrenched themselves to protect them. Three days later French troops attacked the gun emplacements but were easily driven off.

Having landed all of his equipment, Amherst used his engineers and pioneers to construct siege lines and gun emplacements to the west and south of Louisbourg. By early July the fortress and harbour had been surrounded. His heavy guns had been moved ahead of the original siege lines to within six hundred yards of the town. The siege had begun.

The British batteries kept up a constant barrage on the town and fortress, while those on Lighthouse Point fired continuously on the French ships in the harbour. The siege continued with constant skirmishing and French sorties. In one, the Grenadiers of the 17th Foot suffered severely. However the heavy pounding from the British guns was slowly reducing the town to rubble.

At least a third of the garrison had been either wounded or killed, together with many civilians from the town. It was obvious that the fortress could not hold out much longer. The Governor wrote a report to this effect, and dispatched the frigate *Arethuse* to carry the message to France. She slipped out of the harbour on the night of the 15th July on what was really a hopeless task.

On 21st July, the heavy guns of the marine batteries set fire to the French 74-gunship *Entreprenant* which blew up. Fire spread to other ships, the attackers were delighted to see that they were still ablaze all night.

The next day, the Governor's headquarters was hit and that too caught fire. With the demise of the French ships, Boscawen prepared to send six ships of the line into the harbour to bombard the town and defences, unless the Governor surrendered, which the inhabitants urged him to do.

On 26th July, Amherst and Boscawen received a letter from the Governor offering to capitulate. He was given one hour. The terms were harsh; nevertheless he accepted after heated discussions with his senior personnel.

The garrison laid down their arms on the 27th July. British regiments entered the fortress at noon. They had only lost 195 killed while 5,600 French soldiers and sailors were taken prisoner. The British also took 240 cannon. The remaining fortifications were blown up. As it was too late in the season to advance on Quebec, the army wintered locally.

The 22nd Foot, the Cheshire Regiment
40th Foot 1st Battalion, the Prince of Wales's Volunteers (South Lancashire) Regiment

45th Foot 1st Battalion, the Sherwood Foresters (Derbyshire) Regiment
47th Foot 1st Battalion, the Loyal North Lancashire Regiment
48th Foot 1st Battalion, the Northamptonshire Regiment
60th Foot, the King's Royal Rifle Corps
62nd Foot, 1st Battalion, the Duke of Edinburgh's (Wiltshire) Regt.
All received their first battle honour – LOUISBURG*
1st Foot, the Lothian Regiment (the Royal Scots)
15th Foot, the East Yorkshire Regiment
17th Foot, the Leicestershire Regiment
28th Foot, 1st Battalion, the Gloucestershire Regiment
35th Foot, 1st Battalion, the Royal Sussex Regiment

Also received the honour. It was not their first. The award was sanctioned and awarded in 1882.

*

William Pitt was overjoyed when on the 19th August news of the capture of Louisbourg reached London. Disappointment followed four days later, when he was advised regarding the poor showing of Abercromby and the undisciplined retreat of British troops from Ticonderoga. He had hoped that the campaign would have been over by the end of the year.

By the end of 1758, Pitt had recovered his optimism sufficiently to believe that the French dominions in Canada, which they dared to call New France, were within the grasp of the British. He proposed to attack the French in all of their strong posts, believing that a direct assault should be made on Quebec and another against the French further south, taking Montreal.

Major-General Amherst replaced Abercromby and was given overall command in North America. He would move his men up the Hudson River, Lakes George, Champlain and the Richelieu River to Montreal. Another expedition would sweep westwards, through Lake Erie and Lake Ontario towards Fort Niagara and assist Amherst with his assault on Montreal.

---

* LOUISBURG was the British spelling of Louisbourg.

A third attack would be directed against Quebec. Wolfe would command 12,500 regulars and proceed from Louisbourg up the St Lawrence River.

The operation against, and taking of, Fort Niagara, would provide the British with an advanced post, against which any French attempt to re-take Fort DuQuesne would have to be launched. The command was committed to Brigadier John Prideaux, who was colonel of the 55th Foot (2nd Battalion, the Border Regiment) who arrived at Fort Oswego with 2,000 regular troops, which included the 46th Foot (2nd Battalion, the Duke of Cornwall's Light Infantry), where on 27th June he was joined by Sir William Johnson who was leading provincials from New York, and a thousand of his local Indian supporters, who were now engaged in the British service.

Chevalier Pouchot, the French commander of Fort Niagara, was initially unaware of the presence of the British Army as it approached Oswego.

Prideaux and his men landed about a mile from the fort, and by the 20th June, had advanced to within 150 yards, from where they commenced a bombardment of the French position.

The siege had not long been laid before Prideaux was killed in the trenches by the bursting of a shell. The command passed to Johnson who was determined to continue the vigorous measures commenced by Prideaux. The French, alarmed for the safety of the fort, collected about 1,700 of their troops from the outlying posts including Oswego, plus a large body of their Indians to raise the siege.

On 23rd July, Johnson received information regarding the approach of the French relief force. The trenches were guarded by Major John Beckwith with his 44th Foot (1st Battalion, the Essex Regiment). The road on the left of the British line was occupied by light infantry and pickets from the army, reinforced by Grenadiers of the 46th Foot. The line stood firm, whilst the Indians in the British pay, attacked the French flanks.

Several French officers were taken, enabling Johnson to send a message to Pouchot, informing him that the relief force had been defeated. The commander surrendered the fort on 25th July 1759.

Brigadier Thomas Gage, who was sent to succeed Johnson, took his force across Lake Ontario to within sixty miles of Montreal, but failed to progress further. His presence there induced Montcalm on the 10th August to despatch 800 men to guard the western approach to Montreal, thus reducing the garrison of Quebec.

For the assault Wolfe, just 32 years old, now promoted to Major-General for this operation only, was given three brigadiers: Robert Monckton, James Murray and George Townsend. This was an age when commissions were purchased, officers required high birth and money to be elevated to senior positions in the army.

Both Monckton and Murray were younger than Wolfe, both were the sons of peers, but both accepted that they would be subordinate to the new Major-General, however the situation with Townsend was different. He was the nephew of the Duke of Newcastle, and resented that a younger man had been promoted above him; but more important to him, was that a man of a lower family station had been placed above his head.

Having returned to England to recover from a kidney problem, Wolfe sailed back to North America on 14th February with fourteen warships and many smaller craft. Louisbourg harbour was blocked with ice, the fleet sailed on to Halifax, arriving on 30th April.

Vice-Admiral Philip Durell had been given the task of ensuring that the French at Quebec did not receive supplies. Having been held up by ice-floes, he found that when he arrived at the entrance to the St Lawrence on 5th May, he was too late, because five French frigates and many store ships had already sailed into the ice-free gulf and reached the garrison at Quebec.

By May the army was assembled at Louisbourg. Wolfe had expected a force of 12,000 regulars. Instead only about 9,000 were available, these were organised into three brigades.

The force sailed from Louisbourg at the beginning of June. Twenty-nine ships of the line, thirteen frigates and 119 transports entered the Gulf of St Lawrence on the 15th June.

The main fleet joined Durell and followed him through the gulf to the southern shore of the Ile d'Orleans where the final preparations were to be made. On the night of the 25th June, signal fires along the shore, warned the garrison at Quebec that the British had landed and moved to within five miles of them.

Using a telescope from a distance of three miles, Wolfe took his first view of Quebec. It rose on a 300-foot high headland and appeared to be protected by many cannon. To the right, the northern shore rose steeply until, opposite the Ile d'Orleans was the deep gorge of the Montmorency River. Between there and the St Charles River, unseen by Wolfe and unknown to him was a French army of several thousand men. To the west of Quebec for a distance of seven miles, steep cliffs rose above the river to an area of part cultivated land called the Plains of Abraham, the name came from an earlier farmer, Abraham Martin.

Wolfe had hoped to bring Montcalm to a set-piece battle, but having seen the entrenched position of the French, he was unable to decide his next course of action. Townsend averred that this indecision was due to Wolfe being promoted above his ability, whilst Montcalm felt that all he had to do was to stay firm. After all, he believed that his position was impregnable and winter would soon be upon them.

Wolfe had with him the 15th Foot, 28th Foot, 35th Foot, 47th Foot, 48th Foot and 60th Foot, regiments who had fought at Louisbourg and were now quite experienced with North American warfare tactics. The only regiment not at Louisbourg was the 43rd Foot (1st Battalion, the Oxfordshire Light Infantry) they were now with the other regiments on the Ile d'Orleans.

Wolfe decided to hold back from a direct assault and to attack Quebec with many cannon. Townsend moved his brigade onto the Ile d'Orleans, whilst Monckton moved his against the French defenders at Pointe Levis which was directly opposite the town. Batteries were constructed at both locations and from there Quebec was bombarded for the next two months.

Wolfe hoped that this continual barrage against the town would encourage Montcalm to bring his forces to set battle. For although

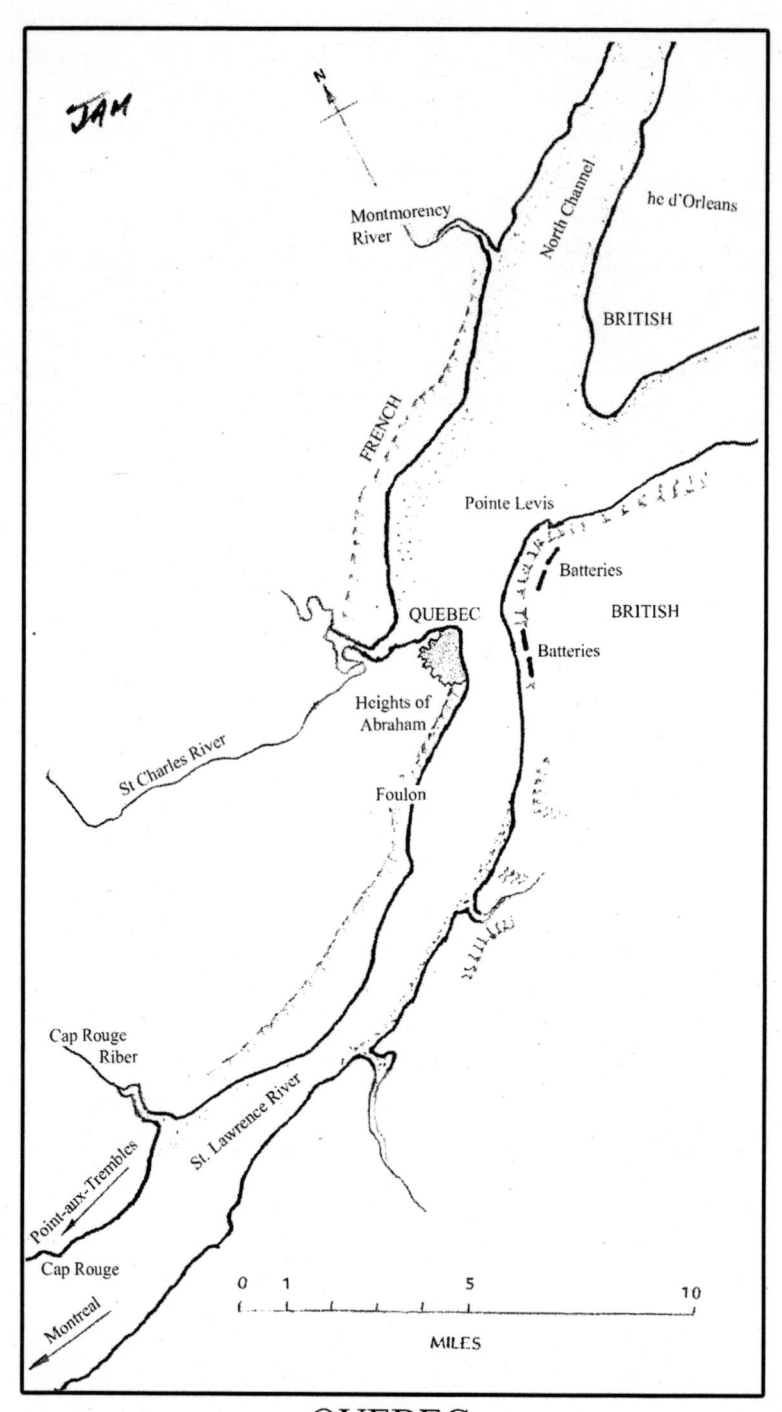

QUEBEC

the French army appeared to have enough men to meet the disciplined British troops, Montcalm knew that many of his were locally raised militia, who were anxious to return to their homes to gather the autumn harvest. He therefore still refused to give Wolfe battle.

To break the stalemate, Wolfe believed it possible to approach Quebec from the north. This would entail crossing the north channel of the St Lawrence and landing north of the Montmorency River. He would cross the mud flats at the mouth and move the ten miles in the direction of the St Charles River, where he hoped that somewhere in between, the French and British armies would face each other.

From the southern side of the St Lawrence, Wolfe sent Monckton south with his troops, marching in full view of Quebec in the hope that it would persuade Montcalm that an invasion would be to the south of the town in the area of Cap Rouge.

The next day Wolfe led the brigades of Murray and Townsend across the river, much to the annoyance of the latter, who believed that he should have led the crossing. The landing was hardly opposed by the French, as was their weak counter-attack, which was easily dealt with by the British.

Once again, Wolfe had failed to engineer the battle that he so required, as Montcalm did not form his army against the invaders. Frustrated, Wolfe decided to put his plan into operation – he would cross the mud flats, but first he had to put out of action the two French redoubts which overlooked the area.

The frigate *Mercury* made soundings in the north channel. Its master James Cook* reported that there was a suitable depth of water, which would allow a large ship of the line to bring its heavy guns to achieve the reduction of the redoubts. This was done by 31st July enabling Murray and Townsend to move across the Montmorency.

Townsend's grenadiers commenced the action before being properly formed, or before the troops intended to support them had

---

* *Captain James Cook was born in Yorkshire in 1728. He circumnavigated the world several times and charted both Australia and New Zealand. He was killed by natives on 14th February 1779 at Kealakua island in the Hawaiian group.*

arrived. The French poured devastating fire on them as they charged up the cliffs. Several hundred were killed and many others were badly wounded. Wolfe, who had been observing the debacle, ordered a retreat. It was his opinion that Townsend had failed to conduct the attack in a co-ordinated manner. Townsend again blamed Wolfe and spread word amongst senior officers that the reverse was all due to the indecision of the General.

The bombardment of Quebec had generally silenced its batteries, which enabled Vice-Admiral Sir Charles Saunders to sail above the town. This move permitted Wolfe to observe the landscape from a close position. What he feared most was landing troops between Quebec and Cap Rouge, before the main body of the regiments could be formed, the leading men would be attacked. He had already seen the result of the action at the Montmorency River.

Montcalm had observed the move by Saunders and thought that it was intended that he should believe that Wolfe would land in the area of Saunder's ships, whereas Wolfe's main force would again land north of Quebec. Montcalm's worry was that his supply line to Montreal could be cut by a relatively small number of British regulars, so he sent 600 men to guard the route at Pointe-aux-Trembles, thirty miles south of Quebec.

Wolfe hoped that if Amherst had taken Montreal he would be able to join in a combined attack on Quebec. Needing to know what progress had been made by the General, he sent Brigadier James Murray with 1,200 men up the St Lawrence. After their second attempt to land, they were involved in a skirmish where they were fortunate enough to take French prisoners, who informed them that Amherst had taken Ticonderoga and also Crown Point.

This information was confirmed by two British officers, who carried letters from Amherst dated 7th August, telling Wolfe that his intention had been to capture Montreal from the south. The 1st Foot had initially marched from New Jersey, while a detachment of the regiment had cleared Cherokee Indians from South Carolina before joining Amherst on his move north.

Amherst had reached the head of Lake George on 21st July. His force of seven regular British regiments, which had included the 17th Foot (1st Battalion, the Leicestershire Regiment) who were without their Grenadiers, these had remained under Wolfe, and the 27th Foot (1st Battalion, the Royal Inniskilling Fusiliers). The force also included many militias from the North American Colonies. A total of 11,000 men disembarked, and marched to surround Ticonderoga.

Unknown to them, Montcalm had ordered the commander to destroy and abandon the fort if the British appeared in strength. Before Amherst could deploy his heavy cannon the fort was destroyed by the French. The British entered the ruins on 26th July. The French moved north, destroying the fort at Crown Point as they went.

Amherst knew that the French had four armed vessels and therefore controlled Lake Champlain. To overcome this, he had to get his boatmen to build ships, a task of at least several months. He would not be able to move on Montreal until the following year. Regiments were later sent to winter quarters, the 27th spent the winter at Crown Point whilst the 55th returned to New York.

It was agreed between Wolfe and Saunders that it would be necessary to move many small ships containing provisions to keep the men supplied for at least six weeks, south past the town of Quebec. By the 3rd September, all of the troops who had earlier crossed the St Lawrence had now returned to the southern side, while the navy moved twenty-two ships carrying 3,600 men south of the town.

Monckton and Townsend moved their regiments westwards along the southern shore of the St Lawrence. Montcalm was baffled by the continual troop movements. He was sure that once again Wolfe was moving men in the hope that the French would become confused, regarding the true intent of the British.

Montcalm had 3,000 men stationed between Cap Rouge and the southern area of Ponte-aux-Trembles who were under the command of Bougainville. They were not all regular soldiers, many were militias who were interested in the current conflict, but were now being employed to prevent the British cutting the supply line from Montreal, which would mean starving Quebec into surrender.

The summer months were slipping by and Wolfe still did not have a definite plan. More ships were sent upriver. Bougainville moved his troops along the bank in line with the British ships. During the next two days, the ships drifted up and down with the tide. The French moved with them, until believing that the whole operation was to exhaust his men, Bougainville finally rested them at Cap Rouge.

Wolfe again surveyed the cliffs and believed that there was a path, the Foulon pass, which meandered from the beach to the cliff top. He thought that it may be possible to scale the path at night. His brigadiers were unimpressed, believing that the climb was impossible. Unperturbed, Wolfe carried on. He ordered the troops who were camped on the shore, to assemble on the beach. The men were not told where they would land. Each man was supplied with provisions for two days.

The troops embarked on the landing craft at 9.00pm. Wolfe issued the order to his men that 'The first body which gets on shore shall at once attack any post in front of him and hold it until the whole army comes up'. Ships from the navy floated up on the tide, the landing craft, hidden by three frigates and smaller vessels, turned at 2 a.m. and drifted downriver again.

Sailors in the leading boats, sought for the jutting rock, the landmark identifying Wolfe's Cove (as it is now called). The first wave of landing craft carried light infantrymen commanded by Colonel William Howe, the Grenadier company of the 45th Foot (1st Battalion, the Sherwood Foresters – [Derbyshire]), Grenadiers of the 17th Foot, Monckton's 15th Foot (East Yorkshire) and Murray's battalions. The boats pulled into the shore at about 4 a.m. The beach was deserted, mainly because the French did not believe that the climb was possible. Colonel William Howe led his picked men ashore. The leading troops scrambled up the cliff path followed by more of the infantry until, within two hours, several thousand men had reached the cliff top.

By morning, Wolfe was able to draw up his men in battle order with his right flank on the cliffs above the St Lawrence. He waited for Montcalm to bring his army against the ranks of the British force. Montcalm remained unmoved for he knew that his army could not withstand the power of the British. Wolfe marched his men to cover any move between Quebec and the St Charles River. One regiment had been left to guard the landing area and to assist the navy to bring up heavy guns to the top of the cliffs.

In typical European fashion, Wolfe drew his regiments of 3,000 men in two lines, forty yards apart, Townsend's battalions on the left,

Murray's in the centre with the 47th Foot (1st Battalion, the Loyal North Lancashire Regiment) who believed that they occupied the position of honour, so much so, that later as an expression of sorrow at the death of Wolfe, the regiment wore a black line in the lace of the epaulettes of its uniform. Monckton was on the right of the line.

There was no sign of the French, until Montcalm with just under 3,000 men advanced up the reverse slope. His cannon opened fire, while the French Canadians and Indians fired and sniped at the British right, who soon suffered from this unexpected source. The 28th Foot (1st Battalion, the Gloucestershire Regiment) fired as the French came to within sixty paces of their line.

British sailors had dragged eight 24-pounders, six 6-pounders and some howitzers, and returned fire on the French who came over the hill at 10 a.m. but moved down the slope in poor order. The British advanced to meet them. Wolfe was on the left of the line, but as he moved to the right he was hit in the wrist, the wound was only slight and did not stop him from encouraging his men.

The French charge continued, most of them discharged their muskets too far away to be effective. When they were only forty yards away, Wolfe gave the order to fire to the motionless British front line who fired as one. The second line, stepping between men of the first, also fired a volley at very close range.

Leading the infantry, Wolfe ordered a bayonet charge. The French troops turned and fled in disorder, leaving a mortally wounded Wolfe on the ground. He had first received a musket ball in the groin, then another in the chest. As Montcalm tried to rally his panic-stricken troops, he too was hit in the groin. He was carried back to Quebec, where he died. Each army had lost its leader.

The battle had only lasted a matter of ten minutes, but the French had lost nearly 1,000 killed or badly wounded, whereas the British had only lost 55 killed.

After the battle the 35th Foot (1st Battalion, the Royal Sussex Regiment) who had been on the British right with Monckton, picked up the white plumes of the Royal Roussillon Regiment of France and stuck them in their own hats, an act which was to lead to the plume being incorporated in the badge of the regiment.

Colonel Hon James Murray, the Lieutenant-Colonel of the 15th Foot was appointed Governor of Quebec, the 15th being included in the garrison of seven thousand soldiers. During the winter of 1759 the troops suffered great hardship due to the lack of fresh provisions and the scarcity of fuel.

2,000 French soldiers spent the winter in Montreal. In the spring of 1760 a large force left Montreal with the intention of taking Quebec back from the British. Murray moved out to meet them, but his force was insufficient to halt the French advance and he was forced to retreat to the town. The French followed, then besieged Quebec from 28th April until mid-May, when a British naval force relieved the town. The French returned to Montreal.

Amherst had wintered in New York and on 14th August with British regulars, supported by men from the colonies, entered the St Lawrence from Lake Ontario with over 5,500 regulars and over four thousand colonials.

He then detached Colonel Haviland of the 55th Foot with over 3,000 men, which included the 27th Foot, the Grenadiers and light companies of his own regiment. They were to capture the Ile aux Noix after a short engagement.

Amherst went on to capture Fort Levi on L'Isle Royale, which after two days of severe fighting, surrendered. After losing men in the rapids and falls, Amherst landed on the Island of Montreal, six miles above the town.

Murray travelled from Quebec. He arrived with just less than 4,000 men on the 6th September and met with Amherst. Montreal was surrounded by a combined army of regular British soldiers and Colonial militia.

Two days later the French surrendered. New France now became Canada under British rule.

On 13th March 1882, the battle honour QUEBEC 1759 was awarded to:

The East Yorkshire Regiment	(15th Foot)
1st Battalion Gloucestershire Regiment	(28th Foot)
1st Battalion Royal Sussex Regiment	(35th Foot)

1st Battalion Oxfordshire Light Infantry (43rd Foot)
1st Battalion Loyal North Lancashire Regiment (47th Foot)
1st Battalion Northamptonshire Regiment (48th Foot)
King's Royal Rifle Corps. 2nd and 3rd Battalions (60th Foot)

CHAPTER XV

SEVEN YEARS WAR 1756–1763
GEORGE III
WEST INDIES 1759–1762

In October 1760 King George the second died. He had been on the throne for 33 years. As his eldest son had died in 1751, his grandson became King George the third.

Having secured Canada, Pitt had even more ambitious plans to deprive the French of their West Indian island possessions especially the islands of Guadeloupe and Martinique. His policy was that at the conclusion of the war, he might be able to exchange Martinique for Minorca, which Britain had lost in 1756.

For a long time, the locations of the islands had placed the French at an advantage, because once past the Leeward Islands, ships could not turn back into the wind, therefore they had to continue westwards until rounding the island of Cuba, which as well as Puerto Rico was controlled by Spain.

The British had a harbour at Kingston on the island of Jamaica, but this did not aid British commercial shipping, which was continually troubled by the French Navy and privateers operating from Martinique.

For the expedition of 1759, the new King's advisors appointed Major-General Thomas Hopson, who unfortunately was old and probably should not have been given command of the 6,000 regular troops, who were to join the eight ships of the line, commandeered by Pitt, for his ambitious drive against the West Indian islands.

As the fleet arrived off Barbados it was joined by a further four ships of the line. The entire force under the command of Commodore Moore sailed for the island of Martinique.

The naval force arrived on the 13th January and commenced a bombardment of the chief port and capital, Fort Royal. This enabled British troops to establish a landing some distance from the town. However, when they tried to bring heavy guns and more regiments ashore, they were repulsed, first by heavy swell and second by ferocious French resistance.

It was decided to abandon the attempt, bring the landing party back to the ships, and seek an easier objective which, the commanders agreed would be the island of Guadeloupe.

Guadeloupe was about thirty miles north of Martinique. It was really two islands, Grand-Terre and Basse-Terre. The islands were divided by a narrow stretch of water.

Basse-Terre had a bay large enough for the British to bring their fleet and commence a bombardment of Fort Royal (also the same name as the chief port in Martinique), which was the main town adjacent to the bay. The shelling from the navy silenced the town guns. The French abandoned their position. British regiments then moved against the island of Grande-Terre, attacking the privateers' base of Pointe-a-Pitre which surrendered.

At the time, the success of the landing and the progress of the British troops was greeted by them with joy, but this was to be followed with mixed feelings. The men were unaccustomed to the climate which bred fever and sickness amongst them. It was not only confined to the men, Major-General Hopson also died of fever.

The command now fell to the Hon John Barrington, who was the first Colonel of the 64th Foot (1st Battalion, the Prince of Wales' [North Staffordshire] Regiment). It was originally the 2nd Battalion of the 11th Foot which was raised in 1756, and two years later had become the 64th Foot. Barrington advanced slowly through the island of Guadeloupe, town by town, dwelling by dwelling until the islands were totally under British control. Disease in the fever-ridden islands was so bad that when the 64th Foot sailed back to England they had

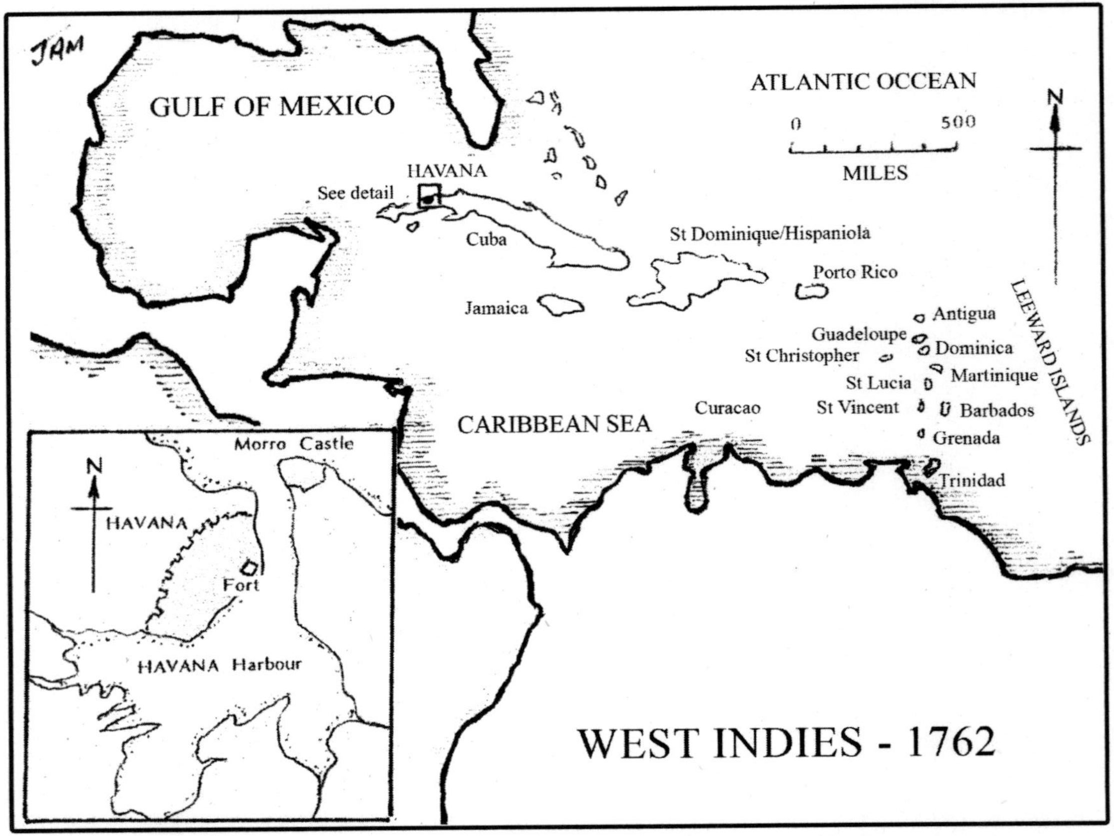
JAM
GULF OF MEXICO
ATLANTIC OCCEAN
0
500
MILES
N
HAVANA
See detail
Cuba
St Dominique/Hispaniola
Porto Rico
Jamaica
Antigua
Guadeloupe
Dominica
St Christopher
Martinique
St Lucia
St Vincent
Barbados
Grenada
Trinidad
Curacao
LEEWARD ISLANDS
CARIBBEAN SEA
Morro Castle
N
HAVANA
Fort
HAVANA Harbour
WEST INDIES - 1762

very few fit men, and had to recruit 787 rank and file to bring the regiment up to strength.

Due to the action at Guadeloupe, the following regiments were, in 1909, granted the battle honour GUADELOUPE 1759:

The Buffs (East Kent Regiment)	(3rd Foot)
The King's Own (Royal Lancashire Regiment)	(4th Foot)
1st Battalion Gloucestershire Regiment	(28th Foot)
1st Battalion South Staffordshire Regiment	(38th Foot)
1st Battalion The Black Watch (Royal Highlanders)	(42nd Foot)
1st Battalion Manchester Regiment	(63rd Foot)
1st Battalion North Staffordshire Regiment (P. of W.)	(64th Foot)
1st Battalion York and Lancaster Regiment	(65th Foot)

Not awarded to the 61st as only part of the regiment was present. The 63rd Foot was granted the right to wear as its badge, the Fleur-de-lis, which at the time was the French national emblem.

Although Pitt was pleased with the success at Guadeloupe, his intention had been to take Martinique. In 1761 he sent an even more powerful expedition against the island. Major-General Robert Monckton would command the army. He had seen action in North America and Canada six years earlier, had also led the right under Wolfe at Quebec, and was considered the obvious man to command the land troops. A large fleet, eighteen ships of the line and fourteen frigates came under 43-year-old Rear-Admiral George Rodney; they carried ten regiments and were to meet at Barbados where the total force assembled. The 28th Foot had moved from Montreal to New York, before joining the main army.

The force landed on Martinique in mid-January 1762 and invested Fort Pigeon, thus preventing its occupants from reinforcing their comrades in Fort Royal, which had been placed under siege by the British, The siege lasted for ten days before the fort surrendered. The army spent some time in the interior, fighting small groups of the French army and supporters until in mid-February, Martinique was totally under the control of the British.

In 1909, the battle honour MARTINIQUE 1762 was awarded to:

The East Yorkshire Regiment	(15th Foot)
The Leicestershire Regiment	(17th Foot)
The Cheshire Regiment	(22nd Foot)
1st Battalion Royal Inniskilling Fusiliers	(27th Foot)
1st Battalion Gloucestershire Regiment	(28th Foot)
1st Battalion Royal Sussex Regiment	(35th Foot)
1st Battalion South Staffordshire Regiment	(38th Foot)
1st Battalion P.W.V. (South Lancashire) Regiment	(40th Foot)
1st Battalion The Black Watch (Royal Highlanders)	(42nd Foot)
1st Battalion Oxfordshire Light Infantry	(43rd Foot)
1st Battalion Northamptonshire Regiment	(48th Foot)
The King's Royal Rifle Corps (3rd Battalion)	(60th Foot()
2nd Battalion The Welsh Regiment	(69th Foot)

On the 18th January 1762, Spain declared war on Britain. William Pitt no longer directly controlled the war. However, such was his power that members of the Government feared criticism, should they not act as he would have expected in his vision for the destruction of the French Empire.

Sir George Pocock was given command of the fleet to take thirty transports to Martinique, which he reached in April. Pocock's selection was an excellent choice, whereas the man to lead the army of 14,000 soldiers was less so. The Earl of Albemarle was 40 years old and his experience was limited to European warfare, which unfortunately did not lend itself to tactics in the West Indies.

The 38th and 69th regiments were not involved in further actions in the West Indies. Instead, Pocock brought with him the 1st Foot (the Lothian Regiment [Royal Scots]), 9th Foot (the Norfolk Regiment), 34th Foot (1st Battalion, the Border Regiment) and 56th Foot (2nd Battalion The Essex Regiment) to join regiments which had already been engaged in the Martinique campaign.

By the 5th June, Pocock had neared the island of Cuba and was about one hundred miles from the intended invasion point, the island's capital, Havana, where there was an extremely large harbour, protected on the east by the castle of Morro and from the west by the Governor's Fort within the city.

As he was aware of the defences at Havana, Pocock anchored his fleet eighteen miles east of the city. From there Albemarle launched the invasion. Once the troops has left the fleet, Pocock sailed to blockade the harbour. Albemarle, showing his inexperience, instead of landing the troops to the west of Havana and directly attacking the city, a move which would probably have yielded a quick victory, with his European tactical thoughts, felt that he had no alternative but to lay siege to the castle of Morro. He landed the troops, led by the 56th Foot (2nd Battalion, the Essex Regiment) without too much resistance, and ordered that his engineers construct batteries. This was achieved by the end of June, enabling the gunners to open fire on the castle at the beginning of July. It did not seem to have been accepted by Albemarle that the conditions in the islands were such that, as it was mid-summer and as the troops had already suffered from disease and fever on Martinique and Guadeloupe, the same could not occur on Cuba. What he really needed, but was not going to get, was a quick victory.

Morro was held by only four hundred defenders, but for six weeks the artillery fired shell after shell on the castle, while the engineers, pioneers and miners drove tunnels which they lined with explosives, under the walls. On 14th August, the castle was blown up. The army moved on to Havana and captured the city fairly easily. Again the troops suffered, as yellow fever raged. Within four weeks over four thousand had died.

One example of this was the 28th Foot. Their losses were such that in 1763 when they sailed back to New York, their strength had been reduced to just 208 officers and men.

Once again, regiments had to wait until 1909 before receiving the battle honour HAVANNAH 1762. Awarded to:

The Lothian Regiment (the Royal Scots)	(1st Foot)
The Norfolk Regiment	(9th Foot)
1st Battalion The Border Regiment	(34th Foot)
2nd Battalion The Essex Regiment	(56th Foot)

Also receiving the award:
15th, 17th, 22nd, 27th, 28th, 35th, 40th, 42nd, 43rd, 48th & 60th

The main part of the 65th Foot returned to England after Guadeloupe, but detached companies took part in the siege of Martinique and Cuba. Their attendance was insufficient to share in the battle honours. For their part played in the capture of Morro, the 56th were awarded the unique battle honour MORO.

Following the fall of Martinique (which the French would recover at the conclusion of peace), the French islands of St Lucia, Grenada and St Vincent also came into British possession

CHAPTER XVI

SEVEN YEARS WAR 1756-1763
GEORGE III
INDIA

Although the Seven Years War commenced in 1756, it is necessary to look at earlier events in India which led to the conflict in that country.

Several European countries had established trading posts in India, mainly located on the coast. The Compagnie des Indes was a French government-controlled organisation, while British trading was carried out by the private English East India Company.

Before the eighteenth century, India had been ruled for at least two hundred years by the Moguls from their capital in Delhi. Their strength enabled the French and British to agree treaties, thereby allowing them to trade in peace. But by 1712, control of the Mogul Empire was beginning to wane. This led to a scramble for power by the various Indian groups, which in turn left the French and British vulnerable.

Joseph Dupleix, the French Governor-General of Pondicherry had long foreseen the coming struggle with Britain. He believed that a strong leader could rule India, and that it should be France. His belief was that a small European force could defeat a much larger number of native troops, but that once under French leadership the local Indians could be trained into an efficient force.

He knew that the Indian leaders were corrupt and were open to bribes. He felt forced to act when in 1740 the Mahrattas murdered the Nawab of the Carnatic. As anarchy spread across India, Bengal was raided; Madras was threatened, as was Bombay in the east.

As the War of the Austrian Succession had broken out in 1743, Dupleix felt justified in approaching the new Nawab and proposed to him, that he should not allow hostilities by others within the Carnatic, for this was where most of the French trading stations were situated.

This agreed, Dupleix promised to hand over Madras to the Nawab, once the French had captured the British trading town. As Dupleix attacked, the Nawab honoured the agreement and stood aside as the French commenced a five day bombardment. The town surrendered on the 10th September 1746. Some British defenders escaped, taking refuge in the nearby Fort St David. One of them was a 21-year-old clerk from the East India Company; his name was Robert Clive.

Having taken Madras, Dupleix reneged on the agreement when he refused to hand the town over to the Nawab. He spent the rest of the year keeping the Indian troops at bay during their frequent attacks. Dupleix then turned his attention to Fort St David, before news reached him that the war against the British had been over for more than a year. Details of the peace treaty from Aix-la-Chapelle, ordered that Madras should be returned to Britain.

Events in the Indian leadership struggle meant that the European traders could not ignore what was happening. They could either fight on their own, try to form an alliance with Indian rulers, or leave the continent. The appeal of trade forced both the French and British to stay. The British were unhappy to sit back and watch as Dupleix attempted to take over as the Mogul Empire collapsed. Indian pretenders seized the Mogul viceroyalty of the Deccan and conquered the Carnatic. With a few French soldiers and two thousand Indian troops, Dupleix placed his own puppets on the throne. They chased the British candidate Mahomet Ali into Trichinopoly, which was instantly besieged.

Robert Clive was aggressive, undisciplined and ruthless. At the age of eighteen he had been sent by boat to India, not as a junior officer in a regular army regiment, but as a junior clerk in the East India Company. In 1750, Clive was 25 years old, fed up with years behind a desk watching British interests being overshadowed by the French in India. Fired with enthusiasm following his experience at the French attack on Madras, he rode into Fort St David and told the Governor of Madras that he would join the HEIC Army if he was given the rank of captain, furthermore he would not require any payment for this appointment. Once he had obtained his commission, Clive received a stroke of good fortune. His superiors in the East India Company had a major disagreement as a result he was given full command.

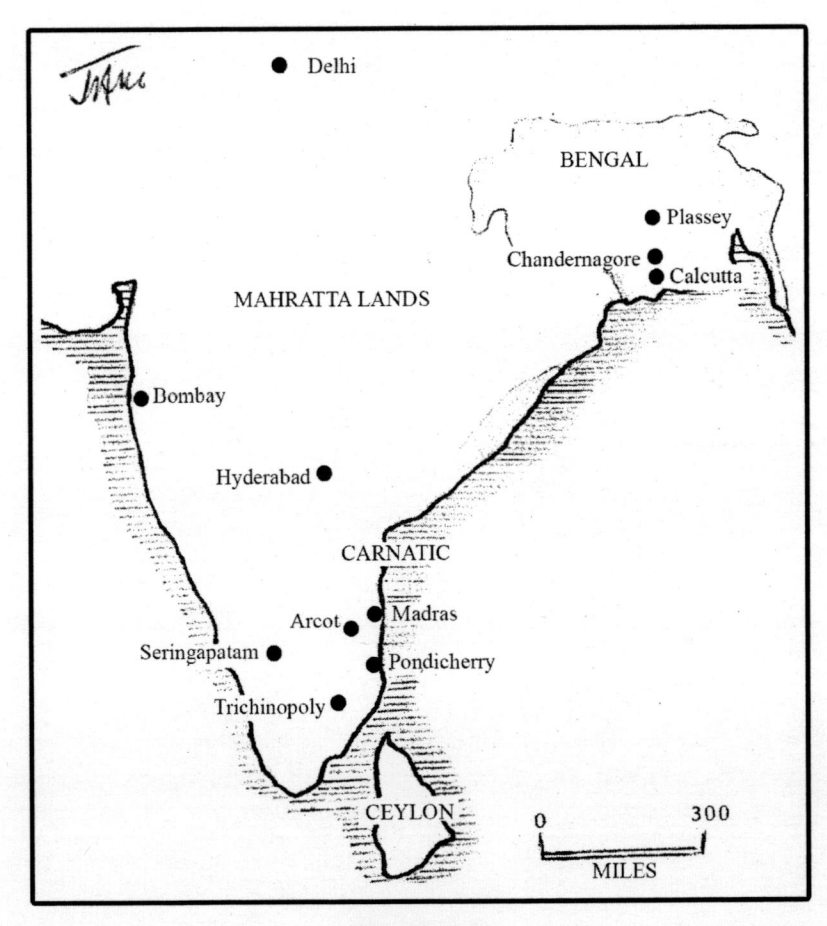

INDIA

He made his way to Trichinopoly where Mahomet Ali was under siege. He believed that relief with the few soldiers that he had under his command, was impossible, therefore he needed to strike a blow elsewhere. He chose Arcot, capital of the Carnatic, which according to his informants had been stripped of troops for the attack on Trichinopoly. Clive's force consisted of eight officers, four of whom had been clerks in the East India Company, leading two hundred Europeans and six hundred Indian sepoys. Marching through the monsoon rains, Clive attacked Chanda Sahib's virtually undefended capital which easily fell. He then moved into the crumbling fortress with only three hundred of his men.

It was not long before Chanda Sahib, dismayed at the loss of his capital, detached ten thousand troops from Trichinopoly to retake the town and fortress. The siege lasted for fifty days. Clive's stand had impressed several Indian chieftains who decided to aid the British. As news of this spread, the Indian besiegers retreated and the siege was lifted. This action was quickly followed by a field battle at nearby Arni, where he defeated a much larger force of French and Indian troops, then the relief of Trichinopoly. During these engagements, Clive impressed, displaying qualities of true leadership. By 1752 Clive and his Indian supporters had occupied much French territory. He returned to England in 1753.

Due to their stubborn resistance at Arcot, in March 1841 the Governor of Madras awarded the HEIC Madras European Regiment (102nd Foot, 1st Battalion Royal Dublin Fusiliers) with the honorary standard* ARCOT, later used by the regiment as a battle honour.

The East India Company believed that Dupleix would cause trouble for them therefore it encouraged the British government to tell the French rulers that he was wildly ambitious, which if left unchecked would ruin both companies. As a result of these discussions, in 1754 Dupleix was recalled to France, he was replaced by the Comte de Lally-Tollendal whose instructions were to share trade with the British.

---

* The custom for the East India Company was to grant 'honorary standards' to their regiments which were in effect battle honours.

In 1755, Clive returned to India as Deputy Governor of Madras, he was anxious to use the Dupleix theory regarding Indian troops being under European leadership, only this time it should be the British who led, displacing the French from central India.

Peace between the British and Indian population in Bengal had generally been kept by the ruling Moslem leader, who had seized and held power for the last fourteen years, yet in 1756 he died. The new Nawab of Bengal was his grandson, Surajah Dowlah** who was 23 years old, unstable, sadistic and treacherous.

One of his first acts was to ignore the treaty that had existed with the East India Company and marched with a very large army on Calcutta. Although the small garrison, mostly English civilians, was taken by surprise, they held out for three days until the fort was destroyed. The Company's employees were imprisoned overnight in a dungeon on 20th June 1756. This became famous as the Black Hole, the number of people said to have been kept in the stifling conditions was 146; this number may have been an attempt by the British to exploit the atrocity, as the true number was probably only 65. What is not in dispute is that only 23 people survived.

Clive had sailed with Admiral Charles Watson, who upon his death was succeeded by Rear-Admiral Sir George Pocock, whose task was to avenge the insult that the British had suffered in Calcutta. In answer to the request from the East India Company, Pitt sent four ships of the line to reinforce Pocock's squadron of three warships.

Pocock played a major role in the bombardment of Calcutta and its seizure. Surajah Dowlah moved his forces north of the fort to join his standing army at Plassey, here with support from the French he appeared impregnable, except that he had upset too many of his own people, including some of his courtiers who now plotted to depose him and set his chief general, Mir Jafar, in his place.

Clive entered into plots and counter-plots to suborn Mir Jafar away from his leader, but as Clive approached Plassey he had not received assurances of support from the general. When he caught up with

---

** Siraj ud-Daulah

Surajah Dowlah, his army consisted of 700 men from the 39th Regiment of Foot (1st Battalion, the Dorsetshire Regiment) and various companies and detachments, namely the EIC Bengal (European) Regiment (101st Foot), EIC 1st Madras European Regiment (102nd Foot), EIC Bombay European Regiment (103rd Foot) also five-hundred sailors with fourteen guns. The Nawab commanded in excess of 50,000 men including 15,000 cavalry, elephants and fifty cannon, maintained and fired by French gunners.

The large Indian armies were not trained to fight to the death, but to intimidate each other into submission. There would be a volley of cannon fire, a brief clash of horsemen, a show of infantry, then the smaller army would give way. Clive was aware of this and he intended to call their bluff.

On 23rd June 1757, Clive took an aggressive stance by attacking and occupying the Nawab's hunting lodge and the nearby walled mango grove and observing the army standing against him. The French gunners commenced firing from as close as two hundred yards, but the trees in the mango grove took the brunt of the gunfire, and also stopped the Indian cavalry charging. The British gunners were fortunate that, by luck, they killed two of the Nawab's commanders.

As the Indian infantry prepared to advance, a sudden downpour drenched the Bengali powder, but the British had taken the precaution of covering their munitions under tarpaulins. Neither Mir-Jafar nor his two fellow conspirators moved their troops in support of the Nawab. Confusion reigned as Surajah Dowlah, sensing treason, ordered his men to retire, instead of an orderly retreat his army fled in panic. The British only lost seven men killed. Clive appointed Mir-Jafar as the new Nawab of Bengal.

During the mid-nineteenth century, for their attendance and action East India Company regiments were awarded the honorary standard PLASSEY these were:

Bengal (European) Regiment (101st Foot)
Bombay European Regiment (103rd Foot)
1st Madras European Regiment (102nd Foot) who also received the Royal Tiger inscribed PLASSEY and BUXAR.

In 1835, the 39th Foot (1st Battalion, the Dorset Regiment) were awarded the battle honour PLASSEY.

The East India Company was now in control of Bengal, while the French were militarily superior in the Carnatic. They were still supported in the neighbouring state of Oudh, to such an extent that Clive decided to move against them wherever they and their Indian puppets were making war against the British.

In 1756, at the start of the war against Britain, the French government sent eight ships under Comte d'Ache and 2,000 regular soldiers to India. With them General Lally attacked and captured the British trading posts at Cuddalore, Fort St David and Arcot and in December 1758 laid siege to Madras. Once more the strength of the British navy more than assisted the land troops. The presence of Pocock kept d'Ache away, as the Frenchman refused to give battle. The effect of this was that Lally was forced to abandon the siege of Madras.

During December 1758 an expedition to the Northern Circars by the EIC Bengal (European) Regiment (101st Foot) resulted in victory for the British. It was a similar story when they moved to the Carnatic, and both actions were responsible for the award in 1894 to the 101st Foot (1st Battalion, the Royal Munster Fusiliers) of the battle honours CONDORE and MASULIPATAM.

Clive appealed to Pitt for help, in response he sent a regiment* on 21st February 1759 under Colonel Sir Eyre Coote. This was a particularly bold action by Pitt against popular feeling, as Britain was under an invasion scare from the French.

Pitt's contribution to British victory in India inadvertently decreased French strength, when they believed that the British were sending ships to capture Mauritius, therefore d'Ache was ordered to take his fleet from the coast of India to protect the island. He sailed from Pondicherry leaving General Lally to defend French interests on his own.

---

* Numbered 84th Foot. It was disbanded after the Seven Years War in 1763.

In November 1759, the Dutch were still operating in a small way in India. British concerns were such that they believed that any outside body would weaken their position. Therefore the Dutch were forced to abandon their Indian interests after their defeat by the British at Badara. This was recognised when, also in 1894 the battle honour BADARA was awarded to the 101st Foot.

In an effort to hold Pondicherry, the Comte de Lally-Tollendal laid siege to the British fort at Wandiwash, sixty miles southeast of Madras. The fort held out for three months giving time for Eyre Coote to march from Madras. Both armies were of equal strength, both were composed of regular troops and sepoys.

Lally opened with his artillery followed by a cavalry charge, he then led his infantry in direct assault. The British fired grapeshot, then concentrated musket fire. A lucky shell exploded the French powder magazine. Lally's front disintegrated and he returned to Pondicherry.

After the victory at Wandiwash, Clive sailed once more for England with the news that French domination in southern India had ended. This battle was recognised, when in 1841 the EIC Madras European Regiment (102nd Foot) was awarded the honorary standard of WANDIWASH.

Colonel Eyre Coote captured French settlements, isolating and laying siege to Pondicherry. Lally waited in vain for the return of d'Ache with French reinforcements, whilst preparing to defend the fort in the hope that they would arrive before it was too late. The British colonel moved slowly, awaiting the end of the rainy season to complete the investment of this last French stronghold. By 6th December 1760 he had established four batteries from which he shelled the town. British warships patrolled the sea in case French supplies and reinforcements attempted to come to the aid of the beleaguered general, who by now only had provisions for a few weeks.

On New Year's Day 1761, the Coromandel coast was struck by a hurricane. Forces from both sides suffered, the strength of the wind so engulfed the European soldiers that they were unable to move to safer ground. Many of the sepoys perished as torrents caused by the heavy rain completely overwhelmed their camp. The cannon were buried under tons of sand and debris as the British batteries were destroyed. When calm returned, the British rebuilt the gun emplacements from where eleven 24-pounders bombarded Pondicherry. Lally capitulated. The fall of their last outpost blasted French hopes of establishing a major trading organisation within India. In 1841 the EIC Madras European Regiment were awarded the honorary standard PONDICHERRY.

In June 1764, Clive returned to India. Much internal conflict had taken place in his absence. He returned as Governor of Bengal and Commander in Chief and in October he moved against the Nawabs of Bengal and Oudh, to show his belief that British dominance in India was paramount. To demonstrate this he led the attack against them at Buxar using 101st and 103rd Regiments, who in 1829 and 1844 respectively were both awarded the honorary standard BUXAR.

The Honourable East India Company raised nine infantry regiments. In 1860-1 they became regiments of the Crown, numbered 101 to 109. Only three are mentioned in the previous text, the remaining regiments were not raised until 1826 or later:

HEIC 1st Battalion Bombay (European) Regiment, claimed to go back to 1661, when a European Corps was formed to garrison Bombay. They became the 103rd Regiment of Foot.

HEIC Madras European Regiment, formed in 1746 (102nd Foot).

HEIC Bengal (European) Regiment, formed in 1756 (101st Foot).

CHAPTER XVII

SEVEN YEARS WAR 1756-1763
GEORGE II
MINDEN

The British infantry fought in only one battle on the continent – Minden – 1st August 1759.

In 1758, six British infantry regiments, six cavalry regiments and supporting artillery under Lieutenant-General Lord George Sackville, had formed part of the force with the Prussian army; they were subordinate to Prince Ferdinand of Brunswick. Their aim was to protect Hanover from French attack, not least because at that time kings of England were also kings of Hanover.

Early in 1759, Ferdinand moved to block two French armies. The French Marshal, the Marquis Louis de Contades with over 60,000 men in the Rhine area and the Duc de Broglie with 20,000 in Hesse, their intention were to move against Hanover. Both French marshals moved on the town of Minden on the 9th July, de Broglie was joined there by de Contades who, because he was the senior Marshal assumed control. Hanover was only 35 miles away.

Ferdinand positioned his army of 45,000 men on the west bank of the river Weser, about 1½ miles north of Minden, with 6,000 men blocking the French supply line. As de Contades realised that his communications with France were endangered, he set out to drive a wedge between the Allies and the river. Towards this end he constructed eight extra bridges across the river; his tactic was to take Ferdinand by surprise. He did not know that this had been compromised when their messenger delivering orders between

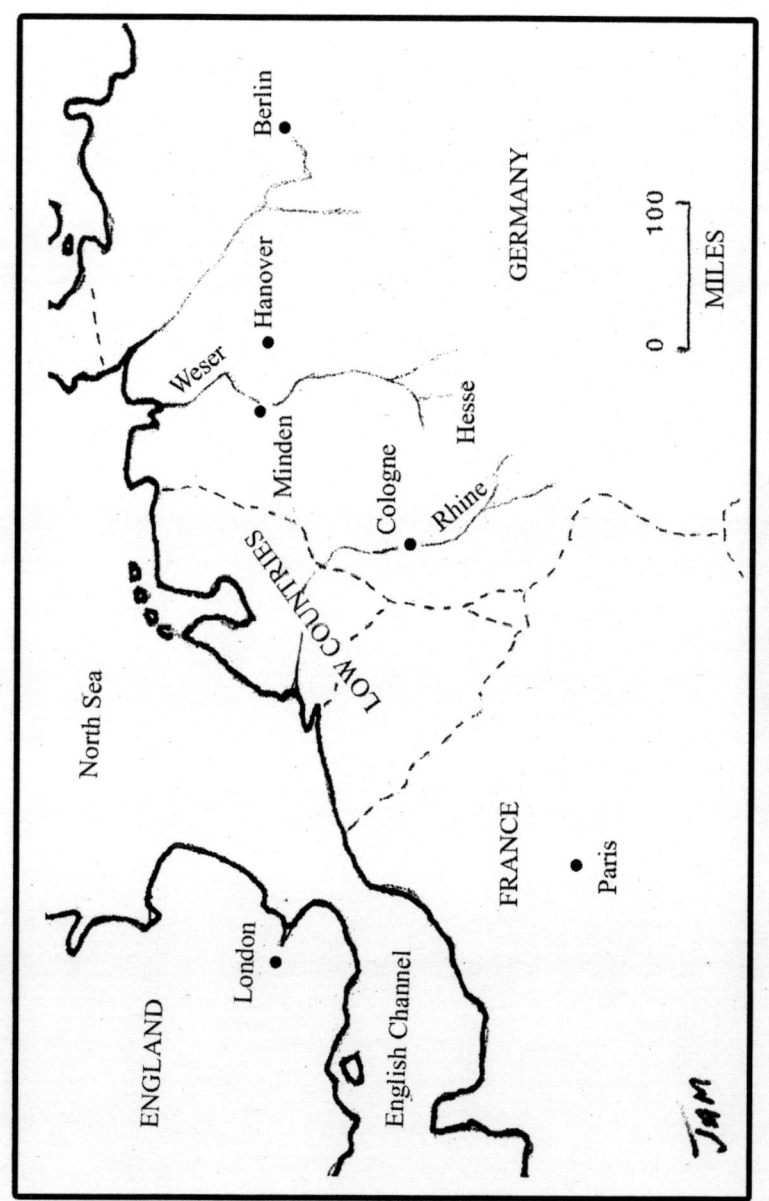

EUROPE 1759

French regimental commanders, revealed their intention to the Allies. Regardless, de Contades decided to attack.

During the night of 31st July the French army commenced their advance. Forewarned, Ferdinand ordered his army to prepare to meet them; he felt that his cavalry needed to be ready by 1 a.m. and the infantry by 3 a.m.

The French position was very strong, their rear was covered by the Weser and to their left was a marsh. The ground in front was good for infantry albeit only 2,000 yards wide. To advance on this relatively narrow front, de Contades changed the accepted practice and placed his cavalry, commanded by the Duke of FitzJames in the centre with his infantry on the flanks. This formation was probably used due to the centre ground being slightly more suitable for his cavalry. At dawn on the 1st August 1759 de Contades ordered the attack.

Ferdinand's army was extended over a three-mile front with the British contingent on the right flank. On the left, in front of the village of Todtenhausen were regiments commanded by Lieutenant-General Wangenheim. Marshal de Contades sent the Duc de Broglie to cut the lines of the Allies, thus isolating Wangenheim and the left flank. As de Broglie advanced, a heavy storm broke and his objective was obscured, slowing his advance and allowing the general to bring his guns into action. The French move stalled, and came to a total standstill.

Ferdinand believed that the French, who were in the process of changing their formation, were vulnerable. He therefore sought to move against them while they were in the act of deployment. His reserve consisted of six British infantry Regiments of Foot, the 12th, 20th, 23rd, 25th, 37th and the 51st, together with three Hanoverian Guards regiments, all under the Hanoverian Sporcken, to whom Ferdinand sent an order through an aide-de-camp that 'when an advance begins, it is to be made with drums beating'. Sporcken took this to mean – advance, drums beating, with such regiments as you have and attack anything in front. It was this misunderstanding which led to the action that covered the Minden regiments with honour.

De Contades saw that his cavalry was being approached by infantry, as from the woods behind the village of Hahlen, emerged red-coated soldiers. On the right of the line were two British infantry brigades well ahead of the main line but oblique to his own, and directly opposite the French cavalry, led by the Marquis de Castries, who became alarmed that the regiment (12th) on the right of the British line was only 100 yards from his own front line.

The British and Hanoverian infantry commanded by the Earl of Waldergrave advanced as ordered with drums beating, under fire from French artillery, their ranks closing as men fell. Eleven squadrons of French cavalry hurled themselves against the infantry, but they carried no firearms, only swords. The British held their fire until the French were within ten paces. The volley smashed the oncoming horsemen who reeled back. As repeated drill had demanded, the infantry closed ranks, reloaded and again moved forward to the beat of drum.

The French attacked again, only to be met by a second volley which had an even greater effect than the first. As horses and men fell, those that could tried to regain their earlier position. It was now 9 a.m. and for the third time de Contades sent his cavalry to overrun the advancing infantry, who met the charge in unwavering line.

As the French cavalry retired, they were pounded by British artillery, the French centre disintegrated. Marshal de Contades, having watched the defeat, later declared that 'I never thought to see a single column of infantry break through three lines of cavalry ranked in order of battle, and tumble them in ruins'.

With the cavalry in retreat, the Count de Lusace, following his earlier orders, brought forward French and Saxon infantry against the British right. The 12th and 37th Formed to face them, and were soon joined by the 20th foot. There was a brief engagement before the remaining rear line British regiments also joined the melee, where together they fired several volleys which forced the enemy to retire.

The remainder of the battle belonged to British and Hanoverian cavalry. The conflict was won as panic turned to rout. Minden was surrendered the next day. The beaten French dispersed over the countryside, a broken rabble having lost over 7,000 men and seventeen standards, British infantry losses were 81 officers and just over 1,300 killed or wounded.

Some accounts vary regarding where and when roses, whatever their colour, were picked and placed in the bonnets of the British infantry. Whatever the truth, roses have since been worn in the hats of 'Minden' regiments on the 1st August each year.

In January 1801 the battle honour MINDEN was awarded to the British infantry regiments who distinguished themselves in the action:

12th Foot – Lieutenant-General Robert Napier – Suffolk Regiment
20th Foot – Major-General William Kingsley – 2nd Battalion Lancashire Fus.
23rd Foot – Lieutenant-General John Huske – Royal Welch Fusiliers
25th Foot – Lieutenant-General The Earl of Home – K.O.S.B.
37th Foot – Lieutenant-General Hon James Stuart – 1st Bn Hampshire Regt.
51st Foot – Major-General Thomas Brudenell – 1st Battalion K.O.Y.L.I.

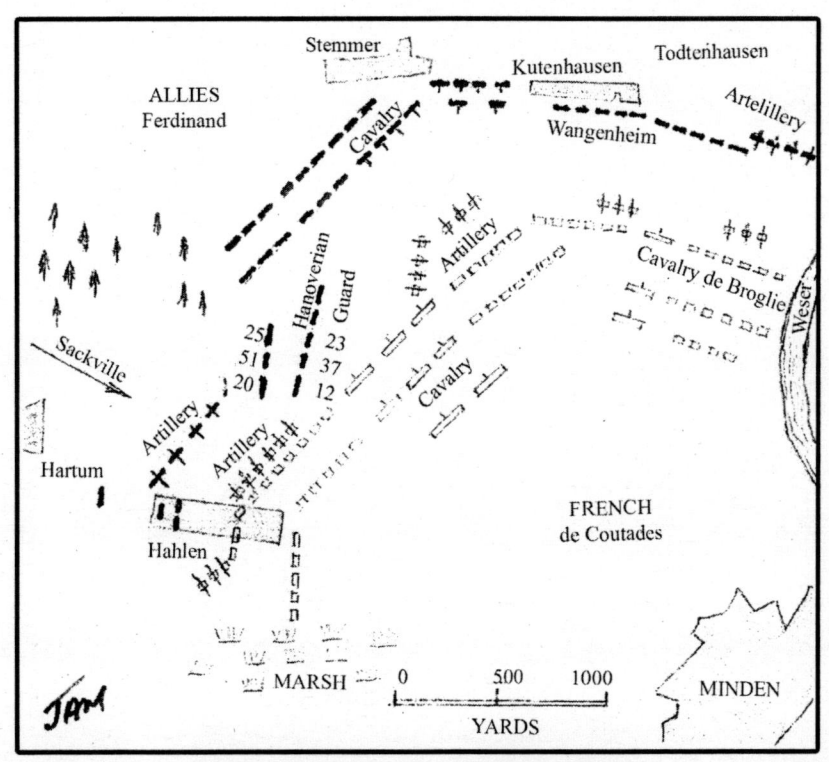

BATTLE OF MINDEN
1st August 1759

CHAPTER XVIII

SEVEN YEARS WAR 1756-1763
GEORGE III
BELLE ILE AND WILHELMSTAHL

The end of the 'Seven Years War' came unofficially in November 1762, but was not formalized until February 1763 with the Treaty of Paris. Actions in the latter stages of 1762 were generally to give greater negotiating power, to whichever of the major parties was in possession of areas at the cessation of the war.

In the autumn of 1760, Pitt proposed the capture of an island off the coast of France. Belle Ile guarded the approach to Quiberon Bay and the Loire estuary. It had little tactical value and if taken, could have caused re-supply problems if the surrounding seas were not controlled by the British navy. Pitt's proposal was agreed.

The navy under the command of Augustus 1st Viscount Keppel, sailed from England in March 1761 with ten ships of the line, eight frigates and at least one hundred transports, carrying about 7,000 troops from the 3rd, 9th, 19th, 21st, 30th, 36th, 67th and 69th Regiments of Foot.

The army was commanded by Major-General Studholme Hodgson who was an officer experienced in European warfare, having served at the battle of Dettingen in 1743.

After an eight-day passage, the flotilla arrived on 6th April, where they found that the French, fearing an attack, had fortified the whole of the island. The British landed in three places, but the defenders repulsed the leading men from the regiments, who sustained heavy casualties, and were forced to retreat to the haven of their transports.

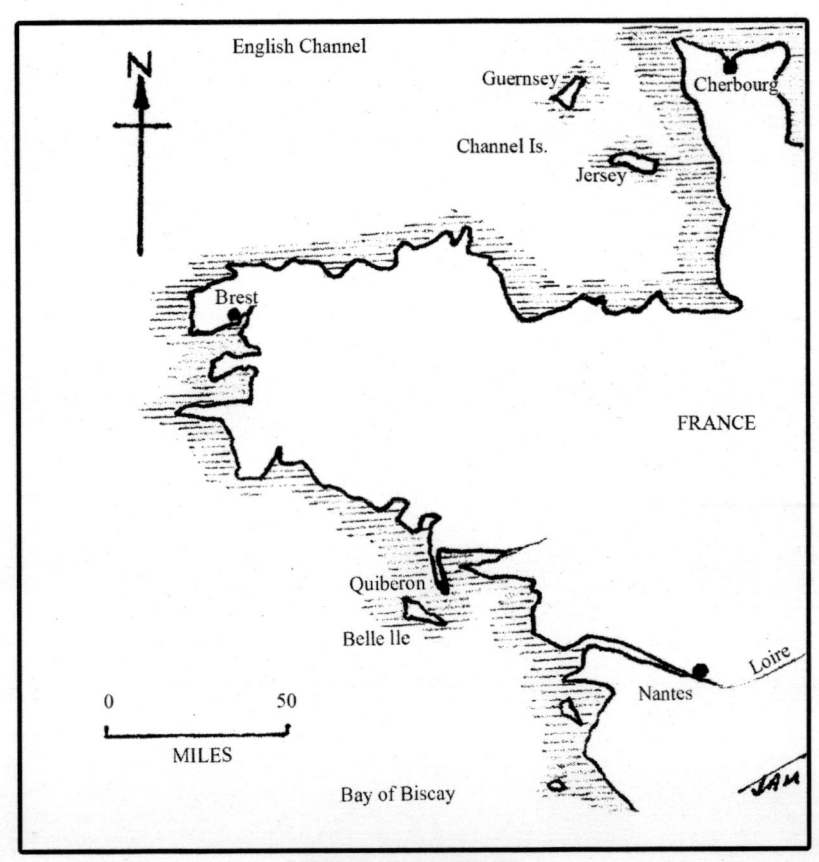

BELLE ILE
June 1761

On the 22nd April the attack was again pressed, and this time Keppel's ships kept up a heavy barrage, enabling the British infantry to land and climb the steep cliffs at Locmaria Point. The leading troops secured a foothold which enabled the main attack to move steadily across the island. Most defences were overrun as French troops retreated to their citadel at Le Palais to which Hodgson laid siege. This lasted until the 7th June, when the garrison surrendered.

As was the custom with an honourably negotiated surrender between European enemies, the French were allowed to march out with drums beating and standards flying, they were then transported to the mainland.

The island was held by the British without further incident until it became part of the negotiations used when peace was declared.

The battle honour BELLEISLE was awarded as late as 1951 to:

3rd Foot – Major-General George Howard – The Buffs, (East Kent Regt}
9th Foot – Major-General William Whitmore – The Norfolk Regt.
19th Foot – Lieutenant-General Lord George Beauclerk – Green Howards.
21st Foot – Lt-Gen The Earl of Panmure – Royal Scots Fusiliers
30th Foot – Lt-Gen The Earl of Loudon – 1st Battalion East Lancs Regt.
36th Foot – Lord Robert Manners – 2nd Battalion Worcestershire Regt.
67th Foot – Hamilton Lambert – 2nd Battalion Hampshire Regt.
69th Foot – Charles Colville – 2nd Battalion Welch Regt.

*

WILHELMSTAHL

The 5th Regiment of Foot, the Northumberland Fusiliers were the only regiment who, in May 1836 were awarded the battle honour WILHELMSTAHL for their involvement in the battle.

In 1762 they had sailed for Germany to join the army of Prince Ferdinand of Brunswick under the Marquis of Granby. At the battle of Wilhelmstahl in Silesia on the 24th June 1762, they oversaw the surrender of more than twice their number of French grenadiers together with their standards.

To celebrate, they took the grenadier caps from the Frenchmen and were afterwards, allowed as a British regiment, to wear a similar pattern, instead of the type worn by other regiments of the British army. To commemorate the victory, Prince Ferdinand presented a snuff box to the commanding officer of the 5th, Lieutenant-Colonel Marly.

CHAPTER XIX

CANADA 1763–1767
GEORGE III

In 1763 the Treaty of Paris granted to Great Britain all of the territory in North America east of the Mississippi, which had previously been held by France.

Following the defeat of the French, the British government decided to reduce the strength of the army which now occupied all of the military posts that had been garrisoned by the French. The only exception to this was Fort Chartres, which was located on the east bank of the Mississippi.

Although by the summer of 1763 when hostilities against the French had ceased, the problems for the British were certainly not over, as local Indians, fired by French propaganda that under the British they would lose their land, were worried. Moreover the amount of strong drink to which many of the Indian nations had become accustomed, brought out a fighting spirit in the youth of the tribes.

In the regions vacated by the French, the Indians had united mainly in the Ottawa area, under a war chief called Pontiac, attacking many farmsteads and small military posts between Lake Erie and Fort Pitt, leaving the only major garrisons, albeit under attack but still held by the British, as Fort Detroit, located upon the straits of Lakes Erie and Huron, also Fort Pitt. Both were garrisoned by the 60th Foot (Royal Americans).

It was considered that both forts should be relieved as a matter of urgency, but following the conditions contained in the Treaty of Paris and the British requirement to honour these terms, a force should also be sent to relieve the French soldiers currently in Fort Chartres. Following the reduction of the army, it was difficult to find sufficient troops to fulfil the relief of all of the areas threatened by the Indians.

The relief of Fort Pitt was considered by the British to be their first requirement. Towards this end, the man chosen for the expedition was Colonel Henry Bouquet, a Swiss officer who already commanded the 1st Battalion of the 60th Regiment of Foot. He was joined by men from the 42nd Foot (Royal Highlanders) and a self-styled 77th Highland Regiment of Militia, in all 956 men.

Bouquet and his column reached Bushy Run in western Pennsylvania at the end of July 1763. He was held up as he approached the narrow pass which ran within steep sides with rising wooded areas ahead. The location was ideal for Indian ambush, but as the regiments stood firm and would not be drawn into attack, a stalemate existed.

After two days, to resolve the situation, Bouquet ordered his advance companies to retire. The Indians, believing that victory was within their grasp, charged in such a random fashion that the disciplined fire from the regular companies of the 42nd and 60th Regiments tore them apart, inflicting a heavy defeat. Bouquet then resumed his march towards Fort Pitt, where his men spent the winter.

Early in the summer of 1764, the regiments under Bouquet, now a brigadier-general, moved into Indian country. These encroachments increased the Indian annoyance prompting them to retaliate with great fury, picking the soft targets of isolated farmsteads. The army ordered Bouquet with eight companies of the 42nd, the Light Infantry of the 60th and 400 Virginian marksmen, together with a detachment of men from Maryland and Pennsylvania, to repel their attacks and quell the uprising.

In February 1764, a column comprising men from the 22nd Foot (the Cheshire Regiment) made an attempt to reach the French still holding Fort Chartres. After many weeks cutting their way through thick undergrowth and forests where they were frequently attacked by small parties of Indians, they had by the 20th of May reached 240 miles north of New Orleans, when another group of Indians attacked their advance party comprising men from the 34th Foot (1st Battalion, the Border Regiment), several of them were killed and, seeing an unequal contest, the officer in charge ordered a retreat.

On the other hand, Bouquet's expedition into the Ohio territory was so successful that the large-scale Indian attacks were greatly reduced. Pontiac continued sporadic operations in the areas now known as Indiana and Illinois, but these soon ceased.

The general cessation of hostilities allowed the British forces in North America under the command of General Thomas Gage to turn their attention to the relief of Fort Chartres. The 42nd arrived at the fort on 17th April 1765 but instead of relieving the garrison, they were threatened by local Indians who had been promised substantial gifts. Unfortunately nothing suitable had arrived, therefore the 42nd retired under cover of darkness. They arrived at New Orleans on 19th June. It was not until the 10th October that the formal surrender of the fort took place as part of the ceremonies marking the official end of hostilities.

A detachment of the 34th took over from the 42nd who, in the summer of 1767 were ordered to embark for Ireland, leaving several of their numbers who wished to stay behind in North America.

Bouquet had earned for himself and the men he led, the credit of having finally broken the French influence and Indian power in the west, giving the British all of the territory west of the Allegheny Mountains.

It is hard to understand why in 1914, after 150 years, that under Army Order No 2, the battle honour NORTH AMERICA 1763/64 was given to:

42nd (Royal Highlanders) Regiment of Foot – The Black Watch
60th (or Royal Americans) – The King's Royal Rifle Corps

This all came under the heading of 'Pontiac's conspiracy', this is totally incorrect, as he hardly became anything other than a local chief looking after his interests and those of his people.

CHAPTER XX

AMERICAN WAR OF INDEPENDENCE
1775–1783
GEORGE III

In this chapter, in the interest of clarity, the 'colonists' or 'rebels' are referred to as Americans.

The conclusion of the Seven Years War in Europe and the Treaty of Paris signed on 10th February 1763, caused the expulsion of the French from North America, and left the territory from Canada to the Gulf of Mexico under British rule.

For over one hundred years, people from Scotland, Ireland, Wales and England had crossed the Atlantic for North America. Over time they had established the thirteen New England colonies. There was one incident which history has termed the 'Boston Massacre'. The trouble began on Friday the 2nd March 1770 when men from the 29th Foot (the Worcestershire Regiment) tried to obtain spare-time work to augment their meagre pay. The regiment had been in Boston for several months, they had not caused any trouble but the locals had objected to the soldiers taking work ahead of them. Three days later, a group of men attacked a sentry on duty, against orders he opened fire killing several people. Hundreds attended the funerals; this led in the area to a deep resentment of British troops.

The colonies belonged to the Crown, but the distance between England and America made communication slow and often confused, leading to a breakdown between them and King George with his advisors in London.

To the Americans, this total lack of interest from the Crown led them to dream of self-government. Against British Government policy, they bought land from the local Indians and set up their own trading companies, which since they no longer had to fear invasion from the French, flourished.

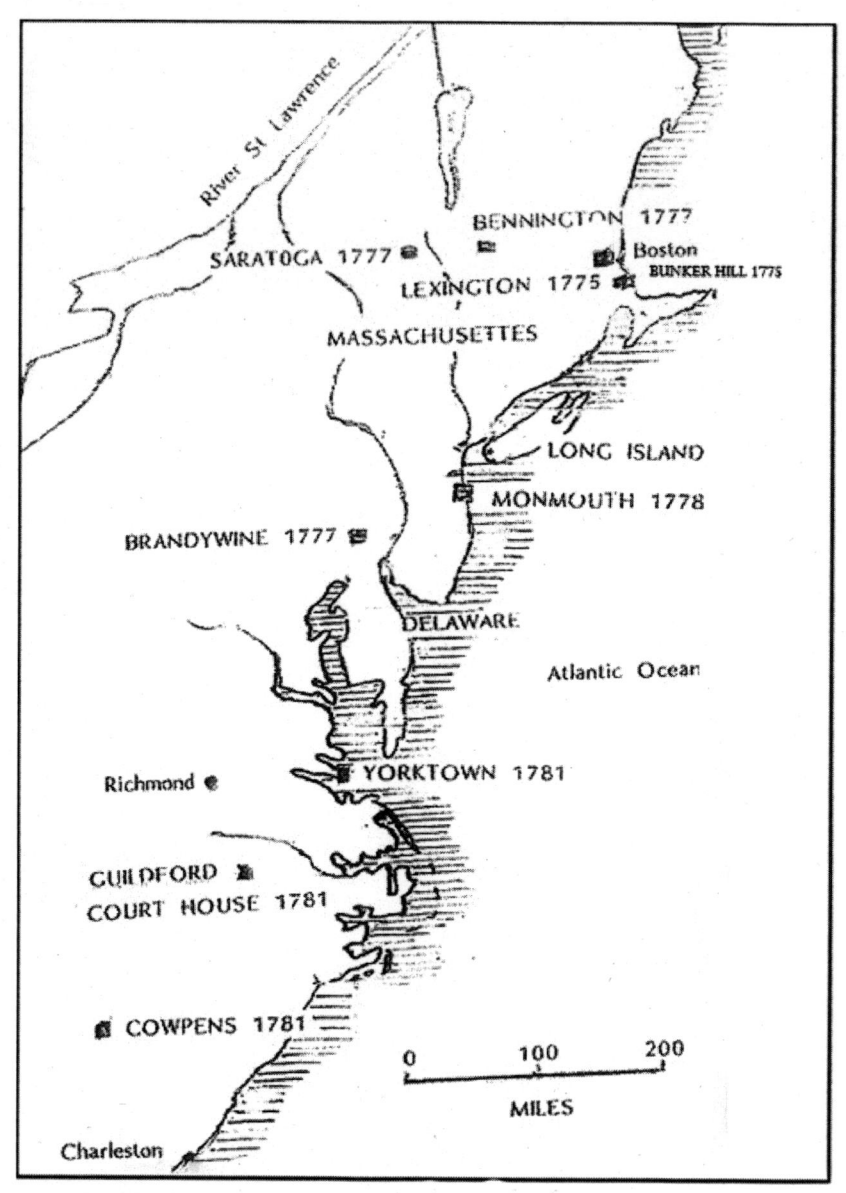

AMERICA - EAST COAST 1781

The King was determined that the colonies should pay for the British troops in garrison there. He therefore imposed taxes, firstly on molasses preventing them selling their produce to the Spanish and French West Indies, but upon imposition of this tax, the Crown still looked for more from the colony.

Completely ignoring American protests as they had no representation in the House of Commons and therefore had no influence in decisions which affected them, they should not be taxed by people who did not understand their new way of life. The Government supported the East India Company who, although facing bankruptcy, had an enormous surplus of tea. Parliament passed an Act authorising the EIC both to ship their tea directly to the colony without having to pay import duties, and to sell through their own agents in America, thus in effect, granting them a monopoly. This united colonial opinion against the Crown, especially amongst the merchants. Loyalists accepted that they owed allegiance to the Crown but many were annoyed that their trade was being badly affected by an out of touch, short-sighted policy of King George and the British Government.

On 16th December 1773 a group of Americans, who had refused to pay the duty on a cargo of tea, dressed as Red Indians and threw a whole consignment of tea into the waters of Boston harbour. History has called this the 'Boston Tea Party'.

When news of this reached London, the British Government misread the attitude of the Americans, believing that Loyalists far outnumbered the few hotheads who were out to cause trouble. To counteract this, Parliament passed a series of acts forcing the Americans to conform to measures set up by the Crown. These Coercion Acts declared that the whole colony was in Crown hands, the Massachusetts Assembly was suspended and the Port of Boston closed. Also passed at the same time was the Quartering Act, designed to prevent occurrences similar to that which had happened in Boston earlier, and which ordered that British troops should be quartered throughout the colony to keep order.

On 5th September 1774 the colonial assemblies held a Congress in Philadelphia. They did not wish to provoke any form of military action, instead, it was agreed to form an association to stop trade with

England unless the Coercion Acts were repealed. A document stating these demands was sent to London where it was badly received and rejected out of hand.

At this time most regiments of foot consisted of ten companies which included a company of light infantry and also a right flank company of grenadiers, in all about 480 men. Total British army strength was just under 50,000 men of which three quarters were infantry. Most were located in England, Scotland or Ireland others were in small garrisons in Africa, India and Gibraltar, whilst only a few thousand were in North America and the West Indies.

The British soldier was armed with a smooth-bore flintlock musket commonly called the Brown Bess, although the derivation of this name is unknown. They also carried a seventeen-inch-long socket bayonet. The muskets and their individual flints were generally the cheapest available, therefore were considered to be inferior by the Americans who used the smaller bore long rifle, which although not made in Kentucky was so called during the hostilities.

Various skirmishes broke out in several places between belligerent Americans and British troops where tactics separated the sides, the British tended to advance in tightly formed ranks with fixed bayonets, this having proved so successful in European warfare, whereas the Americans who knew the county well were used to repelling Indian attacks by shooting from behind cover and retiring when necessary. Both sides followed their own style, often with disastrous outcome.

Every year that passed the danger of conflict grew and the hope of reconciliation receded. It became evident to the Massachusetts Military Governor, General Thomas Gage, that in the spring of 1775 the Americans were collecting military stores at Concord, eighteen miles from Boston. Gage wanted to enforce martial law, but as he only had four thousand troops in Boston he felt that he had to keep any proposed action secret, although it soon became obvious to the inhabitants of Boston that some sort of military expedition was being prepared.

On the night of the 18th April 1775, 800 British troops under the command of Lieutenant-Colonel Francis Smith of the 10th Foot (Lincolnshire Regiment), left Boston and moved under cover of darkness along the road to Concord. The 10th Foot had originally embarked from Ireland in the spring of 1767 and after a short stay in Nova Scotia had been sent to Boston. For this latest operation the men were not told of their destination as it was feared that this would have somehow been conveyed to the Americans. The soldiers were simply ordered to move quickly and quietly out of the town.

The Americans had been on the alert, and a lookout rode to Lexington to give the alarm. The assembly at Concord was warned and the material there was moved to outlying areas. When British troops reached Concord following a skirmish at Lexington, any remaining stores were destroyed. When the troops had completed their duties and tried to retire, they found that the country had risen against them, as a result they had to fight their way back, losing many dead and wounded.

Hostilities had commenced and in a few days the Americans had 20,000 armed men in the field. To take advantage of the situation the American Benedict Arnold, now a captain, proposed to his superiors in Massachusetts that he should mount an expedition against the British at Crown Point and Ticonderoga. Arnold came from a long-established New England family; his great-grandfather had been Governor of Rhode Island in 1663 for fifteen years. Although Arnold received permission for his venture, he failed to encourage enough men to enlist with him, therefore had to join a force under Ethan Allen, who on the 10th May captured Ticonderoga. Following a difference of opinion with his senior officers, Arnold resigned his captaincy under Allen and as a result was placed under General Montgomery.

In the late summer of 1775, Arnold took his column up the Hudson river to invade Canada. By November, after long marches across difficult terrain he had reached within a few miles of Quebec where, to his annoyance, he had to wait for Montgomery to join him. This did not happen until late in December. During this time, Arnold did not fear an encounter with British troops, as he knew that they were only in very small garrisons spread over vast areas. On 31st December the Americans made an assault on Quebec; it was a complete failure, Montgomery was killed and Arnold wounded as the invading force was driven by the British defenders from the area in full retreat.

When news of the American invasion of Canada reached London, it was again considered to be little more than a colony registering a protest. Had Parliament believed that it was more serious it would have been regarded as civil war, a situation where many British officers would have been reluctant to take arms against fellow officers who had been with them during the earlier Seven Years War. This would especially affect those officers who, as Tory Members of Parliament, hoped that this uprising was only a disturbance caused by a few, who were probably Whigs, supporting American loyalists against the Tory Government. Although most officers favoured the Tories, a few were for the Whigs. A good example was Lord Howe, a Whig Member of Parliament who had promised his constituency that he would never serve against the American colonists. However his advancement in the English social order almost certainly later forced him to abandon his principles and take such an appointment.

Following the problems which he had encountered during the return from Concord, Gage decided that he had no option but to stay in Boston. He was aware of the view of the home government that because of his inability to crush what they believed to be a minor disturbance, as the commanding general, he was fairly weak. Therefore they were sending three more generals, William Howe, who as a colonel had led the picked detachment up the cliffs in 1759 at the Battle of Quebec, Major-General Henry Clinton who had served in Europe during the Seven Years War and Major-General John Burgoyne, who in an age where most officers cared little for their men was different, in that he believed it was his duty to see to their well-being.

On 25th May 1775, the generals with infantry reinforcements sailed into Boston harbour, bringing British strength up to just over 6,000 men. Although the Charlestown peninsular was of great strategic importance, it had been evacuated by both sides; first by the Americans who were aware that the British Navy, anchored in the immediate area, could shell them and secondly by the cautious Gage who felt that he had insufficient troops to occupy it in strength.

On the night of the 16th June, taking the initiative the Americans moved men onto the peninsula. In about four hours in total darkness they constructed a shoulder-high earthen fort on Breed's Hill, and in case the British decided to move against them, they sent two companies of sharpshooters into Charlestown to act as snipers. The

Americans' main objective was to move up heavy cannon with which to attack Boston and hopefully drive the British from the town.

The noise of construction which was made by them was considered by the British to be nothing more than a demonstration to unnerve the townsfolk and garrison. Gage decided that he should move in strength to show the Americans that he believed their nocturnal activities were bad manners.

He decided on a frontal attack. In the afternoon of the 17th June 1775, ten light infantry and ten grenadier companies, which Howe had formed into an assault corps directly led by him, marched down to the landing stage. They wore thick scarlet winter uniforms totally unsuitable for the climate and presenting an excellent target for the Americans. They were watched by a large crowd of civilians who were lining the rooftops and vantage points in and around Boston.

It was not until 1.30 p.m. that the first troops departed in naval longboats. The choice of a landing area in the peninsular was influenced by the unavailability to Howe of flat-bottomed landing barges, which would have been able to negotiate a direct crossing over the shallows, instead the force had to move further north to Norton's Point.

As the first wave of troops were rowed from Long Wharf, British cannon on Copp's Hill and the guns of the fleet maintained a covering fire, enabling the light infantry and grenadiers to form a skirmish line. This allowed men from the:

4th Foot (King's Own [Royal Lancashire] Regiment)
5th Foot (Northumberland Fusiliers)
23rd Foot (Royal Welch Fusiliers)
38th Foot (1st Battalion, the South Staffordshire Regiment)
43rd Foot (1st Battalion, the Oxfordshire Light Infantry)
52nd Foot (2nd Battalion, the Oxfordshire Light Infantry).

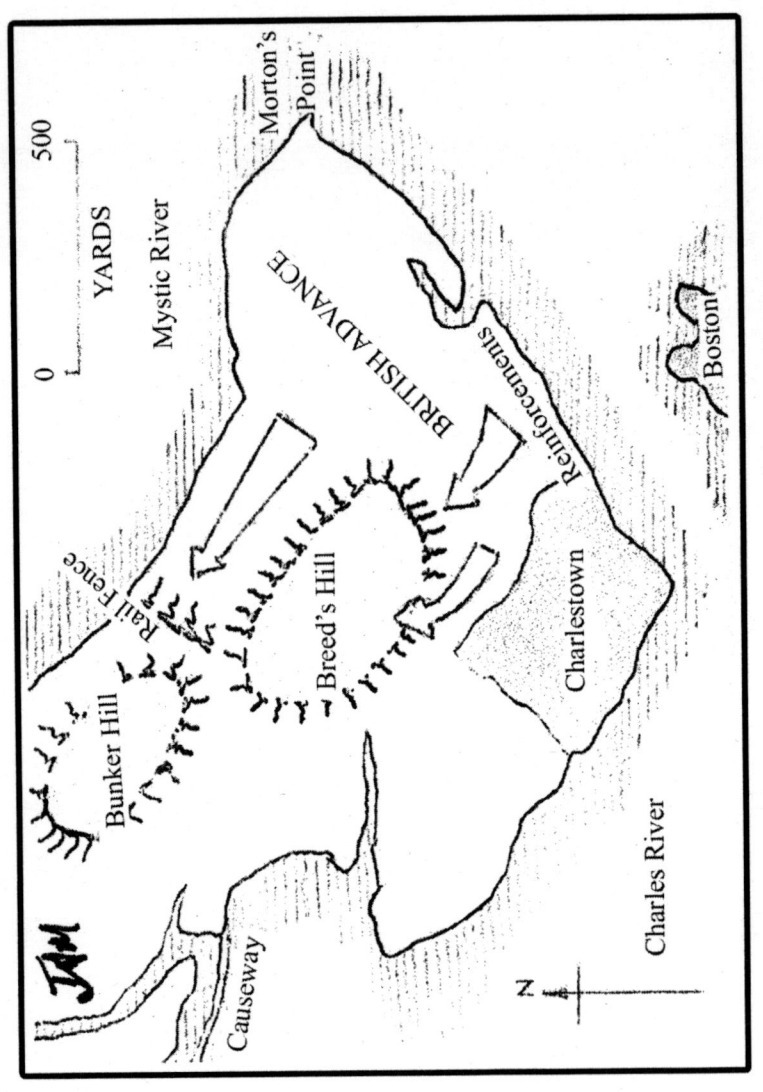

BUNKER HILL 1775

to land unopposed. Once ashore, Howe ordered the men to relax, pile their arms and eat their midday rations. During this delay the situation changed to Howe's disadvantage, as the earthworks on the slopes of Breed's Hill were now fully manned by the Americans. A low stone wall also existed extending down to the Mystic River. Behind it on Bunker Hill another thousand militiamen were preparing defensive positions.

Although the buildings in Charlestown had been set on fire by red-hot shot from the British fleet under Admiral Graves, sniper fire from there was still being directed against the British far left flank. Major Pitcairn from the 10th Foot with Marines and the 47th Foot (1st Battalion, the Loyal North Lancashire Regiment) moved to eliminate this danger from the American sharpshooters, while Brigadier-General Robert Pigot who commanded the left wing composed of the 38th and 43rd Foot regiments moved against the breastwork and redoubt.

Howe's original intention had been to demonstrate to both the watchers in Boston and the Americans, how British infantry could advance in immaculate ranks regardless of enemy fire directed against them until they were within bayonet range, with the damage that that particular weapon could inflict.

Events did not unfold how he had intended, as he led the grenadiers of the 5th and 52nd Foot regiments against the stone wall in his attempt to turn the American flank. Slowly and majestically the British, in three red lines, advanced up the slope towards the American defenders on Bunker Hill. Their progress was hampered by waist-high grass which hid ground made uneven by loose rocks.

An American officer, experienced in the tactics of the British infantry, but also aware that many of his men were short of barricades, ordered his men to hold their fire until the British reached the post, then to aim at the officers first.

The light infantry were the first to feel the effect of the American volley, their second rank stepping over the dead and wounded on the ground. With the next volley more men fell, causing whole ranks to falter and some to retreat. Howe roared his men on with their bayonets; he was supported by regiments under Pigot. Behind the barricades the men from Connecticut fired, the carnage on the British regiments was extensive. Twice the assault was beaten back by well-aimed fire from the Americans. The third attempt succeeded but, of the 10th Foot, every officer was hit and many other ranks killed or wounded.

Clinton sent word to Gage that he was moving to support Howe and that he had ordered the 63rd Foot (1st Battalion, the Manchester Regiment) to be rowed across to land near Charlestown. They were to be joined by the 65th Foot (1st Battalion, the York and Lancaster Regiment) who had been sent to America seven years earlier.

In the forefront of the offensive, Howe regrouped the regiments; he had now been joined by Clinton and the force from Copp's Hill. Howe had lost nearly all of the grenadiers and light infantry, and many companies from the regiments had lost nearly three quarters of their men.

As he neared the objective, Howe was able to wheel his whole force up the hill to take the defenders in flank. The manoeuvre worked, for this time he broke through. American resistance collapsed, they had almost run out of powder. The sight of ranks of British infantry advancing with fixed bayonets was enough to cause the militiamen to run.

Of the three thousand Americans who had held the ridge, nearly a sixth had been killed or severely wounded, mainly in the latter stages of the battle. But British losses were far worse, twenty-seven officers had been killed amongst them was Major Pitcairn of the 10th Foot, a further sixty-three officers had been wounded, some would later die. British soldiers fared far worse, 226 men had been killed with just under a thousand more falling on the slopes.

Howe had captured the hill but it was not the victory that he had envisaged. Many of the British soldiers of all ranks were facing men firing from behind barricades, a practice which they considered unacceptable. Therefore they behaved badly and on several occasions actually broke ranks.

Gage believed that the army had sustained too many casualties and, such was their exhaustion, they were unable to follow up the advantage of the American defeat on Bunker Hill, so any pursuit of the fleeing enemy was abandoned. According to Richard Pope, an officer in the 47th Foot, the remainder of the summer was spent in Boston with 'some style'.

On 3rd July 1775, the Americans confirmed that General Washington should take command of the army currently investing Boston. This was not a difficult task as because of British inactivity, all he had to do was to maintain a presence in the immediate area.

The British Government in London, dismayed at the lack of action by the army to put down 'this civil unrest', blamed Gage, and on 26th September handed the command to Howe. As summer wore on, the fine sunshine days gave way to a cold and wet winter, keeping the troops, albeit short of provisions, in Boston.

Early in 1776, in an effort to break the stalemate General Clinton moved south with a large force. This was followed on 17th March with the evacuation of Boston by the British. At the same time, American delegates at the Second Continental Congress in Philadelphia agreed that if independence was to be achieved, foreign alliances were required, and a formal statement should by issued. It was agreed that a rich Virginian planter, Thomas Jefferson, was the best qualified to create the statement. After days developing the first draft, on 28th June he produced the document. Despite much discussion regarding the content, on the evening of 4th July 1776 the text was formally approved. The Declaration was sighed and the American colonies became independent communities.

There was a skirmish south of Norfolk at Long Bridge where about 900 local Americans formed a barricade. The only British military in the area were sailors and loyalists with a few black troops. The Governor of Virginia called for regular British units and when they arrived, he ordered the officers to move against the Americans.

As the regiments moved along a causeway in single file they were met by very heavy fire again directed towards the officers, many were killed before the Americans retired and dispersed into the countryside. The news of this uprising was conveyed to London. However the Governor of North Carolina assured them that it was only a minor disturbance and that the loyalists in America still fully

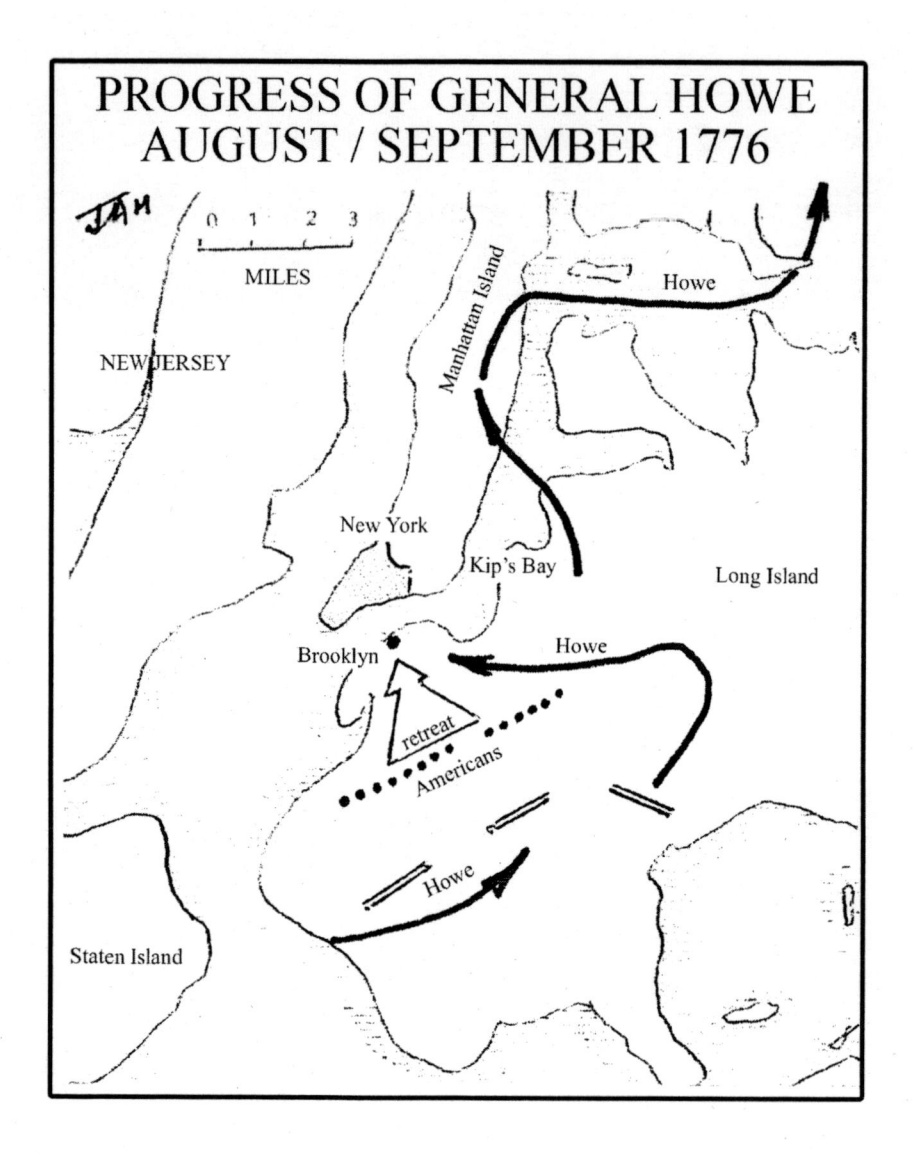

PROGRESS OF GENERAL HOWE AUGUST / SEPTEMBER 1776

supported the Crown, and that there was total support in the colony for England.

One can understand how difficult it was for the British Government in London to accept that the settlers in America did not believe that they should take instructions from men who, they rightly considered, understood little that was happening so far away. It is a demonstration of this shortcoming that the Government believed that the colony was full of loyalists who would support them – regardless of the call for independence.

On the morning of 22nd August 1776, British soldiers crossed the Narrows and landed on Long Island. They included men from the 17th Foot (Leicestershire Regiment), who had landed in Boston on New Year's Day, the 35th Foot (1st Battalion, the Royal Sussex Regiment) who had recently returned to North America, the 10th Foot and the 15th Foot (East Yorkshire Regiment) who had embarked from Ireland and landed in April, also recently drafted from Ireland were the 45th Foot (1st Battalion, the Sherwood Foresters [Derbyshire] Regiment). Another regiment to be involved was the 64th Foot (1st Battalion, the Prince of Wales's [North Staffordshire] Regiment).

Washington had spent the summer on the island preparing defences which, when approached by British troops, enabled them to bring steady fire against the ranks of the regulars, killing about forty of them.

Clinton moved to outflank the Americans, who again fired from behind their earthworks. Although Clinton achieved the objective of forcing the Americans to retire, which allowed him to enter New York, he lost just under four hundred men who fell under the heavy fusillades, with twenty-one officers also killed or badly wounded. Once again the British failed to take advantage of this apparent victory, because of Howe's belief that talks involving the loyalists would produce the best results for the colony and were the thoughts of the Government in London.

There were a few skirmishes towards the end of 1776 at White Plains where the 28th Foot (1st Battalion, the Gloucestershire Regiment), who had sailed for North America in 1775, earned their second

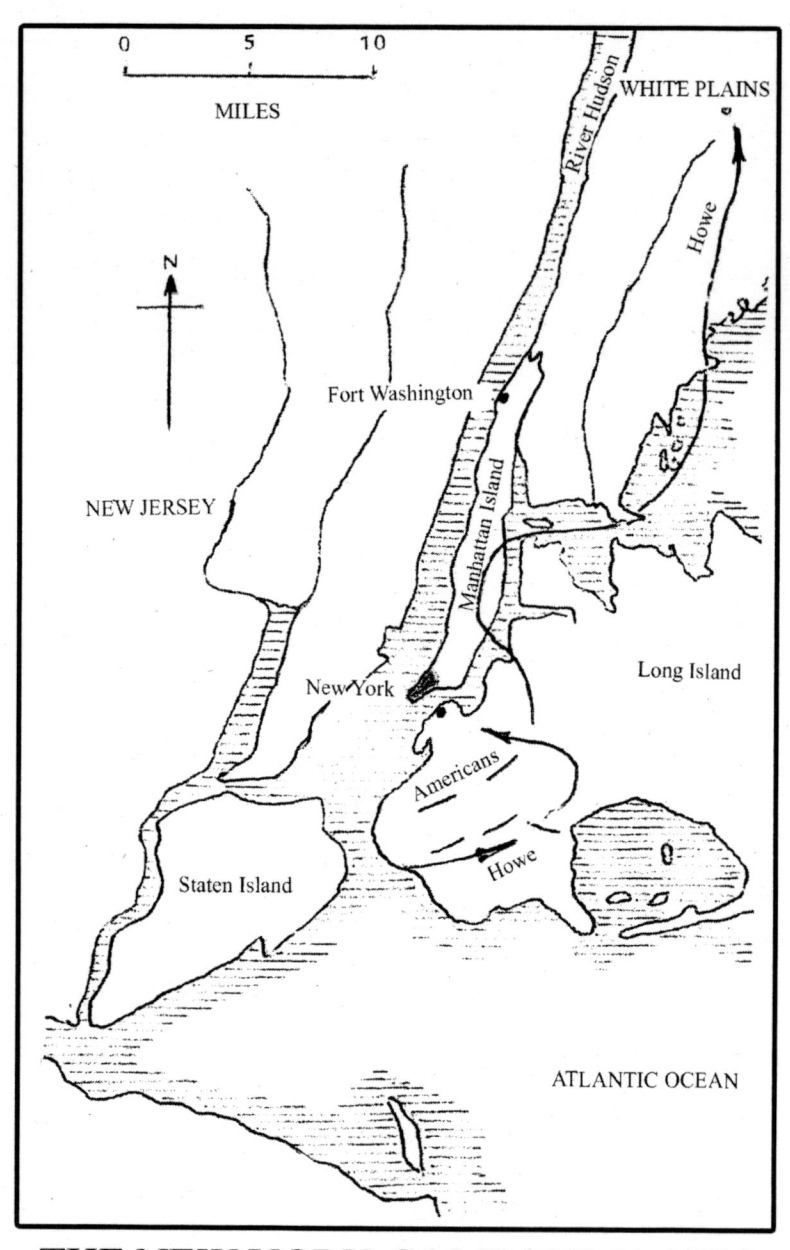

THE NEW YORK CAMPAIGN - 1776

nickname 'The Slashers'. The attack involved crossing the river under fire, the regiment was then faced by a steep cliff upon which were the American positions. The men, unable to climb burdened by their heavy equipment and muskets, were ordered to scramble up without firearms. When at the top they drew their sword bayonets to 'slash' their way through long grass and then drove the Americans from the area. They had also been encouraged by the 13th Foot (Somerset Light Infantry) who took part in the action. Following garrison duty in New York, the 28th were finally sent to the West Indies. Early on the misty morning of 3rd January 1777 the 17th Foot, with a strength of 250 men under Colonel Mawhood marched from Princetown to Trenton with men from the 28th Foot. There they met 3,000 Americans under General Washington. The 17th Foot attacked and drove the American vanguard through an orchard capturing a battery of guns, but then found themselves surrounded. With drums beating and bayonets fixed they broke their way out carrying their Colours, an action which cost over one hundred men killed. Colonel Mawhood was complimented by Washington, but more importantly King George 111 commended the action and awarded the regiment the unbroken laurel wreath surrounding the tiger on their collar badge.

This action had decided little. The winter of 1776 and the spring of 1777, were again spent in stalemate, due to the hierarchy of both sides following the custom of the day, in not believing that warfare should, or could, be carried out during periods of severe weather.

In early August 1777, Howe received information that Washington was at Brandywine Creek with 16,000 men. He set sail, but as the fleet moved south it was met by very stormy weather and indifferent winds before finally arriving on 25th August. Having landed the regiments, Howe learned that Washington was five miles away. It took him sixteen days to assemble the men, their equipment and supplies, delaying the commencement of his advance until 11th September.

Once there, Howe moved a column of over 1,000 men towards the American centre, while the remainder of over 12,000 men including troops from the 10th, 15th, 28th, 45th and 64th Regiments of Foot under Lord Charles Cornwallis* moved against the American right.

Washington advanced against the main British force as he felt that his rear-guard was being threatened. The Americans opened fire which was instantly followed by volleys from the British ranks who drove the Americans back. During this action, the supply of ball and powder within the ranks of the 15th Foot ran short. All soldiers handed theirs to the best shots, while they continued 'snapping' i.e. firing small charges of powder only, then running from tree to tree, hence the nickname 'The Snappers'.

At this stage, the light company of the 57th Foot (Duke of Cambridge's Own [Middlesex] Regiment) took part in a bayonet charge which accounted for 300 killed or wounded and the capture of one hundred prisoners. The Americans were so angered at the use of bayonets that they threatened to grant no quarter to British troops. In defiance and to distinguish them from other regiments, the men of the 57th light company dyed their plumes red. For many years the 57th Foot, as a regiment, wore a red piece of cloth behind their badge, to commemorate this action. It is hard to term this encounter a victory as the British suffered 557 killed or badly wounded, although American losses were over a 1,000 with hundreds taken prisoner. Three days later the army entered Philadelphia.

Three weeks later, Burgoyne commenced his march to join Howe, who appeared unprepared for the combined operation. Washington, once again with spies everywhere, received the same information and made it clear that he intended that no such liaison would take place. To further this, he brought forward additional troops with the intention of defeating Burgoyne.

Washington with an army of 6,000 men took up a strong position just a few miles from Bemis Heights. Burgoyne crossed the Hudson River by a bridge of boats and on 13th September 1777, he advanced in three columns against the American position. He was in command of the centre column, while the left column was under Baron von

---

* Lord Charles Cornwallis became the Earl of Cornwallis after the death of his father in 1762; he was then only 24 years old.

Riedesel with General Philips of the 9th Foot (Norfolk Regiment), they were supported by artillery. The right-hand column was commanded by Brigadier-General Simon Fraser.

By dawn on 17th September, the British advance guard was within four miles of the American lines. The infantry, bayonets gleaming moved against the Americans who, under Arnold tried to turn Burgoyne. The column under Fraser prevented this, and all fronts took part in fierce fighting until the British eventually fell back. By nightfall on this fateful day the British regiments counted their costs. They had lost almost a third of their strength. The 62nd Foot (1st Battalion, the Duke of Edinburgh's [Wiltshire] Regiment) commenced with a complement of almost 400 men but only about sixty survived, such was the accurate fire from the American defenders. The British dead were buried in large pits, the officers in individual graves, although three officers of the 20th Foot (Lancashire Fusiliers) were buried together.

Burgoyne prepared to mount another attack but the weather was against him, he therefore stood his men down. Further up the river, at the head of Lake George, the Americans mounted a surprise attack on the British flotilla which was at anchor, and captured all of the ships including the surrender of men from the 53rd Foot, 1st Battalion, the King's (Shropshire Light Infantry). When news of this misfortune reached Burgoyne near Saratoga, he thought of retreating to safer ground but messengers brought news that Howe had requested that Clinton should create a diversion. This did not happen because Clinton believed that to do so, would leave New York open to the Americans.

On 27th September, Burgoyne sent another message to Clinton reporting that he had only 5,000 men against an American strength estimated in excess of 12,000, armed and ready to attack him. He would try to force his way to Albany, but he required that Clinton would keep him supplied throughout the winter.

Washington, aware of the reduced numbers in the British ranks, decided to attack their camp at Germantown. Within the camp were men from the 10th, 15th, 28th, 45th and 64th Regiments.

In the early hours of the 4th October 1777, the Americans, now reinforced by Continental troops, made a sudden assault in fog so thick that it became impossible for men to identify their opponents. The Americans attached pieces of white cloth or paper to their hats, while the British were in their distinctive uniforms. Three regiments were brought forward from the reserve position, amongst them the 15th Foot, who lost their commanding officer Lieutenant-Colonel John Bird in a successful counter-attack. The engagement lasted barely three hours in which time British losses were over 500 whilst the Americans lost 652 men with 438 men surrendering.

Clinton received reinforcements which enabled him to conduct a series of operations which were totally successful, enabling him to send a message to Burgoyne from Fort Washington on 8th October. A day earlier Burgoyne, rather than retreat, made up his mind to move towards Albany. He was attacked by numerically superior Americans who forced his retreat to Saratoga, which he reached the next day.

On 17th October 1777, having lost many of his senior officers, Burgoyne sought negotiations with the enemy and finally agreed that his remaining men would be allowed to march out of their lines and pile their arms in front of the Americans. The condition, as was the tradition in European warfare, was that the men would be returned to England and take no part in further conflict. The beaten troops, having walked in captivity to Boston, learned that the American Congress did not agree with the terms and the British soldiers were sent to camps as prisoners of war. Upon the surrender the Colours of the 9th Foot were hidden by Lieutenant-Colonel Hill and were later presented to the King when the regiment finally returned to England. The 20th Foot burnt their Colours to stop them from falling into American hands. Officers from the 62nd Foot tore their Colours from their pikes, hiding them. One was restored to the regiment in 1927, apparently found in a farm barn.

Once the disaster a Saratoga became known, it made the official intervention of France more likely. King George III supported his Prime Minister, Lord North and also the mood of the country when the call for volunteers went out. In England many towns undertook to raise battalions at their own expense. Thirty-five regiments were authorized while in Scotland, Lord Macleod raised the 73rd (Highland) Regiment of Foot, titled 'Macleod's Highlanders'. In 1787 they were renumbered 71st Highland Light Infantry (City of Glasgow Regiment), also in Scotland in 1778 Lord Seaforth raised the 78th Highlanders, renumbered in 1786 as the 72nd Foot (1st Battalion Seaforth Highlanders [Rosshire Buffs] the Duke of Albany's). In Wales, the 75th Foot were authorized and came into existence as the Prince of Wales's Regiment, but in line with other fencible regiments, militia and second battalions they were disbanded after the Treaty of Paris in 1783.

As soon as it became known in Philadelphia that Clinton would replace Howe, many were relieved, for it was known that too much of his time had been spent enjoying himself at theatricals, balls and generally leading the high life. Many of his officers and their troops believed that he should have attacked Washington whose army was only twenty miles away, but Howe postulated that to risk lives when Washington was already a spent force was unnecessary.

Clinton arrived in Philadelphia on 8th May 1778. Following the American/French alliance, his first orders were to withdraw his troops to New York. Then because France, Holland and Spain saw their opportunity to move against the Caribbean Islands currently held by the British, he was to send 5,000 men to St Lucia and a further 3,000 to the coast of Florida. The instruction to move to New York was made difficult and dangerous as owing to a lack of transports on the Delaware, he was forced to move his troops overland. Early on the 18th June, he moved ahead of 10,000 troops with a baggage train if hundreds of wagons carrying supplies, equipment and sick men, stretching nearly twelve miles. He was closely followed by Washington.

As they were passing Monmouth County Court House on 28th June, the rear of the column was attacked by at least 6,000 following Americans. The British troops responded forcefully until, as darkness fell, they were given the order to stand down, only to be roused at midnight to resume the march to New York. They had lost nearly 300 officers and men, a figure slightly less than the Americans who, under Washington, abandoned the pursuit and moved north.

In October 1778 the 10th Foot transferred all of its few fit men to other regiments and the remainder, were sent back to Ireland.

Later in 1778, much further south, British activities in Georgia were increasing. The commanding officer of the 2nd Battalion, Fraser's Highlanders was Archibald Campbell the British Member of

Parliament for Stirling, whose father was the Commissioner of the Western Isles. Under Campbell's command were two battalions of Fraser's Highlanders, two German mercenary battalions, Irish and American loyalists. His first move was to visit forts in the area which appeared loyal to the Crown, before sending his men into the local territory, the sight of them brandishing their claymores was enough to persuade any American militia to beat a hasty retreat.

The town of Savannah lay in American hands. Campbell's first move was a feint against their left. When they could not hold their line, he moved forward and his troops swarmed into the town. They took thirty-four American officers and over 400 local men. On 12th May 1779 Campbell's troops reached the outskirts of Charlestown and summoned its surrender. However as he considered that he was not in sufficient strength to force his request, he soon retired.

On 2nd September 1779 a large French fleet packed with French troops approached the shore off Staten Island. Seven days later they moved up the river, forcing the British ships there to retreat before them. They began a bombardment, but after four days of shelling they had to accept that it appeared to have had little effect. Therefore they decided on an immediate assault. A confused melee ensued, the French column sent to take the British from the rear became lost in a swamp, and after hand-to-hand fighting with the 60th Foot (Royal American Regiment), until a very heavy mist fell, unable to continue the conflict, the French and local Americans withdrew.

Following instructions, Clinton sent Colonel Campbell to Georgia, but then felt that he had been left with insufficient troops to strike a decisive blow against the Americans. He became so desperate that he sent an envoy to London, believing that he could not act until reinforcements arrived and complaining that he was constantly being asked to send troops under his command to Canada or the West Indian islands. He was disappointed when reinforcements did arrive in August 1779 because there appeared to be only half of the 6,000 he had been promised and of the men that did arrive most were not of the best quality, while many were suffering from their ordeal at sea.

His difficulties increased when he was again instructed to send a further 2,000 men to Canada, where the attitude of the locals was changing due to the involvement of France in the war. With this further drain on his troop numbers, Clinton believed that New York would be lost should Washington press an attack. The American militia were having their own problems holding men available for Washington, therefore to provide enough men for an assault was not possible.

On 16th June 1779 Spain officially declared war on England, this increased fears that Britain might be invaded by France, prompting the hurried response to raise regiments for the defence of the home nations only. It was believed that once raised, these regiments would enable the transfer of established regiments to be sent abroad, although in the back of the minds of the authorities, was that when earlier in April of that year, sixty newly recruited men from the 71st Highlanders were told that they were to be sent to America. They were of the opinion that they had been recruited to fight the French or Spanish but not against the Americans, who most of the recruits believed to be Scottish emigrants, possibly relations. This was therefore not acceptable. They mutinied against the transfer, declaring their desire to fight, but not against their own.

With his belief that it was impossible to stop the American movement, Clinton requested that he should be recalled to England. This was ignored, and on 10th April 1780 he moved his men out and marched to about twelve miles above Charlestown, where he was joined by Cornwallis, two days later after relentless bombardment the town surrendered. From there messengers brought news that a large French fleet had set sail from France. Clinton's first reaction was that he should return to New York. He was aware that Cornwallis knew of his desire to return to England, and in that event, Cornwallis would take over command of the army.

When Cornwallis learnt that the King would not authorise the change of command, relations between the two generals deteriorated as Clinton left Cornwallis in the south as he returned to New York. Cornwallis then moved his much reduced force which included the 23rd and 71st Regiments together with the 33rd (1st Battalion, the Duke of Wellington's [West Riding] Regiment), taking the town of Camden and moving swiftly against other small towns and settlements, but more importantly, he dealt most severely with men who had joined the American militia, whom he considered as traitors to the British Crown.

The winter months of 1780 saw much suffering amongst British troops, being continually attacked by American sharpshooters, who after one or two discharges of their rifles retreated once the British had located their position. This led to a very uncomfortable existence for the redcoats.

Cornwallis decided that his plan for 1781 was that in the first week in January he would march from Winnsboro with about 1,300 men. Once again the myth that thousands of loyalists in North Carolina would join him led him to move north. He then sent 5,000 men split into small detachments to Camden, Charlestown, Ninety Six, Augusta and Savannah. Heavy fighting took place in March 1781 between the small groups of British soldiers and local militia at Ninety Six, also at the Court House at Guildford, where the British began their attack in serried ranks with fixed bayonets, against sharpshooters moving from tree to tree. The British used field guns firing grape shot, although by this time troops were so spread out that many were hit by their own gunners. No one could claim that they were superior in this conflict, although the British did claim a victory the outcome was anything but that!

Cornwallis continued his march from Wilmington moving north. His men were short of food and many fell ill. On 20th May he arrived at Petersburg where he learnt that the British commander had recently died of fever. Cornwallis took on the extra troops which brought his strength up to 7.000 men. He did not feel that this was enough to maintain control of Virginia and waited for news from Clinton that reinforcements were on their way. Clinton in turn requested that Cornwallis should send men to New York which would strengthen the British position there. Communications between the generals was so poor that neither knew what was the intention of the other, and as both sent and received fresh orders, often arriving much later than intended, much confusion was caused as to what to do next.

Clinton was still annoyed that Cornwallis had moved north. He suggested that as the general was already in Virginia, to enable the British to maintain a base for the fleet he should hold Yorktown. Cornwallis was in a weakened state, his command, now down to 3,000 men who were short of food and with low morale, surrounded by American and French infantry and watching helplessly as their outposts were overrun. He felt that her had no alternative but to save his men and surrender.

On the same day that his request for assistance was answered, Clinton with 7,000 men set sail from New York to relieve the garrison at Yorktown. However, when he received news of the surrender he returned to New York.

When news reached London it was agreed by a noisy Parliament that the war was over. Regiments which had not been sent to Canada or the West Indies returned to Britain, the 45th Foot, by now reduced to less than one hundred all ranks, returned home to Nottingham. This reduction in manpower was typical of all regiments who had taken part in the war.

Eighteen months later on 3rd September 1783 the King's ministers concluded the negotiations which resulted in the Treaty of Paris.

CHAPTER XXI

AMERICAN WAR OF INDEPENDENCE 1775-1783
GEORGE III

West Indies - St Lucia 12th - 28th December 1778.
Europe - Gibraltar 1779 - 1783.

ST LUCIA

Once the French had decided that they should help the Americans, they actively supported the call for independence. In return, one of the agreements was that the Americans would assist them in any operations against the British in the West Indies.

Admiral d'Estaing was given command of a French fleet in 1778 to aid the American struggle. He attempted to seize Rhode Island, but in the autumn he abandoned the project and sailed for the West Indies without the support that the Americans had promised. Here the British had managed to forestall him, for earlier in the year Clinton had been told to make troops available for the West Indies, even though he believed that he might be jeopardizing his own position in North America. Disregarding this, the British Government had decided to take the hitherto French island of St Lucia.

Admiral d'Estaing arrived too late to intercept the British from disembarking troops, the first of which landed on the 12th December. The French fleet did attack the British naval force and was then able to land its own troops in an effort to regain possession of the island.

Upon disembarkation, the 5th Foot (the Northumberland Fusiliers) held a key position and sustained severe and repeated attacks by strong French forces. It was here that after the battle they were able to equip themselves with the white plumes taken from the French dead, thus distinguishing themselves from the remainder of the British infantry for the next 51 years.

The remaining nine regiments held the island against the French, who repeatedly attacked their lines. It was no easy task to repel troops whose island had been invaded by an English army, but for just over two weeks recovery was denied to the French.

For their involvement in the West Indies, it took over 130 years for the following regiments to be awarded the battle honour ST LUCIA 1778:

4th the King's Own (Royal Lancashire Regiment).
5th the Northumberland Fusiliers.
15th the East Yorkshire Regiment.
27th 1st Battalion, the Royal Inniskilling Fusiliers.
28th 1st Battalion, the Gloucestershire Regiment.
32nd 1st Battalion, the Duke of Cornwall's Light Infantry.
35th 1st Battalion, the Royal Sussex Regiment.
40th 1st Battalion, the Prince of Wales's Volunteers (South Lancashire) Regt.
49th 1st Battalion, the Princess Charlotte of Wales's (Berkshire) Regiment.
55th 2nd Battalion, the Border Regiment.

Although in 1881 the 5th Foot are shown as the Northumberland Fusiliers, in 1768 Hugh, Earl Percy, later to become the 2nd Duke of Northumberland became colonel of the regiment. When he retired in 1784 the 5th Foot petitioned to be called the Northumberland Regiment.

There were no battle honours for the actions of regiments on the mainland of America however brave, heroic or Government-backed they might have been!

In 1782 and 1783, the 15th and 28th Regiments sailed back to England, while the 5th Foot returned to Ireland.

GIBRALTAR

When the American War of Independence spread to Europe in 1778, the French moved against Britain in an attempt to challenge her command of the seas. In the following year Spain, with its impressive fleet, joined the French; their primary aim being to recapture the Rock of Gibraltar by preventing supplies reaching both Gibraltar and also Minorca.

In command of the garrison at Gibraltar was General Eliott, with Lieutenant-General Robert Boyd, Colonel of the 39th Foot (1st Battalion, the Dorsetshire Regiment) as Lieutenant Governor. General Eliott had entered the army as an Ensign in the 23rd Fusiliers. He became an engineer in 1737 and an artilleryman two years later. Wounded at Dettingen, he also fought at Fonteney before raising the 15th Light Dragoons in 1759.

By 1779 Gibraltar was invested by a strong Spanish army under the Duke of Crillon, who, together with the Spanish navy, sought to reduce the fortress first by blockade and then by persistent bombardment.

Within the fortress were men from the 12th Foot (Suffolk Regiment) who had been sent to Gibraltar in 1769. The following year they had been joined by the 58th Foot (2nd Battalion the Northamptonshire Regiment) and later men from the 39th Foot (1st Battalion, the Dorsetshire Regiment) and the 56th Foot (2nd Battalion, the Essex Regiment) who in May 1770 had marched from Cork to Dublin, from where they embarked for Gibraltar.

The garrison was originally composed of 5,382 officers and men, of which the 12th Foot had 599, the 39th foot 586, the 56th Foot 587 and the 58th Foot 595. Also at Gibraltar were 1,036 men of the 72nd Royal Manchester (since disbanded) and three Hanoverian regiments, each with an average strength of 450 men.

During the winter of 1778, the Hon George Mackenzie raised the 2nd Battalion of the 73rd Highlanders, (Highland Light Infantry) renumbered 71st in 1786. The 1st Battalion was under the control of his brother Lord MacLeod. In April 1779 the 73rd, under the command of Lieutenant-Colonel Mackenzie, moved from Fort George near Inverness by sea to Portsmouth, then in June again by sea to Plymouth where they stayed until December.

On 8th December 1779, the 73rd embarked on board transports which were held at anchor until the 27th December, when they sailed from Plymouth Sound under convoy of six ships of the line and two frigates. That evening they joined the grand fleet which consisted of twenty-four sail of the line, nine frigates and many more armed ships, store ships and merchantmen, about 150 in total, all under the command of Admiral Sir George Bridges Rodney.

At about 4 o'clock in the morning of 8th January 1780 off Cape Finisterre, seven Spanish warships and sixteen supply ships neared the British fleet, mistaking it for their own. Rodney hoisted a signal ordering a chase, leaving two ships of the line and two frigates to guard his own supply ships and transports. Early in the morning of the next day, the British fleet returned with Spanish ships as prizes. Due to the great number of prisoners, the 73rd'soldiers were ordered to serve as guards on the captured man-of-war.

The fleet resumed its course until, around noon of the 16th January, to the southeast of Cape St Vincent, it was approached by a Spanish fleet of eleven ships of the line intent on stopping supplies reaching Gibraltar. A storm made engagement difficult, but with superior handling, the British ships began to move against those from Spain. The encounter lasted well into the night in a half gale, until six Spanish had been captured and one blown up. Rodney arrived in the Bay of Gibraltar on 23rd January.

On 29th January, the 73rd landed at the New Mole. They had originally been destined for Minorca but as the Governor, General Eliott, believed the garrison to be short of men, he ordered the regiment to disembark and on his own responsibility kept it with him until the end of the siege.

Having unloaded reinforcements and supplies, Rodney departed, taking with him the wives of soldiers and their children who had hitherto resided at Gibraltar.

The siege conducted by the Spanish and French continued, supplies within the garrison were running low and troops were on short rations. In the beginning of October 1780 the defenders

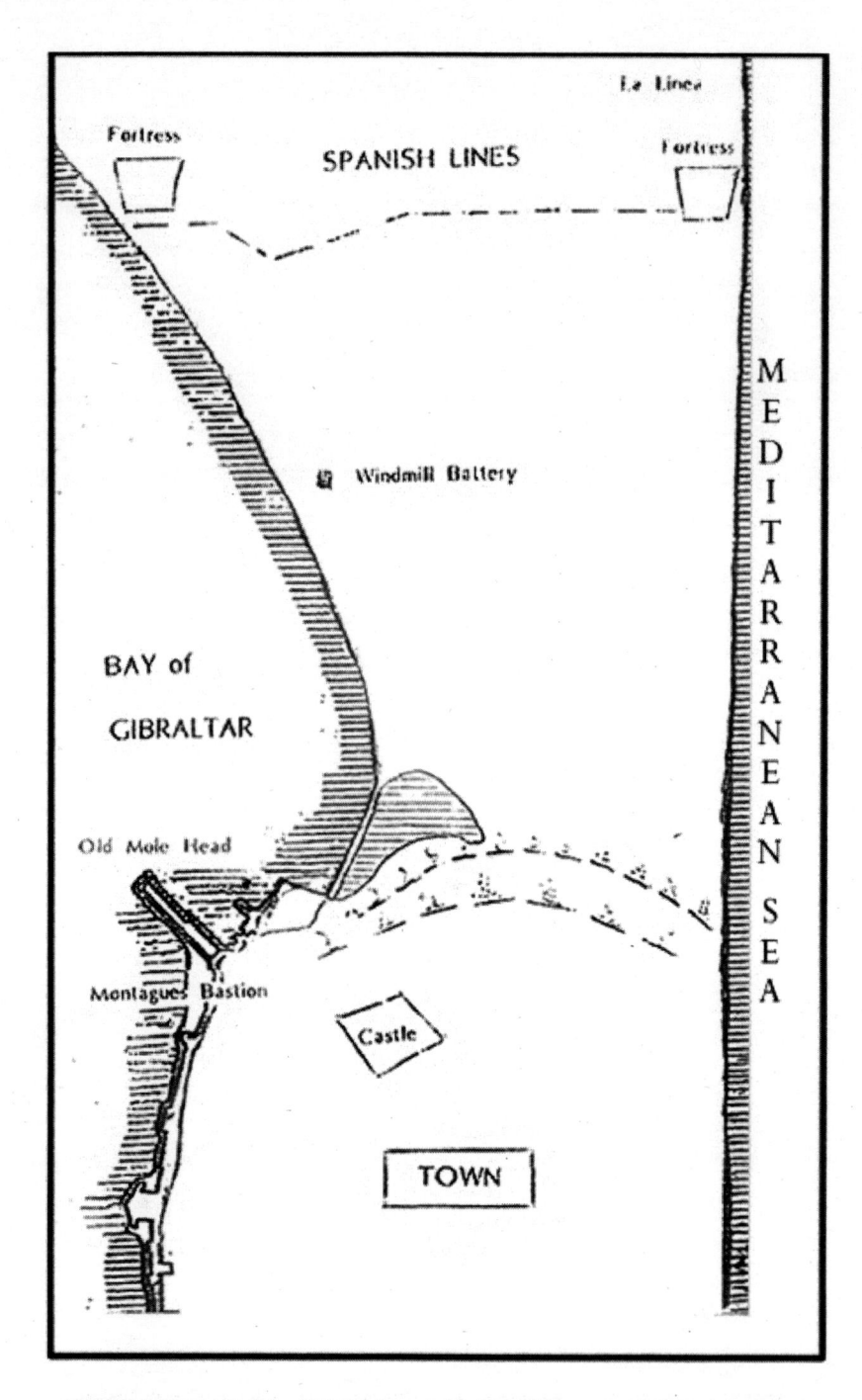

SIEGE OF GIBRALTER 1780-1983

realized that the Spanish were moving to new ground in front of their original lines with the intention of erecting batteries.

Most of the fighting from both sides was conducted by artillery, the British infantry regiments spent their time repairing and improving the defences, a situation which continued until April 1781 when a British fleet, having evaded the French and Spanish blockade, appeared and anchored in the bay.

The sight of the ships angered the Spaniards who believed that their fleet should have prevented the supply ships from reaching the garrison, thus starving it into submission. They opened fire with as much artillery as they had, not only directed at the ships but also at the town and fortress. Their fireballs caused much damage in the town as building after building was incinerated. At this time the 56th Foot with the 12th and 39th Foot were stationed at Montague's Bastion.

By September 1781 the Spaniards had succeeded in establishing several batteries so close to the fortress that they could reach any part of the besieged garrison with withering fire. Because of this, by the end of November, General Eliott believed that he had to attack the Spanish on land, to break a situation where they appeared to be winning. Therefore on the 27th he used 2,200 men under Brigadier-General Ross to move against the Spanish.

Generals Eliott and Ross decided that they would move their infantry forward by stealth in three columns, with the intention of destroying the Spanish siege-works in La Linea.

<u>LEFT COLUMN</u> (Lieutenant-Colonel Trigge) in the front.
72nd Regiment. Grenadiers and light infantry.
12th Regiment.
58th Regiment. Light infantry.

<u>CENTRE COLUMN</u> (Lieutenant-Colonel Dachenhausen, with Major Hamilton 73rd)
The Reserve.
39th Regiment. Grenadiers and light infantry.
56th Regiment. Grenadiers.
73rd Regiment. Grenadiers and light infantry.

RIGHT COLUMN (Lieutenant-Colonel Hugo) in the Rear.
56th Regiment. Light infantry.
With three 'foreign' regiments
All columns contained engineers and artillery.

The advance just before 3 a.m. on 27th November 1781 took the Spanish by surprise. They gave way on every side; much of their work building batteries in recent months was destroyed, their heavy guns were spiked and large mortars rendered useless, their magazine was blown up and the Windmill battery was totally destroyed, marking the end of any chance the Spaniards had of capturing Gibraltar. British losses were slight only four men were killed and twenty-five wounded.

Between the 10th June 1782 and the end of the month the Spanish, encouraged by the capture of Minorca, pounded the Rock continually from long distance, all to little effect.

The Spanish and French increased pressure on the defenders because, by September, ten floating batteries were being constructed. The intention was that these ships would be able to attack the defenders, while remaining immune from the gunners within the Rock.

Large vessels were being dismantled and their sides which would be exposed to British fire fitted with sloping roofs composed of three layers of timbers three feet thick, separated by wet sand and backed by a bed of wet cork. The roofs were further covered by wet hides and central reservoirs of water, from which ran a network of pipes to every exposed part of the vessels' sides. Each of the ships was armed with up to twenty-six guns mounted only on the landward side.

On 13th September the Spanish brought these vessels to their moorings and just after 9 o'clock in the morning opened fire in conjunction with their land batteries. The British fire in return did not at first have any effect on the fortified hulks, so it was agreed to use red-hot shot.

Cannonading continued all day. The British guns in their static positions were able to aim accurately at the Spanish gun apertures, which over the late afternoon were constantly penetrated to such an extent that by 3 o'clock that evening the Spanish fire had greatly slackened, and two hours later had stopped. The flagship of the floating batteries was in flames, and one after another, Spanish ships blew up, forcing their fleet to draw back out of range. Spanish losses were estimated at 2,000 men whereas the garrison only lost sixteen men killed.

In October 1782, Lord Howe arrived with a convoy which included supplies and men from the 25th Foot (King's Own Scottish Borderers) and 54th Foot (2nd Battalion the Dorsetshire Regiment), although his fleet was outnumbered by the French and Spanish fleets, they failed to engage and Howe was able to land men and supplies without being challenged.

On 2nd February 1783 the war came to an end. News of peace arrived at the Rock and on the 6th the siege ended. England recognized the independence of the American colonies and peace was made with France, Spain and Holland. Total losses of the garrison were 1,143, of which 318 were due to death in action or from wounds, 278 were discharged because of wounds and just over 500 died of sickness.

After the conclusion of the war, the 73rd Regiment was ordered to hold themselves in readiness to embark for Britain in order to be discharged, but about the beginning of June 1783, an order was issued by the Government that all who chose to re-enlist out of the 72nd, 73rd and 97th (all to be disbanded) might enter into any other regiment they 'liked best'.

Following their involvement in the siege, the 12th, 39th, 56th and 58th Regiments were in April 1784 awarded the battle honour GIBRALTAR. They also received the Castle and Key emblem, which was taken from the 1502 Seal of Gibraltar. Also taken from the Seal was the motto MONTIS INSIGNIA CALPE which meant Mount of Calpe, the word given by the Ancient Greeks to the Rock of Gibraltar which, along with Abyla across the straits, formed the Pillars of Hercules.

The dates 1779-1783 which follow that of GIBRALTAR were not added until 1908.

The 71st had to wait until 1908 when they received the battle honour GIBRALTAR 1780-1783, thus taking into account their late arrival at the fortress.

CHAPTER XXII

FRENCH REVOLUTIONARY WAR 1793-1801
GEORGE III
MARTINIQUE – ST LUCIA – EUROPE – EGYPT

The masses stormed the Bastille in July 1793. The French King was executed in January 1793.

At the time of Napoleon and the New Revolutionary System in France, history has used the titles of: French Revolutionary War, Napoleonic War and Peninsular War. All cover the period from 1793 to 1814. See chapters XXII, XXIII and XXIV.

Many people in European countries, especially the reformers and radicals in Britain, at first welcomed the French revolution. The mood changed as they heard of the excesses as the mob took control.

MARTINIQUE

The new French republic had two military objectives; the first was in the West Indies where they already had ships and troops, although Britain occupied many of the islands and strategic naval stations.

A force was sent under the British General, Sir Charles Grey, to attack the French-held island of Martinique, which although strongly defended was weakened by the dispersal of their troops throughout the many forts and batteries on the island.

The British force of ten regiments was divided into three brigades. Most had sailed from England, although the 65th Foot (1st Battalion, the York and Lancaster Regiment) were already in the West Indies. The regiments landed at three points, moving against fort after fort forcing surrender.

Two companies of the 15th Foot (East Yorkshire Regiment) stormed Mount Mathurine where the French had erected a large battery; the 15th surprised the French defenders and nearly 300 surrendered, handing over their arms, stores and large guns. The French outposts, the Fort Royal and Fort Courbon were besieged and were ultimately captured. After six weeks of hard fighting, by 23rd March 1794 the island had been taken.

Although regiments suffered casualties during the fighting, more men died of sickness whilst in occupation. The 65th needed more than 300 recruits when it returned to England in 1795. Other regiments followed the same pattern.

For their part in the action, the following regiments were awarded the battle honour MARTINIQUE 1794, but not until 1909:

The Royal Warwickshire Regiment	(6th Foot)
The Norfolk Regiment	(9th Foot)
The East Yorkshire Regiment	(15th Foot)
Royal Scots Fusiliers	(21st Foot)
1st Bn, the Dorsetshire Regiment	(39th Foot)
1st Bn, the Oxfordshire Light Infantry	(43rd Foot)
2nd Bn, the Northamptonshire Regimen	(58th Foot)
1st Bn, the Prince of Wales's North Staffordshire Regt	(64th Foot)
1st Bn, the York and Lancaster Regiment	(65th Foot)
2nd Bn The East Surrey Regiment	(70th Foot)

ST LUCIA

Trouble between the nations continued in the West Indies for several more years, as the occupation of islands remained paramount to both countries, mainly because of the natural harbours which gave support to their fleets.

In November 1795, Sir Ralph Abercromby sailed from England with an expeditionary force, but had to return after seven weeks due to extremely poor weather. Following repairs, the ships sailed again, arriving at the island of Barbados in April of the following year. The main objective was to capture a strongly held hill near the side of the harbour on the neighbouring island of St Lucia. The hill, called The

Morne, was nearly 900 feet high; it was held by a large force of local coloured men under the command of French officers.

The British force consisting of the 27th Regiment (1st Battalion, the Royal Inniskilling Fusiliers) and the 53rd Regiment (1st Battalion, the King's [Shropshire Light Infantry]) landed in a bay just north of the harbour; both regiments under the command of Sir John Moore, moved through thick woodland until they occupied a superior position above the French lines. Moore then led the regiments against the enemy, taking their citadel, therefore control of the island.

The occupation of many of these islands was not necessarily the ideal posting for European troops. As had been the case in Martinique, disease was also rife in St Lucia. When Moore was left in command of the island in June 1796 he had a force of over 4,000 men. By November, five months later, his force had been reduced to a mere thousand men fit for duty.

For their involvement in these actions, the 27th and 53rd were in 1836 and 1825 respectively, awarded the battle honour of St LUCIA 1796 although the date was not added until 1909.

EUROPE

The French main prize was Europe; therefore by the end of 1792, William Pitt, the British Prime Minister, believed that French aggression, especially in the Netherlands, was a threat to British interests and European order. On 1st February 1793 the new French republic declared war on England. It should be noted that at this time the army was still the English, not the British army. The French declaration of war was followed in April against Austria. In November the French urged all countries to revolt against their governments, promising their support in this.

Another massive expansion of the army occurred as a result of the troubles caused by the situation in France. Over twenty new regiments were formed between 1786 and 1794. Many were raised for service in India, some at the expense of the East India Company whilst others were sent to various locations in the West Indies.

It is sometimes difficult to follow where regiments were actually employed, as in the 18th century regimental numbers frequently changed, when regiments were raised and subsequently disbanded with their numbers redistributed to new regiments. As an example, in 1793 the 80th Foot (2nd Battalion, the South Staffordshire Regiment) were raised in Staffordshire by Lieutenant-Colonel, Lord William Henry Paget, (later to become the First Marquis of Anglesey) from the Stafford Militia which was commanded by his father. It was given the title of the 80th Staffordshire Volunteers, and was the third regiment to carry the number 80, all previous regiments having been disbanded.

The 81st (2nd Battalion, the Loyal North Lancashire Regiment) was raised in September 1793 by Major-General Albemarle Bertie as the 83rd (Loyal Lincolnshire Volunteers) Regiment of Foot, their regimental number was changed in 1794 to the 81st Regiment.

The 83rd (1st Battalion, the Royal Irish Rifles) was the third regiment to carry that number. The first had been raised in Ireland in 1758, serving in Portugal before returning home in 1762 to be disbanded a year later. The next became the 83rd (Royal Glasgow Volunteers) formed in 1778 in response to the request for new regiments at the time of the American War of Independence. They went to New York before being demobilized in 1783.

The 84th (2nd Battalion, the York and Lancaster Regiment) was formed in 1793. In 1759 the first 84th Foot had been raised, being sent to India before becoming redundant in 1763. The second regiment to carry the number 84 was a second battalion regiment raised from Scottish emigrants to Canada in 1775. This was disbanded in 1784.

The 85th (2nd Battalion, the King's Shropshire Light Infantry) was raised in Buckinghamshire in 1793 as the Bucks Volunteers. A previous 85th, formed in 1759, was disbanded in 1779.

The first regiment to carry the number 87 was also raised in 1759 as the 87th Keith's Highlanders but lasted for only four years. The second raised in 1779, also lasted for four years.

In 1795 Sir John Doyle raised a new regiment which acquired the number and title of the 87th (the Prince of Wales's Irish), later in 1881 to become the 1st Battalion, the Princess Victoria's (Royal Irish Fusiliers).

The 91st was originally raised by the Duke of Argyll, who was Colonel Duncan Campbell of Lochnell as the 98th (Argyllshire) Regiment of Foot (Highland), it was renumbered in 1798 as 91st (Argyllshire) Regiment of Foot. In 1881 it became the 1st Battalion Princess Louise's (Sutherland and Argyll Highlanders).

In 1794, The Duke of Gordon's son had difficulty recruiting, mainly due to the aftermath of Culloden. However his brother-in-law, Sir Robert Sinclair of Stevenson urged men to join, and was able to review the 100th Regiment (Gordon Highlanders) at Fort George before its departure abroad. It later became the 92nd Foot.

Following the declaration of war, the British Government sent an expeditionary force to the continent. It was led by Frederick, Duke of York and Albany K.G. who was the second son of King George III. Frederick had been carefully schooled for command, therefore it was considered that he was the man to lead the British army against the French.

The British attempted to lay siege to the port of Dunkirk. Although the British army occupied all of the land in the dunes, the navy had not agreed to participate in this particular operation, so it could not therefore really be called a siege because French gunboats continually harassed the British lines.

On 6th September 1793 the French led by General Lazare Carnot, launched an attack against the Austrian lines near Herzele in the Spanish Netherlands (modern Belgium), punching a line in the Allied front and heading the ten miles to the sea. The Duke of York, realizing that if the French continued their advance he would become surrounded, sensibly withdrew. The Allied formation became a rabble, with regiments of the many countries scrambling to gain preferable ground, although after the shock of the French advance, many of the regiments were able to recover some of their composure.

The British, especially the cavalry, challenged the French, notably at Beaumont in April 1794, but it was not until 17th May that infantry regiments took part in an action near the town of Tourcoing, where the British planned a multiple attack on the French whose 40,000 men stood in an exposed position. The British force being small, called upon its allies to support the attack, and hoped that all regiments would be marching in formation, with determined aggression against their opponent's front. It was unfortunate that the plan failed because several of the commanders hesitated, the attack floundered and the French pressed their advantage. The Allies lost over 4,000 killed or wounded with many more captured.

During this time the British army managed to hold its line, when on 23rd May regiments checked the French advance. To annoy them, the colonel of the 14th Foot (the Prince of Wales' Own [West Yorkshire] Regiment) directed that his drummers took up the rhythm of the French revolutionary tune. His regiment received the battle honour TOURNAY; this was also awarded to the 37th Foot (1st Battalion, the Hampshire Regiment) and the 53rd Foot (1st Battalion, the King's or Shropshire Light Infantry).

Following Tourcoing, the campaign in the Netherlands fell apart. The Austrians decided to retreat, generally followed by the remaining Allies.

About this time, the remaining French Royalists who had become troubled by the revolutionary movement, seized Toulon. As he watched the cannon falling short and ineffective, he advised that the direction and military planning left much to be desired. He was a young lieutenant in the French Army, a soldier from a Corsican family; his name was Napoleon Bonaparte, his redirection of the assault was responsible for the retaking of Toulon.

On 1st June 1794, off Ushant, the British Fleet under Lord Howe, which due to the shortage of Marines carried drafts of men from the 2nd Foot (1st Battalion, the Queen's [Royal West Surrey]Regiment) and the 29th Foot (1st Battalion, the Worcestershire Regiment) on board ships of the Royal Navy. They were placed amongst several ships of the line: *Brunswick, Glory, Thunderer* and *Alfred.* As the *Brunswick* went into action, the ship's band which included a drummer of the 29th played a popular air of the time – 'Hearts of Oak'.

The battle lasted about two hours, during which time the French ships either surrendered or were sunk by cannon which holed them below the water line. The action took place 430 miles west of Ushant and because there was no land point after which to name the action, it became known as the Glorious First of June. In 1909 both the 2nd and 29th Regiments received the battle honour NAVAL CROWN, subscribed 1st June 1794.

Napoleon became more and more the major influence in French plans concerning the mainland of Europe. He led troops against the Austrians in their shared border with Italy, and in 1796 was in command of French forces completely routing the Austrian commanders and occupying their territory.

When the French Revolutionary Army overran the Netherlands, the British Government believed that a show of strength might convince the wavering Dutch to revert to their old allegiance. On the 8th August 1799, the British troops under the command of Sir Ralph Abercromby sailed to the Dutch coast. Nineteen days later they arrived below Patten on the Helder; the force consisted of seven regiments with twenty pieces of artillery. The landing was largely unopposed, but due to rough seas, men were lost as one of the landing-craft containing men from the 92nd Regiment capsized, a sergeant and fourteen men drowned. The troops moved on the Helder, which without too much opposition was taken. This was followed when the Dutch Fleet surrendered.

The coast, consisting mainly of flat sandy beaches and sand dunes, covered an area of over twenty miles. It was here that regiments were escorting the artillery along the seashore, when they were attacked by 6,000 French with local Dutch under the French General Brune. The British faced the enemy and after the order to fix bayonets, drove them back to great effect after a series of charges. The action lasted for nearly four hours as regiments on both sides suffered appalling casualties.

The 92nd lost fifteen officers, several other British regiments also lost many of their officers and more than an equal number of men, until it was agreed by both sides that an armistice was the sensible solution. This was followed by an exchange of men from both sides who had been captured. It was agreed that the British would be allowed to evacuate their weary troops. This was carried out and the British returned to England, amongst them was the 79th (The Queen's Own Cameron Highlanders) who had been raised in 1793 by Major Alan Cameron of Erracht as the 79th (Cameron Volunteers) Regiment of Foot.

This action was to lead, between 1814 and 1830, to the award of the battle honour EGMONT OP ZEE to the:

Royal Scots	(1st Foot)
Lancashire Fusiliers	(20th Foot)
King's Own Scottish Borderers	(25th Foot)
1st Battalion, the Royal Berkshire Regiment	(49th Foot)
1st Battalion, the Manchester Regiment	(63rd Foot)
Queen's Own Cameron Highlanders	(79th Foot)
2nd Battalion, the Gordon Highlanders	(92nd Foot)

The award was originally granted to the 92nd on 15th February 1813 as BERGEN-OP-ZOOM.

EGYPT

Having overrun Europe, Napoleon saw his next step as the conquest of the Orient. He was determined to occupy the Near East with the aim of marching to India. His initial intention was the invasion of Egypt. His first move was in 1798 when French troops occupied that country, thus cutting British communications with India.

His ambitions were shattered on 1st August 1798, when the fleet maintaining his links with France was destroyed by Nelson at the Battle of the Nile. Napoleon left his troops behind and returned to France.

Since Nelson's victory, Napoleon's Army in Egypt had been virtually isolated, but still formed a potential menace to British interests in the East. A strong enemy force blocking the short route to India could not be ignored and two armies, one from the Mediterranean, the other from India, were both ordered to converge on Egypt.

It was decided that the forces from Britain would assemble at the island of Malta, and that Turkey would join the assault on the French Army currently occupying Egypt. It was expected that the force under Sir Ralph Abercromby would be composed of 16,000 men, and would land in Egypt in December 1800. The British force duly assembled at

Malta. It consisted of men from the 13th, 18th, 20th, 24th, 26th, 27th, 28th, 44th, 50th, 54th, 89th and 90th Regiments of Foot. The 90th (2nd Battalion, the Cameronians [Scottish Rifles] was raised in 1794 as the 90th (Perthshire Volunteers.)

The 89th (2nd Battalion, the Princess Victoria's, later known as the Royal Irish Fusiliers) had been raided in Dublin in November 1793 by Colonel William Crosbie. It was the third time that the number 89 had been given to a regiment. The first was in 1759 when the 89th (Highland) Regiment of Foot was raised for service in India, it was disbanded in 1765. The second was raised in 1779 as the Worcestershire Volunteers mainly to serve in the West Indies; it only lasted for four years, being disbanded in 1783.

The British force under Abercromby set sail in January 1801. After they arrived, the 1st Battalion of the 27th Foot remained in Malta, but the 2nd Battalion, who had only been formed in May 1800 were with the troops who did not land in Malta but in Marmorice Bay opposite Rhodes.

Sir John Moore, later to be remembered for his humane treatment of his men, and his death at Corunna in 1809, was dispatched to Jaffa in an attempt to co-ordinate the campaign in which the army of the Grand Vizier's Turkish troops appeared to be stalling.

Abercromby used the breathing space to allow his men to recover from the inevitable sickness, which many had suffered during their sea voyage. He eventually became tired of waiting for the Turkish troops and sailed for Egypt, arriving in Aboukir Bay on the 2nd March. But his landing was delayed by a violent storm and it was not until the 8th that troops were able to land on Egyptian soil.

It was agreed that troops from India would be under the command of Major-General Sir David Baird. They would sail from India into the Red Sea and land at Suez. The expeditionary force consisted of 3,000 European soldiers from the 10th, 19th, 80th and the 86th Regiments of Foot.

The 10th Regiment had sailed for India in 1798 and served in Madras, then moving to Bengal before joining the expeditionary force. The 86th (2nd Battalion, the Royal Irish Rifles) had been raised in Shrewsbury on 2nd November 1793, titled General Cuyler's Shropshire Volunteers. The first regiment to carry the number 86 had been raised in Ireland in 1759. It was disbanded in Winchester four years later. The second, raided in England in 1778, was sent to the West Indies. When it returned in 1783 it was disbanded at York.

Shortly after their formation in 1793, the 86th moved to Ireland, before serving as marines until sailing for India, where six companies were to join the expedition to Egypt.

The 61st Regiment was also sent to India, but whilst under sail was diverted to join the force on its way to Egypt, where it expected to land at Suez. The 80th suffered a distressing transfer as portions of the regiment were shipwrecked, although others were more lucky, reaching their destination.

The British under Sir Ralph Abercromby arrived at Aboukir Bay on the 8th March in a fiercely contested landing. He was opposed by a French army of occupation of 30,000 seasoned troops under the command of General Menou, considered to be one of Napoleon's more incompetent generals. As the troops landed they were fired upon by French artillery, firstly by roundshot then grape. Some boats were sunk with men killed, but after three days of heavy fighting a beachhead was established, the French withdrew.

The British then advanced towards Alexandria, halting on a defensive position three miles short of the town. Regiments were again attacked by grapeshot and then by a strong force of cavalry near the Mendora Tower, followed by French musketry, but accurate British fire decimated the French cavalry. This defence was enough

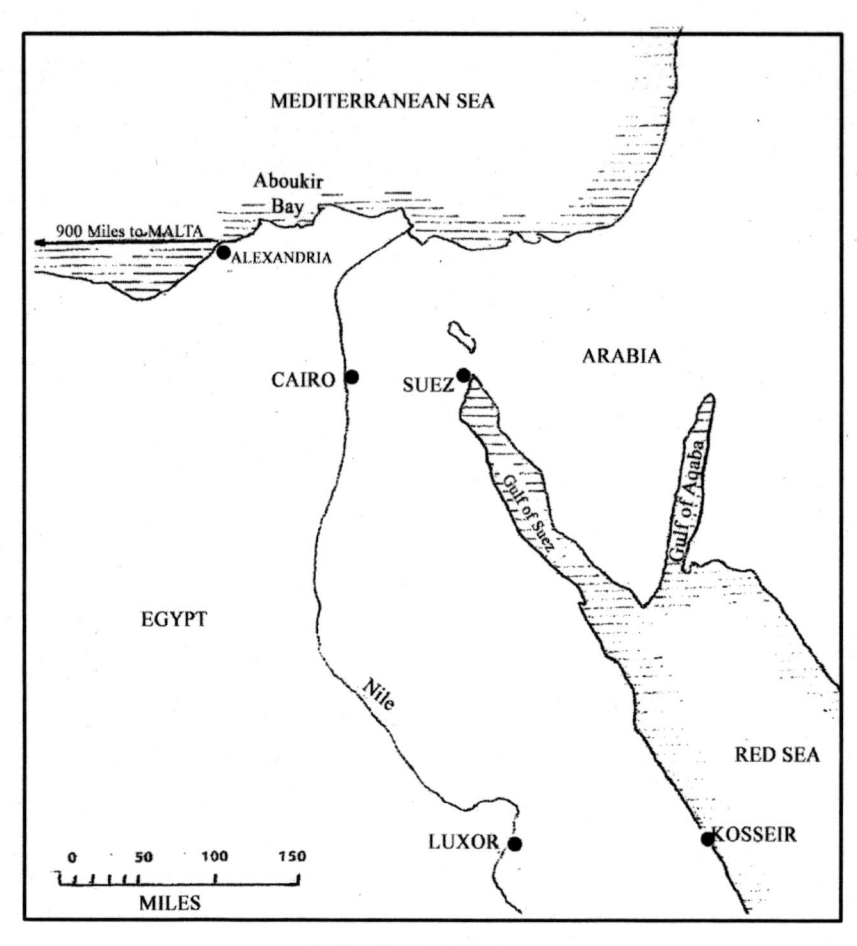

EGYPT 1801

to enable the authorities in February 1813, to award the battle honour MANDORA to the 92nd Regiment, and in March 1817 the same award to the 90th Regiment of Foot.

On the right of the British line were the ancient ruins of the old Roman fort of Canopus, close to the sea. A few hundred yards ahead was a low rocky ridge which covered the approach to the ruins. The 28th were building a redoubt when some hours before dawn on 21st March, the French commander with 1,400 cavalry moved silently out of Alexandria and advanced against the British position. In the darkness the 28th found themselves engaged to their front, while on both of their flanks French columns swept by, cutting them off. But when dawn broke, the French cavalry failed to engage and left it to their infantry to attack from the front and from the flanks, so in both areas they were repulsed. A second body of French cavalry passed by the redoubt and charged towards the rear of the 88th (1st Battalion, the Connaught Rangers), who had been raised in September 1793 and had immediately been named the Connaught Rangers. They were the third regiment to carry the number 88. The first had been raised in 1760 as 88th (Royal Highland Volunteers), who served on the Continent before being disbanded in 1763. The second was raised in October 1779 as Keating's Regiment, disbanded in 1783.

Seeing the threat to the 88th, the commanding officer of the 28th, Lietenant-Colonel Chambers gave the order 'Rear rank 28th Foot, right about face', although encircled, the 28th repelled all attacks, firing a deadly volley which caused the French cavalry to retreat in disorder. After four hours of battle, both sides were short of ammunition and the French retired to Alexandria.

Because of their unique defensive position, the 28th received the distinction of wearing a badge at the back of their headdress as well as in the front. They had lost four officers and seventy men killed or wounded, but a more serious event was that General Abercromby received a mortal wound during the second cavalry charge. He was succeeded by General Hutchinson.

At this point the east side of Alexandria was strongly defended, but the French defences in the west did not appear to be in a complete state. It was decided that an assault should be carried out by the 24th, 26th and 54th Regiments, who then pressed their attack against the guns located close to Alexandria. The 20th carried a French battery, whilst two battalions of the 54th gained the honour of the capture on 21st August of Fort Marabout, which guarded the harbour of Alexandria. By 22nd August 1801, the French within the town were defeated.

Originally the trophy claimed by the 54th was a large artillery piece which they named Marabout. Then on 18th December 1841, the feat was officially recognized when the battle honour MARABOUT was awarded.

In May 1801, the first detachment of the 86th Regiment landed at Suez, at the head of the Red Sea. It had been intended that all regiments would land at Suez, but the monsoon had already commenced and a northeast wind made progress slow. General Baird therefore decided to land at Kosseir, and marched across the desert to the Nile, thence to Cairo.

In June, regiments landed at Kosseir, the distance to Keneh, just south of Luxor was 120 miles, and as five regiments moved towards their destination, the lack of drinking water, added to general fatigue, caused many losses in their ranks. One example was the 10th Regiment who lost one officer and twenty-three men; this loss was typical for most of the others. From Keneh, they moved down the Nile, but when they reached Alexandria, nearly 500 miles away, it had already surrendered to the British. Before they moved on, they received news that Cairo had also fallen.

After the French defeat at Alexandria, the 89th covered the advance of the main army to Cairo. The French were in no position to defend the town, therefore on 26th August, General Menou opened negotiations for surrender. He had completely misunderstood the number or determination of the British. His losses totalled over 4,000 whilst the British dead and wounded were less than 2,000. The 92nd lost thirteen officers and men killed and a further 128 were wounded. This resulted in terms under which on 3rd September, the British took over the French lines and Menou's men followed the Cairo garrison and were evacuated to France.

On 6th July 1802, the following regiments were awarded the battle honour EGYPT 1801, with sphinx:

The Lothian Regiment (the Royal Scots)	(1st Foot)
The Queen's Royal (West Surrey) Regiment	(2nd Foot)
The King's Regiment (Liverpool)	(8th Foot)
The Lincolnshire Regiment	(10th Foot)
Prince Albert's (Somerset Light Infantry)	(13th Foot)
Royal Irish Fusiliers	(18th Foot)
The Lancashire Fusiliers	(20th Foot)
The Royal Welch Fusiliers	(23rd Foot)
The South Wales Borderers	(24th Foot)
The King's Own Borderers	(25th Foot)
1st Bn The Cameronians (Scottish Rifles)	(26th Foot)
1st Bn Royal Inniskilling Fusiliers	(27th Foot)
1st Bn, the Gloucestershire Regiment	(28th Foot)
1st Bn, the East Lancashire Regiment	(30th Foot)
1st Bn, the Prince of Wales's Volunteers (South Lancs) Reg	(40th Foot)
1st Bn, the Black Watch (Royal Highlanders)	(42nd Foot)
1st Bn The Essex Regiment	(44th Foot)
1st Bn, the Queen's Own (Royal West Kent Regiment)	(50th Foot)
2nd Bn, the Dorsetshire Regiment	(54th Foot)
2nd Bn, the Northamptonshire Regiment	(58th Foot)
2nd Bn, the Gloucestershire Regiment	(61st Foot)
The Queen's Own Cameron Highlanders	(79th Foot)
2nd Bn, the South Staffordshire Regiment	(80th Foot)
2nd Bn, the Royal Irish Rifles	(86th Foot)
1st Bn, the Connaught Rangers	(88th Foot)
2nd Bn, the Princess Victoria's (Royal Irish Fusiliers)	(89th Foot)
2nd Bn, the Cameronians (Scottish Rifles)	(90th Foot)
2nd Bn, the Gordon Highlanders	(92nd Foot)
2nd Bn, the Queen's Own (Royal West Kent Regiment	(97th Foot)

In 1801 the 97th Foot was the 97th (Queen's German) Regiment of Foot. Renumbered as 96th in 1816 and disbanded in 1818, when its title was 96th (Queen's Own) Regiment of Foot. A new 96th Foot was raised by the Earl of Ulster in 1824, the honours of the original disbanded regiment were re-granted in 1874.

The 50th (the Queen's Own [Royal West Kent Regiment]) who had taken part in the expedition, were nicknamed 'The Blind Half Hundred', because during the campaign many of their men suffered ophthalmia, which caused temporary and sometimes permanent loss of sight.

CHAPTER XXIII

NAPOLEONIC WAR 1809–1810
GEORGE III
WEST INDIES – MARTINIQUE, GUADELOUPE

At the Peace of Amiens in 1802, the islands of Martinique and Guadeloupe had been returned to the French.

After six years of French occupation, it was decided by the British Government that the island of Martinique should again be under their control. An expedition involving nine Line regiments was sent against the French garrison on the island.

The force was under the command of Lieutenant-General George Beckwith, who was considered to be a great tactician; he divided the regiments into two divisions. They sailed from Barbados on 28th January 1809. The 1st Division landed unopposed on the east coast, while the 2nd Division landed at the south end of the island near the town of St Luce. The island is relatively small, being only 40 miles from north to south and thirteen miles across. There were numerous French troops in occupation, but such was the rapid invasion by the British, that little early organised resistance was encountered.

When regiments from the 2nd Division reached the neighbourhood of Fort Royal, there was a considerable defence by the French. The 15th Foot (the East Yorkshire Regiment) played a major part in taking the area, when they brought up batteries to bombard the French forts.

The 1st Division besieged and then stormed Fort Bambon, where the 8th/63rd (the King's Regiment) captured three French standards. Eventually, on the 24th February the French defenders, seeing that further resistance was hopeless, decided to surrender and once again Martinique fell into the hands of the British.

For their actions, the following regiments were in 1816 or 1817, awarded the battle honour MARTINIQUE 1809, with the date not added until Army Order 295/1909:

The Royal Fusiliers	(7th Foot)
The King's (Liverpool Regiment)	(8th Foot)
The (Prince Albert's) Somerset Light Infantry	(13th Foot)
The East Yorkshire Regiment	(15th Foot)
The Royal Welsh Fusiliers	(23rd Foot)
The King's Own Borderers	(25th Foot)
2nd Battalion the Cameronians (Scottish Rifles)	(90th Foot)
The King's Royal Rifle Corps (3rd Battalion)	(60th Foot)
1st Battalion, the Manchester Regiment	(63rd Foot)

For his part in the capture of the island, the commander of the force, was in 1814, promoted and became General Sir George Beckwith.

GUADELOUPE

Regiments had no sooner recovered from their ordeal in Martinique than some were moved to Granada, where after a few months they were, in January 1810, ordered to Barbados to join a force which was being organized for the capture of the island of Guadeloupe, which like Martinique had been returned to the French in 1802.

Following his success at Martinique, Lieutenant-General Sir George Beckwith was given the command. The expedition sailed for Guadeloupe and as he had successfully done earlier, Beckwith divided his force into two divisions, the 2nd landing near the village of Les Vieux Habitans on the morning of 30th January, the 1st further south.

Although the French were in force on high ground, and in spite of the difficult rugged country encountered by the British, the defenders were forced to retire. British regiments turned both the French right flank, then the left, until the French were forced to concede and their commandant surrendered the island.

This campaign was most creditable to both the British commander and the troops who took part in it, especially as there were very few British casualties. As a mark of appreciation, Sir George Beckwith presented the 15th Foot with a drum-major's staff, with a silver head.

Once again, the health of men in the regiments suffered very severely from the climate in Guadeloupe, and many deaths from fever occurred in the months following their occupation of the island.

As with the battle honour given for Martinique, that for GUADELOUPE 1810 was awarded to three regiments between 1817 and 1819. The only regiment to miss out at this time was the 70th Foot, who were not given the award until 1867. The date 1810 was added to the name, by Army Order 295 in 1909.

The East Yorkshire Regiment	(15th Foot)
1st Battalion, the Manchester Regiment	(63rd Foot)
2nd Battalion, the East Surrey Regiment	(70th Foot)
2nd Battalion, the Cameronians (Scottish Rifles)	(90th Foot)

CHAPTER XXIV

PENINSULAR WAR 1808-1814
GEORGE III
THE SPANISH PENINSULA AND PYRENEES

The war was so called because it was fought over the territories of Spain and Portugal – the Iberian Peninsula.

Following the French invasion of Russia, the Treaty of Tilsit was agreed between the Russian Emperor Alexander and Napoleon. This alliance was not an act of friendship, but was designed to be directed against their common enemy, Britain,

Napoleon's eyes then turned west towards Spain and Portugal, encouraged by the corrupt and ineffectual Spanish royal family. While the British Navy blockaded the coast of Europe, Napoleon closed all ports to British trade. The only country who refused to enforce this embargo was neutral Portugal.

General Andoche Junot was the French commander given the responsibility by Napoleon for invading Portugal, which he commenced in November 1807. Lisbon was soon taken.

King Charles IV of Spain, although easygoing, was dominated by his wife, Maria Luisa, who for at least twenty years had verged on insanity; she was not only influenced by her lover Manuel Godoy but also by the Crown Prince Ferdinand.

The intrigue between the factions played directly into the hands of the French, as in October 1807 both Charles and Ferdinand sought to gain the support of Napoleon, who actually favoured the Crown Prince forcing Charles to abdicate. Godoy accused Ferdinand of being a bastard, causing him to abdicate, this enabled Napoleon to name his elder brother, Joseph, as King of Spain.

Napoleon moved 80,000 troops into Spain on the pretext of reinforcing Junot in Portugal. In May 1808, the Spanish rose in rebellion, closely followed by Portugal. Guerrilla warfare swept both countries causing French troops in Spain to seek shelter in their garrisons, this also isolated Junot in Portugal.

Spain and Portugal appealed for help from Britain, who on 4th July 1808 proclaimed peace with Spain and agreed to mount an expedition to Portugal.

There remained a major problem for the proposed expedition, that of the command. The Official Seniority List was Sir Hew Dalrymple, Sir Harry Burrard, Sir John Moore, Sir John Hope, Sir Kenneth Mackenzie, General Frazer, Lord Paget and the eighth in line was Sir Arthur Wellesley. Most of the men who ranked above Wellesley, except Moore, were either old or inexperienced or both.

Wellesley who had been promoted to Lieutenant-General on 25th April 1808 was in Cork, Ireland preparing to go to Spanish America when he received new orders to proceed with his command of 9,000 men to Portugal. On arrival he would be reinforced by 5,000 men under Major-General Sir Brent Spencer acting as his second-in-command.

With the senior generals still not able to arrive in Portugal before Wellesley, he was told by the Secretary of War, Lord Castlereagh, that until the others arrived, he was to continue against the French in Lisbon on his own initiative.

Wellesley sailed on 12th July, arriving at Oporto on the 24th. The expedition disembarked at Mondego on the 30th where a General Order was carried out in that men from the 60th and 95th Regiments would be attached by companies to infantry brigades. Another rather confusing order directed that attached riflemen with their Baker rifles (the infantry still had Brown Bess muskets) were to be formed on the left of the brigade, but when opposing the enemy they would be on the front, or rear, according to circumstances.

Wellesley remained at Mondego for eight days before marching to Leira. His command consisted of 30,000 well-equipped men which included fourteen Line regiments. On 14th August, Wellesley reached Alcobaca. The next day an engagement took place outside the village of Obidos; an officer from the 5th Battalion, 60th Foot was killed, when a detachment of the 2nd Battalion, 95th Foot clashed with French pickets.

At the same time Lieutenant-General Sir John Moore was sailing back from Sweden and was expected to land at Yarmouth on 15th August. He had been told that neither he nor Wellesley would be in command of the expedition. He should join Wellesley with his 10,000 men, also ships were being sent to Gibraltar where a further 4,000 men were being made ready for the attack. Furthermore, ships were also on their way to Madeira to bring General Beresford and his force, which included the Buffs and artillery.

On the 17th August 1808, the first major action of the Peninsular War took place, when at great cost British regiments drove the French under Junot from their position on the crest of the ridge at Rolica. The battle resulted in the French losing over 600 dead, whilst the British lost 470 men. This was the last battle at which the British Army wore queues, the hanging plaited tail of hair, and powdered hair.

When Wellesley heard that 4,000 British troops were off the coast, he marched to Vimiera to cover the landing which occurred on the 18th, 19th and 20th of August. This was the force under Sir Harry Burrard, to whom Wellesley was to hand over command.

Before this change of command could happen Wellesley, who had been reinforced by two brigades, was attacked by Junot. The nineteen foot regiments stood firm amid heavy casualties, their lines of controlled fire held the French assault which was decisively repulsed. Junot started his retreat to Lisbon. During this battle the 29th Foot ignored the new fashion and still wore their queues and powdered hair.

When Sir Harry Burrard landed late on the 21st August, he immediately moved against Junot's retreating army. His arrival was followed two days later by that of Sir Hew Dalrymple; Wellesley was now outranked by the two generals.

SPAIN & PORTUGAL 1780 - 1783

Junot found himself in a difficult position. The British aim was the removal of French troops from Portugal, therefore talks were set up; the outcome was to become known as the Convention of Cintra. On 31st August, Sir Hew Dalrymple drew up the conditions where, in order to leave Portugal without further conflict, the French required that their 26,000 men were transported by sea to France. This was agreed and the evacuation followed, with Junot and his army being landed from British transports at the west coast, Port of Rochefort.

The release of the French caused so much consternation in England that the three generals were ordered home. Wellesley sailed for Plymouth on 19th September, arriving on 4th October which was also the day that Dalrymple sailed, followed four days later by Burrard.

A military court of enquiry was set up in London. Its findings were that the generals had achieved the objective, at least as far as the Portuguese were concerned, in that the French had been removed from their country with no further loss of life.

For their actions at both locations, the following regiments were awarded the battle honours ROLICA and VIMIERA:

The Northumberland Fusiliers	(5th Foot)
The Royal Warwickshire Regiment	(6th Foot)
The Norfolk Regiment	(9th Foot)
1st Bn The Worcestershire Regiment	29th Foot)
1st Bn, the Duke of Cornwall's Light Infantry	(32nd Foot)
2nd Bn, the Worcestershire Regiment	(36th Foot)
1st Bn, The South Staffordshire Regiment	(38th Foot)
1st Bn Prince of Wales's Volunteers (South Lancs)	(40th Foot)
1st Bn, the Sherwood Foresters (Derbyshire) Regt.	(45th Foot)
The King's Royal Rifle Corps	(60th Foot)
1st Bn, the Highland Light Infantry (City of Glasgow)	(71st Foot)
2nd Bn, Prince of Wales's Volunteers (South Lancs)	(82nd Foot)
1st Bn Princess Louise's, later known as: (Sutherland and Argyll Highlanders)	(91st Foot)
Rifle Regiment	(95th Foot)

The 82nd Foot were raised in 1793 in Stamford by an officer in the suite of the Prince of Wales, later George IV, composed entirely of volunteers, hence the title.

95th Foot. As long-standing early raised regiments carried low regimental numbers, those that were later raised for specific operations, only to be disbanded upon completion, were given higher numbers. Six regiments were to carry the number 95, the latest was in 1823. The 95th who fought in the Peninsular were the fifth, they were disbanded after the War.

Regiments who only fought at VIMIERA were awarded that battle honour:

The Queen's (Royal West Surrey) Regiment	(2nd Foot)
The Lancashire Fusiliers	(20th Foot)
1st Bn, the Oxfordshire Light Infantry	(43rd Foot)
1st Bn, the Queen's Own (Royal West Kent) Regiment	(50th Foot)
2nd Bn, the Oxfordshire Light Infantry	(52nd Foot)

CORUNNA

Sir John Moore arrived from England on 24th August. Landing at Lisbon, he spent just over three weeks before setting up his headquarters at Queluz, about seven miles from Lisbon, with fifteen Line regiments who were still in Portugal.

On 6th October he opened his orders, which had been drafted on 25th September. Due to the command re-organisation following Cintra, he was appointed Commander-in Chief. His orders were to co-operate with the Spanish army for the expulsion of the French from northern Spain. The orders also instructed that he should advance on Madrid.

Moore was to be reinforced by an army from England. This would be 10,000 men under Sir David Baird, who left England and arrived at Corunna in October. Baird commenced landing the troops which included thirteen Line regiments. His orders were to march across the

Galician Mountains, join up with Moore and attack Marshal Soult's Army, before marching against Madrid.

Sir John Moore's column included his Light Brigade, which consisted of the 43rd and 52nd Regiments of Foot who had trained in 1803 in England under Moore. They were joined by the 95th Foot for his march to Madrid.

Believing there was no suitable road which could carry his artillery, Moore split his army in two. The artillery would be escorted by cavalry and this column would be under the command of Sir John Hope, whilst the infantry would be led by Moore himself. The infantry regiments were split into four columns, all following slightly different routes until the army was able to meet the Spanish.

On 13th November Moore reached Salamanca in north-central Spain, about 200 miles from Lisbon, where he stayed for ten days waiting for the artillery to arrive. He then moved to Guarda. Further north Sir David Baird was still moving with his column, following his orders to meet up with Moore ready for the drive to Madrid.

Meanwhile the French were preparing to stop the British advance; Napoleon had entered Spain on 5th November and six days later had moved to Burgos. It was the French belief that the British were intent on cutting Soult's lines of communication, so accordingly brought their combined regiments of nearly 80,000 men against the much smaller British force.

Unfortunately the actions of the Spanish army failed to live up to promises and the joining of the two armies never took place. Moore realized that the Spaniards were not now in a position to assist in any way. He firstly moved south and then confused the French by moving north, but by 28th November he realized that the advance was deeply in trouble, and ordered Baird to fall back to the coast and Sir John Hope to retreat to Ciudad Rodrigo.

Moore decided that he and his columns would join the retreat to Corunna, a 300-mile journey, which, although over difficult terrain and in the midst of winter, gave him the best chance of rescue.

The route entailed crossing mountainous country where snow was falling and winds were cutting into the soldiers' ragged uniforms. As Marshal Soult pressed the pursuit, regiments were compelled to fight rearguard actions, and as the weather deteriorated, and roads became worse, lack of supplies caused the morale of the men to become very strained.

The first regiments reached Corunna on 11th January 1809, but relief ships did not arrive until later in the day when the first two docked. This required that regiments had to be deployed in the two hill ranges overlooking the port. Troops were posted in both areas, and as more transports arrived, Moore began embarking the sick, wounded and cavalry together with their horses, and also some artillery pieces.

Moore remained with his outlying troops, and on 16th January 1809 ordered the main army to begin withdrawing to the transports. However, just before 2 p.m. the French attacked. Two hours later Moore was wounded, the British Line regiments then advanced against the French under the direction of Sir John Hope who had just returned from Ciudad Rodrigo.

Moore was taken into the town of Corunna where he died in the evening. Also killed was the colonel of the 92nd who had been shot in the groin.

When the regiments left the town, the last to leave was Captain Thomas Lloyd Fletcher of the 23rd Foot. He was in the rearguard, and as they passed through the gates, he turned to lock them, but the key would not turn so he inserted a bayonet into the key, and with the aid of a corporal turned it. The keys are now in the Royal Welch Fusiliers' Museum. The next day the transports sailed for England.

Just to indicate how the men suffered during the retreat, the following was described by a sergeant of the 92nd Foot when he landed at Portsmouth. 'I had neither shoes nor stockings but had to walk along the streets bare-footed; the conditions we were in with regard to clothing and cleanliness beggars description. When we came to our billets about six miles from Portsmouth, the inhabitants would not allow us to sleep in their beds, nor sit by their fireside on account of the vermin that infested us; cleaning ourselves was out of the question. It was wretched.'

As well as their battle honours for Rolica and Vimiera, the battle honour CORUNNA was awarded to the 2nd, 5th, 6th, 9th, 20th, 32nd, 36th, 38th, 43rd, 50th, 52nd, 71st, 82nd, 91st and 95th.

Additionally the award was also given to:

The Lothian Regiment (the Royal Scots)	(1st Foot)
The King's Own (Royal Lancashire) Regiment	(4th Foot)
The Prince of Wales's Own (West Yorkshire) Regiment	(14th Foot)
Royal Welch Fusiliers	(23rd Foot)
1st Bn The Cameronians (Scottish Rifles)	(26th Foot)
1st Bn The Gloucestershire Regiment	(28th Foot)
1st Bn, the Black Watch (Royal Highlanders)	(42nd Foot)
1st Bn, the King's Own (Yorkshire Light Infantry)	(51st Foot)
2nd Bn, the East Lancashire Regiment	(59th Foot)
2nd Bn, the Duke of Wellington's (West Riding) Regt	(76th Foot)
The Queen's Own Cameron Highlanders	(79th Foot)
2nd Bn, the Loyal North Lancashire Regiment	(81st Foot)
2nd Bn, the Gordon Highlanders	(92nd Foot)

The 76th Foot was raised in 1787 by Thomas Musgrave. It was also known as the Hindoostan Regiment, raised for service in India at the expense of the East India Company, where it went in 1788 for twenty years, before returning for action in the Peninsular.

DOURO

As a Member of Parliament, Sir Arthur Wellesley knew and understood the mood in the House of Commons, that the Iberian Peninsular especially Portugal should be denied to Napoleon. He was also aware that much debate was taking place as to who should be in overall command. He knew that he was one of the youngest generals and junior in rank to many.

The mood in the country, following news of the death of Sir John Moore and the sight of returning soldiers, was that the army must return to the Peninsula. As more men were required, regiments had to be expanded such that second battalions, which had hitherto only been used for new recruits in training, depot and holding companies, were to be used for general service and sent to Portugal with the Expeditionary Army. Some regiments became so popular that more than two battalions were to be raised.

Wellesley spent much time lobbying leading members of the Government that he should be given overall command, and towards this end he produced a document on how the war should be conducted, which he circulated to them. One of the men who believed that Wellesley was the man to lead was George Canning, the Foreign Secretary who led a campaign to have him given the command. Against much opposition, he won his way and Wellesley was given the role.

Wellesley left England and sailed for Portugal arriving at Lisbon on 22nd April, where he learnt that Marshal Soult had entered Portugal from the north, crossing the River Minho and on the 29th March with 20,000 men had taken and sacked Oporto.

Wellesley moved north with the intention of driving the French from Oporto and thence across the Portuguese border into Spain. On 2nd May he reached Coimbra where he met the troops under his command, and planned his offensive against the French by dividing the infantry into divisions. Units were reorganized to include the Portuguese infantry and placed in separate brigades. He then further split his force into three. Generals Beresford and Mackenzie were ordered to take their separate commands to stop the French from reinforcing Soult.

Wellesley moved his force of 16,000 British and 2,400 Portuguese north towards Oporto, where by 9th May, French outposts were encountered when the British column approached the River Vouga. He crossed with only minimal conflict and continued his progress towards Oporto which he reached on 11th May.

As Wellesley, who in six days had marched 120 miles, approached the town, Soult blew up the last bridge over the River Douro and closed the ferry, taking all boats and barges to the far side believing that this would halt the British advance. However, local Portuguese crossed the river with four wine barges. Twenty-five men of the Light Company of the Buffs crossed and prepared defences, while men of their second and third company followed in the same way.

The French, now aware that the British were crossing in force, launched a heavy attack which was repulsed for over two hours, enabling the rest of the brigade to cross.

The French having lost many men and much equipment were now in full retreat and began to stream from the town, and as the 29th Foot was able to strike into the French flank, Soult retreated towards Amarante.

Before the war was over three Line regiments were awarded the battle honour DOURO after the river where they had been engaged between 10th–12th May 1809:

The Buffs (East Kent) Regiment	(3rd Foot)
1st Bn, the Northamptonshire Regiment	(48th Foot)
2nd Bn, Princess Charlotte of Wales's (Berkshire)	(66th Foot)

TALAVERA

From Oporto in late June 1809, Sir Arthur Wellesley advanced eastwards into Spain up the River Tagus towards Madrid. He had a completely integrated allied army of British and Portuguese regular troops supported, at least in theory, by Spanish irregulars of doubtful reliability, ill equipped, and led by somewhat temperamental commanders.

On 8th July Wellesley entered Plasencia; two days later he went with his senior British officers to plan strategy with Gregorio Cuesta, the Spanish military leader.

The French had three main forces in the area, with 12,000 men garrisoned in Madrid, nearly twice as many were at Talavera under Marshal Claud Victor, and a similar number under Sebastiani at Madridjos. If required, they could in a day or two meet at Toledo, which would give the army strength of over 50,000 men.

Wellesley knew that should the French combine their armies, his smaller force, even with the Portuguese could not withstand an attack. His task was to persuade Cuesta to join with other Spaniards, especially those in the south, to ensure that the French remained as separate units.

Although Cuesta agreed, his word was broken. The Spanish also proved to be ineffective when opposed by French infantry, as they failed to prevent the garrison from the south joining Victor.

On 27th July Wellesley faced with greatly superior numbers fell back down the Tagus to the village of Talavera. The shallow Portina Brook marked the front of the allied line, which consisted of the Spanish infantry led by Cuesta on the right, while in the centre were British regiments; the left was filled with Spanish irregular troops covered by British cavalry. But when later in the afternoon, after time for the Allies to prepare a defensive line, the French discharged their weapons, the Spanish infantry panicked and about 2,000 fled.

Marshal Victor took advantage and attacked the British lines who held firm of Medellin Hill. The fact that night was fast falling helped the British, as the French missed their target in the dark and veered to the right. The effect of the onslaught was lost and the 29th Foot pushed the French back over the brook, before both sides took the opportunity to regroup and rest during the night.

At 5 a.m. the following morning the area was shrouded in fog. French artillery opened with a tremendous barrage and their infantry moved towards the line of British skirmishers, mainly from the 45th Foot and Light Companies from several other regiments, causing them to retreat through the lines of the division commanded by General Sir Charles Stewart.

Stewart moved the men from his regiments into the standard infantry defensive formation – two deep, the line stretched over 900 yards, as the southern French column advanced to within fifty yards, the Brown Bess muskets of the British fired volley after volley. This proved to be too much for the attackers who turned and, in undisciplined fashion, fled. Because the British considered it unwise to follow the retreating troops, the first engagement of the day was over; it was still not 7 a.m.

The infantry on both sides took a welcome break, and throughout the long hot morning, French and British troops took the opportunity to fill their water bottles from the waters of the Portina Brook, which consisted mainly of stagnant pools.

At 11 a.m. French drums were heard by the British, so the order was given to fall in, with the number of troops on both sides, this took some time, but by 1 p.m. French artillery opened fire upon the British front. There were many casualties of which men of the 2nd/83rd Foot took a heavy toll. After this barrage, the French infantry of about

30,000 men advanced against the whole British line. However, to the right the French were having difficulty keeping formation as the rough terrain made any semblance of order impossible.

Further north, 15,000 French troops launched an attack on General Sir John Sherbrooke's 1st Division consisting of eight battalions.

The British regiments were steady, front rank kneeling, enabling the fire from all weapons to be effectively employed.

The French advanced in long columns, which were allowed to approach to within thirty yards before the order was given to open fire. The effect was devastating and, as the French reeled, the British regiments counter-attacked through the smoke with their bayonets. But, following the French, the British overreached themselves and were driven back in disorder by the French second line.

Wellesley moved all available troops to fill the positions left by his disorganised infantry. The French counter-attacked with 10,000 infantry and 7,000 horse. At this juncture General Sir Kenneth Mackenzie, whose brigade consisted of the 4th, 24th and 34th Regiments of Foot, moved into position to stop the French advance. At 75 yards the British fired volley after volley, then with their bayonets moved against the remaining French.

The French withdrew and by 5 p.m. the battle was over, but it was not until early the next day that Marshal Victor withdrew, leaving Wellesley to care for his wounded and bury his dead. This prevented him from following the beaten enemy especially as reinforcements had not arrived until late on the 28th, when General Robert Crauford had brought the Light Division, the 43rd and 52nd Regiments of Foot from Lisbon, marching at speed, and covering the last 42 miles in 26 hours.

Wellesley also received reports that Soult's army was moving south from Galicia, threatening the communication link with Portugal. On 2nd August Soult took Plasencia.

The battle honour TALAVERA was awarded to the following regiments who had previously received awards for earlier battles in the Peninsula: 3rd, 29th, 40th, 45th, 60th, and 66th. Also awarded TALAVERA were the regiments new to the Peninsular:

The Royal Fusiliers (City of London) Regiment	(7th Foot)
The South Wales Borderers	(24th Foot)
1st Bn, the East Surrey Regiment	(31st Foot)
1st Bn, the Northamptonshire Regiment	(48th Foot)
1st Bn, the King's (Shropshire Light Infantry)	(53rd Foot)
2nd Bn, the Gloucestershire Regiment	(61st Foot)
1st Bn, the Royal Irish Rifles	(83rd Foot)
1st Bn, Princess Victoria's (Royal Irish Fusiliers)	(87th Foot)
1st Bn, the Connaught Rangers	(88th Foot)

Wellesley met Cuesta and agreed that the Spanish would stay in the area tending wounded from the Talavera battle, while the British would move against Soult. When Cuesta received information that Victor's army was moving against him, he abandoned his task, left the wounded and fled the area.

The Spanish lost several local engagements to the French, but by mid August, Cuesta had suffered a stroke, causing him to hand over command to General Carlos Areizago. Another change by the end of August elevated Sir Arthur Wellesley to the peerage, although the title was a little verbose* he became the 1st Duke of Wellington.

The Spanish lost yet another battle in November at Alba de Tormes, causing the Central Spanish Junta to abdicate. The effect of this was that guerrilla activities swept Spain until early in 1810 and atrocities were committed throughout the country, as Spanish fortresses surrendered to the French.

BUSACO

In September 1810, Marshal André Masséna was reinforced by regular troops as he led his army into Portugal in pursuit of Wellington. He moved from Almeida to Coimbra and then advanced towards Busaco.

---

* His title, selected in his absence by his brother was Viscount Wellington of Talavera and of Wellington, Baron Douro of Welleslie in the County of Somerset.

His advance was checked by Wellington, who had selected his defensive position on the hillside near Busaco. The area consisted of a ridge of high ground, upon which Wellington had ordered a track to be laid to enable the swift movement of his troops, to cover any weakness in the line.

Wellington's Allied line was nearly nine miles long, running north/south, defended by artillery and seventeen British Line Regiments with Portuguese troops. Expecting an early attack by the French, the British stood to arms at 4 a.m.; the early morning fog covered the area when the first French columns moved against General Sir Thomas Picton's 3rd Division, but as they advanced. British artillery fire took its toll.

The French made their next attack when eleven battalions of infantry moved against the British line about a mile further north. As the French progressed up the slope the 88th Foot met them with the bayonet. In contrast, the 2nd/83rd Foot positioned in the centre under General Sir Brent Spencer, were never closely engaged; their casualties were only one officer and four men slightly wounded. This did not compare with the suffering inflicted on five companies of the 60th Foot, who lost five officers and twenty-two other ranks killed, as well as many wounded including their commanding officer, Colonel Williams who was wounded twice.

Two French columns consisting of seven battalions moved by the slopes against the area defended by Picton's Brigade. The northern French column forced its way to the top of the ridge, where its troops ran along the track cheering until men from General Sir James Leith's command were joined by General Sir Roland Hill's regiments who met the French, again using their bayonets, driving them back down the slope.

Another French column struck at Crawford's Light Division and General Sir Denis Pack's Portuguese Brigade. The Light Division of the 95th, 43rd and 52nd Regiments of Foot overwhelmed them with a bayonet charge, while the 45th Foot distinguished themselves, attacking the French again with their bayonets as the enemy reached the crest of the hill, where they were also attacked by the 3rd/27th Foot, who had only been raised in 1805, known as the Young Inniskillings.

The reverses were too much and Massena withdrew. By not following him, Wellington refused a further engagement, as he believed that at this time the French were too strong to be permanently stopped, so he moved his troops south to the carefully planned defensive position, the lines of Torres Vedras.

For their actions on the ridge, the following regiments were awarded the battle honour BUSACO: 1st, 5th, 7th, 9th 24th, 38th, 42nd, 43rd, 45th, 52nd, 60th, 61st, 74th, 79th, 83rd, 88th and 95th.

The 74th were the 2nd Battalion, the Highland Light Infantry (City of Glasgow) Regiment, raised in 1787 by Major-General Sir Archibald Campbell.

Wellington established his HQ at Pero Negro, behind the fortified lines of Torres Vedras. He believed that Massena would either attack or risk starvation. The French were now separated from safety in Spain by many miles of territory, where Portuguese and Spanish guerrillas operated against any French, especially stragglers.

Further north, Badajoz was held by the Spanish, whose regular army had recently been defeated by Soult, allowing the Frenchman to lay siege to the fortress.

BARROSA

As the British generally spent the winter months in poor circumstances, they were therefore encouraged by the news which arrived from Cadiz. General Thomas Graham, commander of the British contingent, which included the 2nd and 3rd Battalions of the 95th Foot, had on 5th March 1811 launched an attack from the besieged garrison, which resulted in a resounding victory on the heights of Barrosa.

At the battle, the 2nd/87th captured the first French eagle in the Peninsular. In the midst of the fighting, Ensign Edward Keogh saw the eagle of the 8th French Light Infantry, and although he himself was killed in the struggle to take it, his sergeant, Patrick Masterson snatched the trophy despite French efforts to regain it. The Prince Regent directed that the regiment be called 87th (Prince of Wales's Own Irish) Foot. They were to bear by royal command, as a badge of honour on their Regimental Colour, an eagle with a wreath of laurels above the harp, in addition to the plume of the Prince of Wales.

Also in the battle were the 28th Foot, whose commanding officer Lieutenant-Colonel Browne led a composite battalion of grenadiers and light companies, including those of his own regiment. His men were ordered to form the 'forlorn hope' as the Spanish regiments alongside him, refused to face the French. The 28th suffered greatly and only the colonel and one lieutenant survived, from a total of eight officers who had stood against the enemy. But the day was won.

News now reached the British that the siege of Badajoz was over, because the Spanish Governor Jose Imez had treacherously handed the fortress over to Soult.

For the relief of Cadiz the following regiments received the battle honour BARROSA: 28th, 87th and 95th.

2nd Battalion, the Hampshire Regiment　　　　　　　(67th Foot)

FUENTES D'ONOR

In the spring of 1811, Wellington planned to break out of Portugal into Spain. In preparation, on 9th April, the 92nd, 50th and 70th Regiments of Foot had been engaged in a series of skirmishes with the French, who had been massing their forces in Spain.

Soult now controlled Badajoz, and on 1st May Massena crossed the River Agueda at Ciudad Rodrigo with a total of over 50,000 men. He advanced, but Wellington had already prepared his intended battle-site.

Fuentes de Onor lay on the west of the River Dos Casas; it was a straggling hill village situated just south of a ravine. Houses on its narrow streets had been converted by loopholes and barricades into a stronghold, covering the allied left flank. At 2 p.m. on 3rd May the French attack began, as ten battalions crossed the river, they were driven back by the Brigaded Light Division of the 95th, 43rd and 52nd which together with the 2nd/83rd inflicted heavy losses on the French.

A second wave of French infantry moved into the village, at first gaining a foothold, then following heavy fighting, losing ground. The

51st was one of the regiments engaged in the early French advance, when although their casualties were light, their commanding officer ordered that their Colours were burnt rather than fall into French hands. For this, Wellington ordered his court martial, but he was absolved and continued to command his regiment. The 51st left the village when they were moved to join the southern route. Next day, both armies were able to collect their dead and tend to their wounded, with no conflict between the two.

Early in the morning of the following day French infantry, shielded by cavalry, again crossed the river in foggy conditions. The Portuguese defenders were taken completely by surprise, the positions which they held fell to the French. Messena moved against the British, who withdrew, only to reform to a more defensive place.

The next French attack was directly against the village. Using ten battalions they crossed the river but were initially forced back. Then supported by another eighteen battalions, attacked again, engaging the British, where the 2nd/83rd formed part of the defenders including the Scots and Irish and the 88th Foot in Mackinnon's Brigade. The village was again almost taken, but was eventually regained when the French unexpectedly withdrew.

Wellington ordered the British to restore the defences during the night. By 6th May, Massena knew that with the loss of so many of his infantrymen further attacks would be unwise, he, therefore, retired from the area.

The battle honour FUENTES D'ONOR was awarded to:

2nd Battalion, the King's (Shropshire Light Infantry)
    (85th Foot)

also 24th, 42nd, 43rd, 45th, 51st, 52nd, 60th, 71st, 74th, 79th, 83rd, 88th, 92nd and 95th.

Typically, the British soldiery generally referred to the battle, as the 'Fountains of Horror'.

ALBUHERA

Since Badajoz had been taken by the French, and Marshal Soult had returned to Seville, the British under General Beresford were investing the fortress, when news reached him that Soult was moving north to relieve the garrison there. The initial French force was split into two columns, with over 18,000 men in each.

Beresford moved to intercept Soult, the Anglo-Portuguese army also included two Spanish divisions, in all about 20,000 men. The British arrived at Albuhera on 15th May and overnight deployed near the small town. At the same time, also moving south was the British 2nd Division.

At 8 a.m. on the 16th May, the French attacked the British line at Albuhera, while further south the Spanish were attacked by nineteen French regiments. Initially the French were held, but within the hour the Spanish were routed. The 1st British Brigade also suffered many losses.

The weather now played an important part in the next phase of the battle, as torrential rain fell on the British infantry, causing their muskets, which required a dry pan for the powder, to be rendered useless. The French cavalry took advantage, and attacked in a full charge with their sabres, before the British could form a defensive square.

The remainder of the 2nd Brigade lined to the edge of the sunken north road. The French had taken up a position forty yards away on the opposite side. The Colour party of the 29th Foot formed in the centre of their regiment. Ensign Furnace held the King's Colour and Ensign Vance, the Regimental Colour, both men were only 18 years old and it was their first experience of battle, there were also three Colour-Sergeants.

Throughout the morning casualties of the 29th were very heavy, such that the men, following their training rallied to the Colours, unfortunately this enabled the French to concentrate on the massed troops. Two of the Colour-Sergeants were killed. As the Colour party became isolated, the ensigns tried to hide the Colours as their remaining sergeant was killed. British reinforcements arrived and found the Colours amid the bodies of the original Colour party, surrounded by three-quarters of the 29th Regiment who had also fallen. Another regiment which nearly lost their colour was the 3rd Foot. Lt Mathew Latham saved the King's colour, tearing it from its pike and hiding it, despite having his nose sliced off by a French hussar.

Further along the line the commanding officer of the 57th Foot, Colonel Inglis took up his position at the front of his regiment. He was struck by grape-shot in the neck and left breast. As he lay on the ground, he refused to be carried to the rear. Instead he urged his men to hold position, crying, 'Die hard the 57th, die hard'. They had many casualties, out of a complement of 570 men, 428 fell and of their 30 officers only ten remained.

Fortunately the rain had ceased, Beresford moved forward seven British regiments who were now able to use their muskets. Close range encounters were common, as the Redcoats faced two French divisions of 7,800 men. The British lost over four fifths of their men in the exchange, which was slightly fewer than the French.

The 4th Division moved into the attack from the right. They advanced from behind the town and firstly met the French cavalry, then their infantry. The two armies stood at point blank range from each other, the French were met by controlled fire from the British, which caused the French to consider their position. Some men turned and ran, then groups, then whole regiments. The 1st and 2nd Battalions of the 23rd Foot took advantage and stormed the reeling French. The battle was won, but the cost was high; the allies lost 6,000 men of whom 4,000 were British.

The following day, Soult retreated south and Beresford resumed the siege of Badajoz.

The battle honour ALBUHERA was awarded to:

1st Bn, the Border Regiment	(34th Foot)
1st Bn, the Dorsetshire Regiment	(39th Foot)
1st Bn, Duke of Cambridge's Own (Middlesex) Regt	(57th Foot)

also the 3rd, 7th, 23rd, 28th, 29th, 31st, 48th, 60th and 66th.

ARROYO DOS MOLINOS

The summer months of 1811 were used by both sides trying to out-guess what the other would do. Regiments were almost permanently on the march in very bad weather. During this time the 92nd Foot had received a draft from their second battalion in Ireland, to make up their depleted numbers from the most recent conflicts.

Wellington heard that Soult was again intent on relieving the pressure that the British were exerting on the garrison at Badajoz. Soult was joined by the French commander, Marshal Auguste Frederic Marmont, and by mid-June they entered the fortress. Wellington withdrew his forces. He then decided to move against the French in Cuidad Rodrigo but, learning of the strength of enemy forces in the area, retired without combat.

As the year drew on, the Allies settled for an inactive time. But on 28th October, General 'daddy' Hill, an officer respected by his men for his attitude towards them, moved unexpectedly against the small French garrison at Arroyo Dos Molinos, which consisted of only 2,500 men. The French were taken by surprise and the conflict was fought at the foot of a crescent-shaped ridge of a small mountain, in thick mist and heavy rain.

Charging out of the mist, the 71st and 92nd dispersed the French cavalry and as the 34th also became involved, the enemy lost not only all their artillery and baggage, but also their Commanding General and 1,400 of his men.

The battle honour ARROYO DOS MOLINOS was given to the 34th Foot (the Border Regiment). Unlike most of the honours which were awarded during or immediately after the Peninsular War, this was only given to the 34th in 1845. For some unaccountable reason the 71st and 92nd did not receive the honour.

TARIFA

The small town of Tarifa, located on the extreme southern coast of Spain, was defended by two second battalions when it was attacked on New Year's Eve 1811, by French troops.

As the 2nd/47th and 2nd/87th Regiments defended the town using controlled musket fire, spirits were kept high by the pipes and drums of The Prince of Wales's Own Irish (87th) playing 'Garryowen' and 'St Patrick's Day' until the French decided that the attack was unlikely to succeed, and retired.

The battle honour TARIFA was awarded to:

1st Bn, the Loyal North Lancashire Regiment   (47th Foot)
and also the (87th Foot).

The name Tarifa, not only appears on the Colours of the 47th, but also on their regimental buttons.

CIUDAD RODRIGO

Early in January 1812 Wellington received news that the garrison at Ciudad Rodrigo under Marshal Louis Gabriel Suchet, was to be reinforced by 15,000 men from regiments under Marmot. Wellington decided that he should attack the fortress which had been under siege by the British for some time.

The allied plan was to move against the main French defences. At the same time, the Light Company of the 83rd was detached from their regiment to reinforce a Portuguese unit who would deal with the French outposts.

The attack against the main fortress was carried out under darkness during the night of 8th January, when the colonel of the 52nd moved forward with volunteers from his regiment, towards a hill called the Great Teson, an area where the French had built a redoubt. After a brief encounter, the British took the ground, this enabled the attacking troops to dig trenches both directly at, and parallel to, the fortress. This would give them a position close to their objective, enabling them to place siege cannon.

Allied batteries commenced firing in the late afternoon of the 13th. The plan was that shot would batter the walls, causing breaches through which the infantry would carry out the assault. The regiments stood in position to prevent the French from attacking the artillery until their job was done. This was achieved by the 19th when, at 7 a.m., the infantry moved. The bridge over the River Aguedo fell to the troops in the first wave.

The walls had been breached in two main places, the 77th Foot were one of three regiments who led the storming of the left, covering their advance were the 2nd/83rd, whilst the Light Division moved against the right. It was during this attack that their commander General Robert Crauford was killed. As the French resistance failed the fortress fell in two hours. Casualties on both sides were equal, slightly in excess of five hundred each.

The battle honour CIUDAD RODRIGO was awarded to:

2nd Bn, the Duke of Cambridge's Own Middlesex Regt   (77th Foot)
2nd Bn, the Connaught Rangers   (94th Foot)

At the time the 94th was a Highland Regiment in the Scotch Brigade, it was disbanded in 1818. The number 94 was given in 1823 to an Irish Regiment.

Also to receive the battle honour were 5th, 43rd, 45th, 52nd, 60th, 74th, 83rd, 88th and 95th.

BADAJOZ

Since the northern route into Spain had been opened with the fall of Ciudad Rodrigo, the next British aim was to send forces to take the southern route, which was defended by the French at Badajoz.

After their actions at Ciudad Rodrigo, eleven regiments took the long march south. It took eleven days over the mountains, when they would be joined by other regiments, for the combined assault on the fortress of Badajoz.

On St Patrick's Day, the 17th March 1812, the siege began under torrential rain and heavy cloud. When the Allies tried to build breastworks, they were hindered by the weather, where the poor conditions of mud and slime, prevented the construction of solid foundations required for the cannon, and the installation of their siege batteries.

The French were alarmed that British troops were moving against them, and on 19th March, sent men to investigate the strength of the attackers. It took three days before the British had chased them back to their fortress.

Once the siege cannon had been firmly set in position, the artillery kept up a steady bombardment against the walls of the fortress until, on the 6th April, it was reported to Wellington that three breaches had been made. The assault began by mid-morning. The Light and 4th Divisions struck into the breach but, as should have been expected, the French defenders were waiting for the attacking troops to appear.

As the British pressed forward, they were met by massed ranks of infantry, who repulsed the first assault. The 3rd/27th lost a third of their strength in less than two hours, while the 51st were also forced to retire with frightful losses. Over 2,500 men were killed during this operation.

Following the main assault, the 3rd Division which included the 2nd/83rd, was assigned the task of storming the escalade of the castle, this being the highest point in the city. Picton believed that it would be lightly defended, but it was only at great cost that it was finally taken. After many attempts, men slowly gained access, Picton's and Leith's Divisions drove forward at the northern corners of the castle.

Early on 7th April, Allied troops were moving into the town, but still had to take the inner part of the castle. Cautiously they entered the area, where their frustration at the length of the five-week battle took over. An officer of the 45th, after removing the French flag, hoisted his coatee on the flagpole to indicate that the fortress had been taken.

Atrocities committed by the British troops against the population of Badajoz were considered to be the worst in its history. Of the 5,000 strong garrison, only a few escaped the slaughter which followed the fall, The result of the fighting was to compel the French to retire to Salamanca.

The battle honour BADAJOZ was generally awarded within five or six years after the event, to:

1st Bn, the Royal Inniskilling Fusiliers　　　　　　　　(27th Foot)

1st Bn, the East Lancashire Regiment	(30th Foot)
1st Bn, the Essex Regiment	(44th Foot)

also to 4th, 5th, 7th, 23rd, 38th, 40th, 43rd, 45th, 48th, 52nd, 60th, 74th, 77th, 83rd, 88th, 94th and 95th.

ALMAREZ

Having taken Badajoz, Wellington pursued his overall plan to advance into Spain. General Rowland Hill had fought a number of successful local skirmishes, when he was ordered against the French positions on the River Tagus at Almarez which, if taken, would result in links between the French Marshals Soult and Marmont being severed.

Three regiments, the 50th, 71st and 92nd attacked and took Fort Napoleon. For this action they received the battle honour ALMAREZ, which was awarded to the 50th and 71st in 1815, but the 92nd had to wait until 1830 when they received theirs.

1st Bn, the Queen's Own (Royal West Kent Regt)	(50th Foot)
1st Bn, the Highland Light Infantry (City of Glasgow)	(71st Foot)
2nd Bn, the Gordon Highlanders	(92nd Foot)

SALAMANCA

Following months of manoeuvring, July found the opposing armies once more in Spain. The French commander, Marshal Marmont was aware that British troops had moved into Salamanca, a town northwest of Madrid.

The armies clashed about four miles south of Salamanca, an area dominated by two steeply sided hills, the north called the Lesser Arapile was occupied by the British 4th, 5th and 6th Divisions, whilst the southern hill which was about seven miles long was called the Greater Arapile, this hill was south and east of the British position.

The French columns were spread over four miles, their army moving slowly across the top of the Greater Arapile. Their commanders did not realise that their left had started to move before the right was in position. This left a gap in their formation, an advantage which was eagerly seized upon by the British 4th Division who moved against the French, but were themselves greeted by a counter-attack and pushed back.

The 6th Division under General Clinton was ordered to re-take the lost ground. The 61st and 11th Regiments in Hulse's Brigade, were on the British right. As they advanced on the enemy, they drove them back up the hillside. British regiments suffered greatly, as they came under fire from French grape-shot and musketry, but after a fierce struggle, the French retreated.

The 3rd Division on the far British right left Salamanca they included the 2nd/83rd Regiment and moved across the French front, the whole Division marching in three parallel columns. They manoeuvred and formed front to their flank, by simply executing a left turn on the march, and then advanced in brigade order upon the bulk of the French marching column. They overlapped its head which frustrated any attempt by the French to deploy in line of battle. The successive ranks of the French telescoped into each other. Utter confusion turned into rout, and when British heavy dragoons charged, their sabres were used to great effect upon the enemy.

Everywhere the French were withdrawing, leaving a rearguard along the top of the escarpment, the British 6th Division moved against them, but were met by volley after volley resulting in heavy losses. Finally the pressure from all four divisions caused the French to break and flee the field, leaving behind a trophy of Moorish manufacture with a brass Napoleonic eagle on top, captured by the 88th Foot from the French 101st Regiment. Also taken from the enemy by the 30th Foot was the eagle of the French 22nd Regiment.

On a more sombre note, casualties in Hulse's Brigade were the 11th who suffered sixteen officers and 325 men killed or wounded, and the 60th who lost three officers and thirty-five other ranks killed. The 61st started the day with a full complement, of which, only three officers and 78 men survived, their commanding officer Colonel Barlow was killed, and no less than six relays of officers and sergeants were killed under the Colours, which were finally carried during their final assault by Privates Crawford and Coulston.

The battle honour SALAMANCA was mostly awarded to the following regiments within a few years of the event, except the 42nd Foot, to whom it was not given until 1951:

The Devonshire Regiment	(11th Foot)
2nd Bn, the Northamptonshire Regiment	(58th Foot)
1st Bn, the Durham Light Infantry	(68th Foot)

1st, 2nd, 4th, 5th, 7th, 9th, 23rd, 24th, 27th, 30th, 32nd, 36th, 38th, 40th, 42nd, 43rd, 44th, 45th, 48th, 51st, 53rd, 60th, 61st, 74th, 79th, 83rd, 88th, 94th and 95th.

VITTORIA

The campaign of 1813 started late, as the Allied army required to rest after its tiring actions during the previous year. The French too required time, following the loss during 1812 of some of their best units being withdrawn from Spain, as Napoleon attacked Russia, where he lost as many as 28,000 men at Borodino.

The Plain of Vittoria, at the foot of the Pyrenees, is surrounded by mountainous country, crossed by the river Zadorra. Wellington had chosen the area, and decided to attack the 70,000 Frenchmen under Marshal Joudan and King Joseph Bonaparte, before they could properly be brought into line of battle.

The French had left the bridges intact over the river, and hurriedly taken up their positions on the south side, beside the Arinez Hill. The 3rd Division under General Picton, were the 2nd/83rd and 2nd/87th Regiments who had been brigaded together, attacked and charged against the French second line, encouraged by a shouting Picton. The 92nd were also ordered to cross the river, which was achieved, and although the action went on all day, their casualties were only four killed and sixteen wounded.

With the flanks of the 3rd Division now exposed, the order was given for a general advance. The first French gun was taken by the Rifles, consisting of the 95th, 43rd and 52nd Regiments, although the attack was led by the 60th. General Graham leading the 1st Division, moved from the far end of the valley, together with the 2nd/47th in the 5th Division. All divisions thrust aside any French resistance, but in the British 2nd Division, who fought at close quarters with their bayonets the 28th and 39th Regiments suffered severe losses, as did the 3rd/27th who lost more than half of their number killed or wounded.

The French lost their entire artillery of 150 guns and most of their baggage train, containing much treasure, which had been looted over recent years by the French. Instead of following the fleeing enemy, much to the annoyance of Wellington, the British soldiers filled their pockets with much of the loot. They also captured the baton which belonged to Marshal Jourdan. It was dispatched to the Prince Regent, who promptly appointed Wellington a field marshal.

Of the forty-one infantry of the line Regiments who received the battle honour VITTORIA, all had been involved in earlier actions during the War, although many had untried recruits drafted in to bring the ranks up to strength.

1st, 2nd, 3rd, 4th, 5th, 6th, 7th, 9th, 20th, 23rd, 24th, 27th, 28th, 31st, 34th, 38th, 39th, 40th, 43rd, 45th, 47th, 48th, 50th, 51st, 52nd, 53rd, 57th, 58th, 59th, 60th, 66th, 68th, 71st, 74th, 82nd, 83rd, 87th, 88th, 92nd, 94th and 95th.

SAN SEBASTIAN

At the end of June, after the Vittoria campaign, only three places remained under French control in northern Spain, the towns of Vera and Pamplona and the fortress of San Sebastian. The French army rallied in the frontier where Marshal Soult had assumed command, having been dispatched by Napoleon to supersede his brother King Joseph, and Marshal Jourdan.

Operations against San Sebastian continued throughout August. Soult made an attempt to relieve the fortress on 31st August but this was blocked by Spanish troops. One interesting story is shown in the history of the 28th Foot, who during a brief pause in the operations in the mountains sent a sergeant to purchase supplies from the port of San Sebastian. The sergeant took with him a private soldier and a mule. When they arrived at the coast, the sergeant heard that the next day the fortress was to be stormed. He decided to take part in the assault and attached himself to a unit which he knew. He and the private returned to the 28th, not only with the provisions they had been sent to buy, but a letter of recommendation from the brigade commander.

Following five days of heavy bombardment, Allied troops stormed San Sebastian. The castle and port capitulated on the 5th September. For their actions at the battle, the 1st, 4th, 9th, 47th and 59th Regiments received the battle honour SAN SEBASTIAN. Unfortunately, one sergeant and one private was not enough for the award to be given to the 28th.

PYRENEES

After his campaigns in northern Spain, Wellington advanced northwards towards France, but the mountain range of the Pyrenees was a formidable barrier. The French were followed into the mountains, where there were numerous places through which they could march back into Spain. During the course of the pursuit they frequently turned and fought. Now there followed a series of conflicts which came to be known as the Battles of the Pyrenees. The British concentrated on clearing the French from Vera, Pamplona and the village of Sorauren, the latter was eventually taken after heavy fighting, at great cost to the 11th Foot, who helped to repulse a French counter-attack. Pamplona did not capitulate until the end of October.

The Rifles, 95th, 43rd and 52nd were also engaged when they defended the bridge over the River Bidassoa in the Pass of Vera, where they held 5,000 Frenchmen from crossing. Also holding the French fight-back were the 92nd, who together with the 71st, held their position for nine hours, suffering heavy casualties.

The actions in the Pyrenees lasted from the 25th July until 2nd August 1813, where all British foot regiments were mainly responsible for clearing the French from Spain, just moving to the border for the first time.

The 2nd, 3rd, 6th, 7th, 11th, 20th, 23rd, 24th, 27th, 28th, 31st, 32nd, 36th, 39th, 40th, 42nd, 43rd, 45th, 48th, 50th, 51st, 52nd,

53rd, 57th, 58th, 60th, 61st, 66th, 68th, 71st, 74th, 79th, 82nd, 88th, 91st, 92nd, 94th and 95th.

These regiments who had been involved in the engagements were at various times soon after awarded the battle honour PYRENEES, although the 43rd, 52nd, 88th and 95th had to wait until 1910 before they received theirs.

In 1813 the Peninsula was generally clear of the French. Most regiments were now in winter quarters, facing the Pass of Mayo from where they could see France.

Wellington believed that to allow the French, during the winter months, to regroup and strengthen their weary units, would slow, if not completely stall his advance into France. Within twenty miles of the border were two rivers, which he believed he should cross to give him an advantage in the spring, initially to threaten Soult's lines of communication, thereby forcing him to abandon Bayonne and then to aid Wellington's move further into France. He therefore ordered a forward movement of all regiments.

His first objective was the River Nivelle, just eight miles away. The river was strongly defended and as British regiments attacked, the men in the 3rd Division which included the 2nd/83rd successfully crossed the river. Once across the 11th Regiment were ordered to attack a strong redoubt, which had been guarding approaches from the river. They soon took their objective, inflicting severe losses on the enemy.

After the Nivelle had been crossed, British troops drove the French towards the River Nive. Wellington resolved to follow the enemy. The 39th Foot in the 2nd Division, attacked French pickets with running musket fire, until they reached the river.

Just before dawn on the 9th December, the Allies advanced over a four-mile front, the river had three fords and a very flimsy pontoon bridge. Fighting lasted for five days, the French slowly giving way. They defeated the Portuguese at the village of Villefranque before the 39th and 61st Regiments re-took it.

Soult fell back towards Bayonne, and counter-attacked on the 3rd December, before retiring again the next day, until on the 13th, the French attacked with vigour. Although outnumbering the British,

Soult believed that he was being outflanked, he fell back, and as the allies pressed he retreated back into France.

For their involvement in actions at both rivers, the following regiments received the battle honours NIVELLE and NIVE:

3rd, 11th, 28th, 31st, 32nd, 34th, 36th, 39th, 42nd, 43rd, 52nd, 57th, 60th, 66th, 61st, 79th, 91st and 95th.

For regiments who fought at the River Nivelle the battle honour NIVELLE was awarded to the:

2nd, 5th, 6th, 23rd, 24th, 27th, 40th, 45th, 48th, 51st, 53rd, 58th, 68th, 74th, 82nd, 83rd, 87th, 88th and 94th.

For those who fought at the River Nive the battle honour NIVE was awarded to the:

1st, 4th, 9th, 38th, 47th, 50th, 59th, 62nd, 71st, 76th, 84th, 85th, and 92nd.

ORTHES

Early in February 1814, Wellington resumed the offensive and, on the 14th of the month, the final push began around Bayonne. Marshal Soult had to avoid being outflanked, and therefore gave ground as the Allies pressed relentlessly. For thirteen days the Allied army moved further into France. Contact was lost with the retreating French, but Soult took advantage by concentrating his scattered divisions on the heights outside Orthes, where on the 27th February the battle was fought.

The 39th Foot in the 2nd Division was used in the preliminary phase against the French left flank, whilst the 11th Foot crossed the River Gave de Pau in the early morning, and was ordered to attack the heights, where, after a fierce struggle they broke the enemy centre, causing them to fall back.

The 2nd/38th Foot with the 3rd Division, formed part of the main force which vigorously attacked the enemy, often at close quarters, resulting in the regiment losing nine officers wounded from a strength of twenty-two, mainly due to the strong defensive position of the French. At the end of the day Soult realized that his troops were in no condition to continue, he therefore fell back on Toulouse, over 100 miles away.

The regiments of foot who fought in the battle received the battle honour ORTHES, which was awarded to the:

3rd, 5th, 6th, 7th, 11th, 20th, 23rd, 24th, 27th, 28th, 31st, 32nd, 34th, 36th, 39th, 40th, 42nd, 45th, 48th, 50th, 51st, 52nd, 58th, 60th, 61st, 66th, 71st, 74th, 82nd, 83rd, 87th, 88th, 91st, 92nd, 94th and 95th.

TOULOUSE

The French withdrawal continued eastwards, across rolling countryside towards the city of Toulouse, which the enemy had fortified. The British advance was constantly hindered over a period of six weeks, as French artillery and musket fire forced regiments to deploy, until on the 8th April 1814 leading troops crossed the Garonne River, the remainder of the Allied regiments were stretched across an area northwest of the city.

The following day saw the allies taking position against the enemy. Spanish, Portuguese and men from twenty-six British regiments were deployed in various divisions against the defenders. The Spanish launched the first attack just after 6 a.m. on Easter Sunday the 10th April, but it was repulsed. The British were then ordered to move forward, which was met by stiff resistance.

General Picton's 3rd Division was checked, and as his casualties mounted, regiments including the 11th Foot under Brigadier-General Lambert came to their aid. The 61st Foot gained the nickname 'The Flower of Toulouse', because of the 180 men killed or wounded who lay on the field of battle, together with their commanding officer, all in their recently issued scarlet uniforms. The adjutant and two ensigns were the only surviving officers, and after the fighting, only forty other ranks remained.

The British again advanced, the French cavalry charged but were held, and with their infantry were driven back into the city. The French pulled back and, as night approached, Soult and his army were defeated and Toulouse was evacuated.

The battle had been needlessly fought. Nearly 8,000 French, British, Portuguese and Spanish were killed or wounded. Wounds often led to death, following the poor medical services that were available. Napoleon Bonaparte had conceded defeat, but as the highest speed of communication at that time was that of a man on a fast horse, neither side was aware that he had abdicated nearly one week earlier.

TOULOUSE was awarded as a battle honour to the:

3rd, 5th, 7th, 11th, 20th, 23rd, 27th, 28th, 36th, 40th, 42nd, 43rd, 45th, 48th, 52nd, 53rd, 60th, 61st, 74th, 79th, 83rd, 87th, 88th, 91st, 94th and 95th Regiments.

All regiments who had been involved at any stage during the war between 1808 and 1814, and who had been awarded one or more of the battle honours, were at the cessation of hostilities further awarded PENINSULA by Royal authority.

CHAPTER XXV

THE HUNDRED DAYS – WATERLOO 1815
GEORGE III

The Hundred Days – was the time taken, from when Napoleon landed in France to his defeat at Waterloo.

Napoleon was only 44 years old when, following his defeat on the mainland in the war of 1808–1814, he was exiled to the Mediterranean island of Elba. Apparently, he had been told by his mother that he was not meant to die on the island. On the 26th February 1815, Napoleon left Elba, and on 1st March he landed at Cannes with less than a thousand men.

On the 20th March, Napoleon moved into Paris, his supporters were ecstatic, but Europe was again up in arms. He had watched how France had developed under the Bourbon regime, and was convinced that members of his former army would return to fight for him. He was not wrong, as Marshal Ney, leading an army for the Bourbon King changed sides and moved with the army behind Napoleon.

The leaders of other European countries were meeting at the Congress of Vienna when news arrived that Napoleon had returned to France. They each sent word to mobilize their regiments, who must have believed that, after Toulouse, the war with France was over.

The Allied army was gathering in Belgium. Several of the British regiments had to return from their recent postings. Typically the 28th Foot were in Ireland, whilst the 27th Foot had to travel back from North America.

British regiments assembled in and around Brussels where Wellington had recently established his headquarters. He had a total

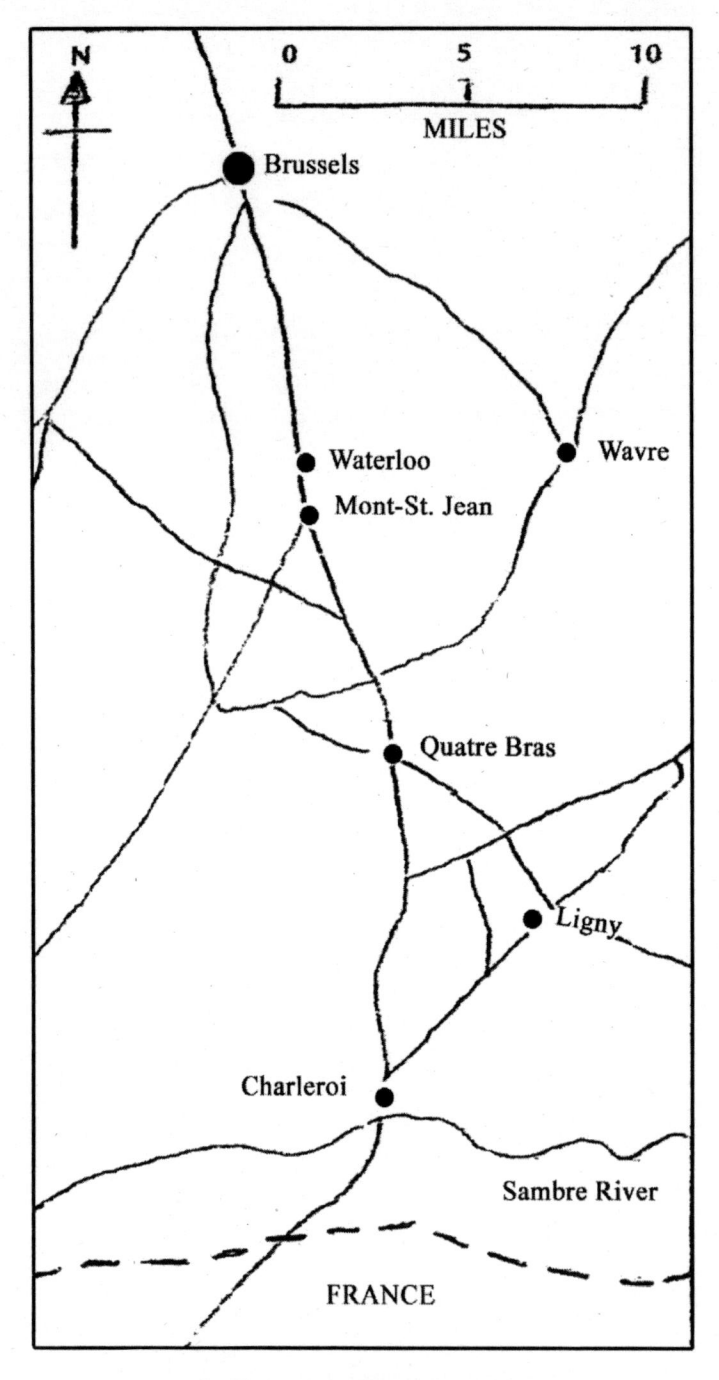

BELGIUM 1815

strength of 93,000 men, although only a third were British, the rest being mostly Dutch and Belgians.

The Prussians, under their 72-year-old commander Marshal Blücher, had gathered over 110,000 men, the intention of the Allies was to attack the French in France. They would gather all of the Allied armies together, and cross into France with 500,000 men, but this would take until July before they were ready.

Napoleon initially tried to open negotiations with Britain, Russia, Austria and Prussia, but he was rebuffed by all of the leaders. He then believed that he should move against the Allies, rather than fight a defensive campaign; for this purpose he had mobilised nearly 130,000 veterans. The Allies were dismayed when they heard that he had crossed the border and was moving towards Charleroi.

Regiment after regiment of Napoleon's light cavalry, closely followed by his infantry, moved northwards and by nightfall on 15th June had pushed beyond Charleroi in a two-pronged advance towards Brussels.

The Allies appeared to be unwittingly playing into Napoleon's hands when Blücher, anxious to act quickly, moved 83,000 men ahead of the British line. Meanwhile a more cautious Wellington, in Brussels, waited for more information regarding the location and intentions of the French.

To allay fears in the Belgian capital, Wellington's officers attended the Duchess of Richmond's ball in full military dress, but at midnight, Wellington learned that Napoleon was moving directly towards Brussels and had advanced further than had been expected. Therefore he ordered his regiments to move on Quatre Bras, but believed that it would only be a holding position, and that he would have to fall back further north towards Waterloo, where he intended to concentrate his forces.

On the morning of the 16th, the 92nd Foot who had earlier arrived in Brussels on the 28th May, together with other regiments including the 28th Foot received orders to move out of Brussels with Lieutenant-General Sir Thomas Picton's 5th Division, their destination the village of Quatre Bras.

Napoleon's initial attack swept Blücher's troops from Charleoi. The Prussians then retreated to the area around Ligny, but Napoleon pressed hard believing that if he could break them, he would easily defeat Wellington. By mid-afternoon the French moved 35,000 troops against Blücher, who was forced from his position. During the rest of the afternoon, close fighting took place in the streets of Ligny, this was followed by the Prussian retreat, northwards towards Wavre.

Guarding the route to Brussels was a force of 8,000 Dutch and Belgium troops at Quatre Bras. Wellington, who had moved quickly by horse from Brussels, arrived behind Allied lines at 10 a.m., to assess the situation.

Marshal Ney moved northwards and at 2.30 p.m. led an assault against the Allied position in the fields outside the village, where his advance troops nearly overwhelmed the Dutch and Belgians. Ney was wary of advancing further, as he knew that Wellington generally kept his main force out of sight, this allowed the British regiments, just before 3 p.m. to gain a position at the crossroads and enabled them to deploy along the east-west road.

The French artillery began to pound the British and then their cuirassiers charged. To relieve the pressure, Sir John Kempt's 8th Brigade, part of Picton's 5th Division advanced to meet them, and charged with bayonet through the high rye grass. This surprised the French, causing them first to check, and then retreat.

Ney was able to regroup, the British formed square and faced French lancers and dragoons with disciplined volleys and the bayonet. Regiments took a heavy toll especially the Scottish, where the 42nd Foot were severely savaged. It was during this time that the 2/69th Foot lost their King's Colour. At sunset the French attacks ceased.

Typical losses to the British are summed up by the 28th Foot, where eleven men were killed and 81 wounded, whereas the 92nd lost their commanding officer killed, along with five officers and 35 other ranks. A further twenty officers and 245 men were wounded. The following day Wellington was able to make an orderly withdrawal from Quatre Bras to the ridge directly in front of Mont St Jean. The retreat was covered by the Rifle Brigade.

On the 17th, Wellington pulled back through heavy rain and thunder. While Ney remained inactive, enabling the Allies to make their ground. At daybreak the following day, the 18th June 1815, an issue of gin was given to the troops. Wellington's plan was to hold firm until Blücher's Prussians could recover sufficiently to drive into the French flank.

When the battle started, the 23rd Foot in the 4th Division was in reserve on the right of the British position, but their colonel, Sir Henry Walton Ellis, soon found a location in which he felt they would be of more use, and moved them up in square just behind the chateau at Hougomont. There the French cavalry charged them several times, but the British held.

Picton's 5th Division formed the left-centre with the farm of La Haye Sainte to the right. The 92nd Foot were placed with a detachment of Belgian troops in reserve, where they came under fire from French artillery all morning. The 27th Foot in Major-General Sir John Lambert's 6th Division stood steady despite increased cavalry action against their square.

Ney led a massive cavalry charge that overran Allied artillery and swirled around the squares of infantry, French cuirassiers, carabineers and the cavalry of the Imperial Guard and 10,000 horsemen poured through the gap between Hougomont and La Haye Sainte. But although they made charge after charge, not a British square was broken.

Under the heavy artillery bombardment sustained by the Belgians, they gave way. The 92nd Foot was then ordered to charge. The men formed four deep, advanced against the French fired one volley and charged; at the same moment the Scots Greys appeared behind them and joined the charge. It was a headlong affair with many of the 92nd clinging to the stirrups of the Greys. The charge lasted only a few minutes, but two Eagles and over a thousand men were captured.

Following the retreat of the Belgian troops, the 27th Foot, whilst holding their square lost so many officers that there were not enough left to command. The 40th Foot offered to lend some of theirs, but Major Hare, commanding the 27th, replied that his sergeants would look after the command.

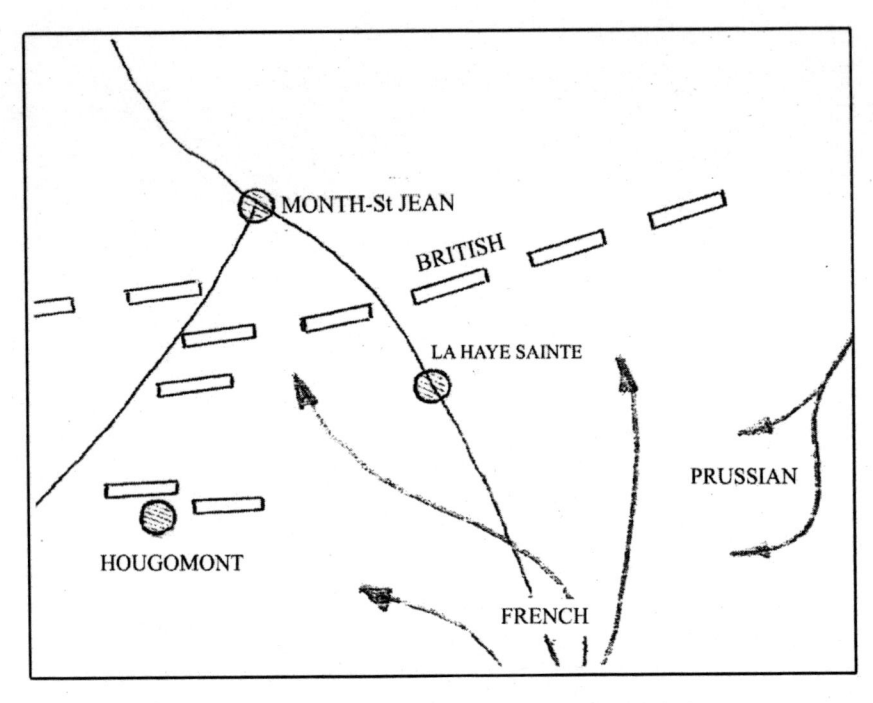

WATERLOO 18TH JUNE 1815

By the evening, the French began to give in to pressure. The British outposts were manned by Lieutenant-General Sir Henry Clinton's 2nd Division which included three battalions of the 95th Foot and the 52nd Foot; whose commanding officer wheeled the regiment. Their 800 bayonets bore down on the veterans of France, who broke and fled.

It was during the evening that Napoleon was informed of the imminent arrival of the Prussians. He flung the last of his reserves, the Imperial Guard against Wellington's army. They were repulsed by the 23rd Foot who took part in the final rout. As a reward for the victory, every man in the 23rd received a medal and prize money: field officers £432.2.4d, privates £2.11.4d.

The Allies had lost over 15,000 killed, wounded or missing, of whom over half were British. Lieutenant-General Sir Thomas Picton was wounded at Quatre Bras, but concealed his injury, only to be shot dead by a musket ball which entered through his top hat at the height of Comte d'Erlon's attack on the 5th Division.

The battle honour WATERLOO was granted to all regiments on the 23rd November 1815, they were advised of this on 8th December 1815.

1st, 4th, 14th, 23rd, 27th, 28th, 30th, 32nd, 33rd, 40th, 42nd, 44th, 51st, 52nd, 69th, 71st, 73rd, 79th, 92nd and 95th.

CHAPTER XXVI

EMPIRE EXPANSION

Queen Victoria came to the throne in 1837

The four decades which followed Waterloo became known as 'The Long Peace', because to the population of Britain, Europe did appear at peace. This encouraged the Government to cut the strength and recruitment of the army, whilst ignoring the requirements of guarding the British Empire.

At home the main duty of the army was the maintenance of civil order. In London, the Bow Street Runners were the first unified, strong and disciplined police force, which was created by Sir Robert Peel in 1829. Peel became Prime Minister for one year only in 1834.

Outside London, where police did not operate, the suppression of riots and civil disturbances was the task of regular troops and yeomanry. This necessitated the movement of regiments in Britain to where they were best required, which accounted to some extent for the dislike of the army by sections of the civil population.

Towards the end of 1821, another duty of the militia was when the Buffs, 3rd (East Kent) Regiment were under orders to provide escorts to accompany batches of convicts to Australia for the penal settlements in New South Wales. The first group aboard the prison ship *Southwalk* left in October, followed by further detachments during 1822 and 1823.

In 1826, whilst commanding the garrison in Australia, Captain Patrick Logan of the 57th (West Middlesex) Regiment discovered a river which was named Logan after him, during which time he explored great tracts of land. There are still standing in Brisbane, buildings which were erected by this officer, who whilst on an expedition was murdered by aborigines in 1830.

On 21st January 1827, Major Edmund Lockyer also of the 57th, claimed for Britain the whole of Western Australia, hoisting the Union Flag at King George Sound.

In 1835 after a short period in the Mediterranean, the 28th (North Gloucestershire) Regiment was posted to Australia. During this time detachments of this regiment were sent to guard the penal settlement at Moreton Bay and from there, following the earlier labours of the 57th, developed to a large extent the present city of Brisbane. The regiment left Australia in 1842, although many of their soldiers remained as settlers, receiving a year's pay and a grant of 300 acres of land.

Other regiments also involved in these duties were the 51st (2nd Yorkshire, West Riding) Regiment who served from 1838 until 1846, the latter in Van Dieman' s Land (Tasmania) and the 17th (Leicestershire) Regiment, who left in 1837 for India together with the King's Regiment.

During this time, many regiments were deployed in lands in the far-flung areas of the British Empire, which stretched from Canada to New Zealand. The main priority though was Asia, especially the Indian continent.

Prior to the Napoleonic War the 17th Regiment was, in 1804, ordered to India and remained there for nineteen years, where they saw active service in remote parts of the country, fighting in Bundlekung in 1807 and again on the River Sutlej one year later, then on the mountainous frontier of Nepal against the warrior Gurkhas.

The 17th first made contact with the Gurkhas who had been carrying out sporadic raids from the principality of Gorkha, against territories policed and garrisoned by the Honourable East India Company (HEIC).

As a result of these incursions, war was declared by the Governor-General in 1814. It was not until 1816 that the 87th (Royal Irish Fusiliers) were one of three British battalions forming the nucleus of the Anglo-Indian Force, which invaded Nepal in the little-known though arduous Gurkha War, in which they took part in the capture of the fortress at Hatteros. Peace was then made.

Because of the fighting qualities of the Gurkhas, four battalions were raised for service with the HEIC under British direction.

ASIA

The MARATHA and PINDARI War

Rebellion against British rule began in 1817 in the region of Nagpore. The first action took place on 5th November at Kirkee, in which the 1st Bombay (European) Regiment, later to become the 103rd HEIC, the 2nd Battalion, the Royal Dublin Fusiliers (disbanded 1922) were engaged together with four Indian regiments. Also in November another disturbance occurred at Seetabuldee, and was dealt with by two of the Indian regiments.

In December, the 1st (Royal Scots) Regiment was the only British regiment to take part in the capture of the Mahratta capital of Nagpore, with no fewer than nine Indian regiments, and in the same month, the action at Maheidpoor where with a different nine Indian regiments, the Royal Scots were joined by the Madras (European) Regiment, later to become the 102nd HE1C, the 1st Battalion, the Royal Dublin Fusiliers (also disbanded in 1922).

The war continued into 1818, where in January two engagements took place mainly only involving Indian regiments, until an uneasy peace was reached. In 1823, the 1st (Royal Scots) were awarded the battle honours NAGPORE and MAHEIDPOOR.

1st BURMESE War

A mixed force of British and Indian regiments moved into Burma in 1824, and spent three years in a campaign fraught by dense tracts of steamy jungle, which had to be traversed to reach the enemy, who had built a number of strongly constructed stockades, which they either abandoned once the Allied troops prepared for attack, or stubbornly defended until they were stormed and destroyed.

The troops were quite unprepared for the appalling climate, especially during the monsoon season. Their supplies were erratic because the local population refused to bring them locally produced provisions. By far the greater part of the enormous casualties to all of the British regiments was caused by the many tropical diseases, of which the worst were scurvy, heatstroke and cholera.

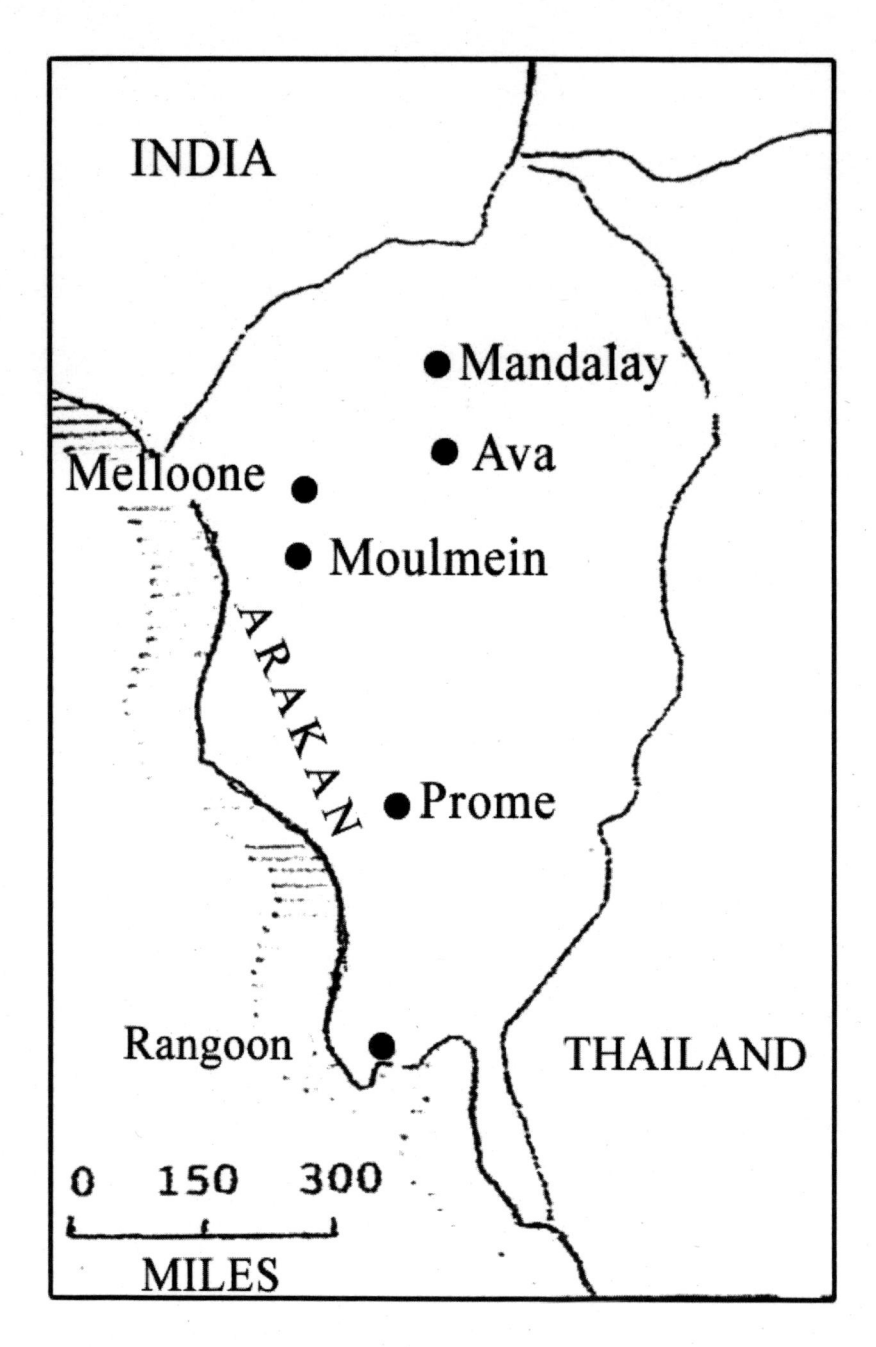

BURMA

At the end of March 1825, the 54th (2nd Battalion Devonshire) Regiment took on its most formidable engagement in the region of Myanmar, with an offensive against Arakan City. In the initial attack, two six-pounder guns were manhandled by the infantry across very difficult ground. Their use, and the action of the Light Company in the final assault, led to the capture of the city.

Also in the region of Myanmar, the 87th took part in the advance to Prome and from there, on 19th January 1826, with the 89th (they later became 1st and 2nd Battalions, the Royal Irish Fusiliers), and other regiments, assisted in the capture of Melloone. Nine days later the position of Moulmein was captured and destroyed.

As well as the casualties from disease, many men from the British Regiments were killed or wounded, although the Burmese army which was totally defeated, suffered very heavy losses themselves, before the war finally ended on 21st February 1826.

The battle honour AVA was awarded to Indian regiments on 22nd April 1826, and to the following British regiments who had been involved in the war, on 6th December 1826:

1st, 13th, 38th, 41st, 44th, 45th, 47th, 54th, 87th, 89th, 102nd

1st AFGHAN War.

To the British Government, who were constantly worried by possible attacks from Russia, Afghanistan was regarded as the natural barrier defending the western approaches to their Indian Empire. To the west, the Iranian Plateau consisted of mountains and desert and to the north, the Hindu Kush stretched for over 600 miles of rocky ground, mostly ice-covered for nearly the whole year.

There were only three passes from Afghanistan into India. In the north there was the Malakand, which was considered almost impassable, and to the south the eighty mile long Bolan Pass. The shortest route was the Khyber which was thirty miles long. It was in some places only yards wide, whilst in others it was the width of a valley. Regardless of its breadth, its entire length was guarded by local tribesmen.

The British were concerned that Russia appeared to be taking areas of land to increase their Empire in the west, which they believed if left unchecked, would eventually lead them into Afghanistan and then India. Towards their aim of learning more about the country and more importantly the identities of its leaders, a small British delegation spent several years gathering the relevant information, which generally revealed that there was conflict between the main Afghan rivals.

In 1826 after a lengthy period of warfare between the various factions, Dost Muhammad came to the throne of Afghanistan. Whilst in their travels, the delegates met Shuja-ul-Mulk who was an Afghan in exile. His plan was to get British support for his return to power, after which he would oppose Russian intervention.

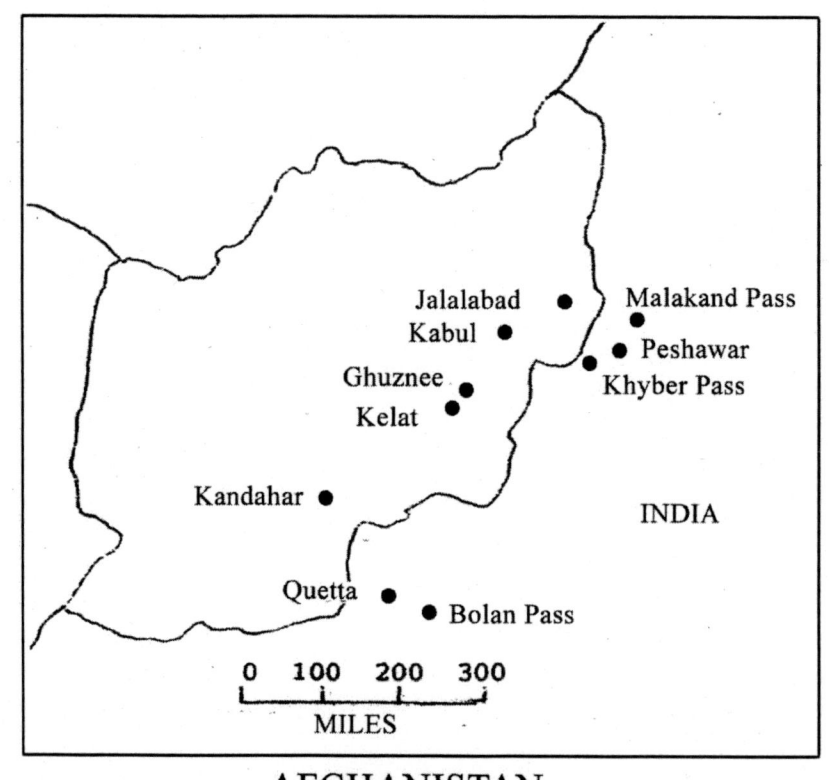

AFGHANISTAN

In 1837 Dost asked the British if they would help him in his desire to restore the ancient Afghan city of Peshawar to his kingdom. The city had been captured four years earlier by his rival Ranjit Singh. The British decided not to back him, he therefore sought help from Russia, who sent an envoy.

Following the action of Dost, the British turned to Shuja believing that if he could regain the throne of Kabul, he would restore the balance of power in Afghanistan. In May 1838, it was agreed that the British would take the lead role assisting Shuja with finance and, more importantly, experienced troops which would include the 17th Foot who had returned to India in 1837 when it joined Sir John Keane's force. Shuja in turn would bring his followers, who he assured would also be hardened fighters. It was known that the local Afghan tribes resented the presence of troops from outside their area, but with Shuja in control problems would be minimized.

On 10th December 1838 the army of the Indus was ready to move. It consisted of 10,000 British and Indian troops and a further 6,000 men who had been collected by Shuja, these were led by British officers. The chosen route into Afghanistan was the southern Bolan Pass, which although a much longer distance from Kabul, had the advantage, although not known at the time, that Dost having assumed that the Khyber would be their preferred route, had deployed his best troops there, to halt the invaders' progress.

From the Bolan Pass the army under the overall command of Sir John Keane travelled westward to Quetta, arriving at the end of March 1839. It was split into two columns. Keane moved his column by sea from Bombay to Karachi. The other column, a Bengal contingent was led by Sir Willoughby Cotton. Leaving Quetta they arrived early in April in Kandahar which was entered without a fight, and where Shuja was made ruler of Afghanistan.

From Kandahar the army moved to Kabul but, before they had reached there, they had to pass the strongest fortress in Central Asia, that of Ghuznee which was garrisoned by Afghan troops under the son of Dost. Its walls were 70 feet high and surrounded by a wide moat; information received from a supporter of Shuja was that a certain gate was vulnerable and that British regiments would be able to storm the stronghold. The 13th Foot moved forward across the rubble which had been created by blasting the walls with powder by the British sappers.

As the light faded, the main force moved forward as the resistance from the defenders became poor, such that they were completely overcome. In this attack, Keane had lost less than 200 of his force. He then advanced towards Kabul, which although defended by Dost's Afghan troops allowed the British to enter. As was the procedure of the day, the army brought its wives, children, servants and followers, probably as many as 12,000, in the belief that Kabul was similar to a relatively friendly Indian city.

The British garrison in Kabul totalled 17,000, of whom all but 700 were Indian troops paid for by the HEIC. The British and their supporters lived as they would have done in India; they believed that the Afghans would take to the British way of life much as the Indians had done.

They carried out typical British pursuits of cricket, hockey, hunting and equestrian activities, whilst ignoring local opposition, unaware that in the countryside, a vast army of Afghans was preparing to remove the invaders and their supporters from their country, regardless of the Afghans who had invited them to their homeland.

The stay in Kabul was financially costly to the British, especially the HEIC, who had maintained the loyalty of the Pathan Ghilzais who commanded the approaches to the Khyber, by giving them an annual payment of £8,000. The HEIC had to economise due to their continual activities in India, the payment to the Ghilzais therefore ceased.

As relations became further strained, one of the brigades of which the 13th Foot were part, was ordered to return to India. On their eastern movement they encountered the full fury of the Ghilzais, and had to fight all the way until they reached Jalalabad, losing much of their baggage and at least 150 men.

In October 1841 the Afghan tribes moved against the British, the barracks and areas occupied by their supporters were besieged, but disciplined firepower from the regular troops made it impossible for the Afghans to enter. Taking stock of the situation it became apparent that very soon food and water, but more especially ammunition would run out. It was decided to leave Kabul even though it was winter, and move through the passes back into India.

One of the problems which faced the regular troops was the thousands of civilians that were retreating with them, as they were attacked from all sides as their journey progressed. Many died in the snow from the horrendous conditions or enemy fire, and only a handful reached Jalalabad. The most graphic example was the medical officer, Dr Brydon who has been depicted reaching the town alone, in a collapsed state.

A few prisoners, mainly white women were taken, these were later released following negotiations in May 1842, when British regiments besieged in Kandahar and Ghuznee were relieved. The fort of Kelat, which was between Kandahar and Kabul had also been under siege; this too was one of those relieved.

Although the Afghans continued their attacks on Jalalabad, they were repulsed by the 13th Foot. When the news reached London, Queen Victoria gave them the title of 13th or Prince Albert's Regiment of Light Infantry.

In 1840 the battle honour GHUZNEE was awarded to the 2nd, 13th, 17th, and 101st, also KHELAT to the 2nd and 17th.

The defence of JALALABAD was also recognised when in 1842 the 13th were awarded that battle honour.

In 1844, together with many Indian regiments, the battle honours of CANDAHAR and GHUZNEE were awarded to the 40th and 41st Regiments and CABOOL 1842 to the 9th, 13th, 31st, 40th and 41st.

The 2nd, 13th, 17th and 101st with eight Indian regiments were awarded the battle honour AFGHANISTAN 1839, although the date was not added until 1914.

CHAPTER XXVII

NEW ZEALAND 1846-1866
QUEEN VICTORIA

The Great Famine of 1845-1847 was responsible for mass emigration from Britain.

During the famine which caused much starvation in Scotland, Ireland and England, the alternative was to stay and starve, or relocate to one of the new countries recently named by the British Government, who would grant limited financial aid to the many who wished to leave Britain to settle in lands, which most believed were owned by the British Empire.

America was the most popular destination, but many believed that Australia was probably more acceptable. Of those bound for the Antipodes, some decided that the climate in New Zealand was more in keeping with that which they enjoyed in their home country. Therefore they took the route further south, encouraged by the British Government who had recently formed a society called the New Zealand Company.

1st MAORI WAR 1846-1847

It was probably wrong to call this a war, although it did involve three British regiments. The recently arrived immigrants had caused much consternation to the locals, especially the Maori chiefs who believed that their warriors should defend their homeland.

There were skirmishes between the Maoris and the British settlers, who believed that having been promised ownership by the

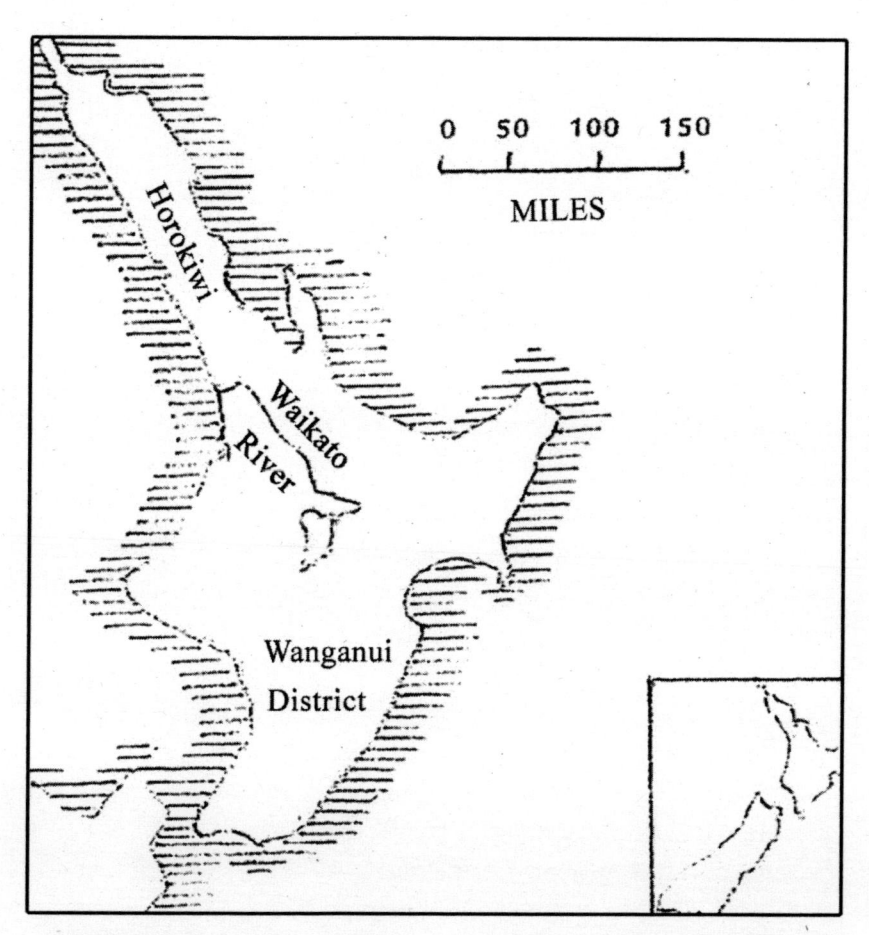

NEW ZEALAND - NORTH ISLAND

Government, that the land was theirs. The conflict became progressively worse, forcing the British to move three regiments into the area, who kept the locals at bay for nearly a decade. The 99th Regiment of Foot (the 99th had been raised in Glasgow in 1824 as the 99th or Lancashire Regiment), together with the 96th Regiment (also raised in 1824 but in Manchester, from a battalion of the 8th Foot (King's) on a temporary basis until placed on the permanent establishment as the 96th Regiment of Foot), the third regiment was the 58th Foot. In 1870 they were awarded the battle honour NEW ZEALAND for their services during 1846-1847.

Following a relatively peaceful time after 1847, trouble again flared between the settlers and the local Maori population over possession of their lands. Several conflicts took place and following the withdrawal of the 58th, 96th and 99th ten years earlier, the British drafted the 12th (Suffolk), 14th (West Yorkshire), 40th (South Lancashire), 57th (Middlesex) and the 65th (Yorks and Lancashire) into New Zealand.

During the 2nd Maori War 1860-1861, Ensign Down and drummer Stagpoole of the 57th both won the Victoria Cross. Stagpoole had a week earlier been awarded the Distinguished Conduct Medal, the only man to win both in one week. However also serving with the 57th was Colour Sergeant George Gardiner VC DCM who earlier was the first recipient of both decorations.

The 65th had arrived in New Zealand in 1846 and was to remain there for nineteen years. They initially replaced the small garrison of the 96th, and were employed in gruelling disturbances in the Horokiwi Valley and also in the Wanganui District. All regiments involved in these operations were in 1870 awarded the battle honour NEW ZEALAND. For bravery in the action of Waikato River in 1863, Colour Sergeant McKenna and Lance Corporal Ryan were both awarded the Victoria Cross.

Trouble flared a year later, which again required British regiments to become involved. The 40th, 57th and 65th were not in the area, but the 12th and 14th were reinforced by the 18th (Royal Irish), 43rd (Ox and Bucks Light Infantry), 50th (Royal West Kent), 68th (Durham Light Infantry) and the 70th (East Surrey), who all received the battle honour NEW ZEALAND.

CHAPTER XXVIII

INDIA 1843–1853
QUEEN VICTORIA

Sikh: a member of a religion founded in the Punjab in the 15th century

Trouble again broke out in India. Conflict with the Sikhs was expected because the Government believed that the security of their Indian Empire was threatened. At the same time problems began in the Mahratta state of Gwalior, which was a small native area wedged in the middle of British territory.

In February 1843, the ruler of the state died leaving no heir. His thirteen-year-old widow adopted a small boy, who with the approval of the Mahratta princes and acceptance by the British, was enthroned as Maharaja which was responsible for the struggle for power. The British Government could not tolerate this latest abuse of their authority and a punitive expedition was inevitable.

The British, who really did not understand the whole culture which existed in India, appointed as Governor General Mama Sahib; this was opposed by the Rani, who had the backing of the Mahratta army, which had at its disposal 40,000 men and over 200 guns.

The British force at Gwalior was less than half the strength of the Mahrattas, consisting of four foot regiments, two lancer regiments and six Indian regiments. The force was split into two columns, the right wing which included the 39th and 40th Regiments, with the 16th Lancers and five Indian regiments, and the left wing with the 3rd and 50th Regiments who also had the 9th Lancers but only one Indian regiment.

The 3rd Regiment had spent twenty-one days moving into position, encumbered by the usual horde of followers. Both the left and right wings made contact during the 28/29 December 1843 but

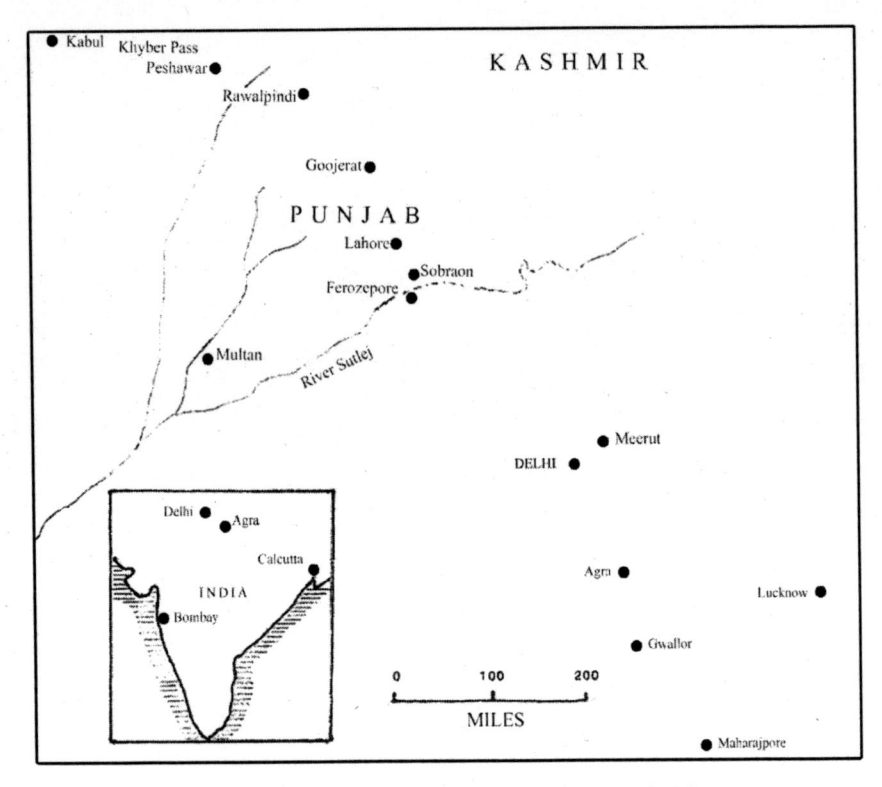

NORTHERN INDIA 1843 - 1853

in separate battles. The 3rd and 50th formed a solid line and drove Mahrattas through the village of Punnier until dusk.

In the action at Maharajpore, the British artillery was outnumbered by the guns of the enemy. The intense Mahratta fire checked the Indian infantry, but the 39th attacked their guns and batteries with the bayonet, then with the 40th moving through their infantry first line, and continuing through the second line. During this attack the 40th lost slightly fewer casualties than the 39th.

For their actions in the Gwalior campaign, the 39th (1st Devons) and 40th (South Lancs) were awarded the battle honour MAHARAJPORE and the 3rd (Buffs) and 50th (Royal West Kent) PUNNIER.

Following the conflict at Gwalior, problems continued. In 1839 the Maharaja, Ranjit Singh died; during his life he had turned the Sikhs in the Punjab into a standing army mainly trained by the French. His territory stretched from Multan to Kashmir and from the north bank of the Sutlej to the border of Afghanistan.

In 1843 his successor was murdered, and the direction which the Sikh army would take became, not only a source of anxiety for the Indian Government, but also for the British, especially as the new Maharaja was an infant whose mother carried ambitions of power, and more importantly did not like the British presence in her country.

To anticipate any internal conflict, the British Government ordered more regiments to assist in the defence of the Empire in India, therefore by December 1844 their force at Umballa numbered 32,500 men and 68 guns. In addition between Umballa and Meerut there were a further 13,000 more troops with 30 guns.

In December, a large Sikh force crossed the Sutlej with the intention of attacking Ferozepore. The British had mobilised seven foot regiments with five Indian regiments; the force also included the British 3rd Hussars.

At Moodkee on the 18th December 1845, the 9th (Norfolk), 31st (Royal Sussex), 50th (Royal West Kent) and the 80th (South Staffs) with the 3rd Hussars and five Indian regiments clashed with the Sikhs. Three days later they were joined by the 29th (Worcestershire), 62nd (Wiltshire) and the 101st (HEIC Bengal) although the five Indian regiments were not at the action against the Sikh insurgents at Ferozepore.

In January 1846, the 31st and 50th with the 53rd (Shropshire Light Infantry) and two Gurkha rifle regiments, together with the 16th Lancers met the Sikhs at Ailwal. Also in January Sir Hugh Gough moved the 9th, 29th, 31st, 50th and 80th with the 16th Lancers and the 10th (Lincolns) with three Gurkha rifle regiments and a further nine Indian regiments opposite the village of Sobraon on the Sutlej. The Sikhs, probably as many as 35,000, were strongly entrenched on the opposite bank. For a month neither moved.

On the morning of 10th February 1846, the British guns opened fire on the Sikhs, which was followed by an advance of the British and Indian regiments, causing the Sikhs to break in confusion with at least 13,000 killed or badly wounded, allowing the regiments to march into and occupy Lahore.

For their part in the battles which were to be known as the 1st Sikh War, battle honours were awarded in 1847 to British foot regiments for MOODKEE 9th, 31st, 50th and 80th.

FEROZESHAH 9th, 29th, 31st, 50th, 62nd, 80th and 101st.

AILWAL 31st, 50th and 53rd.

SOBRAON 9th, 10th, 31st, 50th and 80th.

Not all casualties within regiments were caused in battle. The 28th (Gloucestershire) had been posted to India in 1842 from the healthy climate of Australia. They suffered from cholera and then, after a terrible march across the Kalahari Desert, were deployed against the princes of Scinde. Battle casualties were few, but deaths from heatstroke and disease were tragic and during their first year in India, the 28th lost over 600, including women and children.

For some time after the Sikh defeat at Sobraon, the Punjab remained tolerably quiet, although their leaders were little reconciled to the terms imposed upon them. Trouble soon began in the province of Multan which had only been under British rule for two years. The two British emissaries, who had been sent in April 1848 to support the new Sikh Governor, were murdered and the whole of the western Punjab broke into revolt, calling to expel the British, and backed by the Ameer of Afghanistan.

It took some time to assemble sufficient troops, but by December, the 10th (Lincolns), 32nd (Duke of Cornwall's Light Infantry), 60th (King's Royal Rifle Corps) and 103rd HEIC (Bombay Europeans), also from the Bombay area were twelve Indian regiments. On 27th December the whole force invested Multan, which was then taken by assault on 21st January 1849. The 60th covered the advance and only lost eleven men killed. The regiments then marched to join the army under General Gough.

The 61st (Gloucestershire) sailed from Ireland to Calcutta and in 1848 joined the British force, together with the 24th (South Wales Borderers) who had travelled 350 miles from Agra. Both regiments, with the 29th (Worcestershire) and the 104th HEIC Bengal European (later the 2nd Battalion, the Royal Munster Fusiliers) who with two Indian Bengal infantry regiments took part in the battle of Chillianwallah on 13th January 1849, where they were joined by the

British 3rd and 14th Hussars, the 9th Lancers in the battle which came to be known as the 'Waterloo of India'.

The British/Indian army of slightly less than a thousand men was outnumbered by three times as many Sikhs. Gough moved forward through the heavily wooded area which concealed the Sikh positions; contact was difficult as the British were constantly hit by the enemy's heavy guns.

The British finally made close contact, breaking the power of the Sikh army, which was beaten. The cost to the British should be equated to that of the 24th Regiment, who went into action with 31 officers and 1,065 NCOs and men. Of this establishment thirteen officers and 225 men were killed with many more wounded, they also lost their Queen's Colour but did not believe that it fell into Sikh hands.

The 104th were raised in 1839. Four previous regiments had carried the number 104. The first in 1761-3 (King's Volunteers), the second in 1780-3, then in 1794 (Royal Manchester Volunteers) and in 1806-1817 as the 104th Regiment of Foot, all had been disbanded when the Government of the day deemed them unnecessary.

The army under General Gough arrived at Goojerat and took position against the Sikhs and Afghans, their force was estimated at 60,000 men and over fifty guns. The battle began at 8.30 a.m. on 21st February 1849 with a bombardment from both sides.

After three hours the British commenced an advance, driving the Sikh army backwards. A vigorous pursuit followed, 16,000 Sikhs surrendered with 41 guns at Rawalpindi, The Afghans were driven back all the way to the Khyber Pass, which was reached on the 18th March. With this battle the campaign ended. Some regiments were kept on garrison duties in Peshawar. The 61st spent eight years there, setting the fashion for being the first British regiment to dye their uniforms 'a sort of bluish-brown colour, known as karky'.‡

The battles of 1848-1849 were given the titles of the 2nd Sikh War. British foot regiments, the 10th, 32nd, 60th, 103rd and twelve Indian regiments who fought at Multan were awarded the battle honour MOOLTAN. British hussar and lancer regiments, together

---

‡ Khaki – Urdu meaning dust-coloured

with the 24th, 29th, 61st, 104th and two Indian regiments received the battle honour CHILLIANWALLAH, The final battle at GOOJERAT, earned that battle honour to the hussars and lancer regiments, also to the 10th, 24th, 29th, 32nd, 53rd, 60th, 103rd, 104th and nine Indian regiments.

To commemorate the success of all regiments involved in the three battles they were awarded PUNJAUB. All battle honours were sanctioned for British regiments on 14th December 1852 and for the Indian regiments on 7th October 1853.

CHAPTER XXIX

CRIMEA 1854–1856
QUEEN VICTORIA

The name Crimea brings to mind the Thin Red Line, Charge of the Light Brigade and Florence Nightingale, but there is more ⋯

The war in the Crimea arose from a religious dispute between the Greek and Latin churches about certain rights in Jerusalem, which was then in the possession of the Turks, who also ruled the area that is now Rumania and Bulgaria. The Russians supported the Greek Church, the French the Latin Church.

The Russians, having failed by diplomacy, had in 1853 invaded Turkish territory. The British and French decided to support the Turks, also believing that Russia was attempting to open the route for their fleet to enter the Mediterranean.

An Allied expedition was raised the intention was to seize the Russian Black Sea fleet's base at Sevastopol, which was also the main Russian arsenal for the area. In April 1854 the 23rd Regiment embarked at Southampton for the Crimea where it was one of the first British regiments to land. After spending five months in various camps on the shore of the Black Sea, where men suffered from cholera and dysentery, the combined British and French forces landed in the Crimea.

During the winter of 1854–5 the army endured great hardships from lack of proper food, clothing and shelter in the severe cold weather. Even when men were admitted to hospital, the doctors had totally inadequate means to sustain the flickering life in them, with the result that many died.

This is the war where reports despatched to Queen Victoria regarding the gallantry of her soldiers, were responsible for her decision to institute an award for valour. It was to be called the Victoria Cross.

The main objective of the expedition was the capture and destruction of the Russian fortress, arsenal and docks at Sevastopol.

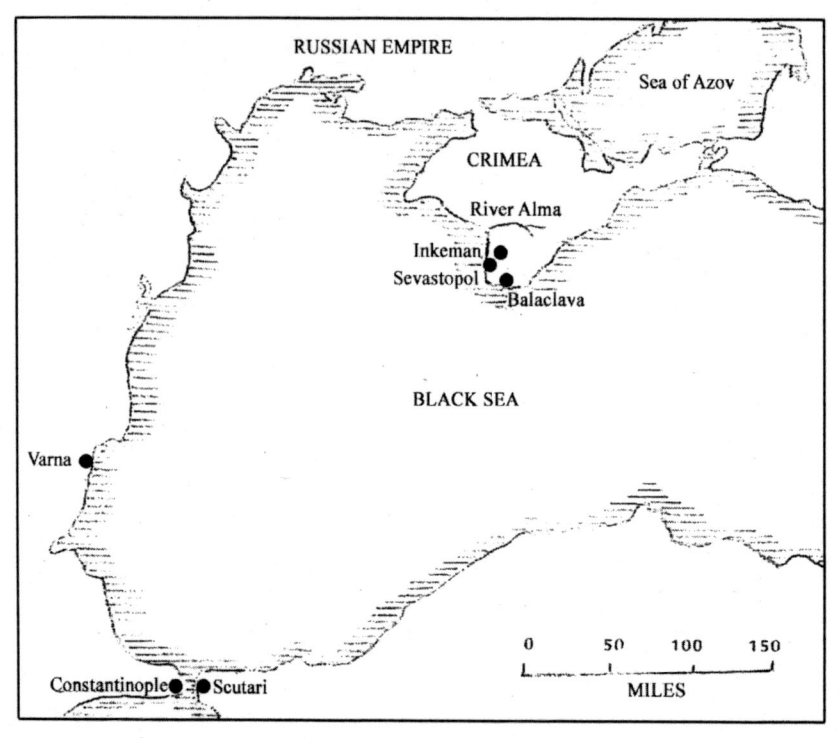

CRIMEA 1854 - 1855

Yet before the Allies could achieve this, the strong Russian force occupying the heights above the River Alma had to be dislodged. At their centre was a large redoubt armed with fourteen heavy guns and garrisoned by a large body of infantry.

The ground between the redoubt and the river was devoid of cover and had steeply sloping banks. On the British side of the river, the cultivated area contained gardens and vineyards, which also concealed Russian skirmishers. Under the fire from the Russian guns, the British deployed, causing the skirmishers to withdraw.

The main objective was the Russian redoubt; it was to be attacked by the Light Division which included the 23rd (Royal Welch Fusiliers) who were in the centre, and that of General Sir Colin Campbell whose 1st Division included the 42nd and 73rd (1st and 2nd Battalions, The Black Watch) and 93rd (2nd Sutherland and Argyle Highlanders) who had been raised in 1800 by the Earl of Sutherland. Both brigades waded waist high through the river, and although the high banks gave temporary cover from the Russian guns, their steepness made it difficult to form a line.

Nevertheless they advanced up the steep slope and under heavy fire the Light Division fell back, until the 1st Division defending a Russian counter-attack, moved against the enemy to capture the position.

During the attack, the 95th (Sherwood Foresters) who had been rearmed with the long Enfield rifle and bayonet, captured a set of Russian drums; also of note was that their Captain MacDonald was saved when a Russian bullet hit the ornament on his cross belt. The 19th (Green Howards) also captured seven Russian drums which belonged to the Minsk, Vladimir and Borodino regiments.

On a more sombre note, the 23rd had thirteen officers and 198 other ranks killed or seriously wounded, whilst the 77th (2nd Battalion, the Duke of Cambridge's Own [Middlesex] Regiment) who had been raised in 1787 for service in India, suffered a similar loss. The regiments now invested Sevastopol and the terrible winter began.

For their actions at the River ALMA, that battle honour was awarded to the twenty-six regiments who took part:

1st, 4th, 7th, 19th, 20th, 21st, 23rd, 28th, 30th, 33rd, 38th, 41st, 42nd, 44th, 47th, 49th, 50th, 55th, 63rd, 68th, 77th, 79th, 88th, 93rd, 95th and Rifle Brigade.

The Allied army had occupied Balaclava since the governor of the castle surrendered to the colonel of the 77th Regiment. The fortress was to be used as a depot from which to besiege Sevastopol. The 93rd was drawn by lot to be the unit which remained at the base, to provide the fatigue parties, and to unload the ships, while other troops were ordered away to defend the line.

Suddenly on the 25th October 1854, the Russians attacked and captured the Turkish defences in front of the British base. Sir Colin Campbell immediately sent the 93rd with a Turkish battalion on each flank, to counter-attack. The Russian fire proved too destructive, Campbell retired them behind a small hill occupied by a British battery, and there the men drew up in line two deep.

At this moment in front of the 93rd appeared a large body of Russian cavalry, part of which charged directly at the battery which was located behind the Scottish regiment. The Turks fled in confusion, but the Highlanders moved to the crest of the hill to meet the charging cavalry with their bayonets fixed. When the Russians were within 500 yards, acting on Sir Colin's order, the 93rd fired two volleys which caused the cavalry to wheel to the left; then the Highlanders' right-hand company changed front and fired a volley into the Russian flank, causing them to break and flee.

For a regiment, who had only been trained to receive cavalry in 'square formation' or 'four deep', their deed was to earn them the nickname 'The Thin Red Line'. They were the only foot regiment to be awarded the battle honour BALACLAVA.

On the morning of the 5th November 1854, the Russians, 30,000 strong attacked British outposts near Inkerman Ridge. Heavy rain had been falling for most of the night, but by early morning it was replaced by mist which soon became dense fog, making the usual military drill impossible. As the enemy moved against the British regiments, fighting was reduced to close range encounters by small groups in hand-to-hand combat, often by individual soldiers unaware of the main scene.

The 68th Foot (Durham Light Infantry) threw off their greatcoats and for recognition, fought in their scarlet tunics. The British were able to gain some semblance of regimental order, and continuous bayonet charges caused the Russians to withdraw.

Regiments were then able to march away from Inkerman towards Sevastopol. The battle honour INKERMAN was awarded to the following British Foot Regiments:

1st, 4th, 7th, 19th, 20th, 21st, 23rd, 28th, 30th, 33rd, 38th, 41st, 44th, 47th, 49th, 50th, 63rd, 68th, 77th, 88th and 95th.

The siege of Sevastopol had lasted since the troop landings in 1854 until September 1855. It is probably wrong to believe that this was a conventional siege, because the fortress and immediate area were never cut off, enabling the Russian defenders to move fairly freely in and out, also to receive supplies, whilst the Allies suffered from the harsh conditions, where losses through sickness and disease far exceeded battle casualties.

The whole campaign against the Russians was one of attrition, fought in the trenches beneath the walls of the fortress. The British had made two attacks on the Redan, a fort before the main fortress, but both were unsuccessful. The Russian fire was so intense that, of the eighteen officers of the 23rd Regiment who started the assault by leading their men across the 285 yards of open ground, only four officers were able to regain their lines; and as no second line was available to reinforce the attack, they were forced to withdraw. The commanding officer of the 38th died from his wounds, whilst the 63rd had 950 casualties.

Most of the regiments took their turn in the trenches, freezing in the terrible winter conditions and suffering from the heat in the summer, with frequent skirmishes from the Russians. The Crimea, especially in the Sevastopol area was the active debut in battle for the 97th (the Queen's Own, [Royal West Kent] Regiment) which had been raised by the Earl of Ulster in 1824, it was not at either the Alma, Balaclava or Inkerman.

The 93rd, from their heroics at Balaclava had taken part in both unsuccessful attacks, and had been selected as the storming party for the third assault, which was never made. The Russians finally had had enough and abandoned the fortress, blowing up the arsenals, magazines, living quarters and the docks. This ended the war, although peace was not signed for six months.

The battle honour SEVASTOPOL was awarded to the:

1st, 3rd, 4th, 7th, 9th, 13th, 14th, 17th, 18th, 19th, 20th, 21st, 23rd, 28th, 30th, 31st, 33rd, 34th, 38th, 39th, 41st, 42nd, 44th, 47th, 48th, 49th, 50th, 55th, 56th, 57th, 62nd, 63rd, 68th, 71st, 72nd, 77th, 79th, 82nd, 88th, 89th, 90th, 93rd, 95th, 97th and Rifle Brigade.

The fact that forty-five foot regiments had taken part, indicated how seriously the British Government had taken the war.

CHAPTER XXX

INDIAN MUTINY 1857–1859
QUEEN VICTORIA

British India at that time was governed not by the Indians, or the British Crown but by the Honourable East India Company (HEIC), a trading concern, who maintained their own military force.

The reasons for the Mutiny were manifold. Britain had lost prestige during the Crimea War, and in India the tribal leaders realized that they no longer ran their own country. The HEIC had originally controlled the populace through Indian princes, but as time passed the Company displayed an almost 'couldn't care less' attitude, resulting in considerable unrest.

The conspirators spread rumours, firstly concerning British power in India, which tradition claimed would last for only one hundred years; they pointed out that Plassey had been fought in June 1757, therefore the time was ready, but more important to the average sepoy was being told that the new Enfield rifles being issued required greased cartridges in place of the old 'Brown Bess' muskets, where a round of ammunition containing the ball and powder had to have the end bitten off before loading into the barrel.

It was alleged that the grease came from either cows, which were sacred to the Hindus, or pig, unclean to Mohammedans. The truth was that the new rifle cartridges did not require greasing.

At Meerut, a town nearly fifty miles northeast of Delhi, there was a dangerous undercurrent of rebellion amongst the native regiments, which was overplayed by the British officers against their men. It was on a Sunday evening the 10th May 1857, whilst the few unarmed British troops were assembling for church parade, that the 3rd Bengal

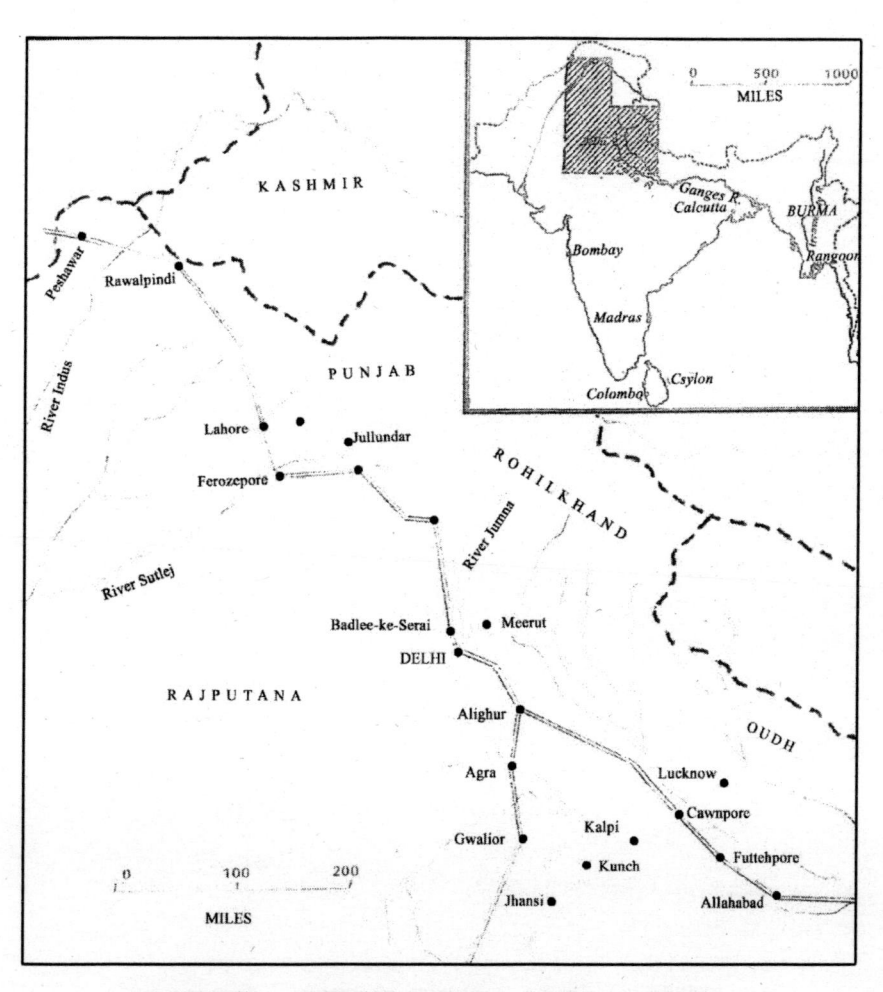

NORTH - WEST INDIA 1857 - 1859

Cavalry who were quartered at Meerut, murdered their European officers and then burst upon the church parade.

There were only two regiments stationed in Meerut, the Royal Scots Dragoon Guards and the 60th Regiment of Foot (the King's Royal Rifle Corps), whose 1st Battalion had been in India since 1845.

When the Mutiny first started, the commanding officer of the 60th, Lieutenant-Colonel John Jones ordered Captain Muter, the senior officer present to instantly dispatch a company to secure the Treasury. The battalion then marched towards the town, being joined by the 6th Carabiniers and a battery of horse artillery, who were the only European troops available. They proceeded to occupy the lines of the native troops, thus preventing the mutineers from establishing themselves in the town, forcing them to retreat to Delhi.

The Mutiny was by no means an insurrection of the entire Indian people, for only a portion of their army rebelled and without the loyalty of the Madras and Bombay regiments, together with the Sikhs and Gurkhas the small British force would not have survived. The main areas of the revolt were generally in the Oudh and Rohilkhand regions also slightly further south.

The 8th (King's Liverpool Regiment) was in Jullundar when the Mutiny broke out. They occupied a nearby fort and drove off nearly 2,000 mutinous Indian soldiers, while the 61st (2nd Battalion, the Gloucestershire Regiment) was in Ferozepore where three regiments of native troops joined the mutineers. The Grenadier Company prevented them from burning the European bungalows or the officers' mess, but the regimental silver was lost, before with other rebels, the mutineers retreated to Delhi.

On 30th/31st May 1857, marching in pursuit, the British troops from Meerut fought two successful actions upon the Hindun River, and on 7th June joined the army under Major-General Henry Barnard who was the divisional commander at Alighur.

As the Mutiny spread, as many as 32, 000 mutineers moved into Delhi, reinstating Bahadur Shar, the last of the Mogul Emperors on the throne. On the 8th June, Barnard's small British force, having been joined by the 8th Regiment, moved towards the city, but on reaching Badlee-ke-Serai it was found that the rebels were in a strongly entrenched position along a ridge overlooking the city. After a brief engagement the area was taken and cleared by British troops; thus began the siege of Delhi.

After several months of minor skirmishes the army received reinforcements which enabled the main assault to begin. On the morning of 14th September, after six days of bombardment, two breaches were made in the walls. Troops including the 60th and 61st Regiments together with the 75th (1st Battalion, the Gordon Highlanders) were able to attack through them, with the 52nd (2nd Battalion, the Oxfordshire Light Infantry) storming the Kashmir Gate.

The assaults were not immediately successful and it was not until nightfall that partial occupation took place. Over the next week, hand-to-hand fighting was continued in the streets and houses until the city was captured. The action was not without casualties; as a typical example, the 60th Regiment with a total strength of 640 all ranks, including 200 reinforcements, sustained 389 men killed or badly wounded.

In September 1663 the following were awarded the battle honour DELHI:

8th The King's (Liverpool) Regiment
52nd 2nd Battalion, the Oxfordshire Light Infantry
60th King's Royal Rifle Corps
61st 2nd Battalion, the Gloucestershire Regiment
75th 1st Battalion, the Gordon Highlanders
101 1st Royal Munster Fusiliers HEIC 1st Bengal (European)
104 2nd Royal Munster Fusiliers HEIC 2nd Bengal (European)
6th Dragoon Guards and 9th Lancers

Later in 1864, thirteen Indian Army regiments and two Gurkah rifle battalions were also awarded the honour.

It would be wrong to assume that the Mutiny centred only on Delhi, as events during 1857 and 1858 were influenced by the high number of ill-advised sepoys joining the mutineers, and the problems encountered by the British commanders, who were faced with insufficient British regiments and an even greater decision for them, on where these were most needed.

The European and loyal native troops were hopelessly outnumbered, and it took several months before regiments could be drafted to the assistance of those already stationed there.

The 108th HEIC (3rd Madras [European] Regiment) were already in India under the control of the East India Company, whilst the 35th (1st Battalion, the Royal Sussex Regiment) were at the outbreak in Burma, it was then moved to Calcutta where they helped to disarm six regiments of local infantry.

The 84th (2nd Battalion, the York and Lancaster Regiment) were in Rangoon with a detachment at Cawnpore. The 38th (1st Battalion, the South Staffordshire Regiment) landed in Calcutta in October which was the same time that the 64th (1st Battalion, the Prince of Wales's later [North Staffordshire Regiment] arrived by sea from Bombay, having been transferred from Persia. The 27th (1st Battalion, the Royal Inniskilling Fusiliers), and the 83rd and 86th (1st and 2nd Battalions, the Royal Irish Rifles), 87th and 89th (1st and 2nd Battalions, the Royal Irish Fusiliers) all moved into India during September.

Lucknow and Cawnpore were two of the main areas of conflict during the Mutiny. At that time one company of the 23rd (Royal Welch Fusiliers) was stationed at Lucknow with their families. They were under siege around the Residency with constant attack for 140 days. The rebels had fortified and loopholed every building on the outskirts of the city.

Sir Colin Campbell, who had taken over as commander-in-chief, in India, assembled a force to the relief of Lucknow and, after much hand-to-hand fighting, the mutineers were driven from the immediate Residency but still occupied the remainder of the city.

The British garrison of 800 men and their families held out at Cawnpore for three weeks against overwhelming odds, and then surrendered only on a promise of safe conduct from the Mutiny leader Nana Sahib, who immediately broke his word and his men slaughtered the entire party, throwing many men, women and children down a well.

By the turn of the year 1857–8, the British could afford to assume a more offensive policy. The 98th (2nd Battalion, the Prince of Wales' [North Staffordshire] Regiment), arrived in Karachi in January and were immediately sent to Nowshera and Campbellpore on the frontier between Peshawar and Rawalpindi to keep that area at peace. While in February, the 80th (2nd Battalion, the South Staffordshire Regiment) landed in Calcutta from South Africa, their destination was Allahabad but their progress, along with all regimental transfers, in the conditions experienced at that time was slow. Two companies were employed as camel corps spending much time assisting hard pressed British columns, although unfortunately, many of their operations were often wild goose chases.

The Ranee of Jhansi was bitterly opposed to the British. The East India Company Resident in the city had dispensed with British troops. The native troops in garrison had mutinied and murdered their British officers, whereupon the Resident, to try to ensure the safety of the remaining Europeans, withdrew to the fort, where they held out for a time until provisions ran out. The Ranee promised safe conduct, this was not kept and women and children were cut to pieces.

On 25th March 1858, the whole of the Central India Field Force which included the 86th Regiment, was drawn up before the walls of Jhansi. The wall was four and a half miles in circumference; it was thick, high and inside was a garrison of 15,000. The British force of 4,500 was under the command of Major-General Sir Hugh Rose who had arrived in India in September the previous year.

The siege batteries opened fire making a breach, but at this juncture news was received by Rose that a rebel relieving force of 22,000 men under its leader Tantia Topee was approaching. After much manoeuvring and disciplined counter-attacks, a disorganized Tantia Topee was driven off.

The breach in the wall was forced and the 86th Regiment moved into the city in hand-to-hand fighting. An entry was made into the palace where the British encountered the Ranee's bodyguard. The palace was captured and the city occupied on 4th April, but the Ranee had fled.

A mobile column was organized and the command was given to Brigadier Henry Havelock who set out from Allahabad and advanced towards Cawnpore where the march was halted by mutineers, but at Futtehpore the British column armed with better rifles inflicted heavy defeat on the rebels. The 64th Regiment lost many men fighting against strong rebel positions covering Cawnpore.

The 8th (King's [Liverpool] Regiment) formed part of the force of 2,800 men to relieve Agra. In a period of 36 hours they force-marched 54 miles, and then defeated the rebel army there of over 7,000. After three days' rest they set off to attack Cawnpore. On the way they were joined by the 23rd and 64th Regiments, and took part in the partial relief of Lucknow where 5,000 British faced 30,000 rebels.

They were then joined by the 93rd (Princess Louise's Highlanders, [Sutherland and Argyll] Highlanders) and the column moved on Cawnpore which was still held by 23,000 rebels. A fierce battle took place, but disciplined British troops overran the mutineers and although suffering many losses, were able to return to Lucknow where total success was attained.

There were areas still in rebel hands in the regions of Oudh and Rohilkhand, but this was patrolled by the Roorkee Field Force of which the 60th Rifle Corps were part, who during April and May operated against the rebels fighting in seven engagements.

The Central Field Force was ordered to take the rebel stronghold of Kalpi. Because daytime temperatures were too high, the army travelled at night. While on the way it was discovered that the Ranee and Topee had managed to get together another army and were holding the town of Kunch, although the rebels then fell back to Kalpi.

A week later Ranee and Topee made a sortie from Kalpi and attacked Rose, who responded strongly, pursuing them back to the town, which Rose found to be deserted, and he strongly but mistakenly believed that the Mutiny was over.

The 92nd (2nd Battalion, the Gordon Highlanders) had landed in Bombay in March 1858 and were part of a force sent to capture Topee, who was becoming more successful at eluding his pursuers. The force also included the 35th Regiment and the 107th HEIC (Bengal Infantry) Regiment, the troops marched on and on through the jungle in intense heat, and at last caught up with him on the road to Rajpore, but he again escaped.

Ranee and Topee met and entered the territory of the ruler of Gwalior, who was loyal to the British. They attacked him and took over his stores and arsenal, persuading his men to join them.

Campbell was attacked by the Gwalior rebel army and only just managed to hold on. In a desperate counter-attack the commanding officer of the 64th (1st Battalion, the North Staffordshire Regiment) was killed together with six other officers.

On its way to the Cape, the 95th (2nd Battalion, the Sherwood Foresters) was diverted to Bombay, and was there attached to the column led by Rose and the Rajputana field force which also included the 83rd Regiment. Following a short siege the fortress of Gwalior fell and the ruler was reinstated. In the fighting the Ranee was killed. The regiments then captured the rebel camp at Koondryee, and in April 1859 took part in the final suppression of the rebels. Topee was finally captured and hanged.

The aftermath brought about much-needed change to how the military in India were organized. The East India Company transferred its control of regiments to the Crown, which meant that its officers no longer could indulge in the lifestyle enjoyed before the Mutiny, and although problems in Asia were still encountered, henceforth they were dealt with by the Crown.

As well as the battle honour DELHI, other Honours were also authorized in 1836.

For their defence of the city, the battle honour LUCKNOW was awarded to the: 5th, 32nd, 64th, 78th, 84th, 90th and 102nd.

And for the relief of the city, the same battle honour was awarded to the: 5th, 8th, 23rd, 53rd, 75th, 82nd, 84th and 93rd.

Finally LUCKNOW was awarded for the capture of the city to the: 5th, 10th, 20th, 23rd, 34th, 38th, 42nd, 53rd, 78th, 79th, 84th, 90th, 93rd, 97th, 101st, 102nd and the Rifle Brigade.

The following regiments who maintained order further south were awarded the battle honour CENTRAL INDIA: 71st, 72nd, 80th, 83rd, 86th, 88th, 95th, 108th and 109th.

CHAPTER XXXI

ZULU WAR 1879
QUEEN VICTORIA

The British Army was equipped with the Model 1879 Martini-Henry .45 calibre single shot rifle.

Zululand lies in the southeast of Africa, located just to the north of Natal, separated from it by the Tugela River and its tributary the Buffalo. It was ruled by the Zulu King Cetshwayo, born about 1827, who controlled their army, which was very organized with regiments drilled in the tactics of the 'chest', the main body, being held back while the 'horns' moving in advance, attacked the flanks and rear, before the 'chest' moved in for the kill.

It was believed that it was only a matter of time before Cetshwayo would try to increase the size of Zululand. This would be achieved by invading Natal; therefore by the end of 1878 the British put into action their plan.

They would need to crush the Zulu nation. The man chosen to command was Lieutenant-General the Honourable Sir Frederic August Thesiger C.B. who arrived in South Africa at King William's town on 4th March 1878. Born in 1827, he had been pushed by his father such that by the age of fifteen he was gazetted in the Rifle Brigade. In 1850 was promoted to lieutenant, then captain and in 1852 as ADC to the Viceroy of India. In 1855 he saw duty in the Crimea and was promoted to brevet major before he commanded the 95th Foot in India. He served as ADC to Queen Victoria and in 1877 was promoted to major-general. He is better known as Lord Chelmsford, a title inherited from his father.

Chelmsford was confident of early success. He had five separate columns which consisted of 16,000 men all from British regiments. They included two battalions of the 24th Foot and single battalions of the 3rd, 4th, 13th and 99th Regiments, as well as two battalions of the 90th Foot. Also in reserve were the 80th located at Luneberg. He kept the 4th Column at Middle Drift and the 5th Column in the Transvaal, available if required.

His main force of three columns crossed the River Tugela on the 11th January 1879. The left column crossed the Buffalo at Rorke's Drift; it contained 1st and 2nd Battalions of the 24th Foot, a field battery, some mounted infantry and two battalions of the Natal Native Contingent, a total of 1,800 European troops and 2,600 native troops. It was commanded by Lieutenant-Colonel Glyn of the 24th and was accompanied by the commander-in-chief, Lord Chelmsford and his staff.

On 20th January, an advance was made to the hill of Isandhlwana about ten miles from Rorke's Drift. The main camp was pitched on the eastern slopes of the hill; a little to the south was a small isolated hill and between the two the road ran westwards towards Rorke's Drift. North of the encampment was broken ground and to the northeast was a range of hills.

During the 21st January, a reconnaissance patrol observed Zulus to the southeast. At 4 a.m. the following day, Lord Chelmsford with companies of the 2nd Battalion 24th Foot, together with artillery and native troops moved out to bring them to battle. No effort had been made by the senior officer Lieutenant-Colonel Pulleine to bring the camp to a state of defensive readiness, apart from ordering the men to fall-in as he believed that there were enough experienced troops to deal with what he thought to be only a small band of Zulus.

Colonel Anthony William Durnford, Royal Engineers, had been born in Ireland in 1830 to an army family (his father was to become a major-general). By the time that Durnford was eighteen, he had been educated in Germany and had passed through the Royal Military Academy as a second lieutenant in the Royal Engineers; he was to become an experienced civil engineering officer, albeit one liable to act in a rash manner.

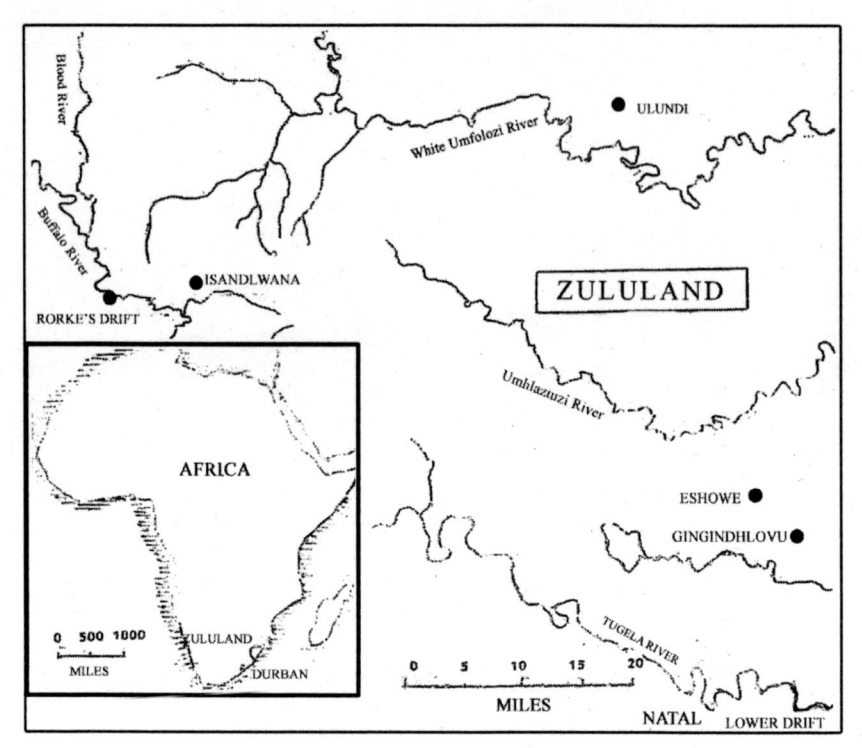

AFRICA 1877-1879

At 10 a.m. Colonel Durnford arrived in camp from Rorke's Drift with a battery troop capable of firing rockets, and several companies of native troops, some mounted. As he was senior to Lieutenant-Colonel Pulleine he immediately took his men out to attack the Zulus, but ordered Pulleine to send a company of the 24th to support him. 'A' Company was despatched to a ridge nearly a mile away to the north. A detachment of mounted infantry from the 80th remained in camp.

About midday, the camp was alerted by the noise of heavy fighting from the direction taken by Durnford; at this point an officer rode in reporting that the situation was most serious and requested a further company to assist 'A' Company. Pulleine reluctantly sent 'F' Company.

Masses of Zulus now advanced towards the camp. Durnford was falling back with his command, as the Zulus adopted their usual fighting technique; their horns moving in advance as the main body was held back. The retreating 24th became engaged with the Zulu right horn, but the entire enemy army was now attacking the camp which was not in any form of battle order.

The regular British infantry in small groups kept up a steady accurate fire, which checked the Zulus many of whom were killed before they could come into contact with the defenders. The main firing line was 400 yards from the camp. As the Zulus continued their onslaught it was realized that each man required more ammunition. Traditionally each soldier carried 70 rounds, and it was unusual in battle to use more than 50; so men were sent to the camp for more.

On reaching the reserve supplies it became almost impossible, firstly to remove the boxes from the kicking and prancing mules and secondly because, once they were placed on the ground, a further problem emerged. The sturdy wooden boxes which held 600 rounds each, had the lids held in place by two strong copper bands, each secured by nine large screws which, in the haste and heat of battle, presented a major problem.

As the main attack continued, the Zulus realized that their numbers were being greatly reduced by the fire from the British and their ranks began to falter. But about 1.15 p.m. the defenders' fire slackened as their ammunition ran out. The Zulus took advantage and rushed, whereupon the native troops broke and fled leaving the hopelessly outnumbered British overwhelmed. The main casualties were from the 24th Foot and a detachment of mounted infantry from the 80th Regiment.

From his command post located in front of the camp, Pulleine witnessed the destruction of five companies of his battalion. When the Zulus broke into the area, he mounted his horse and rode to the guard tent which he entered, to return seconds later with the Queen's Colour of the 1st Battalion, giving it to the adjutant, Lieutenant Melvill and ordering him to take it to a place of safety. Melvill was joined by Lieutenant Coghill, the two men considered using the road to Rorke's Drift but, as it was swarming with Zulus, they turned to the Buffalo, where they were both killed and the Colour was lost.

As for Pulleine, he entered his tent, sat at his field desk and presumably commenced to write his report. At that point a Zulu entered the tent, Pulleine picked up his revolver and fired, hitting the man who jumped over the desk and killed the colonel with his stabbing assegai.

Next day at about 3 p.m. on the 22nd January some of the fugitives from Isandlwana arrived at Rorke's Drift and gave news of the disaster. The post consisted of two stone buildings which were about forty yards apart, the eastern was used as a storehouse which adjoined a strongly built kraal, the other which was slightly larger, was used as a hospital under the control of Surgeon-Major Reynolds, an Irishman who was assisted by one private soldier as an orderly, to look after the thirty men under treatment there. The whole area was mainly rough ground to the front and side of the hospital with uncleared bush and a small garden.

The senior officer was Lieutenant John Chard, a 32-year-old Royal Engineer. His job was in charge of the river crossing regarding the use of the punts, also stabilizing the banks of the drift for which he commanded no British troops, but depended on the services of a few native ferrymen and labourers.

His seniority in the army was due to his length of service of eleven years, which placed him ahead of Lieutenant Bromhead, who commanded 'B' Company of the 2nd Battalion, 24th Regiment. Bromhead was deaf, his career in doubt, and he only remained because of family involvement in the military. He missed commands at drill, was therefore disliked by his men and was usually only given detachment duty guarding regimental supply dumps. He had been left at the post, as part of the permanent garrison with about 80 men from his regiment and 100 men from the Natal Native Contingent (NNC) also a few men from the 1st Battalion 24th and the commissariat.

The garrison at once set to work to loophole and barricade the buildings, block up the gates of the kraal and build a wall of the only material available, mealie bags between the storehouse and hospital.

At about 4 p.m. word was received that the Zulus were advancing towards the Drift in great numbers. The native contingent at once bolted, except for one man, Corporal Friedrich Schiess, a young Swiss, who had been working as an unskilled labourer in Natal. He had served in the Franco-Prussian War and had therefore been accepted into the NNC. The defenders were now reduced to about one hundred men, prompting Chard to reduce the perimeter which he achieved using heavy biscuit boxes to form a new defensive line.

Half an hour later Zulus approached from the southeast, there appeared to be as many as 500, led by a chief on a grey horse. The riflemen of the 24th could not believe that the Zulus were running towards them, and at 500 yards they fired their first volley, watching as the leading runners fell, followed by their chief.

The Zulus continued running towards the defenders, who kept up controlled rifle fire as if they were aiming at targets on the range. Those Zulus who remained, as they got closer, moved into the protection of the garden and bush, where with their stabbing assegais they were able to move forward without being in direct line of fire; from where they were able to rush at the defenders.

Time and again the Zulus, who appeared to be continually reinforced by more impis, swarmed up to the barricades pressing against the hospital and the front defences, under cover from the overgrown garden and bush. Some so close that Lieutenant Bromhead collected the nearest men and drove the attackers off with the bayonet; but on being repulsed, they retired to cover, where they would shout and in unison beat their shields with their assegais.

Once again taking advantage of the cover afforded by the gardens and bush, the Zulus reached the main barricades and fought hand to hand with the defenders who, although better armed, were often required to use their bayonets against the handheld stabbing assegais; after all, the Martini Henry rifle and bayonet was seven feet in length.

At about 6 p.m. the Zulus set fire to the thatched roof of the hospital, which made the building untenable and it therefore had to be evacuated. The problem was that the hospital was divided into rooms, and the only way out involved smashing holes in the partitions between the rooms, before moving to the next.

The Zulus had entered the end room, where they had to be held at bay by bullets and the bayonet, whilst the defenders had to break through the partition walls to gain sanctuary in the next room. This procedure was repeated for the remaining three rooms, until the far one was reached, enabling the men to climb out of the window, leaving several dead.

The defenders now concentrated around the storehouse, where the biscuit box barrier had been built; the area received some protection from the Zulu rifle fire coming from the hills above, where old muskets were used or rifles gained at Isandlwana were aimed at the British. In either case the use of these weapons was so inaccurate and erratic that, apart from annoyance, no harm was done.

The light was fading, but the flames from the hospital roof illuminated the area enabling the defenders to pick their targets. Again and again the Zulus rushed the barricades where they were repulsed. Eventually the stubbornness of the British soldiers and the heavy losses suffered by the Zulus began to produce results. Towards midnight the attacks died out completely.

For gallantry at the defence of Rorke's Drift, the Victoria Cross was awarded to Lieutenant Chard RE, Lieutenant Bromhead and six NCOs and men of the 24th Regiment, also Surgeon-Major Reynolds, Assistant Commissary Dalton and Corporal Schiess of the NNC.

Chelmsford was with his 1st Column at Lower Drift. Following his set-back at Isandlwana he was intent on bringing Cetshwayo to battle. On the other hand the Zulu chief, having heard of the effect of the regimental British fire, especially their main weapon the Martini Henry, was reluctant on a set-piece battle.

Chelmsford's invasion plans took rapid shape. He intended to smash their army in one spectacular victory, thereby capturing their king, ensuring that Natal would not be invaded by the Zulus. The best way of achieving this was to move his army from the Lower Drift, north about sixty miles to the royal kraal at Ulundi.

Colonel Pearson moved his column thirty miles into Zululand. It consisted of 1,400 European troops and 460 NNC, which arrived at the mission station of Eshowe that had been occupied by British missionaries since 1864. There were thousands of Zulus in the area such that communication with the men at Lower Drift had broken down. A runner arrived at Eshowe with the news that Chelmsford would not be able to send reinforcements for at least six weeks. The ring of Zulus on the surrounding hills had thickened therefore Chelmsford did not feel that he was in a position to send a relief force.

It would be incorrect to state that outposts in Zululand were under siege. Eshowe is a good example. The troops within the mission station were able to travel well outside their lines and often did. Zulus were observed in the distance, but they never attacked except for the occasional sniper whose inaccurate fire became only a nuisance. This lack of activity allowed the British to build better fortifications, felling trees and linking existing buildings to the church.

Some of Pearson's mounted troops had earlier discovered Zulu kraals seven miles to the north, so on 1st March, he led 400 men out of the compound at 2 a.m. with the intention of destroying them. They came across the Zulu encampment of forty to fifty huts at dawn. About fifty Zulus ran away, some wearing red tunics acquired at Isandlwana, the huts were set on fire and the British returned by mid-morning.

One problem which existed was that the men had to sleep out in the open on bare ground, although the lucky ones could shelter under the wagons. As the weather was poor with continual rain and damp soggy nights, many suffered very high temperatures leading to fever and the inevitable dysentery which required many being moved to the old church, which had been converted into a hospital. Pearson estimated that his food supply was not in any danger, and if they were not relieved they could last out well into April.

During mid-March it was noticed by the men at Eshowe that flashing lights could be seen from the direction of the Lower Drift, then it became obvious that a heliograph was being used, this enabled communication between the two zones to commence. On 23rd March two Zulus appeared under a white flag, they said that they carried a message from Cetshwayo who enquired why he was being attacked, and they offered safe conduct out of his territory if the British wished to leave. Pearson suspected a trick and ignored it.

The military situation had changed during Chelmsford's time at Lower Drift. The 88th Regiment were the first reinforcements to reach Durban on 6th March, five days later the 57th Regiment arrived from Ceylon, and six days after that they were joined by the 91st Highlanders. The 3rd Battalion, 60th K. R. R. C. was in Colchester when they received sudden orders to embark for South Africa in consequence of the defeat at Isandlwana. They landed at Durban and marched to meet Chelmsford at Lower Drift.

On 25th March, Chelmsford's 1st Column of several British regiments both infantry and mounted, together with Natal contingents also infantry and mounted, a total of nearly three and a half thousand Europeans and over two thousand native troops, moved out of the Lower Drift, north to relieve Eshowe. Following his experience at Isandlwana, Chelmsford ordered that every cart and wagon would carry ammunition boxes, and the lids on all boxes were to be unscrewed. At night, wagons were to form square, outlying pickets were to take up position half a mile in front.

The Zulus, although in large numbers, were spread over much of the local countryside and tended to disappear as the column moved towards them. It was not until the British column was nearing Gingindhlovu that the Zulus decided to defend their homeland.

Early in the morning of 2nd April, the advance pickets reported that Zulus were approaching, but instead of confronting the main body, the British observed that the horns were ahead of them. Six Zulu regiments, two of whom had operated at Isandlwana and Rorke's Drift were attacking; they rushed against the British lines, who at four hundred yards opened fire. The Zulus, regardless that many were falling, stormed up to the muzzles of the British rifles. The Zulu army mostly fled, but some with their Martini Henry rifles fired at random, during these exchanges Lieutenant Johnson of the 99th Regiment was killed in front of his commanding officer and Lieutenant-Colonel F.V. Northey of the 60th Regiment who had received a bullet in the shoulder earlier in the battle, returned to his battalion, but haemorrhaged and died the next day. As the remaining Zulus withdrew they were chased by mounted infantry leaving many wounded and over 700 dead.

The men in Ushowe had observed the whole battle from early morning when the silence had been broken by the sound of artillery. They looked at the battle through telescopes, and saw masses of Zulus pressing on three sides. Pearson prepared to take his column to assist, however, the firing slackened and by 7 p.m. all appeared to be over.

Chelmsford heliographed that he would move to Ushowe the following day, and at 4 p.m. Pearson decided to ride out to meet him with 500 men. When they met there was much congratulation. The 91st Highlanders were the first regiment to march into Ushowe, which was totally relieved the following day. As the British left, the Zulus set fire to the buildings.

Chelmsford returned to Durban on 9th April, where the British establishment had now changed. He believed that the time was now right to take control of the whole of Zululand. As he now commanded 16,000 European troops who were experienced fighters, and around 7,000 natives disciplined in methodical warfare, the Zulus, although still dangerous were now very wary.

On 11th April, the 24th Foot consisting of fifteen officers and 526 men landed at Durban. The regiment had been recruited, and drafted in from other units to their depot at Brecon. With his now vastly strengthened army Chelmsford moved his column northwards towards Ulundi. By July it was reported that Cetshwayo had left the royal kraal.

The British army then attacked the remaining Zulus at Ulundi, who defended the area with vigour, at one time approaching the 80th Regiment at very close range, to be met by devastating volleys from Chelmsford's infantry. Realizing the hopelessness of their situation, the remaining Zulus fled, only to be cut down by British cavalry.

Cetshwayo was still in the area and patrols were sent out looking for him, but he refused to be taken. However, there were not many regions where he could seek sanctuary. He was a proud man who was finally taken by the British. The 3rd/60th and mounted officers of the King's Dragoon Guards escorted Cetshwayo and his wives into the now British camp at Ulundi arriving on 31st August. On 4th September 1879, Cetshwayo was transferred by boat to Natal and captivity in Capetown. The war was over.

The British establishment were not long in recognizing the effort put in by the army because, on 25th July 1882, the following battle honours were awarded to infantry regiments:

SOUTH AFRICA 1877-78-79
24th The South Wales Borderers
88th 1st Battalion, the Connaught Rangers
94th 2nd Battalion, the Connaught Rangers
90th 2nd Battalion, the Cameronians

SOUTH AFRICA 1878–1879
13th Somerset Light Infantry
80th 2nd Battalion, the South Staffordshire Regiment

SOUTH AFRICA 1879
3rd The Buffs (East Kent Regiment)
4th The King's Own (Royal Lancaster Regiment)
21st The Royal Scots Fusiliers
57th 1st Battalion, the Middlesex Regiment
58th 2nd Battalion, the Northamptonshire Regiment
60th The King's Royal Rifle Corps
91st 1st Battalion, Princess Louise's (Sutherland and Argyll Highlanders)
99th 2nd Battalion, the Wiltshire Regiment

CHAPTER XXXII

1881–1899
QUEEN VICTORIA

The General Order 41 of 1881 effective 1st July, to which Secretary of War Mr Edward Cardwell lent his name, provided that every regiment of infantry of the Line should consist of two regular battalions, one to be stationed abroad and maintained at full strength, the other to be kept at home providing drafts for the battalion overseas.

Single battalion regiments were to be combined as necessary, the old numerical titles being abolished, and every regiment was to have a territorial designation based on its recruiting area, now to be known as its Regimental District. In the latter was established the Regimental Depot, while the independent Militia regiments raised within the area, were to be reconstructed as Militia battalions. So from the old regiments of foot and Militia were evolved the new county regiments. Henceforth all regiments were to be referred to by their new designations.

The amalgamations were unpopular with many of the regiments, but it was believed by the Government and senior military personnel that they would give the army a more professional appearance, especially to the general population at all social levels. Although the men were no longer considered to be mere drunken simpletons, public opinion of officers was that generally they were bored wasters, relying on their family position.

It is easy to believe when reading military history, that major battles since Waterloo were all the battles in which the British were involved, but this was not the case, as the Parliament of the day believed that they were now the world police force, and should become involved in every area where, to the British Government, it appeared that the local rulers were incompetent.

As an example of this policy one should go back to 1859, where after long trade talks between the British, French and Chinese had only resulted in stalemate. The British Liberal Government decided early in 1860 that they should send an expeditionary force to China to resolve the situation.

A naval attack on Chinese coastal forts was unsuccessful, therefore early in August a British force of two divisions, 11,000 strong were joined at the request of Napoleon III by 7,000 French troops. Later in August, these arrived at the mouth of the Pei-ha River and laid siege to the Taku forts. The British crossed the river and captured the port of Tongku. Finally at the end of the month the remaining forts were taken.

The Chinese did not oppose the British advance on Pekin, which surrendered. A peace treaty was signed by the three nations on the 24th October.

The battle honour of TAKU FORT was awarded to:

The Lothian Regiment (the Royal Scots)
The Queen's Royal (West Surrey) Regiment
The Buffs (East Kent Regiment)
1st Battalion, the East Surrey Regiment
1st Battalion, the Essex Regiment
The King's Royal Rifle Corps
2nd Battalion, the Hampshire Regiment

Also that of PEKIN 1860 to:
The Lothian Regiment (the Royal Scots)
The Queen's Royal (West Surrey) Regiment
The King's Royal Rifle Corps
2nd Battalion, the Hampshire Regiment
2nd Battalion, the Duke of Edinburgh's (Wiltshire Regiment)

*

Twenty-four British regiments were involved in what was to be termed the Second Afghan War, which took place between 1878-80.

The reason for this large number of regiments was that at the time many were stationed reasonably locally in India or Burma, and also in the relatively immediate location of South Africa.

For many years the Afghan chiefs had been playing the Russians against the Indian Government. In 1879 the British Resident in Kabul became involved in the conflict when his staff and military escort were massacred by local Afghan tribesmen.

A field force under Sir Frederick Roberts was ordered to advance on Kabul but, as ever, the Khyber Pass presented difficulties when advancing to Afghanistan from India, requiring regiments to be sent to cover lines of communication through the pass.

One area which required particular attention was controlled by the Afghans from their fortress of Ali Masjid, which was soon taken by the Leicestershire Regiment (still the 17th Foot), the 1st Battalion, the King's Own (Yorkshire Light Infantry) (51st Foot), the 2nd Battalion, the Loyal North Lancashire Regiment (81st Foot) and the 4th Battalion, the Rifle Brigade (95th Foot).

Meanwhile at Peiwar Kotal on 2nd December 1878, the King's (Liverpool) Regiment (8th Foot) and the 1st Battalion Seaforth Highlanders (Ross-shire Buffs, the Duke of Albany's) (72nd Foot), were making a feint attack while Robert's column outflanked the Afghan position, enabling his later relief of Kandahar by the Royal Fusiliers (City of London Regiment) (7th Foot), the King's Royal Rifle Corps (60th Foot), 2nd Battalion, Princess Charlotte of Wales's (Berkshire Regiment) (66th Foot), 1st Battalion, the Seaforth Highlanders (Ross-shire Buffs, the Duke of Albany's) (72nd Foot) and the 2nd Battalion, the Gordon Highlanders (92nd Foot).

The 2nd Battalion, the Devonshire Regiment (11th Foot) had been in South Africa whence they sailed for India. There they were ordered to Afghanistan. Their task was to march through Scinde and the Bolan Pass during the hottest period of the summer of 1879, resulting in many casualties from fatigue. More deaths were recorded, where the 66th Foot were practically wiped out in a desperate rearguard action at Maiwand on 27th July 1880, where two officers and nine men making a last stand near the village of Khig.

The Battle Honours of ALI MASJID, PEIWAR KOTAL, CHARASIAH, KABUL 1879, AHMAD KHEL, KANDAHAR 1880 and AFGHANISTAN 1878-79, 1878-1880, 1879-1880 were awarded to the regiments who had taken part in the various conflicts.

*

The Suez Canal had opened in 1869, but due to the British buying shares in the company, both Britain and France were now involved both economically and politically. Egypt was at this time nominally a Turkish possession, but Turkey's own troubles and her inefficiency in overseas relations, made her control very poor.

For some time the British had been shoring up the tottering regime of Khedive Ismail, and after riots in Cairo in 1879, they supported his son who was looked on by the Egyptian army officers as a mere tool of British imperialism. It soon became obvious that the local rulers had little control of events; therefore in 1881 a rebellion by the army in Egypt took place led by Colonel Arabi Pasha.

Britain now believed that she should intervene to defend the Suez Canal. Regiments were mobilized and on 8th August 1882, the 1st Battalion, Princess Victoria's (Royal Irish Fusiliers) embarked for Egypt as part of this force. The British Navy bombarded the Egyptian army in Alexandria, closely followed by the landing of the 1st Battalion, the Royal Sussex Regiment and the 1st Battalion, the South Staffordshire Regiment.

The 2nd Battalion, Royal Irish Fusiliers then arrived at Alexandria on 21st August while their 1st Battalion arrived in Ismalia two days later, both formed part of the 2nd Infantry Brigade of the 1st Division under the command of Lord Wolseley. They marched twelve miles during the night and encountered the Egyptians, resulting in the Battle of Tel-el-Kebir on 12th September 1882, securing the freedom for traffic through the Suez Canal.

*

The 1st Battalion, the South Staffordshire Regiment, returned to Egypt from Malta and was sent to the Sudan, where a religious leader

Mohammed Ahmed, the self-styled Mahdi or Messiah, had been waging his holy war in an effort to rid the country of Egyptians and other foreigners.

The British financed a force of 10,000 men of mixed nationality under an Englishman, Colonel Hicks, which moved against the Mahdi, but was wiped out at an engagement at Lake Rahad. Another force under General Baker fared no better at El-Teb against one of the Mahdi's lieutenants, Osman Digna.

The British Government sent General Gordon to the Sudan as Governor-General of the territory. His headquarters was at Khartoum, which was soon besieged. Upon receiving the news the Government decided that strong action was needed.

A force of two columns was assembled, one to move along the main route the River Nile, whilst the other under General Graham would move overland. The 1st Battalion, Gordon Highlanders left Cairo on 16th February 1884, with the main object of seizing the Red Sea port of Suakin. They marched in square formation through the desert, while each night the same discipline existed which at nightfall included the building of a 'zareba' or thorn hedge as a protective barrier.

The first serious action occurred thirteen days later, when at El-Teb the enemy were charged by the 1st Battalion, Black Watch (Royal Highlanders) and the 1st Battalion, the York and Lancaster Regiment who emerged through the smoke which had been caused from concerted British rifle fire. As the two sides engaged, the fighting became hand-to-hand, both sides using anything available including as a last resort the fist, forcing the Sudanese to withdraw leaving many dead.

As regiments moved further south, by 13th March 1884 the engagements at Tamai took place, forcing the Sudanese to retire from the area of Suakin.

The Nile column had an advance guard formed from men of the Black Watch, and the 1st Battalion The South Staffordshire Regiment. The main force which included the 1st Battalion, Princess Victoria's (Royal Irish Fusiliers) and the 1st Battalion, the Royal Sussex, ascended the river under the blazing sun in small boats against the current; even when they were able to set the sails they frequently ran aground, necessitating the unloading of supplies and equipment, which then had to be carried up the rapids.

Believing that the sight of red uniforms as opposed to the newly issued khaki, would deter the local tribesmen from attacking Khartoum, twenty men from the Royal Sussex Regiment were put into two boats and, as arranged, they were wearing red serge coats borrowed from the Guards Camel Regiment. The boats were towed by a steamer towards Khartoum.

Early in January 1885, the Mahdi's local supporters entered Khartoum and made their way to the area occupied by Gordon, who appears to have prepared for his fate. Ignoring calls from the Mahdi for his saving, the dervishes killed him.

Local battles followed involving many regiments; their achievements are recorded in their battle honours. One battle is of note that at Kirbekan when the South Staffordshire Regiment and the Black Watch both lost their GOC and commanding officers.

For some time Egypt and the Sudan remained fairly stable, but during late 1888 trouble clouds were gathering. Regiments were sent to stabilize the situation. In December there was trouble again at Suakin, where a small detachment under Lord Kitchener was threatened by a force of dervishes under their leader Osman Digna.

Three British battalions were in Cairo. The King's Own Scottish Borderers and the Welsh Regiment were rushed to assist, while the Royal Irish Rifles were left to garrison the city. Kitchener was able to move against the dervishes where the modern British equipment proved too much for the local tribesmen, and Osman Digna was beaten.

A British force of Cameron Highlanders, the Seaforth Highlanders, a detachment of the Royal Warwickshire Regiment and the Lincolnshire Regiment marched adjacent to the banks of the River Atbara. Early on the morning of the 8th April 1889, when the regiments were nearing the enemy the British opened fire, driving them back into the jungle. The casualties to the Lincolns were very low, only one sergeant was killed and three officers and fourteen other ranks wounded. Colonel Verner of the Lincolns was wounded leading his men.

The assault continued as the enemy were chased, then finally brought to battle by three brigades, one British and two Sudanese. The battle at Albara probably took less than a few hours, during which time the British lost many officers and 525 other ranks, killed or seriously wounded, which often resulted in death. The dervishes losses were considerably higher, they lost forty emirs and 3,000 killed.

*

In 1885 an expedition was sent to Burma, generally involving regiments from India, to suppress a rebellion by the supporters of King Theebaw and his main tribal leader Bho Shwe, who thought that they should throw off what he believed to be the British yoke.

The campaign which involved ten British regiments and up to forty-three Indian and two Gurkha regiments, became a strenuous and prolonged operation of two years' mainly jungle warfare, where most regiments lost more men from cholera than in action. The King's Own (Yorkshire Light Infantry) lost over 300 men either killed in action or by disease.

The local rebels turned to guerrilla tactics, which meant that regiments did not go into action as single units, but instead used groups of 50 to 200 riflemen as mobile columns. Nevertheless casualties were high, the King's (Liverpool) Regiment had 280 casualties.

One party consisting of men from the 2nd Battalion, the South Wales Borderers, was ordered to move into the area where Bo Shwe was believed to be located. It took a march of sixty-seven miles through heavy rain and over rough terrain, the last fifty-two miles were covered in fourteen hours, enabling the troops to catch the enemy completely by surprise; in the ensuing action Bo Shwe and his supporters were killed,

The war ended when King Theebaw was captured at Mandalay, which resulted in the annexation of Burma to the British Empire.

In 1890 the battle honour BURMA 1885-1887 was awarded to:
The Queen's (Royal West Surrey) Regiment

The King's (Liverpool) Regiment
The Somerset Light Infantry
The Royal Welch Fusiliers
The South Wales Borderers
The Hampshire Regiment
The King's Own (Yorkshire Light Infantry)
The Royal Munster Fusiliers
The Rifle Brigade

The story does not finish with the defeat of the dervishes in 1889, because nine years later another confrontation was to take place. It had taken twenty-three months for Kitchener's army to advance from the Sudanese border, and was to take another three weeks until in early September 1898 the last of his reinforcements were to arrive, enabling him to move against the latest enemy at Omdurman.

His whole force which included men from the Lancashire Fusiliers, Lincolnshire Regiment, Northumberland Fusiliers, Seaforth Highlanders, Cameron Highlanders, Warwickshire Regiment and the Rifle Brigade, with a Maxim Gun detachment from the Inniskilling Fusiliers, also the 21st Lancers and artillery, together with Sudanese and Egyptian troops, all of whom were within striking distance of Abdullahi, the Khalifa and his dervish supporters.

The British line stretched over two miles and was therefore only two deep. The dervishes, estimated at about 50,000 men attacked, but were stopped by artillery and rifle fire before they reached the British.

As the Anglo-Egyptian force moved towards Omdurman, another group of dervishes attacked the Sudanese Brigade breaking through their lines. The situation was critical until the 1st British Brigade came to their rescue, deploying on the threatened flank. Firepower and determination by the Allies caused panic among their foe. The dervishes unused to such disciplined aggression, watched their neighbouring ranks being brought down, fled leaving thousands dead.

The British continued their march to Omdurman which was reached by nightfall.

After the occupation of Omdurman, regiments returned to the Nile and hence to Cairo, to be drafted to their next posting wherever they were needed. As there was no battle honour for Omdurman, regiments were awarded ATBARA and KHARTOUM.

Early in 1895, trouble broke out in the small Indian state of Chitral when it was invaded by Umra Khan, chief of the neighbouring Jandal state with a large force of Pathan tribesmen. His first action was to surround the fort in the capital town of Chitral, placing it in a state of siege. The fort was occupied by the British agent and a small detachment of British troops, who were sent out to deal with the attackers but were repulsed.

A relief force was assembled; seven British regiments with ten Indian and two Gurkha regiments with two mounted Indian lancer regiments, in all about 15,000 men.

The plan was to attack Umra Khan at Chitral. This took place on 3rd April with the main action at Malakand Pass, where the British faced very difficult terrain, consisting of sheer precipices and narrow ledges, which gave the local tribesmen cover with commanding views over the troops in the pass, enabling heavy rifle and musket fire, often using their ancient weapons to be directed towards them.

A further action the following day at Khar, enabled the leading British brigade on 5th April to secure the pass at Malakand with the whole of the relief force. They then moved against Chitral and when they were within sight of the fort, to their surprise the besiegers fled, leaving the area completely, enabling the Seaforth Highlanders and the Buffs to enter the town, assuring the population that the British were still in control.

The battle honour CHITRAL was awarded on 27th July 1897 to:

1st Battalion, the Buffs (East Kent Regiment)
1st Battalion, Bedfordshire Regiment
2nd Battalion, King's Own Scottish Borderers
1st Battalion, East Lancashire Regiment
1st Battalion, King's Royal Rifle Corps
1st Battalion Seaforth Highlanders (Ross-shire Buffs, The Duke of Albany's)
1st Battalion, Gordon Highlanders

The completion of the campaign at Chitral in 1885 did not indicate that peace had returned to the area. Trouble broke out from the Afridi and Orakzai tribesmen in the largest rising against the British on the North-West Frontier, who together with the Mohmand tribesmen then closed the Khyber Pass.

The British Government sent General Sir William Lockhart from England, to take charge of the army from Chitral, who now became the Tirah Expeditionary Force, named after the decision to attack the summer stronghold of the tribesmen at Tirah.

The force numbered 33,000 men, consisting of nine British regiments, four Gurkha and thirteen assorted Indian regiments. Their first engagement on 18th October 1897 was when they fought a rearguard action at Dargai, a village now in Pakistan. The campaign turned out to be a very difficult one, when after a lull, two days later an assault was made on the Dargai Heights, led by the Gurkhas, with the 1st Battalion, the Dorsetshire Regiment and the 2nd Battalion, the Sherwood Foresters (Derbyshire Regiment).

The Gurkhas were repulsed, and early in the afternoon, the Sherwood Foresters were ordered to storm the enemy's entrenchment this proved impossible, owing to the large number of tribesmen lining the edge of the plateau. The Gordon Highlanders were then ordered to take the position, and despite the loss of many men, they finally overran the tribesmen in Dargai.

Following the victory, Lockhart warned the troops that more hard work was ahead, a statement which was proved to be true, because before the end of the year, regiments were engaged in fighting at Maiden, and on 9th November finally in the Bara Valley.

There was further fighting at Shin Kamar, where the tribesmen occupied a very strong defensive position which led the Force into a trap. Only bold action avoided a massacre costing the 2nd Battalion, the King's Own (Yorkshire Light Infantry)* the lives of three

---

*In July 1839, The Honourable Court of Directors of the East India Company, authorized Lieutenant-Colonel Brown-Dyce to raise a new regiment to be known as 2nd Madras European Regiment. In 1861 The European Regiments of the East India Co were converted into regiments of HM General Army whereupon the 2nd Madras

lieutenants and twenty-eight men killed, but by the start of 1898 resistance from the locals was over.

On 15th December 1899 the battle honour TIRAH was awarded to:

1st Battalion, the Queen's (Royal West Surrey) Regiment
1st Battalion, the Devonshire Regiment
2nd Battalion, the Prince of Wales's Own (West Yorkshire) Regiment
2nd Battalion, the Royal Scots Fusiliers
2nd Battalion, the King's Own Scottish Borderers
1st Battalion, the Dorsetshire Regiment
1st Battalion, the Gordon Highlanders
1st Battalion, the Northamptonshire Regiment
2nd Battalion, the Sherwood Foresters (Derbyshire Regiment)

European changed its title to the 105th Foot (Madras Light Infantry). The 105th sailed for India from England in 1887.

EPILOGUE

Actions of British regiments after 1899 are all recorded elsewhere and not dealt with here.

During the late eighteenth century, the attitude of the British Government whether Whig or Tory, was that because of the involvement in the ever-increasing Empire, they had to assume the role of overseeing the known world. This led to many conflicts that were recorded by the following battle honours:

Boxer Rising	China 1900
Punjab Frontier	India 1897–1898
Leone	1897
West Africa	1887–1894
Burmese War	1885–1887
Afghan War	1878–1880
East Africa	1897–1899
West Indies	1880–1900+
New Zealand	1870

The army reforms of 1881 led to a reduction in the number of regiments. From the original 109 foot regiments, amalgamations left only seventy that were available for the engagements at the turn of the century. It must be stated that although there were fewer regiments, many of the new ones had active second and even third battalions.

On 11th October 1899 the Boers in South Africa declared war against the British, who responded with great strength. As well as cavalry, guards and yeomanry, fifty-six Line regiments were engaged in South Africa between 1899–1902. Battle honours were awarded after authorization by Army Order 3 dated 1905.

The next major conflict was the First World War, which Britain entered on the 4th August 1914. It was decided to raise a wartime army, which due to the attitude of the nation, and the support of the young men throughout the country, resulted in an explosion in the number of battalions for existing regiments.

Many regiments were increased from their one or two battalions, for example, the Manchester Regiment who by the end of 1914 had raised forty-two battalions, while the Durham Light Infantry had thirty-seven and most other regiments had in excess of twenty.

War finished in November 1918, when, unless they had earlier been annihilated by pointless bayonet charges against well-fortified enemy trenches, these battalions were disbanded.

The next changes to the British regimental system followed in the wake of civil disturbances. Southern Ireland left the Union in 1922, necessitating the removal of six Irish regiments from the Army List.

There followed the Second World War, when on 3rd September 1939 Britain declared war on Germany. Again battalions were increased to account for the required expansion in manpower. There was no enormous flood of volunteers as in 1914, so conscription was essential from the outbreak.

Following the War, National Service continued until the last man was called up in 1961, to be discharged in May 1963 after the compulsory two years with the colours.

A Government decision to reduce costs and improve efficiency led in 1958/59 to regiments generally from adjacent areas being linked. This reduced the existing sixty-four to only forty-nine.

During the mid-sixties, further amalgamations took place, again linking regiments from neighbouring geographical areas, which led to forty-nine becoming thirty. In 1968 one Scottish regiment was disbanded.

Further major changes took place in 2007, when the Government combined/amalgamated regiments, leaving only six English, two Welsh, one Scottish and one Irish regiment.

THE RIFLES *Regiments of the Line original numbers chart*

THE RIFLES

Regiments of the Line original number		1881	1958	1959 1968	2007
11	North Devonshire Regiment	Dorsetshire Regiment	Devonshire and Dorsetshire Light Infantry		
39	Dorsetshire Regiment				
54	West Norfolk Regiment				
13	Prince Albert's Regiment of Light Infantry	Duke of Cornwall's Light Infantry	Somerset and Cornwell Light Infantry		
32	Cornwall Regiment of Light Infantry				
46	South Devonshire Regiment				
51	2nd Yorkshire West Riding Light Infantry	King's Own Yorkshire Light Infantry		The Light Infantry	The Rifles
105	Madras Light Infantry				
53	Shropshire Regiment	King's Shropshire Light Infantry			
85	King's Light Infantry				
68	Durham Light Infantry	Durham Light Infantry			
106	Bombay Light Infantry				
49	Princess Charlotte of Wales's Hertfordshire Regiment	Princess of Wales's (Berkshire) Regiment	The Duke of Edinburgh's Royal Regiment (Berkshire and Wiltshire)		
66	Berkshire Regiment				
62	Wiltshire Regiment	Duke of Edinburgh's Regiment			
99	Duke of Edinburgh's Regiment				
28	North Gloucestershire Regiment	Gloucestershire Regiment			
61	South Gloucestershire Regiment				
43	Monmouthshire Light Infantry	Oxfordshire Light Infantry	The Royal Green Jackets		
52	Oxfordshire Light Infantry				
60	King's Royal Rifle Corps				
	Rifle Brigade				

1966

ROYAL REGIMENT of SCOTLAND   ROYAL REGIMENT of FUSILIERS

		1881	1882 1887	1936 1959	2007
1	The Lothian Regiment		The Royal Scots (Lothian Regiment)		The Royal Regiment of Scotland
25	The King's Own Borderers		The King' Own Scottish Borderers		
21	The Royal Scots Fusiliers			Royal Highland Fusiliers (Princess Margaret's Own Glasgow and Ayrshire Regiment)	
71	Highland Light Infantry		Highland Light Infantry (City of Glasgow Regt)		
74	Highland Regiment of Foot				
42	Royal Highlanders The Black Watch		The Black Watch (Royal Highlanders)	The Black Watch (Royal Highland Regiment)	
73	Perthshire Regiment of Foot				
75	(Stirlingshire) Regiment of Foot		The Gordon Highlanders		
92	Gordon Highlanders Regiment of Foot				
72	Duke of Albany's Own Highlanders Regiment of Foot		Seaforth Highlanders (Ross-shire Buffs, The Duke of Albany's)		
78	(Highland) Regiment of Foot Ross-shire Buffs				
79	Cameron Highlanders		The Queen's Own Cameron Highlanders		
91	(Princess Louise's Argyllshire Highlanders		Princess Louise's (Sutherland and Argyll Highlanders)	Argyll and Sutherland Highlanders (Princess Louise's)	
93	Sutherland Highlanders Regiment of Foot				
26	Cameronian Regiment		The Cameronians (Scottish Rifles) Disbanded 1969		
90	Perthshire Light Infantry				

1920

5	Royal Northumberland Fusiliers	Royal Regiment of Fusiliers
6	Royal Warwickshire Fusiliers	
7	Royal Fusiliers	
20	Lancashire Fusiliers	

65	2nd Yorkshire North Riding	York and Lancaster Regiment (Disbanded 1969)
84	York and Lancaster	

DUKE OF LANCASTERS   ROYAL ANGLIAN REGIMENT

1881		1958	1968	2007
8	The King's (Liverpool) Regiment	The Manchester Regiment	The King's Regiment (Manchester & Liverpool)	The King's Regiment	Duke of Lancasters
63	(West Suffolk) Regiment of Foot				
96	Regiment of Foot				
4	King's Own Lancashire Regiment	Border Regiment	The King's Own Border Regiment		
34	Cumberland				
55	Westmorland				
30	Cambridgeshire	East Lancashire Regiment	The Lancashire Regiment	The Queen's Lancashire Regiment	
59	Nottinghamshire				
40	Somerset	South Lancashire Regiment			
82	Regiment of Foot				
47	Lancashire	Loyal North Lancashire Regiment			
81	Loyal Lincoln Volunteers				

			1959	1964	
9	Norfolk Regiment (Royal 1935)		1st East Anglian Regiment		Royal Anglian Regiment
12	Suffolk Regiment				
16	Bedfordshire Regiment	Beds & Herts Regiment	3rd East Anglian Regiment		
44	East Essex Regiment	Essex Regiment			
56	West Essex Regiment				
10	Lincolnshire Regiment (Royal 1946)		2nd East Anglian Regiment		
48	Northamptonshire	Northamptonshire Regiment			
58	Rutlandshire				
17	Leicestershire (Royal 1946)				

MERCIANS   PRINCESS of WALES ROYAL REGIMENT

MERCIANS

       1881   1959   2007

#	Regiment (1881)	1959	(post-1959)	Mercians
38	1st Staffordshire Regiment	South Staffordshire Regiment	The Staffordshire Regiment (Prince of Wales's)	Mercians
80	Staffordshire Volunteers			
64	2nd Staffordshire Regiment	Prince of Wales's (North Staffordshire) Regiment		
98	Prince of Wales's Regiment			
29	Worcestershire Regiment	Worcestershire Regiment	Worcestershire and Sherwood Foresters Regiment	
36	Herefordshire Regiment			
45	Nottinghamshire Sherwood Foresters	Sherwood Foresters (Derbyshire Regiment)		
95	Derbyshire Regiment			
22	Cheshire Regiment			

PRINCESS of WALES ROYAL REGIMENT

                              1959   1966

#	Regiment		1959	1966	Princess of Wales Royal Regiment
2	Queen's (Royal West Surrey) Regiment	East Surrey Regiment	Queen's Royal Surrey Regiment		Princess of Wales Royal Regiment
31	(Huntingdon) Regiment				
70	(Surrey) Regiment			The Queen's Regiment	
3	The Buffs (East Kent) Regiment	The Queen's Own (Royal West Kent Regt)	Queen's Own Buffs		
50	Queen's Own				
97	Earl of Wessex				
57	West Middlesex	Middlesex Regiment			
77	East Middlesex				
35	(Royal Sussex) Regiment of Foot	Royal Sussex Regiment			
107	Bengal Infantry (HEIC)				
37	North Hampshire	Hampshire Regiment (Royal 1946)			
67	South Hampshire				

THE YORKSHIRE REGIMENT   ROYAL WELSH

                    1881   1958   2006

14	Prince of Wales's Own (West Yorkshire) Regiment		Prince of Wales's Own Regiment of Yorkshire	The Yorkshire Regiment (Duke of Wellington's)
15	East Yorkshire Regiment			
19	Green Howards			
33	Duke of Wellington's	The Duke of Wellington's West Riding		
76	Hindoostan (HEIC) until 1812			

                    1881   1969   2007

24	(2nd Bn Warwickshire)	South Wales Borderers	Royal Regiment of Wales	Royal Welsh
41	Welsh Regiment	The Welsh Regiment		
69	South Lincolnshire			
23	Royal Welch Fusiliers			

ACKNOWLEDGEMENTS

Note: dates in parenthesis indicate when information was received.

1st Foot

(1972) From Regimental Secretary – *The Royal Scots Handbook*, Paramount Press. Glasgow – 1965.

Scottish Regiments and Uniforms 1660-1914. A. H. Bowling. Almark Publications 1972.

(1976) From Colonel B.A. Fargus OBE – Details 1683 to 1695.

(2003) From David Murphy. The Royal Scots Regimental Museum, Records of the Royal Scots 1715-1745.

2nd Foot

(1973&1976) From Major F. J. Reed – Regimental Sec. RHQ. Titles 1661-1967. Location 1684-1695.

(2003) From Major J. C. Rogers PWRR Curator, General information regarding the 2nd Foot.

(2003) From Major (Retd) A. W. Russell MBE – Association Secretary. Regimental History of the Queen's.

(2003) From Miss S. Higgs – Regimental Museum Attendant.

History of the Second 1715-1799 by Colonel J. Davis – Richard Bentley & Son, London 1895.

3rd Foot

(1973) From Mrs Edith Tyson FMA – Curator, Museum of King's Own Royal Regiment.

Guide book and Museum details of the Buffs. Gibbs & Son, Canterbury 1961.

(1976) From K. G. H. Reedie MA FSA(Scot) AMA – Curator of City Museums, Information on 1685 Rebellion.

(2003) From Major J. C. Rogers. PWRR Curator, General information regarding the 3rd Foot.

(2003) From Miss Katherine Boyce – National Army Museum, Jacobite Rebellions 1715 and 1745.

4th Foot

(1973) From Lieutenant-Colonel R. K. Kay – Curator, Guide to the 4th Foot.

(2003) From Mr S. A. Eastwood – Museum Curator, Regimental Museum, Royal Border Regiment.

Excerpt from *The King's Own, Story of a Royal Regt. 1680-1914.* J. M. Cowper Publisher OUP 1939.

5th Foot

(1973&1976) From Lieutenant-Colonel R. M. Pratt DSO DL, Regimental Secretary, Museum, Alnwick.

Battle Honours, Colonels, Flanders – Story of the Fifth. English Life Publications 1971.

6th Foot

(1976) From Lieutenant-Colonel M. Ryan OBE, Curator, Royal Warwickshire Regimental Museum.

A Brief History of the Warwickshire Fusiliers – Published 1968.

(2003) From Major R. G. Mills, Regimental Area Secretary (Warwickshire), Details re Ireland 1715–1745.

(2004) From Major R. G. Mills, Colonels 1711–1754.

7th Foot

(1973) From C. E. Manser, Chief Clerk, London RHQ. Raising of the Regiment (7th Foot).

(1976) From Regimental Secretary (City of London) Royal Fusiliers. Locations to 1691.

(2003) From Mr C. Crane, Chief Clerk. Historical Records of the 7th or *Royal Regiment of Fusiliers* by Lieutenant-Colonel Percy Groves. – Frederick B. Guerin, Guernsey 1903.

8th Foot
- (1973 and 1976) From Major B. W. R. Baker MC ROII Regimental Secretary.
- *Short History of the King's Regiment* by Lieutenant-Colonel R. P. MacDonald.
- Design Services Advertising, Wilmslow, Cheshire 1971.
- (2003) From Colonel (Retd) M. G. C. Amlot OBE DL. Regimental History.

9th Foot
- (1973) From Regimental Secretary – *The Royal Norfolk Regiment.* Morecambe Bay Printers 1959.
- (1976) From Regimental Secretary – Regimental locations 1685–1694.
- (2003) From Royal Norfolk Regimental Museum. Regimental details 1715–1745.

10th Foot
- (1973) From Major (Retd) E. Jessup Assistant Regimental Secretary.
- *A Short History of the Royal Lincolnshire Regiment.* Heinrich Winkelhagen. Goslar (Germany) 1954.
- (1976) From Major (Retd) E. Jessup. The 10th Foot. 1685–1700.
- (2003) From J. Edmond, Principal Keeper – Museum of Lincolnshire Life – Events in 1715.
- (2004) From J. Edmond, Principal Keeper – Museum of Lincolnshire Life – Colonels.

11th Foot
- (1973) From Lieutenant-Colonel (Retd) D. V. W. Wakely MC. Dorset Military Museum. Short History of the Devonshire regiment, also Short History of the Devonshire and Dorset Regiment.
- C. H. Challacombe Ltd. Well St. Exeter 1968.
- (2009) Peninsular War History.

12th Foot

(1973 and 1976) From Colonel W. A. Heal OBE. Regimental Secretary. Suffolk Regiment Association.

Raising of the 12th Foot and History of the Royal Anglian Regiment.

(2003) From Colonel A. C. Taylor. Area Secretary. Suffolk Regiment Association – History 1715–1745.

(2004) From Colonel A. C. Taylor. Area Secretary. Suffolk Regiment Association – Colonels.

(2008) From Colonel A .C. Taylor. Area Secretary. Suffolk Regiment Association – Gibraltar 1779–1783.

13th Foot

(1973 and 1976) From Lieutenant-Colonel A. C. M. Urwick DL. Hon Curator, Somerset Light Infantry Museum.

A Short History of the Somerset Light Infantry 1685–1954. Young & Son, Chard, Somerset.

(2003) From Major W. J. Spiers. Assistant Regimental Secretary (Museum/Archives).

The Light Infantry, A Brief History. Published by The Light Infantry. Winchester 1994.

From Lieutenant-Colonel D. Eliot. Regimental Secretary (Somerset) Regiment in 1745.

From Lieutenant-Colonel D. Eliot. Regimental Secretary (Somerset) Colonels 1711–1754.

14th Foot

(1973 and 1976) From Major (Retd) H. A. V. Spencer. Regimental Secretary. The Prince of Wales's Own Regiment of Yorkshire.

Dates and titles for the 14th & 15th Foot and the activities of the 14th Foot in 1685–1700.

(2003) From Mrs P. Boyd RHQ. Extracts from History 1715 to 1745 for both the 14th & 15th Foot.

Regiments from 2007 – From 14h Regimental Museum York.

15th Foot
> (1973) From Lieutenant-Colonel F. R. Yorke. Secretary, The East Yorkshire Regiment Association.
> *A Short History of the East Yorkshire Regiment.* Published 1949.
> (1976) From Lieutenant-Colonel (Retd) C. J. Robinson MBE. Secretary, the East Yorkshire Regiment Association. Information Relocation of the Regiment 1685-1690.
> (2003) From Mrs P. Boyd RHQ. Extracts from History in 1715-1745 for both the 14h & 15th Foot.

16th Foot
> (1973) From Regimental Secretary. HQ Royal Anglian Regiment.
> *Story of the Bedfordshire and Hertfordshire Regiment (16th Foot).* Published by Gale and Polden Ltd. The Wellington Press. Aldershot 1958.
> (1976) From Major J. A. Girdwood. Secretary, The Beds and Herts Regiment Association. Actions from period 1688-1691.
> (2003) From Dr Elizabeth Adey. Keeper of Local History. Luton Museum Service. The Story of the Bedfordshire & Hertfordshire Regiment, Volume 1. Chapter IV. 1715-1766.
> From Dr Elizabeth Adey. Colonels 1711-1754

17th Foot
> (1973) From A. MacFadden Regimental Secretary, Royal Anglian Regiment (Leicester & Rutland). The Tigers. *A Short History of the Royal Leicestershire Regiment.* By Major General J. M. K. Spurling CB. CBE. DSO. Published by Leicester Museums 1969.
> From P. Hughes Regimental Secretary. Activities re 17th Foot 1689-1691.
> From Philip R. French, Senior Curator. Later Leicester Newarke Houses Museum.
> *History of the Services of the 17th Foot* by E. A. H. Webb 1714-1722.
> From Philip R. French. Colonels 1711-1754.

18th Foot
> (1976) From War Office library. *Historical Record of the Eighteenth or The Royal Irish Regiment of Foot.* By Richard Cannon. Published by Parker, Furnivall & Parker, London 1848. *The Irish Regiments 1683–1999.* Page 107. 1st & 2nd Royal Irish Regiments by R .C. Harris. (Revised by H R. G. Wilson). Published by Spellmount Ltd. Staplehurst, Kent.

19th Foot
> (1973) From Major G. A. F. Steede RHQ Richmond Yorkshire. Abridged History of the Green Howards.
>
> (1976) From colonel J. M. Forbes JP. DL. Curator, The Green Howards Regimental Museum. Details of the 19th Foot in 1689.
>
> (2003) From Major (Retd) J. R. Chapman MBE. Curator, RHQ and Museum of the Green Howards. Jacobite Rebellions 1715 and 1745.

20th Foot
> (1973) From The Lancashire HQ. Information re History of the Lancashire Fusiliers by Cyril Rey.
>
> (1976) From Major T. P. Shaw MBE. OIC Lancashire HQ RRF. Information re Raising and Location of Regiment from 1690–1702.
>
> From Captain (Retd) J. O'Grady, Curator, Fusiliers' Museum, Lancashire. Information re 1745–1758.

21st Foot
> (1972 and 1976) From Captain (Retd) A. J. Wilson. RHQ Royal Highland Fusiliers. Brief History of The Royal Highland Fusiliers.
>
> From Major (Retd) W. Shaw MBE. Regimental Secretary
>
> *The History Of The Royal Scots Fusiliers 1678–1918* by John Buchan.
>
> Thomas Nelson & Sons Ltd. London, Edinburgh and New York.

22nd Foot
- (1973) From Lieutenant-Colonel C. F. Cooke Regimental Secretary. Short History of the Regiment.
- (1976) From Lieutenant-Colonel (Retd) A. A. Blacoe Regimental Secretary. Details re the Raising of the Regiment.
- (2003) From Geoffrey J. Crump. Honorary Researcher, Cheshire Military Museum. *Ever Glorious – Story of the 22nd (Cheshire) Regiment.* Vol 1 by Bernard Rigby re 1702–1727.

23rd Foot
- (1973 and 1976) From The Regimental Secretary.
- The Royal Welch Fusiliers – Pitkin Pictorials Ltd. London 1974.
- (2003) From Judy Gater, Assistant Officer RHQ Royal Welch Fusiliers. R. W. F. Chapter 1 1703–1759.

24h Foot
- (1973&1976) From Major G. J. B .Egerton DL. Curator, Regimental Museum. *A short History of the South Wales Borderers 24th Foot.* By Western Mail & Echo Ltd. Cardiff.
- (2003) From Celia Green. Customer Services Manager, Regimental Museum. Extract, Locations and actions of the 24th Regiment for 1715 and 1745
- (1973) From Lieutenant-Colonel Hogg, Regimental Secretary. Colonels 1711–1745.

25th Foot
- (1972) From J. Kirtley RHQ. King's Own Scottish Borderers – Short History of the Regiment.
- *Scottish Regiments & Uniforms 1660–1914* A. H. Bowling. Almark Publications 1972.
- (1974) From Lieutenant-Colonel (Retd), Regimental Secretary. Actions in Ireland 1690.
- (2003) From Lt-Colonel C.G.O Hogg DL Regimental Secretary *Extracts from The Records of The King's Own Scottish Borderers 1697–1746* by Capt R. T. Higgins. London 1873.

26th Foot
- (1972) From Lieutenant-Colonel (Retd) J. E. B. Whitehead, Regimental Officer. *History of the Cameronians (Scottish Rifles).* Morecambe Bay Publishers Ltd. Morecambe, Lancashire.
- (1973) From Lieutenant-Colonel (Retd) G. A. M. Soper OBE. Extracts form Regimental History. Ireland 1690.

27th Foot
- (1972) From M. Mulligan, Regimental Office, Royal Irish Rangers. *Outline History of the Royal Irish Rangers.* Printed by Trimble of Armagh 1969. *The Royal Inniskilling Fusiliers 1689–1968* by The Forces Press. Aldershot 1968.
- (2000) From J. M. Dunlop, Curator. Royal Inniskilling Fusiliers Regimental Museum. Raising of the Regiment.
- (2003) From Major (Retd) J. M. Dunlop, Curator. Extracts from Regimental History for 1715 and 1745. *The Irish Regiments 1683–1999.* Page 120. 1st Battalion Royal Inniskilling Fusiliers by R. G. Harris. (Revised by H .R. G. Wilson). Published by Spellmount Ltd. Staplehurst, Kent.
- (2004) From Major (Retd) J. M. Dunlop – Colonels 1711–1754.
- (2005) From Major (Retd) J. M. Dunlop – Seven Years War.

28th Foot
- (1972) From RHQ. A New Short History of the Gloucestershire Regiment 1694–1965. Printed by John Jennings (Gloucester) Ltd.
- Also 1991 English Life Publications. Regiments of Gloucestershire.
- (2003) From G. C. Streatfeild, Curator, Soldiers of Gloucesterhsire Museum. Jacobite Rebellions of 1715 and 1745.

29th Foot
- (1972) From Lieutenant-Colonel C. P. Vaughan DSO. DL. Regimental Secretary. RHQ. The Worcestershire & Sherwood Foresters Regiment. *Short History of the Worcestershire Regiment.* Reliance Printing Works, Halesowen, Worcs. 1970.

(2003) From Lieutenant-Colonel (Retd) C. P. Lowe, Hon Archivist, The Worcestershire Regiment Museum Trust. Locations of the Regiment in 1715 and 1745.

30th Foot

(1972) From Major P. J. Ryan OIC. RHQ *The Lancashire Regiment (Prince of Wales's Volunteers) 1689–1960.* Published by Malcolm Page Ltd. 41 Streatham Hill, London, SW2. 1960.

(1988) From Major (Retd) S. Tipping. Assistant Regimental Secretary. Conditions 1689–1702.

(2009) Peninsular War History.

31st Foot

(1973) From Major F. J. Reed, Regimental Secretary (Queen's Surrey Office). Basic information 1714–1881.

(2003) From Major J. C. Rogers. PWRR Curator, General information regarding the 31st Foot.

(2003) From Major (Retd) A. W. Russell MBE. Association Secretary. Information that the 31st Foot had no involvement in Jacobite Rebellions of 1715 or 1745.

32nd Foot

(1973) From Lieutenant-Colonel (Retd) J. E. E. Fry, Curator Regimental Museum. Basic information on the Duke of Cornwall's Light Infantry.

(2003) From Major W. H. White. Regimental Museum Bodmin. Details of Jacobite Rebellions 1715–1745.

(2003) Major W. J. Spiers. Assistant Regimental Secretary (Museum/Archives). *The Light Infantry, A Brief History.* Published by The Light Infantry, Winchester. 1994.

(2004) Major W. J. Spiers. Colonels 1711–1754.

33rd Foot

(2009) From R. A. Innes Museum Director, The Duke of Wellington's Regiment Museum. Initial information re The Duke of Wellington's Regiment (West Riding).

(2003) From Major D. L. J. Harrap, Regimental Secretary. RHQ. Halifax. Extract from Locations List 1714-1746.

34th Foot

(2009) From Lieutenant-Colonel R. K. May Curator, The Border Regiment Museum. *The Border Regiment. A Brief Summary of 250 years Service. 1702-1952.*

(2003) From Mr S. A. Eastwood B.A. AMA. Curator, The Regimental Museum of The Border Regiment & The King's Own Royal Border Regiment. Historical Account of the 34th & 55th Regiments of Foot for 1719-1752.

(2004) From Mr S. A Eastwood BA. AMA. Colonels 1711-1754.

35th Foot

(1972) From The Museum Curator. Chichester city Museum. *A short History of The Royal Sussex Regiment.* Text by Major J. F. Ainsworth. Photography by C. Howard & Son Ltd. Chichester. English Life Publications Ltd. Derby 1972.

(2003) From Major J. C. Rogers. PWRR Curator, General information regarding the 35th Foot.

(2003) From Richard Callaghan, Curator, Military Museum of Sussex. Location of Regiment 1708-1756.

36th Foot

(1973) From Lieutenant-Colonel C.P.Vaughan DSO. D.L. Reg Sec. The Worcestershire & Sherwood Foresters Regiment. *Short History of the Worcestershire Regiment.* Reliance Printing Works, Halesowen, Worcs 1970.

(2003) From Lieutenant-Colonel (Retd) C. P. Lowe, Hon. Archivist, The Worcestershire Regiment Museum Trust. Extract from *Historical Record of the Thirty-Sixth or the Herefordshire Regiment of Foot 1714-1747* by Richard Cannon. Printed by George E. Eyre & William Spottiswoode Published by Parker, Furnivall & Parker. London. 1853.

37th Foot
- (1973) From Colonel J. M. Clift. Regimental Secretary. Initial Information about The Royal Hampshire Regiment.
- (2003) From Major J. C. Rogers. PWRR Curator, General information re 37th Foot.
- (2003) From Royal Hampshire Regiment Museum. Location of the Regiment 1713–1746.

38th Foot
- (1973) From Colonel (Retd) A. C. B. Cook OBE. RHQ The Staffordshire Regiment. *A short History of the Staffordshire Regiment (Prince of Wales's Own)* Reliance. Printing Works, Halesowen. Worcs. 1972.
- (2003) From Colour Sergeant W. T. Turner. Staffordshire Regimental Museum. Information regarding the Regiment in the West Indies from 1707 until 1764.

39th Foot
- (1973) From Lieutenant-Colonel D. V. W. Wakely MC. Dorset Military Museum. Short History of the Devonshire (11th) & Dorset (39th) Regiments.
- (2003) From Lieutenant -Colonel (Retd) R. A. Leonard. Curator. The Military Museum of Devon & Dorset. Extract from Regimental History – Jacobite Rebellion 1745.
- (2004) From Lieutenant-Colonel (Retd) R. A. Leonard, Colonels 1711–1754.
- (2008) From John Pitman. Keep Military Museum – Gibraltar 1779–1783.

40th Foot
- (1973) From Major P. J. Ryan OIC. RHQ *The Lancashire Regiment (Prince of Wales's Volunteers) 1689–1960.* Published by Malcolm Page Ltd. 41 Streatham Hill, London SW2. 1960. Also *The South Lancashire Regiment. 1717–1956.* Malcolm Page Ltd.
- (2005) From Queen's Lancashire Museum – Seven Years War.

41st Foot
> (2003) From Major Martin Everett TD. The South Wales Borderers and Monmouthshire Regimental Museum of The Royal Regiment of Wales. Locations of 41st Foot 1719–1881.

42nd Foot
> (1972) From Major H. McClark MBE. Assistant Regimental Secretary. The Black Watch. Perth. Initial information re The Black Watch. *Scottish Regiments & Uniforms 1660–1914* by A. A. Bowling. Almark Publications 1972.
>
> (2003) From Thomas S. Smyth. Archivist. The Black Watch. Details of the 43rd in 1745.
>
> (2005) From Thomas S. Smyth. Archivist. Assault on Fort Ticonderoga 1758. Seven Years War.
>
> (2006) From Thomas S. Smyth. Archivist. North America 1750–1780.

43rd Foot
> (1973) From J. M. Leslie, RHQ The Royal Green Jackets. *Short History of The Royal Green Jackets 43rd & 52nd.* Printed by Culverlands Press Ltd, Winnall, Winchester.
>
> (2003) From Colonel (Retd) J. M. A. Tillett. Curator (Oxford) Regimental Museum. Details of the 43rd Foot during the Period 1742–1747.

44th Foot
> (1973) From Major T. R. Stead, DL. Regimental Secretary, RHQ The Royal Anglian Regiment (Essex). History & Traditions of the 3rd East Anglian Regiment (44th Foot). (The Essex Regiment).
>
> (2003) From I. Hook, Keeper of the Essex Regiment Museum. – 1st Battalion The Essex Regiment 1743–1755.
>
> (2005) From I. Hook, Keeper of the Essex Regiment Museum. – Seven Years War 1756–1759.

45th Foot
> (1973) From the Regimental Secretary. Sherwood Foresters Office. *The Sherwood Foresters (Nottinghamshire & Derbyshire Regiment).* Published by English Life Publications Ltd. Lodge Lane, Derby. Printed in Great Britain by Wood Mitchell & Co. Ltd. Stoke on Trent.
>
> (2003) From Major (Retd) J. O. M. Hackett, RHQ. The Worcestershire & Sherwood Foresters Regiment. Information regarding the Regiment's activities 1742-1765.

46th Foot
> (2003) From Major W. H. White, DL. The Regimental Museum, Bodmin. Historical Records of the Forty-Sixth or the Devonshire Regiment of Foot 1740-1748.
>
> (2003) From Major W. J. Spiers. Assistant Secretary (Museum/Archives). *The Light Infantry, A Brief History.* Published by The Light Infantry. Winchester. 1949.
>
> (2005) From Major W. H. White DL. Assault on Fort Ticonderoga. Seven Years War 1758.

47th Foot
> (1972) From P. Rogers, Regimental Secretary, RHQ. The Queen's Lancashire Regiment. *A Short History of The Loyal Regiment.* Published by Malcolm Page Ltd. Publicity House, Streatham Hill, London, SW2.

48th Foot
> (1973) From Major D. Baxter, Hon. Sec. The Northamptonshire Regiment Comrades' Association. The Raising & Details of the 1st & 2nd Battalions.
>
> (2003) From Jacqueline A. Minchinton, Records & Resources Management Officer. Northampton Museum and Art Gallery. Details of the 48th Foot, Chapter II 1742-1755 from *The History of the Northamptonshire Regiment 1742-1934* by Lieutenant-Colonel Russell Gurney, Published by Gale & Polden Ltd. Aldershot. 1935.

49th Foot
> (1988) Medals of The Royal Berkshire Regiment by John Sidney.
> (2003) From Major (Retd) P. J. Ball, The Royal Gloucestershire, Berkshire & Wiltshire Regiment Museum. Details of the Regiment in 1745.

50th Foot
> (1973) From K. J. Collins, Museum and Art Gallery, Maidstone, Kent. Details of the 50th. From The Queen's Own Royal West Kent Regimental Museum.
> (2003) From Major J. C. Rogers, PWRR Curator. General information regarding the 50th Foot.

51st Foot
> (1973) From Colonel N. S. Pope, DSO. MBE. Light Infantry Office (Yorkshire). *A Short History of The King's Own Yorkshire Light Infantry (51st & 105th) 1755-1965.* The Wakefield Express Series Ltd. Express House, Southgate, Wakefield.
> (2003) From Major W. J. Spiers. Assistant Regimental Secretary (Museum/Archives) *The Light Infantry, A Brief History.* Published by The Light Infantry. Winchester. 1994.

52nd Foot
> (1973) From J. M. Leslie, RHQ. The Royal Green Jackets. Short History including Raising of the 52nd.
> (2003) From Colonel (Retd) J. M. A. Tillett, Curator (Oxford) Regimental Museum. Details of Research Addresses.

53rd Foot
> (1973) From Colonel G. M. Thorneycroft, DL. Secretary, Light Infantry Office. Details of raising of the King's Shropshire Light Infantry.
> (2003) From Major W. J. Spiers. Assistant Regimental Secretary Museum/Archives. *The Light Infanrty, a Brief History.* Published by The Light Infantry. Winchester 1994.

54th Foot

(1973) From Lieutenant-Colonel (Retd) D. V. W. Wakely MC. Dorset Military Museum. *Short History of the Devonshire & Dorset Regiment.* C. H. Challacombe Ltd. Well St. Exeter. 1968.

(2003) From Lieutenant-Colonel (Retd) R. A. Leonard, Curator. The Keep Military Museum, Dorchester. Details of Unit Records.

55th Foot

(1973) From Lieutenant-Colonel R. K. May. The Border Regiment Museum. The Border Regiment. A Brief Summary of 250 years Service. 1702–1952.

(2003) From Mr. S. A. Eastwood BA. AMA. Curator. The Regimental Museum of the Border Regiment and The King's Own Royal Border Regiment. Historical Account of the 34th and 55th Regiments of Foot from 1719.

(2005) From Mr. S. A. Eastwood BA AMA. Details regarding the Seven Years War.

56th Foot

(1973) From Major T. R. Stead, DL. Regimental Secretary, HQ The Royal Anglian Regiment (Essex). *History & Traditions of The 3rd East Anglian Regiment. (56th Foot – The Essex Regiment).* Published by Gale & Polden Ltd. The Wellington Press, Aldershot.

(2006) From I. Hook. Keeper of the Essex Regiment Museum. Seven Years War.

57th Foot

(1973) From Major A. E. F. Waldron MBE. Secretary, Regimental Association of the Middlesex Regiment. Short History of The Middlesex Regiment. (The Die Hards).

(2003) From Major J. C. Rogers. PWRR Curator. General information regarding the 57th Foot.

58th Foot
- (1972) From Major D. Baxter, Hon. Sec. The Northamptonshire Regiment Comrades' Association. The Raising and Details of the 1st and 2nd Battalions.
- (2008) From Paul Robinson Museum and Art Gallery – Gibraltar 1779–1783.

59th Foot
- (1973) From Major P. J. Ryan OIC. RHQ *The Lancashire Regiment (Prince of Wales's Volunteers) 1689–1960*. Published by Malcolm Page Ltd. 41 Streatham Hill, London, SW2. 1960.

60th Foot
- (1973) From J. M. Leslie. RHQ. The Royal Green Jackets. The Royal Green Jackets of the Light Division. Printed by Culverlands Press Ltd. Winnall, Winchester. Also A Brief History of The King's Royal Rifle Corps 1755–1948. Published by Gale & Polden Ltd. The Wellington Press, Aldershot. 1948.
- (2009) Peninsular War History.

61st Foot
- (1973) From RHQ. A New Short History of The Gloucestershire Regiment 1694–1965. Printed by John Jennings (Gloucester) Ltd.
- (2003) Regiments of Gloucestershire by English Life Publications.
- (2009) Peninsular War History.

62nd Foot
- (2005) From D. Chilton, Curator 62nd (Wiltshire) Museum. Siege of Louisbourg 1758.

63rd Foot
- (1973) From Major B. W. R. Baker MC. ROII Regimental Secretary. – *A Short History of the King's Regt*. By Lieutenant-Colonel R. P. MacDonald 1917.

(1976)From Major B. W. R. Baker MC. ROII Regimental Secretary. – Regimental History 1685–1696.

64th Foot

(1973) From Colonel H. C. B. Cook OBE. RHQ. The Staffordshire Regiment. *A Short History of The Staffordshire Regiment*, Reliance Printing Works, Halesowen. 1972.

65th Foot

(1972) From Lieutenant-Colonel A. W. Stansfeld MBE. Regimental Secretary. *The York and Lancaster Regiment. A Short History 1758–1968.* Printed by Greenup & Thompson Ltd. Sheffield.

66th Foot

(1988) *Medals of The Royal Berkshire Regiment* by John Sidney.

67th Foot

(2003) From Royal Hampshire Regimental Museum – General Regimental History.

68th Foot

(1973) From Colonel R. B. Humphreys. DL. Reg. Sec. (Durham). Story of The Durham Light Infanty.

(2003) From Major W. J. Spiers. Asst. Reg. Sec. (Museum/Archives). *The Light Infantry, A Brief History.* Published by The Light Infantry, Winchester. 1994.

(2009) Peninsular War History.

69th Foot

(1972) From Major G. J. B. Egerton DL. Curator Regimental Museum (24th Foot). *How the 2nd Battalion of The 24th Foot became 69th Foot.* By Western Mail & Echo Ltd. Cardiff.

70th Foot
(1973) From Major F. J. Reed, Reg. Sec. (Queen's Surrey Office). Basic information 1758–1881.
(2003) From Major J. C. Rogers, PWRR Curator. General information regarding the 70th Foot.

71st Foot
(1972) From Captain (Retd) A. J. Wilson, RHQ Royal Highland Fusiliers. Brief History of the 71st Foot.
(1976) From *Scottish Regiments & Uniforms 1660–1914*, by A. H. Bowling. Almark Publications 1972.

72nd Foot
(1973) From RHQ Queen's Own Highlanders (Seaforth and Camerons) – History of the 72nd Foot.
(2003) From Lieutenant-Colonel (Retd) A. M. Cumming OBE. RHQ the Highlanders. Basic details of the 72nd Foot.

73rd Foot
(2003) From Thomas S. Smyth. Archivist. The Black Watch. Location of Archival Material.

74th Foot
(1972) From Captain (Retd) A. J. Wilson RHQ Royal Highland Fusiliers. A Brief History.

75th Foot
(1972) From RHQ The Gordon Highlanders by Christopher Sinclair-Stevenson – Hamish Hamilton, London 1968.
(1992) From Captain (Retd) C. Harrison RHQ – General Sir Ian S. M. Hamilton GCB. GCMG. DSO. TD.
(2003) From Lieutenant-Colonel (Retd) A. M. Cumming OBE. RHQ The Highlanders. Details of the 75th Foot.

76th Foot
> (2003) From Major D. L. J. Harrap Reg. Sec. RHQ Halifax. Details of the 76th Foot.

77th Foot
> (1972) From Major A. E. F. Waldron MBE. Sec. The Middlesex Reg. History of the Die Hards.

78th Foot
> (1973) From RHQ Queen's Own Highlanders (Seaforth and Camerons). History of the 78th (Highland Regiment of Foot) or The Ross-Shire Buffs.
> (2003) From Lieutenant-Colonel (Retd) A. M. Cumming OBE RHQ The Highlanders. Details of the 78th Foot.

79th Foot
> (1973) From RHQ Queen's Own Highlanders (Seaforth and Camerons). History of the 79th Regiment of Foot.
> (2003) From Lieutenant-Colonel (Retd) A. M. Cumming OBE RHQ The Highlanders. Basic Details of the 79th Foot.

80th Foot
> (1972) From Colonel (Retd) H. C. B. Cook, OBE. RHQ. The Staffordshire Regiment. A Short History of The Staffordshire Regiment (the Prince of Wales's Own).

81st Foot
> (1973) From P. Rogers, Reg. Sec. RHQ The Queen's Lancashire Regiment. *Short History of The Loyal Regiment.* Published by Malcolm Page Ltd. Publicity House, Streatham Hill, London. SW2.

82nd Foot
> (1972) From Major P. J. Ryan, OIC RHQ *The Lancashire Regiment (Prince of Wales's Volunteers 1689–1960)* Published by Malcolm Page Ltd. 41 Streatham Hill, London. SW2. 1960.

Also the South Lancashire Regiment 1717-1956. Malcolm Page Ltd. London. SW2.

83rd Foot

(1972) From Major (Retd) R. W. Connell, MBE. Asst. Reg. Sec. RHQ The Royal Irish Rangers.

History of The Royal Ulster Rifles 1793-1957. Prepared by Lieutenant-Colonel M. J P. M. Corbally. Published by The Paramount Press, Waterloo St. Glasgow. Printed by The Herald Press, Arbroath.

(1973) From M. Mulligan, Regimental Office, Royal Irish Rangers. *Outline History of The Royal Irish Rangers.* Printed by Trimble of Armagh. 1969.

(2003) From Captain J. Knox MBE. Curator, Royal Ulster Rifles Regimental Museum. Details of The Regiment from 1793-1968.

The Irish Regiments 1683-1999. Page 140. 1st Battalion Royal Irish Rifles by R. G. Harris. ((Revised by H. R. G.Wilson). Published by Spellmount Ltd. Staplehurst, Kent.

(2008) Peninsular War History.

84th Foot

(1973) From Lieutenant-Colonel A. W. Stansfeld MBE. Reg. Sec. RHQ The York & Lancaster Regiment. *A Short History of The York & Lancaster Regiment.* Printed by Greenup & Thompson Ltd. Sheffield.

85th Foot

(1972) From Colonel G. M. Thornycroft, DL. Secretary, Light Infantry Office. Details of Raising of The King's Own Shropshire Light Infantry.

86th Foot

(1973) From Major (Retd) R. W. Connel MBE. Asst. Reg. Sec. RHQ The Royal Irish Rangers. *History of The Royal Ulster Rifles 1793-1957* Prepared by Lieutenant-Colonel M. J. P.

M.Corbally. Published by Paramount Press, Waterloo St. Glasgow printed by The Herald Press, Arbroath.

(1973) From M. Mulligan, Regimental Office, Royal Irish Rangers. *Outline History of The Royal Irish Royal Irish Rangers.* Printed by Trimble of Armagh. 1969.

(2003) From Captain J. Knox, MBE. Curator, Royal Ulster Rifles Regimental Museum. Details of The Regiment 1793-1968. *The Irish Regiments 1683-1999.* Page 143. 2nd Battalion Royal Irish Rifles. By R. G. Harris. (Revised by H. R. G. Wilson). Published by Spellmount Ltd. Staplehurst, Kent.

87th Foot

(1973) From Major G. A. N. Boyne, JP. Curator, The Royal Irish Fusiliers Regimental Museum. *Outline History of The Royal Irish Fusiliers (Princess Victoria's).* Gale & Polden Ltd. The Welling Press. Aldershot. 1955.

(1973) From M. Mulligan, Regimental Office. Royal Irish Rangers. *Outline History of The Royal Irish Rangers.* Printed by Trimble of Armagh. 1969. *The Irish Regiments 1683-1999.* Page 157. 1st Battalion Royal Irish Fusiliers by R. G. Harris (Revised by H. R. G.Wilson). Published by Spellmount Ltd. Staplehurst, Kent.

88th Foot

The Irish Regiments 1683-1999. Page 176. 1st Battalion The Connaught Rangers by R. G. Harris (Revised by H. R. G. Wilson). Published by Spellmount Ltd. Staplehurst, Kent.

(2008) Peninsular War History.

89th Foot

(1973) From Major G. A. N. Boyne, PJ. Curator, The Royal Irish Fusiliers Regimental Museum. *Outline History of The Royal Irish Fusiliers (Princess Victoria's).* Gale & Polden Ltd. The Wellington Press, Aldershot. 1955.

(1973) From M. Mulligan. Regimental Office. Royal Irish Rangers. *Outline History of The Royal Irish Rangers.* Printed by Trimble of Armagh. 1969. *The Irish Regiments 1683-1999.* Page 162.

2nd Battalion Royal Irish Fusiliers by R. G. Harris (Revised by H. R. G. Wilson). Published by Spellmount Ltd. Staplehurst, Kent.

90th Foot

(1972) From Lieutenant-Colonel (Retd) J. E. B. Whitehead, Regimental Officer. *History of The Cameronians (Scottish Rifles)*. Morecambe Bay Publishers Ltd. Morecambe. Lancs.

91st Foot

Scottish Regiments & Uniforms 1660–1914 by A. H. Bowling. Almark Publications. 1972.

(1973) From RHQ the Argyll & Sutherland Highlanders. The Castle, Stirling. *The History of The Argyll & Sutherland Highlanders (Princess Louise's). 1794–1963*. By Lieutenant-Colonel G. I. Malcolm of Poltalloch. Printed by Learmonth & Son. Stirling. 1965.

92nd Foot

Scottish Regiments & Uniforms 1660–1914 by A. H. Bowling. Almark Publications. 1972.

(1973) From RHQ the Gordon Highlanders. *The Gordon Highlanders* by Christopher Sinclair-Stevenson. Famous Regiments Series. Hamish Hamiliton, London. 1968.

(2003) From Lieutenant-Colonel (Retd) A. M. Cumming OBE. RHQ The Highlanders. Basic Details of the 92nd Foot.

93th Foot

Scottish Regiments & Uniforms 1660–1914 by A. H. Bowling. Almark Publications. 1972.

(1973) From RHQ the Argyll and Sutherland Highlanders. The Castle, Stirling. *The History of the Argyll and Sutherland Highlanders (Princess Louise's) 1794–1963*. By Lieutenant-Colonel G. I. Malcolm of Poltalloch. Printed by A. Learmonth & Son, Stirling. 1965.

94th Foot
> *The Irish Regiments 1683–1999.* Page 183. 2nd Battalion the Connaught Rangers by R. G. Harris. (Revised by H. R. G. Wilson). Published by Spellmount Ltd. Staplehurst, Kent.

95th Foot
> (1972) From the Regimental Secretary. Sherwood Foresters Office. *The Sherwood Foresters (Nottinghamshire & Derbyshire Regiment).* Published by English Life Publications Ltd. Lodge Lane, Derby. Printed in Great Britain by Wood Mitchell & Co. Ltd, Stoke on Trent.

96th Foot
> (1973 and 1976) From Major B. W. R. Baker, MC. ROII Regimental Secretary. *Short History Of The King's Regiment* by Lieutenant-Colonel R. P. MacDonald. Design Services Advertising, Wilmslow, Cheshire. 1971.

97th Foot
> (1972) From Kenneth J. Collins, Museum & Art Gallery, Maidstone, Kent. Details of the 50th/97th From The Queen's Own Royal West Kent Regimental Museum.

98th Foot
> (1973) (1973) From Colonel (Retd) H. C. B. Cook, OBE. RHQ The Staffordshire Regiment. *A Short History of The Staffordshire Regiment (the Prince of Wales's Own).* Reliance Printing Works, Halesowen, Worcestershire. 1972.

99th Foot
> (2003) From Curator (Wiltshire) Museum. – History of Regiment.

100th Foot
> *The Irish Regiments 1683–1999.* Page 192. 1st Battalion Prince of Wales's Leinster Regiment by R. G. Harris (Revised by H. R. G.Wilson). Published by Spellmount Ltd. Staplehurst, Kent.

101st Foot
> The Irish Regiments 1683–1999. Page 204. 1st Battalion Royal Munster Fusiliers by R. G. Harris. (Revised by H. R. G. Wilson). Published by Spellmount Ltd. Staplehurst, Kent.

102nd Foot
> *The Irish Regiments 1683–1999.* Page 217. 1st Battalion Royal Dublin Fusiliers by R. G. Harris. (Revised by H. R. G. Wilson). Published by Spellmount Ltd. Staplehurst, Kent.

103rd Foot
> *The Irish Regiments 1683–1999.* Page 217. 2nd Battalion Royal Dublin Fusiliers by R. G. Harris. (Revised by H. R. G. Wilson). Published by Spellmount Ltd. Staplehurst, Kent.

104th Foot
> *The Irish Regiments 1683–1999.* Page 204. 2nd Battalion Royal Munster Fusiliers by R. G. Harris. (Revised by H. R. G. Wilson). Published by Spellmount Ltd. Staplehurst, Kent.

105th Foot
> (1972) From Colonel N. S. Pope, DSO. MBE. Light Infantry Office (Yorkshire). *A Short History of the King's Own Yorkshire Light Infantry (51st/105th) 1755–1965.* The Wakefield Express Series Ltd. Express House, Southgate, Wakefield.

106th Foot
> (1973) From Colonel R. B. Humphreys, DL. Reg. Sec. (Durham). Story of The Durham Light Infantry.

107th Foot
> (1973) From The Museum Curator. Chichester city Museum. *A Short History of The Royal Sussex Regiment.* Text by Major J. Ainsworth. Photography by C. Howard & Son Ltd. Chichester. English Life Publications Ltd. Derby. 1972.

108th Foot
> (1973) From M. Mulligan. Regimental Office. Royal Irish Rangers. *Outline History of the Royal Irish Rangers*. Printed by Trimble of Armagh. 1969. *The Irish Regiments 1683–1999*. Page 128. 2nd Battalion Royal Inniskilling Fusiliers by R.G.Harris. (Revised by H.R.G.Wilson). Published by Spellmount Ltd. Staplehurst, Kent.

109th Foot
> *The Irish Regiments 1683–1999*. Page 192. 2nd Battalion Prince of Wales's Leinster Regiment by R. G. Harris. (Revised by H. R. G. Wilson). Published by Spellmount Ltd. Staplehurst, Kent.